Lecture Notes in Computer Science 5119

Commenced Publication in 1973
Founding and Former Series Editors:
Gerhard Goos, Juris Hartmanis, and Jan v~~ ~

Samuel Kounev   Ian Gorton   Kai Sachs (Eds.)

Performance Evaluation: Metrics, Models and Benchmarks

SPEC International Performance Evaluation Workshop,
SIPEW 2008
Darmstadt, Germany, June 27-28, 2008
Proceedings

 Springer

Volume Editors

Samuel Kounev
University of Cambridge
Computer Laboratory
William Gates Building, 15 JJ Thomson Avenue, Cambridge, CB3 0FD, UK
E-mail: skounev@acm.org

Ian Gorton
Pacific Northwest National Laboratory
Computational and Information Sciences
PO Box 999, MS: K7-90, Richland, WA, 99352, USA
E-mail: ian.gorton@pnl.gov

Kai Sachs
TU Darmstadt
Department of Computer Science, Databases and Distributed Systems Group
Hochschulstr. 10, 64289 Darmstadt, Germany
E-mail: sachs@dvs.tu-darmstadt.de

Library of Congress Control Number: Applied for

CR Subject Classification (1998): D.2.4, C.2.4, F.3, D.4, C.4

LNCS Sublibrary: SL 2 – Programming and Software Engineering

ISSN   0302-9743
ISBN-10   3-540-69813-2 Springer Berlin Heidelberg New York
ISBN-13   978-3-540-69813-5 Springer Berlin Heidelberg New York

Springer is a part of Springer Science+Business Media

springer.com

© Springer-Verlag Berlin Heidelberg 2008
Printed in Germany

Typesetting: Camera-ready by author, data conversion by Scientific Publishing Services, Chennai, India
Printed on acid-free paper   SPIN: 12321483   06/3180   5 4 3 2 1 0

Preface

This volume contains the papers presented at the SPEC International Performance Evaluation Workshop held June 27–28 in Darmstadt, Germany.

From 39 submitted papers, 16 were selected for publication. Each submitted paper was reviewed by three Program Committee members. The accepted papers cover a range of different topics in performance evaluation with a good balance between theoretical and practical contributions. The final workshop program, as well as this volume, is organized in five subject areas:

- Models for Software Performance Engineering
- Benchmarks and Workload Characterization
- Profiling, Monitoring and Optimization
- Web Services and Service-Oriented Architectures
- Power and Performance

We were pleased to have Mor Harchol-Balter, Murray Woodside and Ulrich Marquard give two keynote speeches and an invited talk, respectively. Prof. Harchol-Balter spoke about her recent work on scheduling for server farms, while Prof. Woodside spoke about the relationship between performance models and performance data. Dr. Marquard gave a talk on the SAP standard application benchmarks.

Many people contributed to the success of the workshop. First of all, we would like to thank the members of the Program Committee for reviewing and evaluating the submitted papers and helping us to put together a high-quality workshop program. Many thanks also to Alejandro Buchmann from the Technische Universität Darmstadt and John Henning from Sun Microsystems for serving as General Chairs of the workshop and providing advice on many organizational issues.

We would like to thank the publisher, Springer, for their cooperation and support. Thanks also to Pablo Guerrero, Christof Leng and Marion Braun from the Technische Universität Darmstadt for designing the workshop website and for their support with organizational matters. Furthermore, we would like to thank our sponsors, SAP AG, Deutsche Telekom and Sun Microsystems for their generous donations. Last but not least, we greatly appreciate the cooperation of SPEC's management and the SPEC office, in particular, the OSG Chair Alan Adamson, SPEC President Walter Bays, Kathy Power and Dianne Rice for their continued support.

May 2008

Samuel Kounev
Ian Gorton
Kai Sachs

Organization

SIPEW 2008 was organized by the department of Computer Science, TU Darmstadt and SPEC (Standard Performance Evaluation Corporation) in cooperation with IEEE, IEEE Computer Society, Gesellschaft für Informatik (G.I.), MMB and Informationstechnische Gesellschaft im VDE (ITG).

Executive Committee

General Co-chairs	Alejandro Buchmann (TU Darmstadt, Germany)
	John Henning (Sun Microsystems, USA)
PC Co-chairs	Samuel Kounev (University of Cambridge, UK)
	Ian Gorton (Pacific Northwest National Laboratory, USA)
Organizing Chair	Kai Sachs (TU Darmstadt, Germany)

Program Committee

Alan Adamson	IBM, Canada
Virgílio Almeida	Federal University of Minas Gerais, Brazil
Simonetta Balsamo	Università Ca' Foscari di Venezia, Italy
Falko Bause	TU Dortmund, Germany
Umesh Bellur	Indian Institute of Technology Bombay, India
Jeremy Bradley	Imperial College London, UK
Gaurav Caprihan	Oracle, India
Shiping Chen	CSIRO ICT Centre, Australia
Vittorio Cortellessa	Universita' dell'Aquila, Italy
Andrea D'Ambrogio	University of Rome "Tor Vergata", Italy
Lieven Eeckhout	Ghent University, Belgium
Rudolf Eigenmann	Purdue University, USA
Stephen Gilmore	University of Edinburgh, UK
Mor Harchol-Balter	Carnegie Mellon University, USA
John Henning	Sun Microsystems, USA
Helen Karatza	Aristotle University of Thessaloniki, Greece
David Lilja	University of Minnesota in Minneapolis, USA
Christoph Lindemann	University of Leipzig, Germany
Daniel Menascé	George Mason University, USA
José Merseguer	Universidad de Zaragoza, Spain
John Murphy	University College Dublin, Ireland
Harald Müller	SAP, Germany
Dorina Petriu	Carleton University, Canada

Steve Realmuto	BEA Systems, USA
Jeff Reilly	Intel, USA
Kai Sachs	TU Darmstadt, Germany
Gary Sevitsky	IBM T.J. Watson Research Center, USA
George Tharakan	Sun Microsystems, USA
Nigel Thomas	University of Newcastle, UK
Petr Tuma	Charles University in Prague, Czech Republic
Reinhold Weicker	formerly Fujitsu Siemens, Germany
Katinka Wolter	Humboldt Universität zu Berlin, Germany
Murray	Carleton University, Canada

External Reviewers

Varsha Apte
Adriana Chis
Allan Clark
Om Damani
Uli Harder
Henrique Jorge Amorim Holanda
Jan Kriege
Lucian Patcas
Diego Perez
Bernhard Riedhofer
Mirco Tribastone
Itamar Viana
Samir Zeort

Sponsors

SAP AG, Germany
Deutsche Telekom, Germany
Sun Microsystems, Germany

Table of Contents

Web Services and Service-Oriented Architectures

Power and Performance

Profiling, Monitoring and Optimization

Scheduling for Server Farms:
Approaches and Open Problems

Mor Harchol-Balter

Computer Science Department
Carnegie Mellon University
Pittsburgh, PA, 15213, USA

Server farms are ubiquitous in applications ranging from Web server farms to high-performance supercomputing systems to call centers. The popularity of the server farm architecture is understandable, as it allows for increased performance, while being cost-effective and easily scalable.

Given the prevalence of server farms, it is surprising that even at this late date so little is understood regarding their performance as compared with their single-server counterpart, particularly with respect to scheduling. Part of the problem is that there are at least three disjoint communities studying scheduling in server farms, including the SIGMETRICS community, the INFORMS community, and the SPAA/STOC/FOCS community, all of which have different approaches and goals. One of our goals in this talk is to make researchers aware of results in these different communities.

Our primary focus is the evaluation of different routing/dispatching policies in server farms. The emphasis will be on *intuition*, so that the talk is accessible to newcomers as well as old-timers. In surveying the newest results, we will also present some practical open problems.

Since server farms are composed of many individual servers, each operating under some scheduling policy, we will begin by briefly examining single-server systems, and the effect of scheduling therein. Here we will pay particular attention to the effect of heavy-tailed job size distributions witnessed in computer system environments [1,2,3,4], in determining which scheduling policies are most effective in practice. We will point out several counter-intuitive results, such as the fact that scheduling policies that favor short jobs may actually help long jobs as well [5,6,7,8,9], and the fact that scheduling results in closed system models can be very different from those in open system models [10].

We will then move on to studying server farm models representative of those used in supercomputing and manufacturing. These involve non-preemptive, First-Come-First-Serve (FCFS) scheduling at the individual servers. We will see that the mean response time of such FCFS server farms can vary by orders of magnitude depending on the routing/dispatching policy used for assigning jobs to servers [11]. We will question common wisdoms, like whether load should be balanced among identical servers [12]. We will also discuss the benefits of cycle stealing in such models [13,14,15,16], and what one can do when the size of jobs isn't known a priori [17].

S. Kounev, I. Gorton, and K. Sachs (Eds.): SIPEW 2008, LNCS 5119, pp. 1–3, 2008.
© Springer-Verlag Berlin Heidelberg 2008

We next turn to server farm models that are representative of Web server farms. Here the individual servers all employ Processor-Sharing (PS) service order, which is a preemptive time-sharing scheduling policy. Examples of such server farms include the Cisco Local Director product, the IBM Network Dispatcher, Microsoft SharePoint, and F5 Labs BIG/IP. We first show that the desired routing/dispatching policy for minimizing mean response time in the case of PS server farms can be very different from that for FCFS server farms. We then focus on a particularly good policy, Join-the-Shortest-Queue, and discuss some existing approximations in the literature (e.g., [18,19,20]) and some new approximations that apply to the case of PS server farms [21].

Finally, we turn to the question of what server farm architectures are optimal for minimizing mean response time. Here we consider server farms where the individual servers employ Shortest-Remaining-Processing-Time (SRPT) scheduling, or there is a central SRPT queue. Such models are very difficult to analyze stochastically. The closest stochastic result is for a server farm with a central priority queue [22]. Primary work on SRPT server farms is dominated by the STOC/FOCS/SPAA community, which uses competitive ratios as its metric. We will describe server farm architectures that appear to be optimal, but aren't, and discuss their competitive ratios, both for the case of a central queue model [23] and an immediate-dispatch model [24]. These results motivate future research directions for researchers in the stochastic community.

References

1. Harchol-Balter, M., Downey, A.: Exploiting process lifetime distributions for dynamic load balancing. ACM Transactions on Computer Systems 15(3) (1997)
2. Barford, P., Crovella, M.E.: Generating representative Web workloads for network and server performance evaluation. In: ACM SIGMETRICS Conference, pp. 151–160 (July 1998)
3. Shaikh, A., Rexford, J., Shin, K.G.: Load-sensitive routing of long-lived ip flows. In: Proceedings of SIGCOMM (September 1999)
4. Schroeder, B., Harchol-Balter, M.: Evaluation of task assignment policies for supercomputing servers: The case for load unbalancing and fairness. Cluster Computing: The journal of Networks, Software Tools, and Applications 7(2), 151–161 (2004)
5. Harchol-Balter, M., Schroeder, B., Bansal, N., Agrawal, M.: Size-based Scheduling to Improve Web Performance. Transactions of Computer Systems 21(2), 207–233 (2003)
6. Wierman, A., Harchol-Balter, M.: Classifying Scheduling Policies with respect to Unfairness in an M/GI/1. In: Proceedings of the ACM Sigmetrics Conference on Measurement and Modeling of Computer Systems (SIGMETRICS), pp. 238–249 (June 2003)
7. Brown, P.: Comparing FB and PS Scheduling Policies. In: Eighth Workkshop on Mathematical Performance Modeling and Analysis (MAMA 2006) (June 2006)
8. Schroeder, B., Harchol-Balter, M.: Web servers under overload: How scheduling can help. ACMTOIT 6(1) (February 2006)
9. Yang, C.W., Wierman, A., Shakkottai, S., Harchol-Balter, M.: Tail asymptotics for policies favoring short jobs in a many-flows regime. In: ACM Sigmetrics 2006 Conference on Measurement and Modeling of Computer Systems (2006)

10. Schroeder, B., Wierman, A., Harchol-Balter, M.: Closed versus Open System Models: a Cautionary Tale. In: Proceedings of Networked Systems Design and Implementation (NSDI 2006), pp. 239–252 (May 2006)
11. Harchol-Balter, M., Crovella, M., Murta, C.: On Choosing a Task Assignment Policy for a Distributed Server System. IEEE Journal of Parallel and Distributed Computing 59, 204–228 (1999)
12. Harchol-Balter, M., Vesilo, R.: To Balance or Unbalance Load in Size-Interval Task Allocation (in submission, 2008)
13. Osogami, T., Harchol-Balter, M., Scheller-Wolf, A.: Analysis of cycle stealing with switching times and thresholds. Performance Evaluation 61(4), 369–374 (2005)
14. Fayole, G., Iasnogorodski, R.: Two coupled processors: the reduction to a reimann-hilbert problem. Zeitschrift für Wahrscheinlichkeitstheorie und verwandte Gebiete 47, 325–351 (1979)
15. Foley, R., McDonald, D.: Exact asymptotics of a queueing network with a cross-trained server. In: Proceedings of INFORMS Annual Meeting (2003)
16. Borst, S., Boxma, O., van Uitert, M.: The asymptotic workload behavior of two coupled queues. Queueing Systems: Theory and Applications 43, 81–102 (2003)
17. Harchol-Balter, M.: Task Assignment with Unknown Duration. Journal of the ACM 49(2), 260–288 (2002)
18. Nelson, R.D., Philips, T.K.: An Approximation to the Response Time for Shortest Queue Routing. In: ACM SIGMETRICS Conference, pp. 181–189 (May 1989)
19. Nelson, R.D., Philips, T.K.: An Approximation for the Mean Response Time for Shortest Queue Routing with General Interarrival and Service Times. Performance Evaluation 17, 123–139 (1993)
20. Wessels, J., Adan, I., Zijm, W.: Analysis of the asymmetric shortest queue problem. Queueing Systems: Theory and Applications 8, 1–58 (1991)
21. Gupta, V., Harchol-Balter, M., Sigman, K., Whitt, W.: Analysis of join-the-shortest-queue routing for web server farms. In: PERFORMANCE 2007 Conference. IFIP WG 7.3 International Symposium on Computer Modeling, Measurement and Evaluation, Cologne, Germany (October 2007)
22. Harchol-Balter, M., Osogami, T., Scheller-Wolf, A., Wierman, A.: Multi-server queueing systems with multiple priority classes. Queueing Systems: Theory and Applications 51(3-4), 331–360 (2005)
23. Leonardi, S., Raz, D.: Approximating total flow time on parallel machines. In: ACM Symposium on Theory of Computing, pp. 110–119 (1997)
24. Avrahami, N., Azar, Y.: Minimizing total flow time and total completion time with immediate dispatching. In: ACM Symposium on Parallel Algorithms and Architectures (SPAA 1997), pp. 11–18 (2003)

SAP Standard Application Benchmarks - IT Benchmarks with a Business Focus

Ulrich Marquard and Clarissa Götz

Performance, Data Management & Scalability, SAP AG
{ulrich.marquard, clarissa.goetz}@sap.com

Abstract. SAP is the world's leading provider of business software. It delivers a comprehensive range of software products and services to its customers: Companies from all types of industries, ranging from small businesses to large, multinational enterprises engaged in global markets. The hardware and software requirements of these businesses are as diverse as the companies themselves, but for most customers they boil down to two key performance indicators: Throughput, of importance mainly for background processing, for example overnight payroll calculations, and response time, of relevance to end users actively engaged on the system. For over 15 years SAP and its hardware and technology partners have developed and used benchmarks to test the performance and scalability of both SAP solutions and the hardware they run on. The SAP Standard Application Benchmarks, first certified as such in 1995, help SAP and its partners prove that their software and hardware components scale up (and down) with their customers' business needs, and support customers in configuring SAP Business Solutions for their productive systems.

1 The Acid Tests for Business Technology: Reliability, Predictability and Scalability

Since the early 1990s, SAP has been running load tests in cooperation with its hardware and technology partners to look into the performance behavior across applications, releases, and hardware platforms. Very quickly it became evident that these load tests had to be standardized to ensure reliable, reproducible and high-quality results. The concept of the *SAP Standard Application Benchmarks* was developed, and a standard process for running and certifying these benchmarks deployed. This framework included clear process definitions, criteria for permissible system configuration and tuning, a standardized environment and a set of benchmark tools to enable the benchmarks to be implemented on different platforms. Also, an independent governing body was established to oversee the certification of the benchmarks and their continued development in response to evolving market needs.

But top performance or performance under extreme load is not all that matters to SAP's customers. Another mission critical criterion is that the behavior

S. Kounev, I. Gorton, and K. Sachs (Eds.): SIPEW 2008, LNCS 5119, pp. 4–8, 2008.

of a business solution remains predictable and reliable as the business volume increases and decreases in the course of a business day, week, month, etc. Scalability is the key word: only if a system is scalable can it be sized appropriately. In sizing, performance results established for a certain system load are used as the basis for extrapolating or interpolating hardware resource requirements for higher or lower business volumes. Thus, the most important reasons why SAP Standard Application Benchmarks are extensively used by SAP, partners and customers are:

- Performance and Scalability - The SAP Standard Application Benchmarks help both SAP and its hardware and technology partners demonstrate the performance, scalability and manageability of even extraordinarily large installations. SAP and its partners have a joint commitment to performance-optimize their technologies and to pass the resulting performance gains on to their customers' businesses, with impressive results: There are configurations available on the market today that would enable an online retail company to turn over $170 million in only one hour's worth of sales order processing, at an average sales price of $10 per sales order item.
- Sizing - By analyzing the benchmarking results that are published at the SAP Benchmarking Web site [4], customers are able to anticipate how a particular hardware and software configuration behaves under high load. Since the SAP Standard Application Benchmarks are also the basis for SAP's sizing methodology[1], they help SAP customers define a system configuration that fits their specific business needs.

An additional important aspect of scalability inherent in the SAP Standard Application Benchmarks is that they create a *scalable load*. As a result, small servers or even laptop computers can be tested with the same benchmark that is used to test very large systems consisting of dozens of servers and hundreds of CPUs.

Moreover, the load that is generated during the run of an SAP Standard Application Benchmark can be predicted with high accuracy, and this is of great advantage for the certification process. A typical check during benchmark certification would be, for example, to validate whether the statistics show that the number of database inserts for a particular table are as expected. *Reproducible load* leads to reproducible results and this consistency, in turn, gives a good indication of the validity and reliability of the benchmarking results. Benchmarks executed on basically the same hardware thus tend to generate very similar results. Tests run internally at SAP with series of benchmarks have shown that the measured accuracy is roughly 1%, which means that performance optimizations within the range of 1% can be measured and validated.

---

[1] SAP provides a well-defined sizing methodology and an online sizing tool, the Quick Sizer, which help customers in their sizing processes. For more information see [1].

2   Methodology and Principles Behind the SAP Standard Application Benchmarks

The SAP Standard Application Benchmarks differ from other IT benchmarks: rather than testing for technical throughput figures such as "transactions / hour" they combine the measurement of system performance with a business application that is productively used in customer implementations. By executing actual business processes, they render application-specific and business-relevant performance indicators, for example, the number of users that can work simultaneously in the system, user interactions per hour, or business throughput figures such as fully processed order line items per hour.

The architecture of the SAP Standard Application Benchmarks is designed in a way that makes it transparent for the system under test as to whether the generated load originates from simulated or real users. This keeps the benchmark results free from distorting artifacts and helps achieve realistic, business-relevant results. For example, all monitoring tools that are activated in productive systems are also enabled for the benchmark, and the benchmark driver is located on an external system, thus producing no additional load or making any influence on load balancing.

Defined in business application terms (for example, "fully processed order line items per hour"), the measured throughput is then mapped onto the resource consumption of the most prominent hardware components (incl. CPU and memory) and the result expressed in a hardware-independent unit of measurement: the *SAP Application Performance Standard (SAPS)*. This unit is derived from the SAP Sales and Distribution (SD) Benchmark, SAP's most important and frequently used benchmark, and is defined as:

$$2,000 \text{ fully processed order line items per hour} = 100 \text{ SAPS}$$

Translated back into technical terms this equals 6000 dialog steps/screen changes or 2400 SAP transactions. Since all benchmark scripts, including that of the SAP SD Benchmark, have remained virtually unchanged over the years, it is possible to track the performance progress of IT technology: SAPS figures have increased 50 fold between 1996 and 2006 (from about 600 to 30000), roughly mirroring the stipulations set forth in Moore's Law[2] (see Figure 1).

The stability of benchmark scripts also enables a comparative evaluation across different platform versions, software releases, or architectures. SAP uses these scripts for quality assurance within its own development community, e.g. to monitor resource consumption during development of a new release, to analyze different system configurations and parameter settings, and to verify hardware sizing. The hardware and technology partners use the SAP Standard Application Benchmarks in their QA efforts, as well, for example, to run tests for new servers.

---

[2] Moore initially stipulated a doubling of transistor counts every year [3], but later redefined the period to two years.

Number of SAPS, two-tier configuration

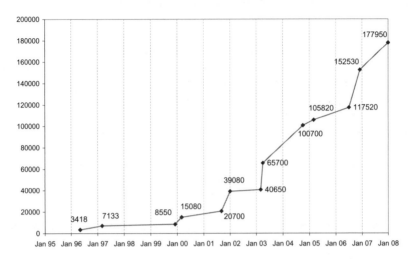

Fig. 1. Development of SAPS achieved for 2-tier configurations (i.e. application server and database server co-located on one system); for details see [4]

3   Shaping the SAP Standard Application Benchmarks

The stability, integrity and agility of the SAP Standard Application Benchmarks are no coincidence. An expert set of people are the motor behind the benchmarks, most notably the *SAP Benchmark Council*. This independent body, consisting of members from SAP and its hardware and technology partners, governs the SAP Standard Application Benchmarks and all related development, certification and publication processes.

The SAP Benchmark Council started in March 1993 as a relatively informal meeting of representatives from SAP and its hardware and technology partners, and was officially inaugurated in 1995. The council meets once per month; its responsibilities include monitoring all activities regarding benchmarking, defining benchmark rules and processes and ensuring the strict adherence to them, as well as controlling the content and publication of the benchmarks. SAP certifies all benchmarks submitted by the partners on behalf of the SAP Benchmark Council and publishes the results at the SAP Benchmarking Web site [4].

To meet the challenges presented by rapid technological change and to reconcile the potentially differing opinions of this multi-vendor assembly, the SAP Benchmark Council uses the principle of spin-off work groups to investigate new topics, discuss the challenges they present to benchmarking, and come up with solutions that benefit customers and can be adopted by all parties involved. These work groups are made up of experts from interested partners and meet on an as-needed basis to create proposals on how a particular requirement can be integrated into the benchmarking process. Virtualization, multi-core computing and Green IT are only a few of the most recent topics on the agenda.

The principles on which the SAP Benchmark Council is founded are both simple and effective: All members have the same rights and responsibilities. This, paired with a common understanding and a selfimposed restraint, ensures that no partner can push through a personal agenda unilaterally. In this way, the SAP Benchmark Council remains flexible and agile, while at the same time ensuring continuity and reliability for customers, partners, and SAP. Fair play is also guaranteed by the fact that each partner can obtain a benchmark submission from another partner for review. This right to disclosure and each partners readiness to hand over this potentially sensitive data to other partners discourages illicit tuning and ensures that the benchmarking processes and results are above-board (for an overview of manipulation detection methods see [2]).

Combined, these principles and methods help maintain the high level of credibility and visibility of the SAP Standard Application Benchmarks in the industry, and all involved - SAP, partners and customers - have a vested interest in keeping it that way.

4   Conclusion

The SAP Standard Application Benchmarks have established themselves as some of the most credible and popular application benchmarks in the industry, not least of all because they combine the measurement of system performance with business applications as they are productively used by customers. A standard process and an independent governing body for the definition, execution, submission and certification of these benchmarks - the SAP Benchmark Council - ensure that the benchmarks are portable across all major platforms and operating systems, and that they generate reproducible and publishable results whose integrity is beyond doubt.

References

1. Janssen, S., Marquard, U.: Sizing SAP Systems. Galileo Press, Bonn, Germany (2007)
2. Klein, M.: Manipulation Detection of Benchmark Results for Mobile Devices. Diploma thesis, Institut für Telematik (ITM), Telecooperation Office (TecO), Universität Karlsruhe (TH), Germany (2008)
3. Moore, G.E.: Cramming more components onto integrated circuits. Electronics Magazine 38(8), 114–117 (1965)
4. SAP Standard Application Benchmarks, http://www.sap.com/benchmark

The Relationship of Performance Models to Data

Murray Woodside

Carleton University, Ottawa, Canada
cmw@sce.carleton.ca

Abstract. Performance engineering of software could benefit from a closer integration of the use of performance models, and the use of measured data. Models can contribute to early warning of problems, exploration of solutions, and scalability evaluation, and when they are fitted to data they can summarize the data as a special powerful form of fitted function. Present industrial practice virtually ignores models, because of the effort to create them, and concern about how well they fit the system when it is implemented. The first concern is being met by automated generation from software specifications. The second concern can be met by fitting the models to data as it becomes available. This will adapt the model to the new situation and validate it, in a single step. The present paper summarizes the fitting process, using standard tools of nonlinear regression analysis, and shows it in action on examples of queueing and extended queueing models. The examples are a background for a discussion about the relationship between the models, and measurement data.

1 Motivation

Software performance modeling and measurement are insufficiently integrated. Roughly speaking we may say that measurement is used to test software and to identify performance problems, often in laboratory conditions; modeling is used for prior analysis of planned systems (when there are no measurements available), for capacity and scalability analysis (exploiting the capability to model large deployments), and for insight into deep problems. There are a number of exceptions; one is in tracking performance models for adaptation of time-varying systems (e.g. [19]).

In [20] the potential benefits of more strongly unifying these two aspects of performance analysis were identified as

- end-to-end performance process unifying prior estimates with testing/debugging and capacity modeling
- better quality models calibrated frequently and routinely from data, using a strong and maintained connection between the model and the system,
- more efficient measurement, by using models to plan the measurement trials.

The weak link here seems to be the calibration of models from data. Long experience in creating models teaches how difficult it can be to determine their parameters empirically. Some critical kinds of data are often difficult to obtain, notably the CPU

S. Kounev, I. Gorton, and K. Sachs (Eds.): SIPEW 2008, LNCS 5119, pp. 9–28, 2008.

demands of particular operations. However, recent work on tracking model parameter values with a Kalman Filter estimator has indicated how data-gathering can be eased by use of a suitable estimator [20]. That work was for tracking parameters which are changing. This paper considers a different problem, modeling a system which is not changing, but which is operated under different workloads and configurations. It describes a simple framework for estimating a model by nonlinear regression, and some properties of the resulting model (including how it differs from one made up from expert knowledge alone). Standard statistical concepts provide a bridge between the practice of measurement and the practice of modeling.

The reduction of difficulty comes from indirect estimation of model parameters, using only measurements at the interfaces of the system. A prime example is the difficulty of estimating the CPU demand of a particular operation. Direct measurement requires source-code instrumentation (as in profiling, for instance) but a model-based estimator only requires accessible performance measures such as operation response times, and then estimates the CPU demand to fit the measured values.

Recent efforts to calibrate CPU demands from accessible measures include [10] and [3], in which individual operations were measured in separate benchmark experiments, and the patent application [16], which applies an optimization technique to fit a queueing model to data. The patent motivation includes the rationale:

> "There should be a simple method to estimate the parameters of the model, given high-level system measurements obtained by external monitors, rather than adding instrumentation with detailed level measurement probes to applications." [16]

The present paper combines ideas from statistics textbooks and the performance modeling literature, and shows how they might be able to unify the practice of performance engineering of software. Its methods can be applied to *any* performance modeling formalism. Relevant background for modeling is given by Smith and Williams [14], Balsamo et al [1], and in the proceedings of the WOSP conference [21]. Representative material on measurement is provided in the Paradyn papers by Miller and co-workers (e.g. [11]), and by the online tutorial [2].

2   Software Performance Analysis

2.1   A Unified Process

The vision of a unified process, which this paper intends to support, is sketched in Figure 1 reproduced from [20]. Performance predictions and data feed a common data repository with a united definition of the semantics of predicted, measured and required values, defined during requirements analysis. Performance values are derived early and evolve with the design and the product. Performance knowledge can be leveraged, rather than being abandoned soon after it is produced. The awkward fact that performance is a moving target and one never measures or models the same system

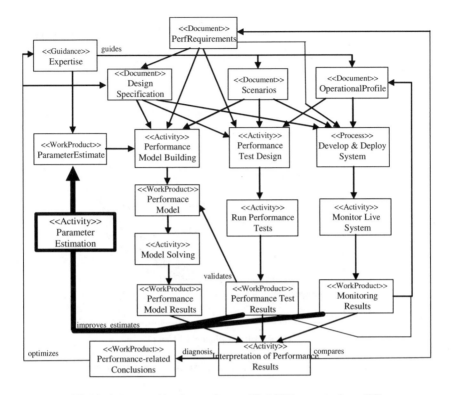

Fig. 1. A proposed landscape for a unified SPE process, from [20]

twice, is covered by versioning the data in synchrony with versions of the design, the run-time configuration and the code.

The estimators described in this paper provide the links shown by the very heavy arrows, by which parameter values are calibrated from data from a test or an operational system. These links maintain the parameters of the model as the software is completed and make the model available for planning deployments and new versions of the system.

The estimators form a bridge between what we will term a data-centric view of performance, on the right-hand side of Figure 1, and a model-centric view, on the left.

2.2 Data-Centric View

An extreme data-centric view is that only measurement data is significant, because only the data can capture the full complexity and interactions of the system. Measurements are carried out in tests or trials, in which a controlled and instrumented configuration is operated under a specified workload, and as much data is recorded as possible, including performance measurements at system interfaces, and measures on internal operations.

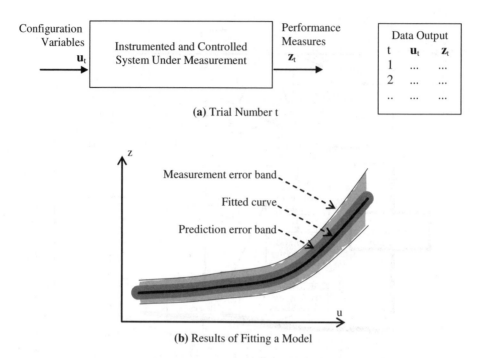

(a) Trial Number t

(b) Results of Fitting a Model

Fig. 2. Inputs and outputs of a system performance measurement trial

A high-level view of system measurement is sketched in Figure 2(a), showing the inputs and outputs of a single measurement test or trial, identified as trial number t:

- $\mathbf{u}_t$, a vector of *controlled parameters* whose values can be assigned in a measurement experiment or a proposed configuration. These are system parameters that could be significant for performance. They might include the number of processor cores, the size of a thread pool, cache or buffer pool, the size of files to be transferred or of database transactions. Qualitative attributes of a configuration, such as the use of a particular middleware or component, or the presence/absence of some feature, can be included through categorical variables in u, but will not be considered here.
- $\mathbf{z}_t$, a vector of measured values of any performance quantities of interest. These can be average values, percentiles of delay distributions or any other well-defined measure. We assume the system is stationary, and for any value of the controlled parameters the measures have defined and repeatable values apart from sampling error due to a finite measurement period.

A series of measurement trials gives a tabulated relationship between the controlled variables **u** and the measured responses **z**, which for one component of each can be plotted as shown in Figure 2(b). The measurement errors are indicated as a shaded band.

Many kinds of measurement systems have been used. We can categorize types of data into four groups, in increasing order of difficulty to obtain it:

1. data gathered by the operating system, such as processor and process utilizations, and I/O counts
2. data collected at system interfaces by timers and counters,
3. profiling data on CPU usage by operation, down to quite fine grained methods, using embedded source code instrumentation (in for instance Purify [4]) or stack sampling (as in gprof).
4. Logical resource usage, such as critical section monitoring in Paradyn [12].

In much of the performance analysis of commercial software it is not practical to use the more sophisticated tools in groups 3 and 4, because of time and cost, and because source code is not available for third-party components. And those tools often distort the system by introducing significant fine-grained costs. Field measurements are often restricted to groups 1 and 2, and even in the lab there is an advantage in only requiring the simpler forms of instrumentation.

In measurements to support the model fitting described below, the performance measures are delays measured at component and messaging interfaces, and utilizations of processors and processes. If a model is fitted to the data, shown as a solid line, its predictions also have a prediction error indicated by the darker shaded band. This band is narrower than the measurement error band, because the fitting process smooths out the errors of individual measurements.

2.3 Model-Centric View

The model-centric view seeks an abstraction that captures the essence of the system performance in its simplest form. Performance models often do not start from data. For example, to provide insight into performance issues during the system design phase, performance models can be created based entirely on the design and on expert judgment [14]. A given model has a structure, based on the elements of the design, and parameters which describe what the system will do. (The particular modeling method to be used is not our focus here, but is surveyed in [1].) We should regard the model calculation as a vector function $\mathbf{h}(\mathbf{x}, \mathbf{u})$, as illustrated in Figure 3:

$\mathbf{u}$ = configuration parameters as before
$\mathbf{x}$ = parameter values in the model, which must be obtained by some process
$\mathbf{y}$ = vector of predicted performance measures = $\mathbf{h}(\mathbf{x}, \mathbf{u})$

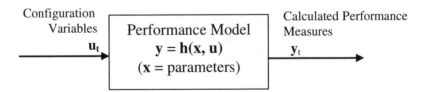

Fig. 3. Performance model as a function

Despite the difficulties in obtaining parameter values, Smith and Williams (who have developed procedures for gathering structure and parameters for early models) show that the results have many practical uses in practice [14]. Their approach includes the important notion of expressing a parameter as an interval expressing expert judgment as a range of values parameter value in the range [min, most likely value, max].

Using these interval values we can show the model predictions as a plot with a central value and an uncertainty band, for parameters within these intervals, similar to the darker band in Figure 2(b).

It may be confidently stated that good insight into structure is often available, but the parameter values are often problematic. *The main barrier to usability of these early models lies in lack of confidence in the parameter values.*

The Bridge: Estimation

To fit a model to experimental data it is common to estimate its parameters directly, by measuring the property represented by the parameter. For CPU demand parameters (for instance) this often requires recording the CPU associated with each operation, as in profiling. Other kinds of parameters include the relative frequency of different operation invocations or messages, and the sizes of data objects.

Here we consider a more general version of estimation, which includes direct estimation as a special case. We assume a model structure is determined, within the chosen formalism, from expert knowledge or system design documents. To this structure we attach three kinds of parameters:

- *assumed parameters*, whose values are known and do not vary during the estimation process or in planned deployments. We will not consider these further here; they are lumped in with the structure.
- controlled parameter vector $\mathbf{u}$, as above, taking value $\mathbf{u_t}$ in trial t,
- estimated parameter vector $\mathbf{x}$, assumed to be constant.

and performance measures of interest, given by

- vector $\mathbf{y}$ for the model and
- vector $\mathbf{z_t}$ for measurement trial t, also as above.

The result of a series of trials is a pair of sequences $\mathbf{z_t}$ and $\mathbf{u_t}$ for t = 1,...Tmax.

A standard basis for estimation, which we will use, is to maximize the likelihood of the model. We assume that the measurements $\mathbf{z}$ are determined by an unknown function $\mathbf{h(x, u)}$ (to be found) plus a measurement error vector $\mathbf{v}$:

$$\mathbf{z_t} = \mathbf{h(x, u_t)} + \mathbf{v_t}$$

Assuming that vector $\mathbf{u_t}$ is independent over time with a joint normal distribution with mean zero and covariance matrix $\mathbf{R}$, we obtain the maximum-likelihood estimate as the vector $\mathbf{x}$ that minimizes E($\mathbf{x}$):

$$\hat{\mathbf{x}} = \arg \min E(\mathbf{x}), \quad E(\mathbf{x}) = \Sigma_t (\mathbf{y_t} - \mathbf{z_t})^T \mathbf{R}^{-1}(\mathbf{y_t} - \mathbf{z_t})$$

If we only know $\mathbf{R}$ to within a constant, the constant can also be estimated. If components of $\mathbf{v}$ are independent with the same variance, $\mathbf{R}$ is proportional to $\mathbf{I}$ and $\hat{\mathbf{x}}$ is the familiar least squares estimator. Estimates made with $\mathbf{I}$ in place of $\mathbf{R}$ (that is, plain least-squares estimates) are unbiased but less accurate.

This is a standard optimization problem, which can be solved in many ways. Many of these exploit the special structure of $E(\mathbf{x})$, which is a quadratic form. A standard approach, treated in statistics texts such as [8], is Gauss-Newton iteration which gives an approximate solution through a series of linear regressions. Gauss-Newton iteration was used to analyze the example given below. Since it is not a widely-known procedure, the adaptation of Gauss-Newton iteration to performance models is given in detail in the Appendix.

If $\mathbf{x_t}$ is not assumed to be constant, then it can be modeled as a function of time (provided the trials are regularly spaced in time) and estimated with an optimal filter such as the Kalman filter; this case is not considered further here.

2.4 Inference: Knowledge and Uncertainty

A major impediment to the use of any kind of model (not just a performance model) is the feeling, in a potential user, that one should not trust the predictions if one does not understand the limitations of the model. A substantial part of these limitations is, the prediction uncertainty due to inaccurate parameter values, and these can be estimated as confidence intervals. This informs the potential user of the accuracy, which may be different for different measures coming from the model, and poor accuracy may identify the need for more information, depending on the decisions to be made. It also places the predictions into a familiar framework of statistical predictions and statistical quality control, which industrial decision makers can deal with. For example, if one can give the probability of missing a performance target by different amounts, it enriches the consideration of risk.

Within these confidence bounds, the model becomes a representation of the data.

Using the approximate maximum likelihood and non-linear regression framework considered here, estimation errors and prediction errors are effectively assumed to be normally distributed. Normality is a reasonable assumption for measurement errors which are averages or sums, due to the central limit theorem. However the nonlinearity of the model reduces the validity of the assumption for estimation and prediction errors.

The most basic and familiar representation of uncertainty takes the form of confidence intervals, which are found as part of the standard inference results for regression:

- confidence intervals for the parameters $\mathbf{x} = \hat{\mathbf{x}} \pm \mathbf{CIx}$
- confidence intervals for the predictions $\mathbf{y} = \mathbf{h}(\hat{\mathbf{x}}, u) \pm \mathbf{CIy}$

where the vector $\mathbf{CIx}$ is the confidence interval half-widths for $\mathbf{x}$. As we will see, parameters that make little difference to the prediction tend to be estimated with large confidence limits.

3 Illustration: Queueing Model

The small queueing network model shown in Figure 4 will be considered as the first example. It represents a small Web server with its disk (node 2) and a separate node for CGI application service (node 3). A response includes all the work done between visits to the "Users" node in the Figure, which represents the operation in which a user responds to one system output and generates the next request to the system. Users have a characteristic "think" time for this operation, which will be set to zero here. Service times are assumed to be exponential. We consider one controllable parameter, three demand parameters to be estimated, and four measures.

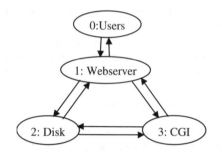

Fig. 4. A small queueing model

Then the queueing model has four parameters:

$\mathbf{u}$ = N = the number of active jobs, assumed to be constant (so this is a "closed" model), with default value 4,

$\mathbf{x}$ = [x(1), x(2), x(3)] = the total average demands for service by nodes 1, 2 and 3, with actual values [2, 3, 4] sec/response.

$\mathbf{y}$ = [y(1), y(2), y(3), y(4)] = [T(1), T(2), T(3), f], where T(i) is the mean response time of node i, totalled over a user response, and f is the throughput of user requests.

The model is assumed to satisfy the separability conditions for product form queueing networks, which means that it can be solved by Mean Value Analysis (MVA) [5].

The data for illustrating the use of nonlinear regression were obtained by simulating the same queueing network for different durations, and with different numbers of users, as shown in Figure 5. Clearly this oversimplifies the fitting problem, since the performance model ought to fit to some degree. However it serves to demonstrate that the method can find the right model, and it illustrates the important issue of accuracy of the fitted parameters.

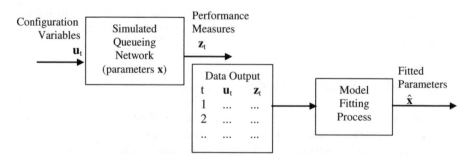

Fig. 5. Configuration of the Computations for the Illustration

To simulate measured data, the system was simulated for 10 trials, each of duration S time units, with from 1 to 10 users; node 3 approaches saturation at a population of about 8. S was varied from 1000 time units to 100000, and the total simulation time was varied from 10^4 to 10^7 time units. The throughput ranged from about 0.1/time unit with one user, to 0.25 with 10 users, so a trial of length 1000 includes between 100 and 250 responses. In the estimation, analytic derivatives were computed for the H matrix by extending the MVA algorithm as described in [19].

Two sets of experiments were performed with zero "think time" at node 0, and with a mean think time of 10 units. Table 1 shows the demand parameter estimates and their confidence intervals. Since the random think time introduces additional variation in the data, it is not surprising that most confidence intervals are a little wider for the second set.

Table 1. Queue Model Parameter Estimates and their Confidence Intervals

Expt/Trials/ Length of Trial	Think Z	$\hat{x}(1) \pm CIx(1)$		$\hat{x}(2) \pm CIx(2)$		$\hat{x}(3) \pm CIx(3)$	
A1/10/1000000	0	2.003	0.0109	3.005	0.0108	4.005	0.0087
A2/10/100000	0	1.992	0.0223	2.989	0.0222	4.011	0.0178
A3/100/10000	0	2.011	0.039	3.077	0.038	4.044	0.031
A4/10/10000	0	2.018	0.018	2.994	0.018	4.004	0.014
A5/10/1000	0	2.182	0.204	2.967	0.217	3.848	0.181
B1/10/1000000	10	2.005	0.0089	2.994	0.0097	4.009	0.0081
B2/10/100000	10	2.003	0.0215	3.010	0.0234	4.036	0.0194
B3/100/10000	10	2.001	0.025	2.999	0.027	3.941	0.023
B4/10/10000	10	1.939	0.072	2.944	0.078	3.925	0.065
B5/10/1000	10	1.854	0.221	2.798	0.247	3.980	0.188

From the results in Table 1, we can see that:
- The confidence intervals are tighter for the largest demand values (server 3), which corresponds to the most saturated resources. This is very natural, since the regression is controlled by the sensitivity of the performance measures to the parameters. This is shown by the sensitivity matrix H, which at convergence (in experiment B5, but the others are similar) is

$$H = \begin{array}{ccc} \mathbf{2.9219} & -0.3164 & -1.8522 \\ -0.1388 & \mathbf{5.6991} & -3.5126 \\ -0.4019 & -1.7367 & \mathbf{10.3132} \\ -0.0044 & -0.0119 & -0.0474 \end{array}$$

The columns represent the sensitivity of the four measures (three node response times and one throughput) to the three node CPU demands. The bold values show that each server response time is most sensitive to its own service time, but the other values show larger magnitudes in column 3 than the other columns. In particular row 4 showing sensitivity of overall system performance, has its largest element in column 3.
- Although server 2 is more heavily utilized than server 1, (and its demand shows greater sensitivity in the H matrix) the confidence intervals for their demands are similar, since neither is determining for performance.

- Longer measurement trials give more accurate estimates, which is not surprising since the measurement error is less. However Table 1 does not provide very consistent advice on how much better the accuracy will be. Estimates by averaging improve their accuracy in the ratio of the square root of the estimation time, but these estimates improve more slowly (a factor of 10 more simulation time gives only a factor of 2 or less reduction in the confidence interval width).
- It is interesting that dividing the total trial time into 100 shorter trials gave worse confidence intervals, than 10 trials each ten times as long. Possibly end effects in the simulations (start-up of the queues) account for this.

The response-time predictions of the model for populations from 1 to 20 are plotted in Figure 6, for Expt. 5 with the shortest simulations, including 95% confidence intervals. We see an increasing error band because the parameter errors are amplified at larger populations, Essentially they reflect the percentage error in the demand parameters, particularly the dominant one.

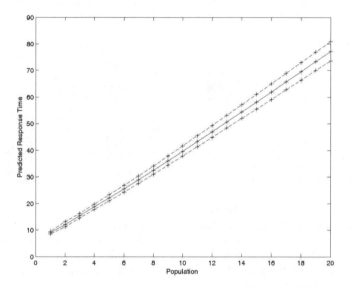

Fig. 6. Output predictions of the queue model found for Case B5, with 95% confidence intervals

3.1 Structure

A recurring question is, have we captured all the structure of the system? In a classical queueing model, this means, is there another queueing resource that is not provided for in the model. Given the very straighforward structure of queueing models, one can easily add a node and fit its demand. The data used for the tests in this section was generated by a simulation of a three-queue model. If we attempt to fit a fourth queue, we can test to see if the fit is significantly better. Table 2 shows results for fitting four service demands to the same data as used in experiments B1 (long measurement runs) and B5 (short runs, giving larger measurement errors). The sums of squares criterion $E(C_i)$ is given for these results to compare to the value $E(B_i)$ for a three-queue model. We can see there is no reduction.

Table 2. Results for fitting models with four queues when the system has only three

Expt	$\hat{\mathbf{x}}$ (1)± CIx(1)		$\hat{\mathbf{x}}$ (2)± CIx(2)		$\hat{\mathbf{x}}$ (3)± CIx(3)		$\hat{\mathbf{x}}$ (4)± CIx(4)		E for Ci	E for Bi
C1(as B1)	2.005	0.009	2.994	0.010	4.010	0.009	0.005	0.201	2.577	2.579
C5(as B5)	1.858	0.231	2.808	0.263	4.006	0.203	0.470	4.127	1482	1481

It is easy to see that the fourth queue in this model is not useful or significant to the fit. One giveaway (that the fourth queue is not very significant) is that the confidence interval half-width is much larger than the fitted demand. When the data is very accurate, in C1, the fitted value is also near zero, but when it is less accurate as in C5, the fitted value is quite a lot more than zero. Some delay due to servers 1 and 2 is evidently being accounted for in this case by the extra ghost server.

The significance is tested using the sums of squared errors E. The test statistics are:

For C1: [(E(B1) - E(C1))/1]/[E(B1)/36] = [0.001]/[2.579/36] = 0.014
For C5: [(E(B5) - E(C5))/1]/[E(B5)/36] = [-1]/[1481/36] = -0.024

The test statistic cannot be negative in linear regression, where the model is a sum of terms each with a coefficient. However this is a nonlinear regression in which the model is not a sum of terms, and we are comparing the results of two independent approximate minimizations. Even so the model with additional parameters should give a smaller E; the fact that we obtained a larger sum of squares must be due to approximation error. The critical value at the 95% level is F(1,36,0.95) = 4.14. Case C1 is two orders of magnitude from significance, and case C2 also does not indicate significance.

4   Illustration with a Layered Model

Real software systems have a lot more structure to their resource use, than a classical queueing network model. The layered queueing network (LQN) formalism [5][6][12] captures the nested use of resources, including logical resources such as process threads, buffers, and locks, and does so in a formalism that represents large-scale aspects of the software architecture, such as concurrent processes.

Figure 7 shows an example LQN representing a web application. The bold rectangles represent concurrent processes (called *tasks* in LQN terminology) with the attached rectangles representing their externally invoked operations (called *entries*), and associated to oval symbols representing their host processors. Entries are labeled with their CPU demand, in suitable time units, and in the figure the entry labels show both a symbolic name prefixed by $, and a value. The name identifies a parameter which was estimated, and the value is the value used in the simulation to generate the data. We can later judge the estimation process by how close it comes to the original value. Entries call or request service from other entries, indicated by arrows; the solid arrowheads here indicate that the caller waits for the response (blocking calls). An entry may have a second phase or delayed operation, after it sends a response to its requester, so here the entry appOp shows host demands and database requests for two phases.

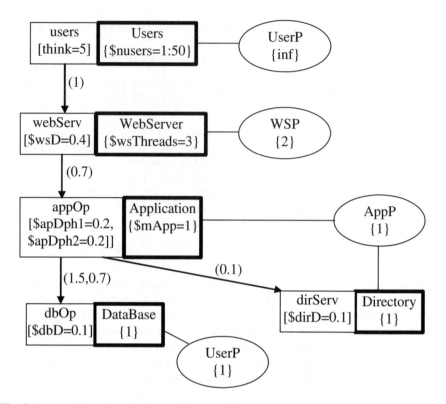

Fig. 7. Layered Queueing model used for the illustration. The parameters with $name were estimated; the numbers show the values used in the simulation.

The servers in an LQN include both the tasks and the processors. Processors can have a relative rate (not shown) and a multiplicity, in curly brackets (to represent multicore or symmetric multiprocessors), and tasks can also have a multiplicity (shown in curly brackets) representing the size of a finite thread pool. The Users are a special class of task, that does not serve any requests, and represent the customers to the system. An infinite processor represents one processor per task.

This model was simulated to generate data for 10 trials, using numbers of users from 5 to 50 in steps of 10. For estimation of the seven parameters, the configuration vector **u** again consisted of the number of users. Estimation was by Gauss-Newton iteration of the nonlinear regression problem, as described in theAppendix. The derivatives needed for the H matrix were computed by finite differences, after rerunning the analytic solver for a slightly (1%) perturbed value of the parameter, for parameters with real values. Parameters with integer values ($wsThreads and $mApp) were perturbed by 1 unit.

Table 3 shows the results for the parameters with the half confidence interval below each result, for two experiments. In experiment D1 there were 10 trials of duration 1000 units, in experiment D2 there were 10 trials of 100000 units. Under the name of each estimated variable is given, in brackets, the value of the variable in the simulation. This is the "correct" value for the variable, and the estimate should be close to this value.

Table 3. Results for fitting seven parameters of the LQN in Fig 6 to data generated by simulation

Expt./ Trial length	$dirD	$WSD	$appDph1	$appDph2	$dbD	$mApp	$wsThreads	E
Correct value	0.1	0.4	0.2	0.2	0.1	1	3	
D1/1000	0.695	0.559	0.192	0.234	0.101	1.000	3.000	0.5935
Confidence Int. ±	0.693	0.138	0.021	0.232	0.002	0.207	0.050	
Conf. Int. as %	100%	25%	11%	100%	2%	21%	16%	
D2/100000	0.378	0.608	0.195	0.111	0.100	1.000	3.000	0.1960
Confidence Int. ±	0.367	0.059	0.011	0.202	0.001	0.140	0.024	
Conf. Int. as %	97%	10%	6%	182%	1%	14%	8%	

The results show that

- All the confidence intervals cover the correct values of the parameters. That is, the estimation technique was able to recover the parameter values, given the correct model structure. This is a basic requirement for a trustworthy estimator.
- The longer experiments produced only moderately more accurate results. In estimating a mean value, 100 times as many samples (as in experiment C2) would give a confidence interval only 1/10 as wide; here the ratios are no better than 1/3 and mostly worse than that. This suggests that more short experiments are more worthwhile.
- Curiously, one result has lower accuracy for the longer experiment, the second phase demand of the application task App. Since the second phase does not block the web server, it only affects the visible performance through congestion of App. However as App is quite busy (96% utilized, see below), the performance might be expected to be sensitive to this parameter.
- The most accurately estimated parameters were the demands for the database and application phase 1. We can see that lower-layer parameters are more accurately estimated. Since they block higher-layer tasks, they influence the performance.
- The resource utilizations show push-back between the layers, as is well-known for software bottlenecks. The utilizations with 50 users are:
  - processor utilizations:
    - WSP: 0.88 (for a dual processor, that is maximum utilization of 2.0)
    - AppP: 0.61
    - DBP: 0.34
  - task utilizations:
    - WS: 3.0 (for three threads)
    - App: 0.96
    - DB: 0.34
    - Dir: 0.04

The App task is virtually saturated, and waiting for it introduces delays which make the WS task also saturated (the push-back). But the servers below the App task (its processor and the database server) are not heavily utilized.

The most sensitive parameters (indicated by the percentage confidence interval widths) are the App processor and database server, which determine the holding time of the App task for one service, and thus the system throughput and delay.

- One parameter dirD is of marginal significance, based on its confidence interval. If we examine the LQN we see that the directory service is a relatively light load on processor AppP, so apparently it doesn't have enough impact to be accurately estimated. The accuracy of estimation, relative to the actual value of 0.1, is also poor.
- The estimation of integer parameters was successful. The confidence intervals are found in the conventional way, but are only of interest if the half-width is near to or greater than 1.

Experiment D2 was repeated for a test with a longer user think time (15 units instead of 5). Provided the correct think time was used as a controlled parameter in the calculations for fitting, the estimated parameters and confidence intervals were identical. The predicted performance for think times of 5 and 15 units are plotted in Figure 8 with their 95% confidence intervals.

Equally, the model can be used to extrapolate from these experimental conditions to different values of population, think time, and demands of operations for resources.

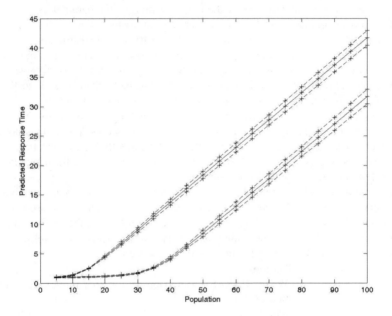

Fig. 8. Response time predictions for two values of the user think time (5 units and 15 units)

5   Exploiting the Model

A brief summary of uses of the model is (see also Figure 1):

1. Performance test design: the equation for confidence intervals (in the appendix) shows that they depend on the covariances R and sensitivities H (which come from the model). H can be affected by the configuration used to gather test data, and should be chosen so that configurations that give high sensitivities to all the desired parameters, should be combined. The duration of performance tests can also be chosen, to give adequate accuracy.

2. Performance problem diagnosis and analysis of improvements: where performance is inadequate, solutions at the architecture level can be analysed by changes to the performance model.
3. Scalability analysis: scope out the space of probably configurations to identify scalability limitations, by creating models of large configurations, built from sub-models for components. This is straightforward for LQN models, where each process has a submodel. Different kinds of scaling strategy can be analysed.
4. Product configurations for individual clients can be evaluated, using a mature calibrated model of the product.
5. Product upgrade analysis: when new features are planned, estimates for their workload can be included in an existing model for a quick evaluation of their impact; this can be refined using prototypes.
6. Product performance management: some techniques for adaptive control of service configurations use a model of the application, with parameters that are updated online to track changes in system usage, efficiency or load (e.g. [8]).

5.1 Validity of the Model

The fitting process effectively validates the model for the operational conditions under which the data is gathered, and for nearby conditions within the range of the configuration parameters. In this range we may say the model is used for interpolation in the data. Of course additional validation may be done by additional measurements within that range.

Many of the uses listed above require extrapolation from the data, and here is where performance models are most useful. The advantage of fitting a performance model instead of a polynomial or some other arbitrary function, comes from its realistic underlying resource-usage semantics. So, how can we maintain confidence in the predictions of the model.

Roughly speaking there are two ways the model may fail in extrapolation. First, as we move away from the fitted range the confidence interval of predictions becomes wider, as seen in Figures 6 and 8. This is understandable and can simply be recorded. Second, some resource which was not included in the model, or which was not heavily enough utilized to be accurately modeled, may become an active constraint in a larger configuration. Consider for instance if the directory server in Figure 7 were shared among 30 replicas of the application, it would be an important limitation. Or imagine a database buffer pool which is not restricting at the scales of the test, but which becomes a constraint in larger systems. Some comments follow:

1. Many parameters which are insensitive in small-scale testing are always insensitive, and therefore their accuracy is not critical. The model itself can be used to calculate the sensitivity in large-scale versions, if it is a concern.
2. Resources which may become critical in larger deployments should be identified based on system expertise, and perhaps tests can be constructed which stress those resources.
3. Traffic statistics, both the intervals between arrivals and the distribution of demands made on applications, can challenge the assumptions of the performance modeling tools. Long-tailed distributions for arrivals and demands, and correlations between successive demands, are examples. These possibilities should not be

ignored in any case, as they typically require more reserve capacity to handle them with adequate performance. If they occur they also may require a more sophisticated model. However the methods for parameter estimation would be the same, as shown here.

5.2 Simplified Models

Regression modeling usually seeks to fit the simplest model that can explain the data. One indicator of having excessive model structure and parameters is, fitted values with large confidence intervals, as shown for queueing models in Table 2. However an LQN model is simplified not by removing a single parameter, but by removing or approximating a structural unit, a task or subset of tasks. A suitable approximation for elements left out of a model is to introduce a pure delay in the holding time of an affected resource, or in the response time. This delay can be fitted, and has a similar role to fitting a constant in linear regression.

6 Conclusions

Performance models can be maintained in sync with a developing product, by calibrating their parameters from performance test data. The estimation techniques described here use standard statistical methods, and non-intrusive monitoring to obtain test data. The limitations of prediction accuracy can also be estimated.

Acknowledgements

This research was supported by the Natural Sciences and Engineering Research Council of Canada (NSERC), the Ontario Centres of Excellence (OCE), and by the IBM Centre for Advanced Studies, Toronto.

References

[1] Balsamo, S., DiMarco, A., Inverardi, P., Simeoni, M.: Model-based Performance Prediction in Software Development. IEEE Trans. on Software Eng. 30(5), 295–310 (2004)
[2] Barber, S.: Beyond performance testing, parts 1-14, IBM DeveloperWorks, Rational Technical Library (2004), http://www-128.ibm.com/developerworks/rational/library/4169.html
[3] Bogardi-Meszoly, A., Levendovszky, T., Charaf, H., Hashimoto, T.: Improved Evaluation Algorithm for Performance Prediction with Error Analysis. In: Proc. 11th Int. Conf. on Intelligent Engineering Systems, pp. 301–306 (2007)
[4] IBM, IBM Rational PurifyPlus, Purify, PureCoverage, and Quantify: Getting Started, G126-5339-00 (May 2002)
[5] Franks, G., Majumdar, S., Neilson, J., Petriu, D., Rolia, J., Woodside, M.: Performance Analysis of Distributed Server Systems. In: Proc. Sixth International Conference on Software Quality (6ICSQ), Ottawa, pp. 15–26 (1996)
[6] Franks, G., Petriu, D., Woodside, M., Xu, J., Tregunno, P.: Layered bottlenecks and their mitigation. In: Proc of 3rd Int. Conference on Quantitative Evaluation of Systems QEST 2006, Riverside, CA, September 2006, pp. 103–114 (2006)

[7]   Jain, R.: The Art of Computer Systems Performance Analysis. John Wiley & Sons Inc., Chichester (1991)

[8]   Kutner, M.H., Nachtsheim, C.J., Neter, J., Li, W.: Applied Linear Statistical Models, 5th edn. McGraw-Hill, New York (2005)

[9]   Litoiu, M., Zheng, T., Woodside, M.: Service System Resource Management Based on a Tracked Layered Performance Model. In: Proc. IEEE Int. Conf. on Autonomic Computing, Dublin (June 2006)

[10] Liu, Y., Fekete, A., Gorton, I.: Design-Level Performance Prediction of Component-Based Applications. IEEE Trans. on Software Engineering 31(11), 928–941 (2005)

[11] Miller, B.P., Callaghan, M.D., Cargille, J.M., Hollingsworth, J.K., Irvin, R.B., Karavanic, K.L., Kunchithapadam, K., Newhall, T.: The Paradyn Parallel Performance Measurement Tool. IEEE Computer 28(11), 37–46 (1995)

[12] Rolia, J.A., Sevcik, K.C.: The Method of Layers. IEEE Trans. on Software Engineering 21(8), 689–700 (1995)

[13] Roth, P.C., Miller, B.P.: On-line Automated Performance diagnosis on Thousands of Processes. In: ACM SigPLAN Symp. on Principles and Practices of Parallel Programming (PPOPP 2006), New York (March 2006)

[14] Smith, C.U., Williams, L.G.: Performance Solutions. Addison-Wesley, Reading (2002)

[15] Storm, A.J., Garcia-Arellano, C., Lightstone, S.S., Diao, Y., Surendra, M.: Adaptive self-tuning memory in DB2. In: Proc. 32nd Int. Conf. on Very large databases, Seoul, pp. 1081–1092 (2006)

[16] Tantawi, A.N.: Method and system for dynamic performance modeling of computer application services. USA, Patent Application 20070299638 (2007)

[17] Vugrin, K.W., Swiler, L.P., Roberts, R.M., Stucky-Mack, N.J., Sullivan, S.P.: Confidence Region Estimation: Techniques for Nonlinear Regression: Three Case Studies. Sandia Laboratories Report SAND2005-6893 (October 2005)

[18] Woodside, M., Petriu, D.C., Petriu, D.B., Shen, H., Israr, T., Merseguer, J.: Performance by Unified Model Analysis (PUMA). In: Proc. WOSP 2005, Mallorca, pp. 1–12 (2005)

[19] Woodside, C.M., Zheng, T., Litoiu, M.: The Use of Optimal Filters to Track Parameters of Performance Models. In: Proc. 2nd Int. Conf. on Quantitative Evaluation of Systems, Torino, Italy, pp. 74–84 (2005)

[20] Woodside, M., Franks, G., Petriu, D.C.: The Future of Software Performance Engineering. In: Proc Future of Software Engineering 2007, at ICSE 2007, May 2007, pp. 171–187, Order Number P2829. IEEE Computer Society, Los Alamitos (2007)

[21] WOSP, The Proceedings of the ACM International Workshop on Software and Performance. ACM Press (1998-2007)

Appendix: Nonlinear Regression

Various numerical minimization techniques can be used to find $\hat{\mathbf{x}}$. A simple one which gives some insight into the nature of the problem is a simple gradient descent. We form the derivative vector $\partial E(\mathbf{x})/\partial \mathbf{x}$:

$$\partial E(\mathbf{x})/\partial \mathbf{x} = -2 \, \Sigma_t \, \mathbf{H}^T(\mathbf{x}; \mathbf{u}_t) \, \mathbf{R}^{-1} \, \mathbf{e}_t,$$

where $\mathbf{H}(\mathbf{x}; \mathbf{u}_t) = \partial \mathbf{h}(\mathbf{x}; \mathbf{u}_t)/\partial \mathbf{x}$, and from any starting point $\mathbf{x}$ we make a *gradient descent step* proportional to the negative gradient:

$$\mathbf{x}^{new} = \mathbf{x} + \Delta\mathbf{x} = \mathbf{x} - a \, \partial E(\mathbf{x})/\partial \mathbf{x} = \mathbf{x} + (2a) \, \Sigma_t \, \mathbf{H}^T(\mathbf{x}; \mathbf{u}_t) \, \mathbf{R}^{-1} \, [\mathbf{z}(t) - \mathbf{h}(\mathbf{x}; \mathbf{u}_t)]$$

where a is the constant of proportionality, or step size control parameter. If this is repeated until x converges, we have *simple gradient descent*.

Various quasi-Newton methods are better. They use an approximation to the Hessian matrix E_{xx} (the matrix of second derivatives of $E(\mathbf{x})$):

$$E_{xx} = \partial^2 E(\mathbf{x})/\partial \mathbf{x}^2 = -2 \, \Sigma_t \, \partial \mathbf{H}^T(\mathbf{x}; \mathbf{u}_t)/\partial \mathbf{x} \, \mathbf{R}^{-1}\mathbf{e} + 2 \, \Sigma_t \, \mathbf{H}(\mathbf{x}; \mathbf{u}_t)^T \mathbf{R}^{-1}\mathbf{H}(\mathbf{x}; \mathbf{u}_t)$$

$$\approx 2 \, \Sigma_t \, \mathbf{H}(\mathbf{x}; \mathbf{u}_t)^T \mathbf{R}^{-1} \, \mathbf{H}(\mathbf{x}; \mathbf{u}_t)$$

The first term is ignored because it is small when the residuals are small, for instance near the best fit (if the fit is good). Then the step size is determined by E_{xx}. For example, by differentiating a quadratic approximation for $E(\mathbf{x})$ (a Taylor expansion around the point x)), we could choose the minimum of the approximation, which is at

$$\mathbf{x}^{new} = \mathbf{x} + \Delta \mathbf{x} = \mathbf{x} - E_{xx} \, \partial E(\mathbf{x})/\partial \mathbf{x}$$

Other quasi-Newton methods can also be applied to $E(\mathbf{x})$. Some of them build a Hessian approximation from information gathered over several steps.

Successive Linear Regressions

The same iterative algorithm is obtained by considering a sequence of weighted least-squares problems based on linearizing $\mathbf{h}(\mathbf{x}; \mathbf{u})$ about the current estimates of x. One output of this interpretation is a standard calculation for the sampling covariance of the estimates x, which gives confidence intervals.

Ordinary regression equations can be written based on the Taylor expansion around any current estimate x as (referring to [8] Chapter 13):

$$\mathbf{z}_t = \mathbf{h}(\mathbf{x}; \mathbf{u}_t) + \mathbf{H}(\mathbf{x}; \mathbf{u}_t)(\Delta \mathbf{x}) + \mathbf{v}_t$$

(where v is still the hypothetical random error term) and finding the increment $\Delta \mathbf{x}$ to minimize the weighted sum of squares for this linear model. We put all the observations into a single partitioned vector of mT components, and similarly all the residuals e, random errors v, the predictions h, and also put the sensitivities H into a single partitioned matrix, giving (using the notation of Kutner et al, chapter 13):

$\mathbf{Y}$ = vector combining the T error vectors $\mathbf{e}_t = \mathbf{z}_t - \mathbf{h}(\mathbf{x}; \mathbf{u}_t)$ at the current starting estimate x

$\mathbf{D}$ = matrix combining the $\mathbf{H}$ matrices computed at x

$\mathbf{W}$ = a matrix with T "$\mathbf{R}^{-1}$" matrices on its diagonal, one for each period

These partitioned matrices look like this:

$$Y = \begin{pmatrix} e_1 \\ \dots \\ e_t \\ \dots \\ e_T \end{pmatrix}, \qquad D = \begin{pmatrix} H(x,u_1) \\ \dots \\ H(x,u_t) \\ \dots \\ H(x,u_T) \end{pmatrix}, \qquad W = \begin{pmatrix} R^{-1} & 0 & \dots & 0 \\ 0 & R^{-1} & \dots & 0 \\ \dots & \dots & \dots & \dots \\ 0 & 0 & \dots & R^{-1} \end{pmatrix}$$

and the model to be fitted in the neighborhood of some starting estimate $\mathbf{x}$ is

$$\mathbf{Y} = \mathbf{D}\,\Delta\mathbf{x} + \mathbf{v},$$

where the elements of $\mathbf{D}$ are treated as the observations. Now by conventional least-squares solution the value of $\Delta\mathbf{x}$ which minimizes the weighted sum of squares $(\mathbf{Y} - \mathbf{D}\,\Delta\mathbf{x})^{T}\mathbf{W}(\mathbf{Y} - \mathbf{D}\,\Delta\mathbf{x})$ is

$$\Delta\mathbf{x} = (\mathbf{D}^{T}\mathbf{W}\mathbf{D})^{-1}\,\mathbf{D}^{T}\mathbf{W}\mathbf{Y}$$
$$\hat{\mathbf{x}}^{\,new} = \hat{\mathbf{x}} + \Delta\mathbf{x}$$

and this is used to update $\hat{\mathbf{x}}$, and to iterate to convergence. It may be more convenient to see it in terms of sums over the matrices and vectors for each measurement period, by expanding the partitioned matrices:

$$\Delta\mathbf{x} = (\Sigma_t\,\mathbf{H}_t^{T}\mathbf{R}^{-1}\mathbf{H}_t)^{-1}\,\Sigma_t\mathbf{H}_t^{T}\mathbf{R}^{-1}\mathbf{e}_t$$

Remember that $\mathbf{H}$ and $\mathbf{e}$ are those values for the starting estimate $\mathbf{x}$ for this step, and $\mathbf{H}_t$ is different for each step because $\mathbf{u}_t$ is different.

The covariance matrix of $\Delta\mathbf{x}$ (and thus of the solution) is

$$\mathbf{P} = (mse)\,(\mathbf{D}^{T}\mathbf{W}\mathbf{D})^{-1} = (mse)\,(\Sigma_t\,\mathbf{H}_t^{T}\mathbf{R}^{-1}\mathbf{H}_t)^{-1}$$

where mse estimates a scale factor for the covariance, given by:

$$mse = (\mathbf{Y}^{T}\mathbf{W}\mathbf{Y} - \Delta\mathbf{x}^{T}\mathbf{D}^{T}\mathbf{W}\mathbf{Y})/(mT - n) = (\,\Sigma_t\,\mathbf{e}_t^{T}\mathbf{R}^{-1}\mathbf{e}_t - \Delta\mathbf{x}^{T}\,\Sigma_t\mathbf{H}_t^{T}\mathbf{R}^{-1}\mathbf{e}_t\,)/(mT - n)$$

which as the iteration converges and $\Delta\mathbf{x}$ goes to zero, becomes:

$$mse = \mathbf{Y}^{T}\mathbf{W}\mathbf{Y}/(mT - n) = (\Sigma_t\,\mathbf{e}_t^{T}\mathbf{R}^{-1}\mathbf{e}_t\,)/(mT - n)$$

The factor $(mT - n)$ is the degrees of freedom remaining in the data after fitting n parameters to mT measured values.

Confidence Intervals

The converged solution $\hat{\mathbf{x}}$ of the above linear approximation can be used to give conventional confidence interval estimates for each parameter separately. Under the assumptions we have made (normality of measurement errors, and approximate linearity of h(x,u)), the posterior distribution of $\mathbf{x}$ is normal with covariance matrix $\mathbf{P}$. Then the confidence interval at level α for the kth parameter is

$$\hat{\mathbf{x}}_k \pm t(1 - \alpha/2;\ mT\text{-}n)\,(\text{sqrt}(P_{kk}))$$

where t in this equation is the t-statistic with $(mT\text{-}n)$ degrees of freedom (measured values - fitted parameters), and P_{kk} is the estimated variance of $\Delta\mathbf{x}_k$, a diagonal element of $\mathbf{P}$.

According to the linearization of $\mathbf{h}$, a small deviation $\Delta\mathbf{y}$ of the predicted performance $\mathbf{y}$, due to a small deviation $\Delta\mathbf{x}$ in $\mathbf{x}$, is given by

$$\Delta\mathbf{y} = \mathbf{H}\,\Delta\mathbf{x}$$

Therefore the approximate distribution of the predictions $\mathbf{y}$ of the performance model, for the fitted parameters $\hat{\mathbf{x}}$ and a given $\mathbf{u}$, is also normal with mean $\hat{\mathbf{y}} = \mathbf{h}(\hat{\mathbf{x}},\mathbf{u})$ and covariance matrix $\mathbf{C}$:

$$C = Cov(y) = H(\hat{x}, u) P H^T(\hat{x}, u)$$

From this we can derive a confidence interval for the prediction y_i as

$$\hat{y}_i + t(1-\alpha/2; mT\text{-}n) (sqrt(C_{ii}))$$

When we want to state a combined uncertainty interval for a set of parameters (e.g. all of them at once) it is called a *confidence region*. Based on the normality approximation for the estimated parameters and the predicted performance values, both of these vectors have ellipsoidal confidence regions, bounded by contours of the normal distribution, which are given by

for parameters: $(x - \hat{x})^T P^{-1}(x - \hat{x}) = $ constant

for predictions: $(y - \hat{y})^T C^{-1}(y - \hat{y}) = $ constant

A simpler approach is to consider a rectangular subspace or box bounded by the intersection of the separate intervals. The "Bonferroni" approximation assumes this has a probability given by the product of the probabilities associated with each parameter separately. For instance if there are three parameters with 95% confidence intervals, the intersection of these only has probability no greater than $0.95^3 = 0.857$. (It may be less because of interaction effects between the parameter estimates.) With this approach, a conservative confidence region for n parameters at level α is given by the intersection of separate estimates at level α/n. Examples of more exact confidence regions, showing interactions between the variables, and references are given in [17].

Comparison of Structures

Two models M1 and M2 of different structures may be compared, to evaluate if one is significantly better fit than the other, using a standard F test. Suppose the values of E are E1 and E2 (E2 < E1), and the number of fitted parameters are respectively n1 and n2 (n2 > n1), then M1 is judged to be significantly better at the level α if

$$[(E2 - E1)/(n2 - n1)]/[E2/(mT - n2 - 1)] > F(n2 - n1, mT - n - 1, \alpha)$$

where F( ) is the F-statistic with degrees of freedom (n2-n1, mT - n - 1) corresponding to the degrees of freedom in the two mean squares [8]. A model with more parameters should not be able to give a larger residual error, so the fraction should always be positive.

Extracting Response Times from Fluid Analysis of Performance Models

Jeremy T. Bradley, Richard Hayden, William J. Knottenbelt, and Tamas Suto

Department of Computing, Imperial College London
180 Queen's Gate, London SW7 2BZ, United Kingdom
{jb,rh,wjk,suto}@doc.ic.ac.uk

Abstract. Recent developments in the analysis of stochastic process algebra models allow for transient measures of very large models to be extracted. By performing so-called *fluid analysis* of stochastic process algebra models, it is now feasible to analyse systems of size 10^{1000} states and beyond. This paper seeks to extend the type of measure that can be extracted from this style of fluid analysis. We present a systematic transformation of a PEPA model that will allow us to extract measures analogous to response times. We end by extracting these response-time measures from a PEPA model of a healthcare system.

1 Introduction

The ability to calculate response-time or passage-time measures in quantitative analysis is important in many industrial systems. Response-time quantiles form the basis of many service level agreements (SLAs) in the telecommunications and other industries, e.g. a broadband connection should be successfully established within 2 seconds, 95% of the time.

However such industrial-scale systems require huge state-space analysis capability. If using traditional explicit state-space performance techniques, we quickly exceed the capability of Markov chain response-time analysers [1] to be able to generate and analyse the state space.

Recently, so-called *fluid* techniques have been developed to cope with the state-space explosion. This approach, typically, approximates the state space with a sequence of time-varying real variables and describes their evolution by a set of differential equations [2]. This sounds at first to be a panacea, but these techniques typically produce transient component counts at a given time instant. What we would like to do is reproduce useful response-time measures while taking advantage of the massive state-space capability of the fluid analysis techniques.

In this paper, we present a combination of these approaches by looking at how response-time measures might be extracted from fluid analysis of a stochastic process algebra model, PEPA. We show how, by modifying the state space of the model in a systematic fashion, we can transform the problem of response time extraction from fluid models to one of component time-to-extinction measurement.

S. Kounev, I. Gorton, and K. Sachs (Eds.): SIPEW 2008, LNCS 5119, pp. 29–43, 2008.

2   Stochastic Process Algebra and Fluid Modelling

2.1   PEPA

PEPA [3] as a performance modelling formalism has been used to study a wide variety of systems: multimedia applications [4], mobile phone usage [5], GRID scheduling [6], production cell efficiency [7] and web-server clusters [8] amongst others. The definitive reference for the language is [3].

As in all process algebras, systems are represented in PEPA as the composition of *components* which undertake *actions*. In PEPA the actions are assumed to have a duration, or delay. Thus the expression $(\alpha, r).P$ denotes a component which can undertake an α action at rate r to evolve into a component P. Here $\alpha \in \mathcal{A}$ where $\mathcal{A}$ is the set of action types. The rate r is interpreted as a random delay which samples from an exponential random variable with parameter, r.

PEPA has a small set of combinators, allowing system descriptions to be built up as the concurrent execution and interaction of simple sequential components. The syntax of the type of PEPA model considered in this paper may be formally specified using the following grammar:

$$S ::= (\alpha, r).S \mid S + S \mid C_S$$
$$P ::= P \bowtie_L P \mid P/L \mid C$$

where S denotes a *sequential component* and P denotes a *model component* which executes in parallel. C stands for a constant which denotes either a sequential component or a model component as introduced by a definition. C_S stands for constants which denote sequential components. The effect of this syntactic separation between these types of constants is to constrain legal PEPA components to be cooperations of sequential processes.

More information and structured operational semantics on PEPA can be found in [3]. A brief discussion of the basic PEPA operators is given below:

Prefix. The basic mechanism for describing the behaviour of a system with a PEPA model is to give a component a designated first action using the prefix combinator, denoted by a full stop, which was introduced above. As explained, $(\alpha, r).P$ carries out an α action with rate r, and it subsequently behaves as P.

Choice. The component $P + Q$ represents a system which may behave either as P or as Q. The activities of both P and Q are enabled. The first activity to complete distinguishes one of them: the other is discarded. The system will behave as the derivative resulting from the evolution of the chosen component.

Constant. It is convenient to be able to assign names to patterns of behaviour associated with components. Constants are components whose meaning is given by a defining equation. The notation for this is $X \stackrel{def}{=} E$. The name X is in scope in the expression on the right hand side meaning that, for example, $X \stackrel{def}{=} (\alpha, r).X$ performs α at rate r forever.

Hiding. The possibility to abstract away some aspects of a component's behaviour is provided by the hiding operator, denoted P/L. Here, the set L identifies those activities which are to be considered internal or private to the component and which will appear as the unknown type τ.

Cooperation. We write $P \bowtie_L Q$ to denote cooperation between P and Q over L. The set which is used as the subscript to the cooperation symbol, the *cooperation set* L, determines those activities on which the components are forced to synchronise. For action types not in L, the components proceed independently and concurrently with their enabled activities. We write $P \parallel Q$ as an abbreviation for $P \bowtie_L Q$ when L is empty. Further, particularly useful in fluid analysis is, $P[n]$ which is shorthand for the parallel cooperation of n P-components, $\underbrace{P \parallel \cdots \parallel P}_{n}$.

In process cooperation, if a component enables an activity whose action type is in the cooperation set it will not be able to proceed with that activity until the other component also enables an activity of that type. The two components then proceed together to complete the *shared activity*. Once enabled, the rate of a shared activity has to be altered to reflect the slower component in a cooperation.

In some cases, when a shared activity is known to be completely dependent only on one component in the cooperation, then the other component will be made *passive* with respect to that activity. This means that the rate of the activity is left unspecified (denoted $\top$) and is determined upon cooperation, by the rate of the activity in the other component. All passive actions must be synchronised in the final model.

Within the cooperation framework, PEPA respects the definition of *bounded capacity*: that is, a component cannot be made to perform an activity faster by cooperation, so the rate of a shared activity is the minimum of the apparent rates of the activity in the cooperating components.

The definition of the derivative set of a component will be needed later in the paper. The derivative set, $ds(C)$, is the set of states that can be reached from a the state C. In the case, where C is a state in a strongly connected sequential component, $ds(C)$ represents the state space of that component.

2.2   Fluid Analysis

Traditionally, stochastic process algebras such as PEPA have been analysed by expanding the model description and extracting the global state space. The underlying mathematical model of a PEPA-generated state space is a continuous-time Markov chain or CTMC. The CTMC can be analysed for steady-state measures, transient measures or response-time measures and related back to the original PEPA model. This process suffers from the state-space explosion problem.

In previous fluid modelling papers [2,9], a PEPA model was translated into a set of ordinary differential equations which were then solved. The results gave measures that roughly equated to mean transient measures in some cases.[1] What we seek to achieve here is a type of response-time result that can be extracted from the fluid analysis of a PEPA model.

Fluid modelling of process models refers to a continuum representation of the underlying discrete state space. Deriving such a representation from a performance-annotated process model, such as PEPA, gives a description of the flow of components from one derivative state to the next over time.

The first description of fluid analysis of PEPA models was presented by Hillston [2]. This has since been expanded upon [9,10] but in this paper we keep to the subset of PEPA originally considered by Hillston [2] for translation to a fluid model.

In brief, we will summarise how the fluid model is constructed from a PEPA model that displays a large degree of parallelism. In [2], Hillston shows how a class of PEPA models can be analysed using coupled ordinary differential equations (ODEs). In this section, we summarise the numerical vector form representation and ODE analysis of PEPA models.

Cooperating models of identical non-synchronising agents of the form, for example:

$$\underbrace{P \parallel P \parallel \cdots \parallel P}_{n}$$

are more succinctly represented by a vector which describes the *number* of components in a given derivative state. That is to say, suppose P has two other derivative states, P' and P'', in its component description. A triple (v_1, v_2, v_3) could be used to represent there being v_1 components in state P, v_2 in state P' and v_3 in state P'' in the cooperation above. This creates an aggregation of the original explicit state space where, for example, the states $P' \parallel P \parallel \cdots \parallel P$ and $P \parallel P' \parallel \cdots \parallel P$ are combined with other states where there is only a single P' component in cooperation with P components.

Clearly $v_1 + v_2 + v_3 = n$, the total number of components in the cooperation. The ordering of the derivative states within the expression above makes no difference to the observable behaviour. Thus there is no loss of information in simply counting derivatives in this way rather than recording their relative positions. Moreover it has the effect of reducing the state-space representation to an aggregated form (described in [11]) which requires a vector representation of size $|ds(P)|$, the number of derivative states of P, rather than one of size n, in the unaggregated form.

We demonstrate this aggregation with the generic example of an n-processor/m-resource system given in [2]. We have a processor component, $Proc_0$, which can perform a $task1$ action at rate r_1 and become a $Proc_1$ component. From there the $Proc_1$ component performs a $task2$ action at rate r_2 to return to state $Proc_0$. The Res_0 component performs similarly to switch between states Res_0 and Res_1. The final system comprises n processor components in parallel cooperating over the $task_1$ action with m resource components, also in parallel.

---

[1] The exact relationship between the deterministic solution of the fluid model and the traditional probabilistic analysis of the CTMC is the subject of current research.

This means that in order for a single $Proc_0$ component to perform a $task_1$ action, it has to synchronise with a single Res_0 component.

$$Proc_0 \stackrel{def}{=} (task1, r_1).Proc_1$$
$$Proc_1 \stackrel{def}{=} (task2, r_2).Proc_0$$
$$Res_0 \stackrel{def}{=} (task1, r_1).Res_1$$
$$Res_1 \stackrel{def}{=} (reset, s).Res_0$$
$$System \stackrel{def}{=} Proc_0[n] \underset{\{task1\}}{\bowtie} Res_0[m] \tag{1}$$

This model would usually be translated into an underlying CTMC according to the operational semantic rules of PEPA, given in [3]. For even small values of m and n this results in an massive CTMC state-space. An aggregate state $((n - 1, 1), (m, 0))$ would represent a possible state where there were $n - 1$ processor components in state $Proc_0$, one in state $Proc_1$, m resource components in state Res_0, and none in state Res_1.[2]

Hillston [2] further goes on to show how a set of ODEs can be constructed which can represent the discrete number of components in a given state with a continuous state-space approximation. This is particularly useful in agent-oriented models which typically have many thousands of similar components in parallel. For this type of model, this type of aggregation is essential if the resulting state-space explosion is to be avoided.

2.3 Numerical Vector Form and ODE Generation

Consider a PEPA model made up of component types C_i, such that the system equation has the form:

$$C_1[n_1] \underset{L}{\bowtie} C_2[n_2] \underset{L}{\bowtie} \cdots \underset{L}{\bowtie} C_m[n_m] \tag{2}$$

where $C[n]$ is the parallel composition of n C-components. Take C_{ij} to be the jth derivative state of component C_i. The cooperation set L is made up of common actions to C_i for $1 \leq i \leq m$. Now a numerical vector form for such a model would consist of $(v_{ij} : 1 \leq i \leq m, 1 \leq j \leq |ds(C_i)|)$ where v_{ij} is the number of C_{ij} components in the system at a given time. A set of coupled differential equations can be created to describe the time-variation of v_{ij} as follows:

$$\frac{dv_{ij}(t)}{dt} = - \sum_{k : C_{ij} \xrightarrow{(a,\cdot)} C_{ik}} \text{rate of } a\text{-action leaving } C_{ij}$$

$$+ \sum_{k : C_{ik} \xrightarrow{(b,\cdot)} C_{ij}} \text{rate of } b\text{-action leaving } C_{ik} \tag{3}$$

---

[2] For comparison, $m = n = 100$ would generate an explicit CTMC state-space of 2^{200} states, but an aggregate state-space of only 101^2 states.

To make this specific to PEPA models of the type in Equation (2), we need a few preliminary definitions. Let us define $Ex(C)$ to be the set of action/rate pairs or activities (a, r) that are enabled by derivative state, C. Similarly, define the set of entry activities, $En(C)$, to be the set of action/rate pairs (b, s) that lead to state C, that is, for some C', there exists a one-step evolution $C' \xrightarrow{(b,s)} C$. It is also assumed in [2] that if, for some component type C_i, a derivative state enables an a-action, then no other derivative state of C_i can enable that same action. We follow that restriction here for simplicity, but further work on extending the expressiveness of fluid translation is on-going [9,10].

From these definitions, we can create a more precise version of Equation (3):

$$\frac{\mathrm{d}v_{ij}(t)}{\mathrm{d}t} = - \sum_{(a,r) \in Ex(C_{ij})} r \times \min\{v_{kl} \ : \ C_{kl} \xrightarrow{(a,r)} \}$$

$$+ \sum_{(b,s) \in En(C_{ij})} s \times \min\{v_{kl} \ : \ C_{kl} \xrightarrow{(b,s)} \} \tag{4}$$

This formulation deals with PEPA models that cooperate actively and do so with constituent components enabling shared actions with the same rate. That is:

$$P \underset{\{a\}}{\bowtie} Q \text{ where } P \xrightarrow{(a,\lambda)} P' \text{ and } Q \xrightarrow{(a,\lambda)} Q'$$

This can be generalised straightforwardly to heterogeneous rates in cooperation where:

$$P \underset{\{a\}}{\bowtie} Q \text{ where } P \xrightarrow{(a,\lambda)} P' \text{ and } Q \xrightarrow{(a,\mu)} Q'$$

by a small modification to the ODE formula to:

$$\frac{\mathrm{d}v_{ij}(t)}{\mathrm{d}t} = - \sum_{(a,r_p) \in Ex(C_{ij})} \min\{r_p v_{kl} \ : \ C_{kl} \xrightarrow{(a,r_p)} \}$$

$$+ \sum_{(b,s_p) \in En(C_{ij})} \min\{s_p v_{kl} \ : \ C_{kl} \xrightarrow{(b,s_p)} \} \tag{5}$$

where $\{r_p\}$ and $\{s_p\}$ represent the set of distinct rates of a-actions and b-actions as enabled by the derivatives of the component-types C_i.

For the subset of PEPA worked with in this paper, the solution of these sets of ordinary differential equations, for a particular model, represents an approximation to the mean number of components at time t.

3   Response-Time Generation

The standard definition of a response time random variable in a Markov chain is set up as below.

Consider a finite, irreducible, continuous-time Markov process, $\{X(t) \ : \ t \geq 0\}$. $X(t)$ denotes the state of the Markov process at time $t \geq 0$. $N(t)$ denotes the number of state-transitions that have occurred by time t.

The first passage-time from a source state i at time 0 into a non-empty set of target states j is:

$$P_{ij} = \inf\{u > 0 \ : \ X(u) \in j, N(u) > 0 \mid X(0) = i\} \tag{6}$$

for a stationary time-homogeneous Markov process.

Loosely, this can be considered as the time-to-absorption from state i to one of the states in j. What we propose in this paper, is to construct a similar concept in the fluid analysis of a PEPA model of the type of Equation (2).

One of the standard techniques for extracting response-time distributions from CTMCs, is to make states in the target set, j, absorbing and perform transient analysis on the resulting modified chain [12].

Our approach is to perform a similar absorbing modification, but at the PEPA abstraction level rather than at the CTMC level, and then solve the resulting fluid model. The time-to-absorption measure which represents the response time in the original CTMC calculation is translated into the component extinction-time in the new fluid model.

3.1 Constructing an Absorbing PEPA Model

First, we will set up a basic PEPA absorption operator, $\triangleright$, which can be used systematically to modify any PEPA model in preparation for extracting a response-time measure.

We will only consider response times in terms of transitions of individual component types, e.g. how long before all the voters have voted, or all the clients have received service.

This translates into finding the response time for n_i components of type C_i, to have entered one of the states $H = \{C_{ij} \ : \ j \in j\}$, having started in state C_{i1}, where j represents the set of target states in the component type being considered. Taking a PEPA model of the form:

$$C_1[n_1] \underset{L}{\bowtie} C_2[n_2] \underset{L}{\bowtie} \cdots \underset{L}{\bowtie} C_m[n_m] \tag{7}$$

Given a set, $H = \{C_{ij} \ : \ j \in j\}$, of component states that we wish to make absorbing, we apply the absorption operator recursively over the PEPA syntax:

$$((a,\lambda).P) \triangleright_{(U)} H = \begin{cases} (a,\lambda).\mathsf{Stop} & : \text{ if } P \in H \\ (a,\lambda).(P \triangleright_{(U \cup \{P\})} H) : & \text{ if } P \notin H, P \notin U \\ (a,\lambda).P & : \text{ if } P \notin H, P \in U \end{cases}$$

$$(P + Q) \triangleright_{(U)} H = (P \triangleright_{(U)} H) + (Q \triangleright_{(U)} H)$$
$$(P \backslash L) \triangleright H = (P \triangleright H) \backslash L$$
$$(P \underset{L}{\bowtie} Q) \triangleright H = (P \triangleright H) \underset{L}{\bowtie} (Q \triangleright H)$$

$P \triangleright H$ is shorthand for $P \triangleright_{(\emptyset)} H$ where the indexed set keeps track of previously visited component states. The operator defined above, recurses across the PEPA description and on encountering a component state in the set H, it replaces it

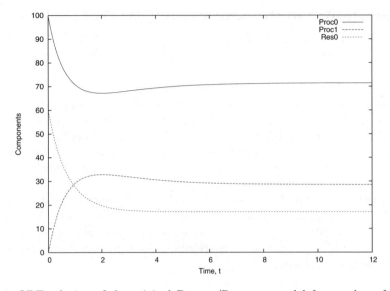

Fig. 1. ODE solution of the original Process/Resource model for number of $Proc_0$, $Proc_1$, Res_0 components

with the absorbing state Stop. We assume that derivative states are uniquely labelled across the component types to avoid multiple component types being made absorbing. If this is not the case then a simple relabelling can be applied in advance of this transformation.

In this paper, we are considering simple response times that are expressed in terms of one component type only. We will only consider derivative states in H that come from the same component type C_i for any i (as given by the definition of H).

Having absorbing states in PEPA is unusual as PEPA models usually have irreducible underlying CTMCs. The absorbing state in this instance is Stop, and a discussion of absorbing states in PEPA can be found in [13].

3.2   Processor–Resource Example

We use the earlier example of an n-processor/m-resource system from Equation (1). We require the response time of n $Proc$-components making the transition from $Proc_0$ to $Proc_0$ again. To achieve this, we apply the absorption operator to the PEPA model $System \rhd H$ with $H = \{Proc_0\}$. This gives an absorbed model:

$$Proc_0 \stackrel{def}{=} (task1, r_1).Proc_1$$
$$Proc_1 \stackrel{def}{=} (task2, r_2).\mathsf{Stop}$$
$$Res_0 \stackrel{def}{=} (task1, r_1).Res_1$$
$$Res_1 \stackrel{def}{=} (reset, s).Res_0$$
$$System \stackrel{def}{=} Proc_0[n] \underset{\{task1\}}{\bowtie} Res_0[m]$$

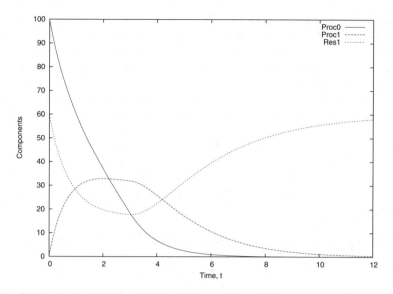

Fig. 2. ODE solution of the absorbed Process/Resource model with response time measured at 11.515s

By way of comparison, solving the ODEs generated by the original model gives the plot in Figure 1. Solving the ODEs for the absorbing version gives Figure 2. In both cases $n = 100$, $m = 60$, $r_1 = 1.0$, $r_2 = 0.6$ and $s = 0.4$.

In Figure 2, we see the count of $Proc_0$ and $Proc_1$ components drop to 0 as would be expected in an absorbing model. We count the moment of absorption as the moment at which $< 0.5\%$ of the components remain in either state $Proc_0$ or $Proc_1$. This is measured at time 11.52 and represents a response-time measure for the time taken for $n = 100$ $Proc$-components to transit from state $Proc_0$ to $Proc_0$ while cooperating with the Res-components.

4   Worked Example: Healthcare System

The healthcare system in this section is a model of an accident and emergency department, first presented as a stochastic Petri net model in [14].

The system consists of patients, doctors and nurses, where patients who fall ill, are assessed by nurses before being sent to doctors for tests, treatment or surgery. The purpose of the system is to assess how fluctuations in the numbers of resources in the system, the number of nurses and doctors, affect the overall response-time for treatment.

$$System \stackrel{def}{=} Patient[P] \bowtie_{L} (Nurse[N] \;||\; Doctor[D])$$

where $L = \{$ *see_nurse, complete_assessment, see_emergency_nurse, eemergency_assessment, see_doctor, discharge_treated_patient, surgery, recover* $\}$.

The attentive reader will note that this system equation is not explicitly of the form of Equation (2), that we require for this particular style of fluid analysis. However, since the *Doctor* and *Nurse* components do not synchronise on any actions, we can effectively treat the $(Nurse[N] \parallel Doctor[D])$ cooperation as a single component group.

The nurses in the system can either see a standard patient or an emergency admittance. In each case an assessment is made before handing on for treatment.

$$Nurse \stackrel{def}{=} (see\_nurse, r_4).(complete\_assessment, r_5).Nurse$$
$$+ (see\_emergency\_nurse, r_6).(emergency\_assessment, r_7).Nurse$$

The doctors in the system can either see and treat the patient or admit the patient for surgery.

$$Doctor \stackrel{def}{=} (see\_doctor, r_8).(discharge\_treated\_patient, r_{11}).Doctor$$
$$+ (surgery, r_9).(recover, r_{12}).Doctor$$

Finally, the patients are of two types – either standard walk-in arrivals or emergency cases. They cooperate with the nurses and the doctors over the shared actions before being discharged.

$$Patient \stackrel{def}{=} (fall\_ill, r_1).Ill$$
$$Ill \stackrel{def}{=} (walk\_in\_arrival, r_2).Waiting\_room$$
$$+ (ambulance\_arrival, r_3).Trolley$$
$$Waiting\_room \stackrel{def}{=} (see\_nurse, r_4).Patient\_assessment$$
$$Patient\_assessment \stackrel{def}{=} (complete\_assessment, r_5).Waiting\_to\_be\_treated$$
$$Trolley \stackrel{def}{=} (see\_emergency\_nurse, r_6).Ambulance\_assessment$$
$$Ambulance\_assessment \stackrel{def}{=} (emergency\_assessment, r_7).Waiting\_to\_be\_treated$$
$$Waiting\_to\_be\_treated \stackrel{def}{=} (see\_doctor, r_8).Treated\_by\_doctor$$
$$+ (surgery, r_9).Surgery\_done$$
$$+ (perform\_lab\_tests, r_{10}).Tests\_done$$
$$Treated\_by\_doctor \stackrel{def}{=} (discharge\_treated\_patient, r_{11}).Patient$$
$$Surgery\_done \stackrel{def}{=} (recover, r_{12}).Patient\_Recovered$$
$$Patient\_Recovered \stackrel{def}{=} (discharge\_recovered\_patient, r_{13}).Patient$$
$$Tests\_done \stackrel{def}{=} (evaluate\_results, r_{14}).Waiting\_to\_be\_treated$$

Using the techniques of Section 2.3, we construct a system of 17 coupled ODEs (for 16 derivative states of the original model plus the newly-introduced absorbing state) for $P = 100$ patients, $N = 30$ nurses, $D = 5$ doctors.[3] Such a

---

[3] The following rate values are used throughout this paper $r_1 = 1$, $r_2 = 4$, $r_3 = 3$, $r_4 = r_5 = r_6 = r_7 = r_{11} = r_{14} = 10$, $r_8 = 5$, $r_9 = r_{10} = r_{12} = 3$ and $r_{13} = 8$.

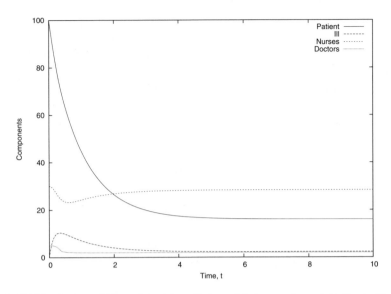

Fig. 3. ODE solution of the original hospital model for number of *Patient*, *Ill*, *Nurse* and *Doctor* components

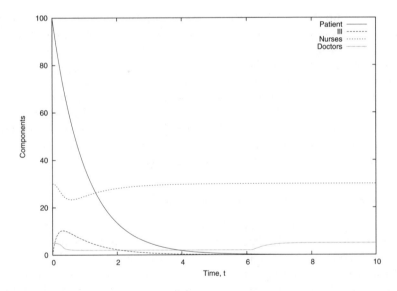

Fig. 4. ODE solution of the hospital model for patient response-time metric

system is well beyond the capability of existing explicit state-space techniques to analyse due to the size of the underlying CTMC. Without modification, we obtain solutions for patients, ill patients, nurses and doctors in Figure 3.

Now we seek the response-time measure for the time taken for $P = 100$ patients to pass through the system and go from state *Patient* back to state

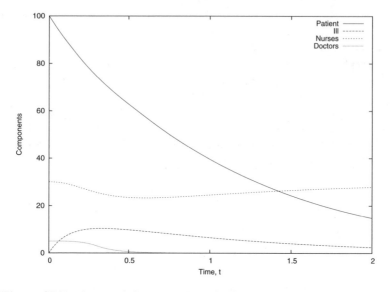

Fig. 5. ODE solution of the hospital model for patient response-time metric

Patient. We set up the absorbing PEPA model with the transformation $System \triangleright$ $\{Patient\}$. Plotting the new set of 18 resulting ODEs gives Figure 4, and on examining the data, we obtain the measure that it takes 7.17 hours for all 100 patients to progress through the system.

Finally, we seek a response-time measure on the progress of doctors in the model. Similarly, we calculate the response-time for $D = 5$ doctors to go from state *Doctor* to state *Doctor*. We set up the absorbing PEPA model with the transformation $System \triangleright \{Doctor\}$. Plotting the new set of 18 resulting ODEs gives Figure 5, and on examining the data, we obtain the measure that it takes 1.84 hours for all 5 doctors to process at least 1 patient.

4.1   Comparison with a CTMC-Derived Passage Time

Given the motivations behind developing such techniques of fluid analysis, it is of course computationally infeasible to compute passage times in the usual manner[4] for models of the magnitude of that just presented. In this section, we consider a scaled down form of the healthcare model (5 patients, 3 nurses and 2 doctors: about 24 million states). This will allow a comparison of the quantity computed using the new technique presented here against the CTMC-derived passage time.

We work again with response-time measure of the healthcare model obtained via the transformation $System \triangleright \{Patient\}$. Figure 6 shows the CDF for the CTMC-derived time of passage from the initial state to that in which all *Patient* components have reached the Stop state. Since we defined the point of absorption

---

[4] Using the standard uniformisation technique of the underlying CTMC.

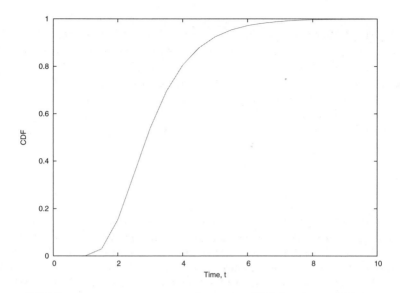

Fig. 6. CTMC passage time to patient absorption CDF for the small hospital model

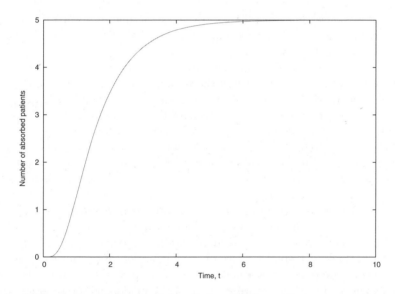

Fig. 7. ODE solution of the small hospital model for patient response-time metric, showing only the variable for the patient absorbing state (Stop)

for the ODE-derived solution to be when the sum of the continuous variables counting the states of the patients reaches 0.5% of the original component population, it makes at least intuitive sense to look at the 99.5% quantile of the corresponding CTMC passage time. Examining the data, we see that in the direct CTMC passage-time calculation it takes approximately 7.6 hours for 99.5% of the *Patient* components to absorb. Figure 7 shows the result of integrating the 18 ODEs for the model. In this case, it takes about 6.13 hours for 99.5% of the original patient population to be absorbed.

A general observation from this preliminary comparison is that the absorbing fluid model appears to absorb more quickly than the equivalent CTMC cumulative distribution function of the passage-time. Work is on-going to characterise this relationship more formally but it appears that it may be a justifiable result in many cases.

5   Conclusion

Fluid analysis of stochastic process algebra models is a powerful analytic tool for obtaining quantitative analysis of massive state-space models. We have summarised existing fluid techniques for a popular process algebra, PEPA, and pointed out that the type of measure that is obtainable from the standard fluid analysis [2] is restricted to a form of transient analysis. We have shown, in this paper, how it might be possible to express and extract response-time style measures from fluid analysis of stochastic process algebra models. We did this by using an analogous absorbing state technique to that used in the explicit state-space analysis of response times in CTMCs. By constructing an absorption operator for the PEPA language, we have a simple tool for allowing general PEPA models to be analysed for fluid-generated response times.

In this paper, we looked for the absorption of 99.5% of the components under consideration in the system to extract the response time. We compared that with the equivalent 99.5% CDF quantile measurement in a 24 million state CTMC version of a healthcare system. We postulate that the fluid-generated response time will tend to underestimate the CTMC response-time measure in general, but further work is required in this area to show this. We would like to establish a relationship with the mean response-time measurement of traditional CTMC analysis. We are also looking to generate variance and higher moment metrics for the response-time measure extracted in this way.

Finally, there is the potential for constructing more expressive measures on more general models. Currently, we only look for movement of an entire population of component types from one state to another. It would be a clear advantage to be able to look at response times of a combination of partial movements of populations of components types. We see no reason why this approach should not be extended directly to more general PEPA models as the fluid semantics are defined for those models.

Acknowledgements

The authors would like to thank Allan Clark for help with ipc and Jane Hillston for advice over fluid mean response time calculations. In addition, we would like to credit the anonymous referees for helpful comments which improved the paper. Jeremy Bradley, William Knottenbelt and Tamas Suto are supported in part by the EPSRC grant GRAIL, ref. EP/D505933/1.

References

1. Bradley, J.T., Dingle, N.J., Gilmore, S.T., Knottenbelt, W.J.: Extracting passage times from PEPA models with the HYDRA tool: a case study. In: Jarvis, S.A. (ed.) UKPEW 2003, Proceedings of 19th Annual UK Performance Engineering Workshop, University of Warwick, pp. 79–90 (July 2003)
2. Hillston, J.: Fluid flow approximation of PEPA models. In: QEST 2005, Proceedings of the 2nd International Conference on Quantitative Evaluation of Systems, Torino, pp. 33–42. IEEE Computer Society Press, Los Alamitos (2005)
3. Hillston, J.: A Compositional Approach to Performance Modelling. Distinguished Dissertations in Computer Science, vol. 12. CUP (1996)
4. Bowman, H., Bryans, J.W., Derrick, J.: Analysis of a multimedia stream using stochastic process algebras. The Computer Journal 44(4), 230–245 (2001)
5. Fourneau, J.M., Kloul, L., Valois, F.: Performance modelling of hierarchical cellular networks using PEPA. Performance Evaluation 50(2–3), 83–99 (2002)
6. Thomas, N., Bradley, J.T., Knottenbelt, W.J.: Stochastic analysis of scheduling strategies in a GRID-based resource model. IEE Software Engineering 151(5), 232–239 (2004)
7. Holton, D.R.W.: A PEPA specification of an industrial production cell. In: Gilmore, S., Hillston, J. (eds.) Process Algebra and Performance Modelling Workshop, Edinburgh, June 1995. The Computer Journal, vol. 38(7), pp. 542–551. CEPIS (1995)
8. Bradley, J.T., Dingle, N.J., Gilmore, S.T., Knottenbelt, W.J.: Derivation of passage-time densities in PEPA models using ipc: the Imperial PEPA Compiler. In: Kotsis, G. (ed.) MASCOTS 2003, Proceedings of the 11th IEEE/ACM International Symposium on Modeling, Analysis and Simulation of Computer and Telecommunications Systems, University of Central Florida, pp. 344–351. IEEE Computer Society Press, Los Alamitos (2003)
9. Bradley, J.T., Gilmore, S.T., Hillston, J.: Analysing distributed internet worm attacks using continuous state-space approximation of process algebra models. Journal of Computer and System Sciences (in press, 2007)
10. Hayden, R.: Addressing the state space explosion problem for PEPA models through fluid-flow approximation. Technical report, Ugrad. project report, Imperial College London (2007)
11. Gilmore, S., Hillston, J., Ribaudo, M.: An efficient algorithm for aggregating PEPA models. IEEE Transactions on Software Engineering 27(5), 449–464 (2001)
12. Dingle, N.J., Harrison, P.G., Knottenbelt, W.J.: Uniformization and hypergraph partitioning for the distributed computation of response time densities in very large Markov models. Journal of Parallel and Distributed Computing 64(8), 908–920 (2004)
13. Thomas, N., Bradley, J.T.: Terminating processes in PEPA. In: Djemame, K., Kara, M. (eds.) UKPEW 2001, Proceedings of 17th Annual UK Performance Evaluation Workshop, Leeds, July 2001, pp. 143–154 (2001)
14. Suto, T., Bradley, J.T., Knottenbelt, W.J.: Performance Trees: Expressiveness and quantitative semantics. In: QEST 2007, 4th International Conference on the Quantitative Evaluation of Systems, pp. 41–50. IEEE, Los Alamitos (2007)

Approximate Solution of a PEPA Model of a Key Distribution Centre

Yishi Zhao and Nigel Thomas

School of Computing Science, Newcastle University, UK
{Yishi.Zhao,Nigel.Thomas}@ncl.ac.uk

Abstract. In this paper we explore the trade-off between security and performance in considering a model of a key distribution centre. The model is specified using the Markovian process algebra PEPA. The basic model suffers from the commonly encountered state space explosion problem, and so we apply some model reduction techniques and approximation to give a form of the model which is more scalable. The system is analysed numerically and results derived from the approximation are compared with simulation.

1 Introduction

One of the more intriguing areas of performance engineering to emerge over recent years has been the study of the overhead introduced by making a system secure. It is clear that in order to add more functionality to a system that more execution time is required. However, in the case of security, the benefit accrued from any additional overhead is not easy to quantify and so it is very hard for the performance engineer to argue that a particular performance target should take precedence over a security goal. One area where alternative secure solutions exist is in cryptography, where there may be a choice of algorithm, or even a choice of key length, which will greatly influence the performance of the system. For this reason cryptographic protocols are one of the few areas of security to have received much attention from the performance community [4,5,8]. To date this work has been largely limited to measurement and has not addressed the underlying causes of delay which might be understood by modelling or detailed code analysis.

In this paper we tackle a different, but related, problem in the area of the performance - security trade-off, namely key exchange. Our initial inspiration for this work has been the study of the wide mouth frog protocol by Buchholz *et al* [2]. The authors used the stochastic process algebra PEPA to analyse timing properties of the protocol. Although their motivation was to investigate timing attacks, the models developed in [2] showed how authentication protocols can be modelled effectively in PEPA.

The paper is organised as follows. In the next section we introduce the system to be modelled, the key distribution centre (KDC). This is followed by a brief overview of the Markovian process algebra PEPA. Section 4 introduces the

S. Kounev, I. Gorton, and K. Sachs (Eds.): SIPEW 2008, LNCS 5119, pp. 44–57, 2008.

basic model of the KDC, followed by a simplified (equivalent) version and an approximation in Section 5. Some numerical results are presented in Section 6, including comparison of the approximation results with simulation. Finally some conclusions are drawn and areas of further work described.

2   Key Distribution Centre

We now describe the specific problem we seek to model. This is the secure exchange of secret keys (also known as symmetric keys) using a trusted third party known as a key distribution centre (KDC). The protocol is illustrated below, following the description in [10].

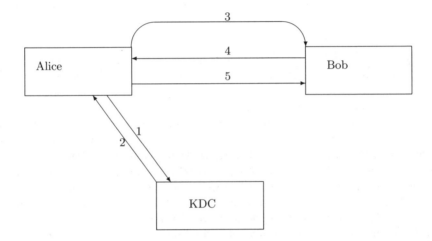

Fig. 1. Key Distribution Scenario

- Alice and KDC share a key K_A
- Bob and KDC share a key K_B

1. Alice sends request to KDC with nonce N_1
2. $E\{K_A\}[K_S|request|N_1|E\{K_B\}[K_S|ID_A]]$
   - K_S is a session key for Alice and Bob to use.
   - Alice can't decrypt the part encoded with Bob's key, she can only send it on.
3. $E\{K_B\}[K_S|ID_A]$
4. $E\{K_S\}[N_2]$
5. $E\{K_S\}[f(N_2)]$

where,

- N_1 and N_2 are nonces (random items of data),
- ID_A is a unique identifier for Alice,

- $E\{K_A\}[X]$ denotes that the data X is encrypted using the key K_A, and
- $f(N_2)$ denotes a predefined function applied to the nonce N_2, signifying that Alice has read the encrypted message sent by Bob.

The key features of this protocol are that only Alice can read the message sent by the KDC (2) as only Alice and the KDC know the key K_A. Included in this message is another message further encrypted with K_B, the key shared by Bob and the KDC. Alice cannot read this message, but instead forwards it to Bob (3). This message tells Bob that Alice is genuine (i.e. has communicated with the KDC and displays a correct ID) and informs Bob of the session key; only Bob can read this message. Alice and Bob now both know the session key K_S and the remainder of the protocol ensures that Bob trusts Alice and the session key (and Alice trusts Bob).

3   PEPA

In this paper we model the performance of the key distribution centre using the Markovian process algebra PEPA. This approach has a number of advantages over a direct approach of using Markov chains. As a formal specification, a PEPA model can be derived automatically from, and compared automatically with, formal definitions of the protocol we are modelling. Functional properties of the model, such as deadlock freeness, can also be checked automatically. These attributes of the model specification are particularly important in the field of security, where correctness is vital if security properties are to be maintained. Furthermore, the analysis of the model we are considering here is based on formulating progressive simplified versions of the model. Because of the formal nature of the specification we can apply formal transformations to the model based on known concepts of equivalence. Therefore we know that the approximate model we derive shares certain properties with the original model. In brief, we know, and can prove, that the approximation is still a valid model of the original protocol. This would not be possible if we simply chose the approximation by some expert intuition or arrived at it by some less formal means.

A formal presentation of PEPA is given in [6], in this section a brief informal summary is presented. PEPA, being a Markovian Process Algebra, only supports actions that occur with rates that are negative exponentially distributed. Specifications written in PEPA represent Markov processes and can be mapped to a continuous time Markov chain (CTMC). Systems are specified in PEPA in terms of *activities* and *components*. An activity (α, r) is described by the type of the activity, α, and the rate of the associated negative exponential distribution, r. This rate may be any positive real number, or given as unspecified using the symbol $\top$.

The syntax for describing components is given as:

$$(\alpha, r).P \mid P + Q \mid P/L \mid P \underset{\mathcal{L}}{\bowtie} Q \mid A$$

The component $(\alpha, r).P$ performs the activity of type α at rate r and then behaves like P. The component $P + Q$ behaves either like P or like Q, the resultant behaviour being given by the first activity to complete.

The component P/L behaves exactly like P except that the activities in the set L are concealed, their type is not visible and instead appears as the unknown type τ.

Concurrent components can be synchronised, $P \bowtie_{\mathcal{L}} Q$, such that activities in the cooperation set $\mathcal{L}$ involve the participation of both components. In PEPA the shared activity occurs at the slowest of the rates of the participants and if a rate is unspecified in a component, the component is passive with respect to activities of that type. $A \stackrel{def}{=} P$ gives the constant A the behaviour of the component P.

In this paper we consider only models which are cyclic, that is, every derivative of components P and Q are reachable in the model description $P \bowtie_{\mathcal{L}} Q$. Necessary conditions for a cyclic model may be defined on the component and model definitions without recourse to the entire state space of the model.

4   The Models

This scheme can be easily modelled for a single pair of clients in PEPA [6] as follows (*Model 1*).

$$KDC \stackrel{def}{=} (request, \top).(response, r_p).KDC$$

$$Alice \stackrel{def}{=} (request, r_q).(response, \top).Alice'$$

$$Alice' \stackrel{def}{=} (sendBob, r_B).(sendAlice, \top).(confirm, r_c).Alice''$$

$$Alice'' \stackrel{def}{=} (usekey, r_u).Alice$$

$$Bob \stackrel{def}{=} (sendBob, \top).(sendAlice, r_A).(confirm, \top).Bob'$$

$$Bob' \stackrel{def}{=} (usekey, \top).Bob$$

$$System \stackrel{def}{=} KDC \bowtie_{\mathcal{L}} Alice \bowtie_{\mathcal{K}} Bob$$

Where, $\mathcal{L} = \{request, response\}$, $\mathcal{K} = \{sendBob, sendAlice, confirm, usekey\}$.

In Model 1, above, Alice's behaviour is separated into getting a session key (Alice), authentication with Bob (*Alice'*) and using the session key (*Alice''*). Similarly Bob's behaviour is separated into the key exchange and authentication with Alice (*Bob*) and the use of the session key (*Bob'*). In this model Alice only requests (and uses) one session key at a time. Thus the model is limited such that if Alice wishes to start a new session, she must first finish the previous session. This observation will be important when considering models with multiple clients.

According to Stallings [10]:

> "*The more frequently session keys are exchanged, the more secure they are, because the opponent has less cipher text to work with for any given session key. On the other hand, the distribution of session keys delays the start of any exchange and places a burden on network capacity. A security manager must try to balance these competing considerations in determining the lifetime of a particular session key.*"

In brief, this means there is a trade-off to be achieved between performance and security in the handling of session keys. In our model (above), this would be represented by varying the values of r_u and r_q. If these values are high then keys are being refreshed more regularly, putting more demand on the KDC and the network.

In our work we are primarily interested in studying the performance of the KDC, rather than the network. In [11] we developed three approaches to modelling multiple clients requesting session keys from the KDC. These approaches all formally represent the same protocol definition and are notionally equivalent at the syntactic level (they have a form of *bisimilarity*). However, they are not isomorphic and hence can give different values for important performance metrics. In the most intuitive version, presented in this paper, multiple clients are manually added using different names with parallel requests and responses allowed; meaning that the KDC can receive (and queue) several distinct requests before responding to them. A model with N pairs of clients is illustrated in Figure 2.

This approach can be modelled in PEPA as follows (*Model 2*).

$$KDC \stackrel{def}{=} (request_1, \top).KDC_1 + (request_2, \top).KDC_2$$
$$+ \cdots + (request_N), \top).KDC_N$$

$$KDC_1 \stackrel{def}{=} (response_1, r_p).KDC + (request_2, \top).KDC_{N+1}$$
$$+ \cdots + (request_N, \top).KDC_{2N-1}$$
$$\cdots$$

$$KDC_{2^N} \stackrel{def}{=} (response_1, r_p/N).KDC_{2^N-N} + (response_2, r_p/N).KDC_{2^N-N+1}$$
$$+ \cdots + (response_N, r_p/N).KDC_{2^N-1}$$

$$Alice_i \stackrel{def}{=} (request_i, r_q).(response_i, \top).(sendB_i, r_B).(sendA_i, \top).$$
$$(confirm_i, r_c).(usekey_i, r_u).Alice_i \ , \ 1 \le i \le N$$
$$Bob_i \stackrel{def}{=} (sendB_i, \top).(sendA_i, r_A).(confirm_i, \top).(usekey_i, \top).Bob_i$$
$$, \ 1 \le i \le N$$

$$System \stackrel{def}{=} KDC \bowtie_{\mathcal{K}} ((Alice_1 \bowtie_{\mathcal{L}_1} Bob_1)|| \cdots ||(Alice_N \bowtie_{\mathcal{L}_N} Bob_N)$$

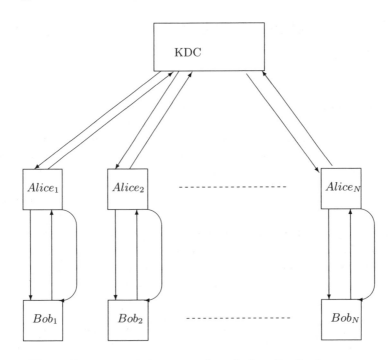

Fig. 2. Diagrammatic representation of a key distribution centre

Where,

$$\mathcal{K} = \{request_1, response_1, \cdots, request_N, response_N\}$$

and

$$\mathcal{L}_i = \{sendB_i, sendA_i, confirm_i, usekey_i\}$$

In Model 2 we introduce the possibility that the KDC is serving multiple requests from multiple Alices. Each Alice still only makes one request at a time and each request is served by the KDC (we are not overly concerned here about the order of service). Note that due to the semantics of the specification events occur sequentially and not simultaneously. In addition we do not allow batched requests.

Specific notation in Model 2 is introduced as follows. The subscript j in KDC_j corresponds to a binary representation of the request status of node i, such that the ith bit is 1 if $Alice_i$ is awaiting a response from the KDC and 0 otherwise. The rate of each $response_i$ action in KDC_j is r_p divided by the number of $response_i$'s enabled.

It is worth observing here that Model 2 is cumbersome to specify; if we want to consider an extra client that no only needs to be specified as new $Alice_j$ and Bob_j components, but also the KDC component needs to be modified to incorporate the additional behaviours, $request_j$ and $response_j$.

5   Model Simplification and Approximation

Model 2 suffers from the commonly encountered state space explosion problem. For each Alice (and corresponding Bob) the state space is multiplied by another 6 behaviours, hence the state space is 6^N, where N is the number of client pairs (Alice+Bob). With $N = 9$ the state space has already grown to over 1 million states; if N is only 5, the solution still involves matrices with over 60 million elements (although admittedly mostly zeros). Even the best distributed Markov chain solvers generally only tackle state spaces of a few million states at most. To counter this, and to make the model easier to specify and understand, we have applied some simplification techniques to derive a form of the model which gives the same results for key steady state metrics. This approach is based on the concept known as bisimulation; whereby two models may be said to be equivalent if any sequence of actions that is possible in one model, has an equivalent sequence of actions (at the same rate) in the other model (*strong* bisimulation requires that equivalent actions have the same name, which is not the case here). This leads us to an alternative representation of the model as follows (*Model 3*).

$$KDC \stackrel{def}{=} (request, \top).KDC + (response, r_p).KDC$$

$$Alice \stackrel{def}{=} (request, r_q).(response, \top).Alice'$$

$$Alice' \stackrel{def}{=} (sendBob, r_B).(sendAlice, \top).(confirm, r_c).Alice''$$

$$Alice'' \stackrel{def}{=} (usekey, r_u).Alice$$

$$Bob \stackrel{def}{=} (sendBob, \top).(sendAlice, r_A).(confirm, \top).Bob'$$

$$Bob' \stackrel{def}{=} (usekey, \top).Bob$$

$$System \stackrel{def}{=} KDC \underset{\mathcal{L}}{\bowtie} \left(Alice \underset{\mathcal{K}}{\bowtie} Bob || \ldots || Alice \underset{\mathcal{K}}{\bowtie} Bob \right)$$

Where, $\mathcal{L} = \{request, response\}$, $\mathcal{K} = \{sendBob, sendAlice, confirm, usekey\}$.

Clearly the component *Bob* is almost redundant, and the sharing for the action *request* and its enabling in *KDC* has no effect on the behaviour of the model. Hence an even simpler equivalent specification would be (*Model 4*):

$$KDC \stackrel{def}{=} (response, r_p).KDC$$

$$Alice \stackrel{def}{=} (request, r_q).(response, \top).Alice'$$

$$Alice' \stackrel{def}{=} (sendBob, r_B).(sendAlice, r_A).(confirm, r_c).Alice''$$

$$Alice'' \stackrel{def}{=} (usekey, r_u).Alice$$

$$System \stackrel{def}{=} KDC \underset{response}{\bowtie} (Alice||\dots||Alice)$$

This model and the preceding one are clearly isomorphic, i.e. they have equivalent CTMCs with a one-to-one mapping between states and transitions. We can now apply the well known approximation technique of combining successive internal actions into a single action with a modified rate. This is equivalent to lumping states in the underlying Markov chain (Hillston [6] introduced the *weak isomorphism* equivalence for exactly this purpose). Thus we obtain the following simple form of the model (*Model 5*).

$$KDC \stackrel{def}{=} (response, r_p).KDC$$

$$Alice \stackrel{def}{=} (response, \top).(\tau, r_x).Alice$$

$$System \stackrel{def}{=} KDC \underset{response}{\bowtie} (Alice||\dots||Alice)$$

Where r_x is given by

$$r_x = \left(\frac{1}{r_q} + \frac{1}{r_B} + \frac{1}{r_A} + \frac{1}{r_c} + \frac{1}{r_u} \right)^{-1}$$

Model 5 is equivalent to a simple closed queueing system with one queueing station (the KDC) and an exponential delay after service before returning to the queue. It is a simple matter to write down the balance equations for such a system.

$$r_p \Pi_i = (N + 1 - i) r_x \Pi_{i-1} \ , \ 1 \leq i \leq N$$

where Π_i is the steady state probability that there are exactly i jobs waiting for a response from the KDC and N is the number of pairs of clients (the number of instances of *Alice* in the above PEPA model specification). Thus it is possible to derive expressions for the average utilisation of the KDC and the average number of requests waiting for a response.

$$U = 1 - \left[N! \sum_{i=0}^{N} \frac{\rho^i}{(N-i)!} \right]^{-1}$$

and,

$$L = N!(1 - U) \sum_{i=1}^{N} \frac{\rho^i i}{(N-i)!}$$

where $\rho = r_x / r_p$.

This approximation is, in fact, an $M/M/1/./N$ queue and the throughput and average response time are easily computed from the above expressions (see Mitrani [9] pages 195-197).

$$T = (N - L)r_x$$

and

$$W = \frac{N}{T} - \frac{1}{r_x}$$

6 Numerical Results

The approximation is now compared with simulation results for the full model. The simulation was written in Java using the roulette wheel approach. The simulation has been verified numerically against the PEPA model using the PEPA Workbench [3] for small numbers of clients ($N \leq 6$). The PEPA Workbench will not give results for larger models due to problems with performing computations on the large matrices involved, hence the need for the simulation. Initially in the experiments which follow, the parameters are set to 1.0 (except r_u=1.1 for numerical computation reasons in the PEPA Workbench) and other parameters are varied as shown.

In Figure 3 we show the utilisation (of the KDC) varied against the numbers of client pairs for both the simulation and the approximation for various values of r_p. Increasing the value of r_p in this way is equivalent to replacing the KDC with a faster server. In Figure 4 we show the average response time (average waiting time plus average service time) of the KDC for the same systems. Clearly, for both metrics, there is a very close match between the simulation and the approximation. Hence, in Figures 5 and 6, we show the percentage error, given as (approximation-simulation)/simulation, for both metrics to provide a greater insight into the accuracy of the approximation. This shows that the approximation and simulation agree to within 2% for the utilisation and within 4% for average response time. In all cases the simulation is run to a terminating condition of a 95% confidence interval. Not surprisingly this becomes increasingly more difficult to attain as N increases, hence the run-time increases with N.

The most significant difference between the simulation and the approximation is the time it takes to derive results. The simulation took several weeks to code and each run takes in excess of 10 hours (we are not claiming this to be the most efficient simulation possible) whereas the approximation was coded into MS Excel in less than half an hour and results are almost instantaneous. It is worth noting that these metrics are based on long run averages, which we would expect the approximation to be fairly accurate in predicting, particularly utilisation. If the measure of interest was a transient measure then the lumping of states might not give such an accurate picture. Furthermore, if we wished to predict the end to end performance of the protocol, i.e. from *request* to *confirm*, then we would need to perform a slightly different approximation which separates the *usekey* action from the other lumped actions.

The results show that there is obviously a benefit from increasing the server speed at the KDC, but the increase in server speed is not necessarily exactly

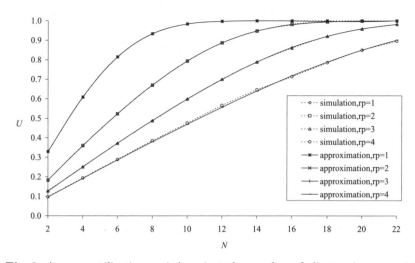

Fig. 3. Average utilisation varied against the number of client pairs. $r_u = 1.1$, $r_A = r_B = r_c = r_q = 1$.

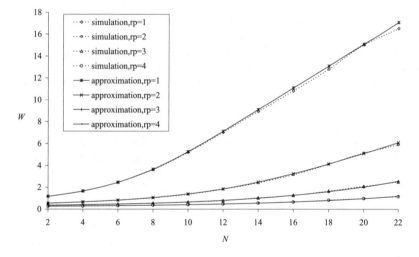

Fig. 4. Average response time varied against the number of client pairs. $r_u = 1.1$, $r_A = r_B = r_c = r_q = 1$.

proportional to the increase in capacity. For example, if we have a target maximum utilisation of 0.65, then with $r_p = 1$ the KDC can cope with at most 4 client pairs. If we increase the server rate to $r_p = 3$ then the capacity is 10 client pairs, not 12 as we might intuitively expect. However, if we specify the maximum average response time to be 2, then $r_p = 1$ gives the capacity as 4, $r_p = 2$ gives 12, and $r_p = 3$ gives the capacity as 18 client pairs. Clearly in this case the increase in server speed from $r_p = 1$ to $r_p = 2$, or $r_p = 3$, has a

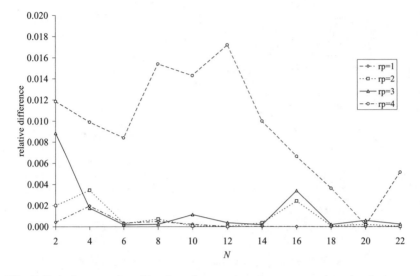

Fig. 5. Relative error in utilisation of approximation compared to simulation. $r_u = 1.1$, $r_A = r_B = r_c = r_q = 1$.

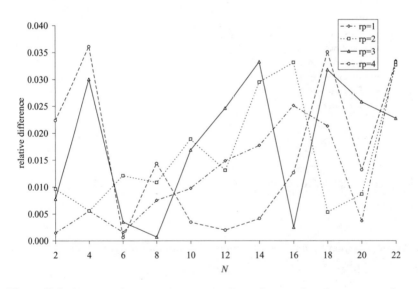

Fig. 6. Relative error in average response time of approximation compared to simulation. $r_u = 1.1$, $r_A = r_B = r_c = r_q = 1$.

significantly greater impact on the client capacity than we might expect. Note also that, whilst intuitively we may consider that it is possible that a greater impact could be made by considering multiple KDC severs, we know that for a simple $M/M/k$ queue it is preferable to have one fast server than two of half

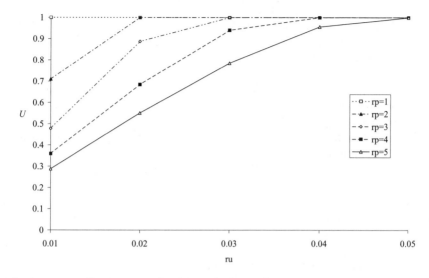

Fig. 7. Average utilisation varied against the rate of session key use, r_u $r_q = r_A = r_B = r_c = 1$, $N = 150$

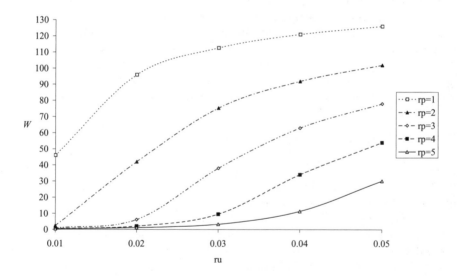

Fig. 8. Average Response time varied against the rate of session key use, r_u $r_q = r_A = r_B = r_c = 1$, $N = 150$

the speed. Clearly therefore we would rather double the speed of the processor, than double the number of processors at the KDC (although doing both would clearly be beneficial).

In the above experiments the duration for which the session key is used is set to be approximately the same as the durations for any other action. We have done this so that we can explore the behaviour of the KDC when it is heavily loaded, despite only having a small number of client pairs. Clearly this is not a practical scenario and having established the accuracy of the approximation we can now go on to consider larger systems with a greater duration of the use of the session key. Note that although in theory the approximation scales very well, in practise there can be numerical problems relating to the representation and manipulation of large factorials, hence in this instance we have restricted the experimentation to $N = 150$ ($150! \approx 5.7 * 10^{262}$)

Figures 7 and 8 show the utilisation and average response time for various values of r_u and r_p when $N = 150$. When the use rate is low ($r_u = 0.01$) the performance is good for $r_p > 2$ (in fact the response time for $r_p = 2$ is more than five times that of $r_p = 5$, although this is not clear in the graph). However, increasing the use rate has a dramatic effect on both the utilisation and the average response time. The systems rapidly become saturated, except $r_p = 5$ (and to a lesser extent $r_p = 4$) which grows more gently. At $r_u = 0.05$ all the systems are saturated (100% utilisation). A similar picture is evident for the average response time. For $r_p = 5$ the average response time increases exponentially. However, for $r_p = 1$, where the response time is obviously much greater, the increase is inversely exponential, i.e. the rate of increase decreases as r_u increases. This is because $r_p = 1$ is already saturated at $r_u = 0.01$ and so a large number of clients are already spending a long time in the queue awaiting a response from the KDC. Hence, decreasing the time they use the session key does not greatly change their overall behaviour (which is already dominated by queueing). The other cases of $1 < r_u < 5$ fall between these extremes, with the saturation point being clearly evident in the plot of the average response time.

7   Conclusion and Further Work

In this paper we have shown how a key distribution centre can be modelled and analysed using the Markovian process algebra PEPA. The intuitive means of modelling the protocol is cumbersome and suffers from state space explosion, preventing meaningful analysis with significant numbers of clients. We have taken two approaches to coping with this problem; first we have implemented a simulation of the model and secondly we have attempted to approximate the system behaviour with a much simpler model. The approximation shows good accuracy of prediction compared with simulation, scales exceptionally well and is extremely fast to compute.

This study is the first step into looking at performance modelling of a range of authentication mechanisms using PEPA and simulation. Such a study will provide a greater understanding in the overhead inherent in these mechanisms and may possibly identify some means by which accepted mechanisms can be improved. The next step is to explore the use of ordinary differential equation analysis [7] and stochastic simulation methods from computational systems biology [1] as an alternative mechanism to coping with the state space explosion problem. We then seek to apply the lessons learnt to a class of non-repudiation protocols.

The analysis in this paper demonstrates the rather obvious point that a more powerful key distribution centre improves the performance. By adding a cost to the provision of service and a (negative) cost to the time a job spends in the queue, it would be possible to demonstrate the trade-off in service provision and compute and optimum service capacity. Potentially we would also be able to use such a mechanism to set quality of service bounds such that a service could be guaranteed to be completed within a given time frame with a given probability if a certain amount of computational power is provided at the KDC.

References

1. Bradley, J., Gilmore, S., Thomas, N.: Performance analysis of Stochastic Process Algebra models using Stochastic Simulation. In: 20th IEEE International Parallel and Distributed Processing Symposium. IEEE Computer Society, Los Alamitos (2006)
2. Buchholtz, M., Gilmore, S., Hillston, J., Nielson, F.: Securing statically-verified communications protocols against timing attacks. Electronic Notes in Theoretical Computer Science 128(4) (2005)
3. Clark, G., Gilmore, S., Hillston, J., Thomas, N.: Experiences with the PEPA Performance Modelling Tools. IEE Proceedings - Software 146(1), 11–19 (1999)
4. Dick, S., Thomas, N.: Performance analysis of PGP. In: Ball, F. (ed.) 22nd UK Performance Engineering Workshop (UKPEW), Bournemouth University (2006)
5. Freeman, W., Miller, E.: An Experimental Analysis of Cryptographic Overhead in Performance-critical Systems. In: 7th International Symposium on Modeling, Analysis and Simulation of Computer and Telecommunication Systems (MASCOTS), IEEE Computer Society, Los Alamitos (1999)
6. Hillston, J.: A Compositional Approach to Performance Modelling. Cambridge University Press, Cambridge (1996)
7. Hillston, J.: Fluid flow approximation of PEPA models. In: 4th International Conference on Quantitative Evaluation of Systems (QEST 2005), pp. 33–43. IEEE Computer Society, Los Alamitos (2005)
8. Lamprecht, C., van Moorsel, A., Tomlinson, P., Thomas, N.: Investigating the efficiency of cryptographic algorithms in online transactions. International Journal of Simulation: Systems, Science & Technology 7(2), 63–75 (2006)
9. Mitrani, I.: Probabilistic Modelling. Cambridge University Press, Cambridge (1998)
10. Stallings, W.: Cryptography and Network Security: Principles and Practice. Prentice-Hall, Englewood Cliffs (1999)
11. Zhao, Y., Thomas, N.: Modelling secure secret key exchange using stochastic process algebra. In: Pereira, E., Pereira, R. (eds.) 23rd UK Performance Engineering Workshop, Edge Hill University (2007)

A Model Transformation
from the Palladio Component Model
to Layered Queueing Networks

Heiko Koziolek[1] and Ralf Reussner[2]

[1] Graduate School Trustsoft*
University of Oldenburg, Germany
[2] Chair for Software Design and Quality
University of Karlsruhe, Germany
{koziolek,reussner}@ipd.uka.de

Abstract. For component-based performance engineering, software component developers individually create performance specifications of their components. Software architects compose these specifications to architectural models. This enables assessing the possible fulfilment of performance requirements without the need to purchase and deploy the component implementations. Many existing performance models do not support component-based performance engineering but offer efficient solvers. On the other hand, component-based performance engineering approaches often lack tool support. We present a model transformation combining the advanced component concepts of the Palladio Component Model (PCM) with the efficient performance solvers of Layered Queueing Networks (LQN). Joining the tool-set for PCM specifications with the tool-set for LQN solution is an important step to carry component-based performance engineering into industrial practice. We validate the correctness of the transformation by mapping the PCM model of a component-based architecture to an LQN and conduct performance predictions.

1 Introduction

Although the computational power of modern hardware is constantly increasing, many IT companies still face serious performance problems in their systems. This can lead to reduced user satisfaction and high maintenance costs [30].

The increasing complexity of modern software systems makes it hard to analyse performance properties at low abstraction levels. The idea of component-based software performance engineering (CBSPE) is to let software architects reason on the performance properties of their systems during design time at an architectural level using performance specifications provided by different component vendors. This enables them to manage the complexity of the performance model, to identify performance-critical components, and to avoid poor designs.

* This work is supported by the German Research Foundation (DFG), grants GRK 1076/1 and RE 1674/1-2.

S. Kounev, I. Gorton, and K. Sachs (Eds.): SIPEW 2008, LNCS 5119, pp. 58–78, 2008.
© Springer-Verlag Berlin Heidelberg 2008

For component developers, it is not trivial to supply performance specifications of their components. As components shall be composed and deployed independently, component developers cannot make assumptions on how software architects compose components with others, how components will be deployed, and how users will execute them. All these factors influence the performance properties of a component. Therefore, component developers have to supply *parametrised* specifications, which software architects can adapt to different environments.

Researchers have proposed several approaches with parametrised specifications to support CBSPE (e.g., [5,9,6]). However, none of these approaches has reached industrial maturity due to still limited parametrisation concepts and due to a lack of tool support [16]. The Palladio Component Model (PCM) [4] is another proposal for CBSPE. It features component performance specification parametrised for different resource environments, usage profiles, and calls to required services. There is a discrete-event simulator for performance analysis of PCM instances, which, however, can be time-consuming for non-trivial systems.

Approaches for CBSPE can build on analytical methods for monolithic performance models, after the software architect has composed the individual component performance specifications, and tools have resolved their parametrisations. A mature monolithic performance model for distributed software systems with an efficient analytical solver is provided by Layered Queueing Networks (LQNs) [25]. Although there is an extension for LQNs to support CBSPE [32], its parametrisation concept is still limited. Therefore, we do not use this extension in this work.

In this paper, we introduce a fully automated model transformation from PCM to LQN. Software architects can use this transformation and the connected LQN solver to assess the performance of a PCM instance. With the PCM as input model, they can easily change parameter values in the PCM instance and analyse different settings. Because the LQN solver relies on Mean-Value-Analysis (MVA) and carries out an approximative performance prediction, it allows quicker performance analysis than running the PCM discrete-event simulator in many cases.

The contributions of the paper are (i) a model transformation from PCM to LQN, and (ii) a case study, where the transformation helped to analyse the performance of a component-based system. A part of the transformation (i.e., solving parameter dependencies) can be reused for other model transformations. To the best of our knowledge the transformation in this paper is the first implemented and validated transformation from a component-based modelling language to LQNs.

The remainder of this paper is organised as follows: Section 2 surveys related work in the area of component-based performance engineering and model transformations for LQN. Section 3 briefly introduces the basic concepts of PCM and LQN. Section 4 describes the two-step model transformation involving the solution of parameter dependencies and the mapping to LQNs. Section 5 presents a case study applying the transformation on the model of a component-based system. Section 6 discusses limitations of the transformation, before Section 7 concludes the paper.

2   Related Work

The area of software performance engineering (SPE) originates from the pioneering work of Connie Smith [26]. Balsamo et al. [1] have surveyed several approaches for SPE, which use annotated, UML-like design models and transform them into performance models, such as queueing networks, stochastic process algebra, or stochastic Petri nets. Becker et al. [3] compare different approaches for CBSPE.

Several approaches introduce model transformations targeting LQNs. The source models are annotated UML diagrams [23,8,31,12], Use Case Maps [22], and CSM [21]. These approaches do not support the specifics of component-based systems. Grassi et al. [11] have defined the intermediate modelling language KLAPER, which shall ease model transformations between different component-based design models and performance models. A KLAPER to LQN mapping is under development, and the work in this paper could be adapted to incorporate this mapping. However, the performance annotations in KLAPER so far do not follow defined semantics, which complicates automatic transformations.

Though some researchers have used LQNs to model component-based systems (e.g. [28,29]), these approaches create single monolithic models, from which individual component specifications cannot be reused for different systems, because they lack the necessary parametrisation.

Wu et al. [32] have extended LQNs with the Component-based Modeling Language (CBML), which adds explicit provided and required interfaces to parts of LQNs and therefore enables replacing these parts with other LQN parts conforming to the same interfaces. This extension also features a form of parametrisation, which for example allows adapting the number of thread instances available to a component. The parametrisation however does not refer to input or output parameters of a component service, which is supported by the PCM.

Besides LQNs, other performance models have been used to analyse the performance of component-based software systems. Liu et al. [18] focus on EJB-based systems and have created a benchmark for application servers. Combining the benchmark results with an application model yields a queueing network, which allows analysing an application architecture for different workloads. The performance models created by this approach rely on certain EJB patterns and are hardly reusable in different settings. Kounev [15] uses Queueing Petri Nets (QPN) to model the SPEC jAppServer 2004, which consists of several software components. However, the resulting model is monolithic and cannot be decomposed into individual, reusable models for single components.

3   Foundations

3.1   Palladio Component Model

The Palladio Component Model (PCM) is a meta-model for the specification of component-based software systems and especially targets performance predictions [4]. Besides the specification of software components (according to

Szyperski's definition [27]) and connectors, it additionally allows modelling hardware resources and resource demands of components. While UML models annotated with the UML SPT profile [19] could be used to model similar information as in the PCM, the PCM includes more advanced component concepts than the UML and features a parametrisation concept, which enables independent modelling by different component developers.

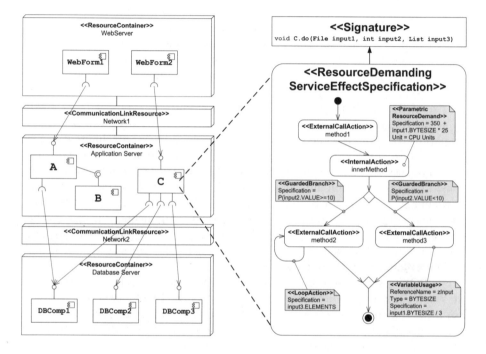

Fig. 1. A simple example PCM Instance

The PCM is divided into several sub-models targeting specific developer roles. Component developers specify behavioural abstractions of their components and put them into repositories. Software architects retrieve these specifications during design time and compose them to the model of a complete software system. System deployers provide a model that specifies the hardware environment and the allocation of components to resources. Finally, domain experts use the PCM to specify the usage of the system in terms of number of users, user flow, and input parameters.

As the PCM contains more than 100 meta-classes, we only provide a simple example for a PCM instance here (Fig. 1) in a UML-like concrete syntax to give the reader an idea of the PCM's modelling capabilities (more details in [4]). The figure's left hand side contains an example component-based software architecture (provided by a software architect) and its allocation to hardware resources (provided by a system deployer).

Each component may include an abstract behavioural description for each of its provided services (specified by the component developer), which is called Resource Demanding Service Effect Specification (RDSEFF). It specifies the resource demands of the service and its calls to required services. Fig. 1 depicts an RDSEFF for the service do of the component C on the right hand side. The service first calls an external service method1 and then uses the CPU of the application server (internalMethod). The component developer specifies the resource demand in an abstract unit ("CPU-Units"), which can be converted into a timing values once the system deployer has specified the execution time for a CPU unit. A single internal action can represent a large amount of code in a single model element, thereby creating an abstraction from the implementation.

In this case, the resource demand is specified including a dependency to the size of the service's input parameter input1. Once the domain expert specifies the size of this input parameter for the given application context (e.g., 1000), the actual resource demand can be resolved (e.g., 25350 CPU Units). Because of the parametrisation, the specification can be easily adapted for different usages and hardware environments (not shown here) if the component is reused. Besides parametrised resource demands, RDSEFFs also allow parametrised branch transitions, loop iteration numbers, and input parameters to required services as shown in Fig. 1. The RDSEFF parametrisation allows modelling performance annotations in dependency to the data flow between components, whereas in other approaches (e.g., LQNs) the parametrisation only refers to single components. There are several extensions for the PCM (e.g., [13,2]) to reflect performance-relevant influences by the middleware.

The PCM is specified in Ecore from the Eclipse Modelling Framework. There are several graphical editors for the specification of PCM instances. There is also a discrete event simulation for PCM instances called SimuCom [4], which enables deriving performance metrics such as response times, throughputs, and resource demands of a complete system model, but can be time-consuming for large models, because it supports arbitrary distributed service times. Finally, several reverse engineering tools are under development [7,14], which shall semi-automatically derive components and RDSEFFs given arbitrary Java code.

3.2 Layered Queueing Networks

Layered Queueing Networks (LQN) [10] are a performance model in the class of extended queueing networks. Other than plain QNs, LQNs model software entities and their communication explicitly in a hierarchical structure. Like the PCM, LQNs target the performance analysis of distributed business informations systems, but unlike the PCM they do not support independent specification of individual software components. There is an approximative, analytical solver based on Mean-Value Analysis (MVA) for LQNs including M/M/n queues [25].

As an example, Fig. 2 shows a simple LQN instance in the standard concrete syntax. It is an acyclic graph and consists of *processors* (circles) and *tasks* (parallelograms). Processors model hardware entities such as CPUs, hard disks, or networks. Tasks model software entities, such as components, application servers, databases, semaphores, or buffers. Tasks are arranged in a layered hierarchy, where tasks from upper layers may send requests to tasks from lower layers. Both processors and tasks contain a request queue (not depicted in the figure), from which they serve waiting requests according to a specific scheduling discipline (e.g., FCFS or Processor Sharing).

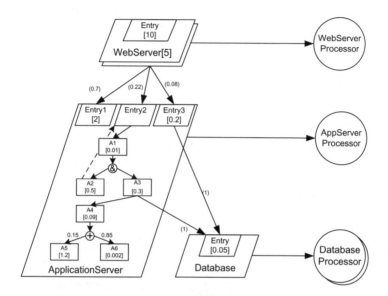

Fig. 2. A simple example LQN Instance

Each task can contain multiple *entries*, which model the services provided by the software entity. Entries either directly specify a resource demand to the underlying processor of the tasks, or include a control flow graph containing multiple *activities*, which issue such demands. Both entries and activities can also make calls to the entries of tasks on lowers layers of the LQNs. These calls can be synchronous (i.e., blocking the caller) or asynchronous (i.e., the control flow of the caller continues immediately after issuing the request).

The control flow graphs for activities support sequences, branches, loops, and forks. Other than in the PCM, branch probabilities and loop iteration numbers have to be specified as constant values and cannot depend on input parameters. Resource demands by activities or entries specify execution times as mean values of exponential distributions.

If an entry does not include a control flow graph, its execution may consists of up to three so-called *phases*, where each phase can request processing from the underlying processor or call other entries. The implicit semantics of the first phase is that the caller of the entry containing the phase blocks until it is finished. The entry then generates a reply for the caller, after which the caller continues execution. Concurrently, the entry executes the second and third phase asynchronously from the caller. This models a common communication pattern in distributed systems, which tries to ensure a high responsiveness by returning control to clients as early as possible.

The top-most tasks in an LQN are called reference tasks. They model clients and may include open or closed workloads. Open workloads specify an arrival rate for incoming requests and do not bound the number of requests issued to the system. Closed workloads specify a bounded number of users circulating in the system (the user population). After completing execution of all requests, a user re-enters the system after a given think time.

4   Model Transformation

4.1   Process

The model transformation and solution process from PCM instances to LQN instances contains multiple steps (Fig. 3). First the different developer roles specify their parts of the PCM instance. After the domain expert has created the usage model, the PCM instance is complete and can be checked automatically for syntactical inconsistencies.

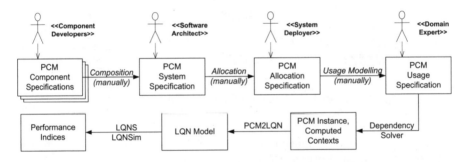

Fig. 3. Modelling and Transformation Process

The Dependency Solver (DS) takes the complete PCM model as input and propagates parameter values specified in the usage model through all RDSEFFs, substituting parameter references in these specifications with the actual values (Section 4.2). This step creates resource demands, branch probabilities, and loop iteration numbers without parameter dependencies. Afterwards, the tool PCM2LQN is responsible for mapping the model to an LQN instance (Section 4.3) and executing the LQN solver for the performance prediction. The tool-chain is fully automated after starting the DS and embedded into the PCM bench.

4.2   Transformation 1: Dependency Solver

The DS combines the sub-models from the different developer roles and removes the parametrisation from RDSEFF instances, so that they are prepared for a

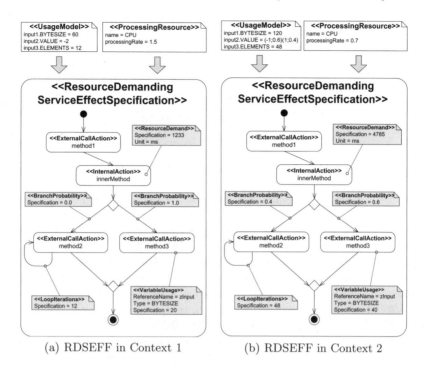

(a) RDSEFF in Context 1   (b) RDSEFF in Context 2

Fig. 4. Output of the Dependency Solver

mapping to a performance model. To clarify this process, we will first briefly describe the PCM context model.

The PCM strictly separates information about the context (i.e., the composition, allocation, and usage) of a component from its own behavioural specification, because this information is unknown to the component developer. Software architects create a so-called *assembly context* for each component instance they compose into an architecture. It stores the component instance's binding to other components. There can be multiple assembly contexts for a single component type in an architecture, as a software architect can use multiple instances of the same component in the same architecture.

System deployers create a so-called *allocation context* for each *assembly context* specifying the component instance's deployment to a particular hardware resource. The usage of a component (i.e., the number of invocations and the used parameter values) only needs to be specified at the system boundaries for components directly interacting with users. The domain expert creates a so-called usage model, which stores this information. The DS then traverses all RDSEFFs using the binding specification from the assembly contexts and propagates the parameter values from the usage model through the architecture.

Consider the example in Fig. 4. It depicts the output of the Dependency Solver after processing the RDSEFF from Fig. 1 in two different contexts using the usage model and processing resource specification at the top of the figure.

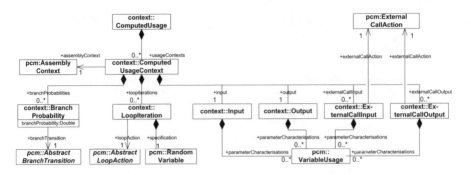

Fig. 5. Computed Usage Context (Meta-Model)

For example, the `ResourceDemand` of the left-hand side RDSEFF results from
the `ParametricResourceDemand` $(350 + \text{input1.BYTESIZE} * 25)$ seen before in
Fig. 1. The DS has substituted the actual parameter value specified in above's
usage model $(350 + 60 * 25 = 1850)$ and divided the expression by the processing
rate from the processing resource $(1850/1.5 = 1233)$.

The PCM allows component developers to specify parameter dependencies
referring to the value, bytesize, length (for collections), or other performance-
relevant properties of a parameter [16]. The dependencies may include arithmetic expressions $(+,-,*,/)$ on resource demands or loop iteration numbers, and
boolean expressions $(=, <, >, \leq, \geq, AND, OR)$ on branching guards (cf. Fig. 1).

The PCM does not only support characterising parameter values with constant values, but also probability distributions. For example, the domain expert
could specify `a.BYTESIZE = IntPMF[(10;0.2) (20;0.3) (30;0.5)]` in the usage model, meaning that the size of a in bytes is 10 with a probability of 0.2.
Then, solving the parameter dependency for the example $(2 * \text{a.BYTESIZE})$ by
the DS would result in a `RandomVariable` with the value: `IntPMF[(20;0.2)
(30;0.3) (40;0.5)]`.

Notice that parameter dependencies need not exactly reflect the precise, actual dependencies given by the code of the component, which is for example
often impractical for large components. A coarse abstraction of the dependency
focussing on the performance impact of a parameter is often sufficient.

The DS stores all solved expressions for parameter dependencies in the so-
called "computed context model", which is a decorator model for the PCM.
It includes a computed usage context model (meta-model in Fig. 5), which
stores solved expressions for branch probabilities, loop iteration numbers and
input/output parameter values. Furthermore it includes a computed allocation
model (meta-model in Fig. 6), which stores solved expressions for resource demands. These models are separated, because they result from different information sources (i.e., the domain expert and the system deployer).

The model traversal by the DS starts with RDSEFFs of components at the
system boundaries. If these RDSEFFs contains calls to other RDSEFFs, the DS
successively also traverses those RDSEFFs. Upon finishing the traversal of an

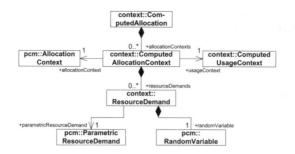

Fig. 6. Computed Allocation Context (Meta-Model)

RDSEFFs, the DS returns to the calling RDSEFF and creates the `External-CallOutput` specification of the `ComputedUsageContext`, which may include a solved parameter dependency to the return value or output parameter characterisations specified in the called RDSEFF. The DS traverses each loop body in the RDSEFF only once, which is sufficient for solving the parameter dependencies.

After the DS has traversed the whole model and created all computed context models, this decorated PCM instance is ready for the transformation into a performance model. A more detailed description of the DS can be found in [16]. Although the following only describes the mapping to LQNs, transformations to other performance models can be applied at this point. For example, there is a transformation to Stochastic Regular Expressions [17].

4.3   Transformation 2: PCM2LQN

The second transformation PCM2LQN maps a PCM instance decorated with computed contexts to an LQN instance. This transformation is documented in detail in [16]. Due to space reasons, this papers describes the mapping with an example, provides an overview of the complete mapping, and highlights challenges of the transformation due to semantic gaps between PCM and LQN.

Example. Fig. 7 demonstrates how PCM2LQN maps the RDSEFF from Fig. 4(b) into an LQN. Each RDSEFF is mapped into an LQN task with a task activity graph. Although PCM2LQN could map all RDSEFFs of a single component to a single LQN task with multiple entry activity graphs, this has not been implemented, as the LQN solvers so far do not support entry activity graphs.

PCM2LQN transforms each `ExternalCallAction` into an LQN activity with zero host demand and a synchronous call to the task representing the called RDSEFF. The activities A1 and A4 in the example have resulted from this mapping.

PCM `InternalActions` model computations by a component service, which execute on the resources the component is deployed on. Every `InternalAction` can contain several `ResourceDemands` directed at specific resources, such as a

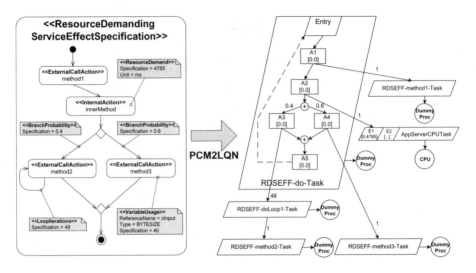

Fig. 7. PCM2LQN Example: Transforming an RDSEFF to LQN fragments

CPU or hard disk. PCM2LQN creates an activity for the `InternalAction` and for each `ResourceDemand` (A2 in the example) and connects them sequentially.

RDSEFFs can reference multiple resources, but LQN tasks can run only on a single LQN processor. Thus, PCM2LQN converts PCM `ResourceDemands` to LQN entries, which are added to the task running on the processor created for the resource referenced by the `ResourceDemand` (E1 in the example). The activities created for the resource demand call these entries synchronously.

For the host execution demand of those entries, PCM2LQN either directly uses the PCM resource demand specification if is a constant or computes its expected value if is a probability distribution. This step is necessary as LQNs only support mean value resource demands. It lowers the accuracy of the model as information about the distribution gets lost.

The control flow constructs of branch and sequence can directly be mapped to their counterparts in LQN task graphs. PCM2LQN accesses the computed usage context for a given RDSEFF to retrieve the branch probabilities (0.4 and 0.6 in the example) and uses them in the task graph.

Although LQN activity graphs support loops, these loops may only contain a sequence of activities, but not branches or nested loops. PCM `Loop` bodies instead allow arbitrary behaviour. Therefore PCM2LQN creates a new LQN task for each loop body. Within this task, the LQN can include arbitrary behaviour and model the PCM loop body.

The tasks created for the loop body is called as often as the specified number of loop iterations (48 in the example). If the number of loop iterations is specified with a probability distribution, PCM2LQN uses its expected value for the number of calls to the loop body task.

The tasks created for RDSEFFs and loop bodies run on dummy LQN processors, which they do not use. PCM2LQN creates these processors to make the model valid for the LQN solvers. Only the LQN processors created for PCM `ProcessingResources` are actually used by LQN tasks. Their mapping is straight forward, as PCM2LQN can directly map their processing rates to the speed-factor of LQN processors, and their scheduling policies to LQN scheduling policies.

Mapping Overview. Tab. 1 depicts a complete overview of the transformation. The first column refers to meta-classes from the PCM. The second and third column refer to the corresponding meta-classes from the LQN meta-model. The second column contains the main classes of the mapping, and the third column contains additionally created classes to make the LQN instance syntactically correct or to model control flow precedence.

In addition to the meta-classes, the values contained in the brackets refer to attributes of these classes. The table only includes the attributes of a meta-class if PCM2LQN maps to another value than the default value (documented in [24]), otherwise the attribute is left out in the table for brevity. For example, for an `Activity` of a LQN the default `hostDemand` is zero, therefore all `Activities` without a `hostDemand` attribute in the table have an implicit `hostDemand` of zero.

Several LQN classes reference each other using strings, which refer to the `name` attribute of other classes. The LQN's `Precedence` classes use this mechanism to connect individual `Activities` to an activity graph. The table does not include all reference strings used in the transformation as they add little value to understanding the transformation.

The mapping for PCM usage models is similar to mapping of RDSEFFs. With them, domain experts specify user behaviour in terms of workload, scenarios, and calls to RDSEFFs. PCM2LQN maps the included `ClosedWorkloads` to LQN reference tasks (i.e., scheduling=ref). Such tasks only emit requests, and cannot serve requests themselves. The attribute `population` (i.e., the number of concurrent users) of the `ClosedWorkload` is equivalent to the multiplicity attribute of the new reference task. The attribute `thinkTime` (i.e., the time a user waits before re-entering a scenario after completing it) is mapped to the LQN task think time.

PCM `OpenWorkloads` are also mapped to reference tasks. However, in this case their think time is 0.0 and their multiplicity is 1 (i.e., the default values). PCM2LQN transforms the `OpenWorkload`'s `interArrivalTime` into a rate using the expected value of the specified probability distribution. This rate is used as the open arrival rate for the entry in the newly created reference task. PCM2LQN maps the rest of the usage model similarly to RDSEFFs, therefore we omit a detailed description.

In addition to the mappings shown in the example PCM2LQN also supports mapping RDSEFF `ForkActions`. They model the invocation of threads and their concurrent execution. The mapping to LQNs is similar to the mapping for branches. PCM2LQN uses an AND precedence to create the fork and creates new tasks for the forked behaviours. After they have finished execution, another precedence merges the forked control flow together again. So far, the mapping only supports synchronous forks.

Table 1. Transformation PCM2LQN

PCM	LQN	LQN - supplemental
ResourceEnvironment		
prs:ProcessingResourceSpecification	Processor (scheduling=prs.schedulingPolicy, speedFactor=prs.processingRate)	Task, Entry
UsageModel		
cw:ClosedWorkload	Task (scheduling=ref, thinkTime=expectedValue(cw.thinkTime), multiplicity=cw.population)	Processor, Entry
ow:OpenWorkload	Task (scheduling=ref), Entry (openArrivalRate=1/expectedValue(ow.interArrivalTime))	Processor
sb:ScenarioBehaviour	TaskActivityGraph	
elsc:EntryLevelSystemCall	Activity(synchCall)	Precedence (pre=elsc, post=elsc.successor)
d:Delay	Activity(thinkTime=expectedValue(d.userDelay))	Precedence (pre=d, post=d.successor)
b:Branch	Activity, Precedence(pre=b, postOR=bt_1..n), Precedence (preOR=bt_1..n, post=b.successor)	
bt:BranchTransition	ActivityOr(prob=bt.branchProbability)	
l:Loop	Activity (synchCall, callsMean=expectedValue(l.iterations))	Processor, Task, Entry, Precedence (pre=l, post=l.successor)
RDSEFF		
rdb:ResourceDemandingBehaviour	TaskGraph	Processor, Task, Entry
st:StartAction	-	
sp:StopAction	ReplyActivity, ReplyEntry	
eca:ExternalCallAction	Activity(synchCall)	Precedence (pre=eca, post=eca.successor)
ba:BranchAction	Activity, Precedence(pre=ba, postOR=abt_1..n), Precedence (preOR=abt_1..n, post=ba.successor)	
abt:AbstractBranchTransition	ActivityOr(prob=computedUsageContext(abt).branchProbability)	
la:LoopAction	Activity (synchCall, callsMean= expectedValue(computedUsageContext(l). iterations))	Processor, Task, Entry, Precedence (pre=la, post=la.successor)
cia:CollectionIteratorAction	Activity (synchCall, callsMean= expectedValue(computedUsageContext(cia). iterations))	Processor, Task, Entry, Precedence (pre=cia, post=cia.successor)
ia:InternalAction	Activity(hostDemand=0)	Precedence (pre=ia, post='first prd'), Precedence (pre='last prd', post=ia.successor)
prd:ParametricResourceDemand	Activity(synchCall), Entry, PhaseActivity(hostDemand=expectedValue(computedUsageContext(prd).resourceDemand))	Precedence (pre=prd, post='next prd')
sva:SetVariableAction	-	
fa:ForkAction, sp:SynchronisationPoint	Activity, Precedence(pre=fa, postAND=rdb_1..n), Precedence (preAND=rdb_1..n, post=fa.successor)	
pr:PassiveResource	Task(schedDisc=semaphore), Entry (signal), Entry (wait)	
aa:AcquireAction	Activity(synchCall, dest='wait')	Precedence (pre=aa, post=aa.successor)
ra:ReleaseAction	Activity(synchCall, dest='signal')	Precedence (pre=ra, post=ra.successor)

In the PCM, components can have `PassiveResources`, which can be used to model semaphores or thread pools. LQNs use special tasks to model semaphores. These tasks have the scheduling discipline 'semaphore' and contain two entries named 'wait' and 'signal'. The first entry allows requesting the semaphore, while the second entry models returning the semaphore. PCM2LQN creates such a task for each `PassiveResource` in the PCM instance. The `AcquireAction` and `ReleaseActions` are mapped to activities with synchronous calls to the 'wait' entry or 'signal' entry respectively.

Prototypical Implementation. PCM2LQN uses three visitors (implemented in Java) to traverse the PCM's `ResourceEnvironment`, `UsageModel`, and `RDSEFF` models. The navigation between the RDSEFFs is managed by using the assembly contexts and looking up the connected components in the PCM `System` specification.

PCM2LQN creates instances of an LQN meta-model in Ecore. This meta-model has been generated with EMF from the LQN-XML schema provided with the LQN tools (Version 3.12, cf. [24]). Once the visitors of PCM2LQN have traversed the whole PCM instance, an object representation of the LQN instance has been created. Using the XML serialisation of EMF, PCM2LQN then saves this representation to an XML file, which is the input of the LQN solvers.

5   Case Study

The following case study serves to demonstrate the correctness of the model transformation introduced in this paper. We have modelled a component-based software system as a PCM instance and used the Dependency Solver described in Section 4.2 as well as PCM2LQN described in Section 4.3 to generate an LQN and run the LQN solvers for performance analysis. Additionally, the case study points out the benefits of a parametrised, component-based performance specification as the PCM, which enables model reuse and analysis of the impact of different usage profiles, hardware resources, and component compositions to performance.

The case study investigates the so-called "Business Reporting System" (BRS), which is loosely based on an industrial system. We only present performance predictions based on the model and do not provide comparisons with measured data. The validity of LQN performance predictions have been shown in former studies (e.g., [10]) and are out of scope for this paper. We assume that the PCM instance of the BRS with its control flow and resource demands reflects the performance properties of the modelled system well.

The BRS is a 4-tier, web-based system to monitor and manage business data. On a high abstraction level, it consists of 5 software components (Fig. 8 at the top). Clients either request business reports or specific entries from the database via the `WebServer`. A `Scheduler` connects the `WebServer` with an `ApplicationServer`. The latter contains a component `ReportingEngine`, which manages the creation of reports, and a component `Cache`, which buffers data from the database for quick access. Both, the `ReportingEngine` and the `Cache` query the component `Database`, which stores a configurable amount of entries in its tables.

Fig. 8 shows PCM RDSEFFs for services of the `WebServer`, `Reporting-Engine`, and `Database` at the bottom. The whole model consists of nine

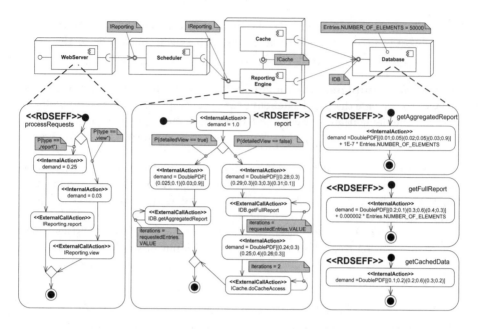

Fig. 8. Business Reporting System (Palladio Component Model)

RDSEFFs, some have been omitted for brevity[1]. The first RDSEFF process-Requests includes parameter dependencies, which determine branch probabilities according to the probabilities specified in the PCM usage model for the type of requested services (i.e., report or view). It also contains some constant resource demands to the WebServer's CPU.

The second depicted RDSEFF (report) from the ReportingEngine chooses a branch depending on whether the users request detailed reports or not. Detailed reports result in longer calls to the database. As the BRS also allows users to specify the number of entries in the generated reports, the loops in this RDSEFF are iterated as many times as the number of requested entries. Finally, this RDSEFF contains resource demands specified as probability density functions (PDF).

The three RDSEFFs on the right hand side of the figure represent services from the database system and do not include calls to other components. The resource demands specified in the upper two RDSEFFs depend on the number of entries specified in the Database. A larger number of entries results in longer queries. The component developer of the Database has made this relationship explicit, so that different software architects can adjust the model to their anticipated number of entries in the database.

The full PCM instance of the BRS additionally includes an usage model and a resource environment model, which are not illustrated here. Network traffic is considered negligible in the model.

---

[1] The full PCM instance of the BRS system as well as PCM2LQN are available for download at http://www.palladio-approach.net.

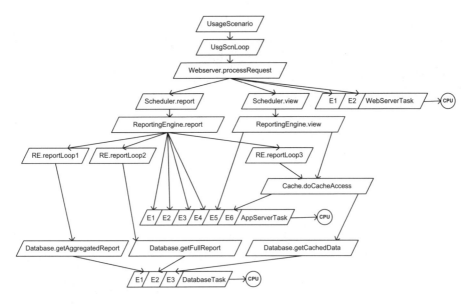

Fig. 9. Business Reporting System (Layered Queueing Network, Schematic Illustration)

Running the formerly described model transformations on the PCM instance of the BRS yields the LQN, schematically depicted in Fig. 9. The illustration only shows entries including non-zero host demands to the underlying processors, and only shows processors which are actually used by task. The complete model contains a processor for each task to make it valid for the solvers. The illustration also does not display the task activity graphs generated for the RDSEFFs.

Notice, how the loops of the RDSEFFs result in additional tasks and how the resource demands of RDSEFFs result in LQN entries as described in Section 4.3. For example, PCM2LQN has mapped the four resource demands of the RDSEFF `process` (seen in Fig. 8) to the entries E1-E4 of the `AppServerTask` in Fig. 9. PCM2LQN determines the expected values for the probability density functions specified in the RDSEFFs and uses them in the LQN.

In our performance analysis, we predict the performance of the system for different usage profiles. This only requires changing the PCM usage model and not the PCM RDSEFFs, as the dependency solver automatically determines the branch probabilities, loop iterations numbers and resource demands for a given usage model. Here, we do not alter other possible parameters of the model, such as the speed of hardware resources or the composition of the components to keep the case study managable.

Tab. 2 contains the three usage profiles used for the prediction. Users can change the type of requests, the number of entries per request, and decide whether they want detailed reports or not. Additionally, the number of entries in the database is part of the usage profiles and needs to be specified by the software architect. Here, the three usage profiles are not based on specific realistic settings, and only serve to demonstrate the prediction capabilities of the model.

Table 2. Usage Profiles for the Business Reporting System

	Usage Profile 1	Usage Profile 2	Usage Profile 3
Type of request	25% report,75% view	40% report, 60% view	10% report, 90% view
Number of requested entries	10	5	7
Detailed reports	20% yes, 80% no	70% yes, 30% no	10% yes, 90% no
Entries in Database	50000	10000	100000

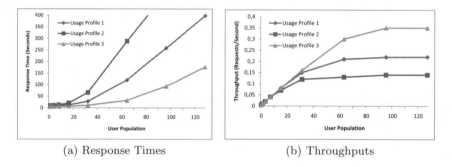

(a) Response Times   (b) Throughputs

Fig. 10. Performance Indices Business Reporting System

Running the transformation and the LQN solver for all usage profiles took less than 5 seconds in each case. We analysed the response time and throughput of the system for the different usage profile and an increasing user population (Fig.10). In some cases with a higher user population (> 60 users), the LQN solver did not converge, so that we used the LQN simulator to obtain the depicted results. The curves indicate that the system will be saturated for more than 64 users (usage profile 1), or more than 32 users (usage profile 2), or more than 96 users (usage profile 3).

6   Limitations

The model transformation introduced in this paper enables solving PCM instances with LQN solvers. It is beneficial for software architects, who can quickly analyse the performance properties of their design models. The parametrisation in PCM instances enables them to easily change the modelled usage profile, hardware environment, or component assembly and assess different design alternatives. However, there are still some open issues for the transformation:

– **Information Loss:** Some information within a PCM instance is lost when mapping to an LQN. For example, PCM2LQN computes the expected values of general distribution functions specified in an PCM instance and uses them in the LQN to specify resource demands and loop iteration numbers. Therefore, using LQN solvers for performance prediction is not useful if general distributions functions are of interest.

- **Exploiting more LQN constructs:** LQNs support more communication concepts between software entities than the PCM. For example, they allow asynchronous communication, forwarding of requests, and multiple phases. It is desirable to extend the PCM in the future to support more of these concepts, so that a larger number of systems can be analysed.
- **Incorporating Intermediate Modelling Languages:** KLAPER [11] and CSM [21] are intermediate modelling languages, which shall ease the implementation between design-oriented models, such as the PCM, and analysis-oriented models, such as LQNs. Transformations from these languages to LQNs are planned, but not yet implemented. Once these transformations become available, the model transformation should be adapted to incorporate them.
- **Solver Feedback:** Mapping PCM instances to LQN instances and running the solver has been fully automated and integrated into the PCM bench. However, the current implementation simply prints the textual solver results to the screen, so that the performance analyst has to interpret them. For the future, a more sophisticated feedback of the solver results into the PCM instance would be desirable, so that LQNs become fully transparent for the analyst.
- **Standardised Transformation Language:** We have implemented the both the Dependency Solver and PCM2LQN as ad-hoc Java transformations. Once engines for standardised transformations languages such as QVT become available, it is desirable to use QVT to implement the transformation.
- **Standardised Design Model:** Instead of UML, the PCM is a proprietary modelling language specifically designed for the performance analysis of component-based software systems. So far, existing UML models cannot be reused without manual overhead when specifying a PCM instance. A transformation from UML models to PCM instances could enable reusing parts of existing UML models and lower the reservation of using the PCM in industry.

7   Conclusions

The model transformation introduced in this paper connects efficient performance solvers for monolithic software architectures to a component-based performance modelling language. The transformation bridges differences of LQNs and PCM instances, by for example mapping distribution functions to expected values and allowing components to access multiple resources. We have embedded the transformation into the PCM bench for modelling and analysing PCM instances, so that performance analysts can use the LQN solvers for quick performance predictions. While the solvers are more efficient than the current PCM simulator SimuCom, they only deliver mean-value performance indices instead of distribution functions.

Having component-based, parametrised performance specifications such as in the PCM has several benefits. It allows reusing the performance specification in different contexts such as hardware environments, usage profiles and component assemblies. PCM RDSEFFs shall be stored in public repositories, so that different software architects can incorporate them into their architectural models. The parametrisation allows the different participating developer roles to model independently from each other. As RDSEFFs specify resource demands, loop iteration numbers, and branch probabilities in dependency to parameter values, it is easily possible to adjust the specification for different usage profiles. This is usually not possible in monolithic models (e.g., annotated UML diagrams), where for example the dependency between a branch probability and input parameters is not explicitly specified.

For the future, we plan to implement the transformation in a standardised transformation language such as QVT [20]. It is also desirable to map PCM instances into intermediate modelling languages such as CSM [21] or KLAPER [11] to enable transformation into even more performance models and exploit the specifics of these models. Another area of improvement is the feedback of the solver results into the PCM model, so that the performance models become fully transparent for software architects.

References

1. Balsamo, S., DiMarco, A., Inverardi, P., Simeoni, M.: Model-based performance prediction in software development: A survey. IEEE Trans. Softw. Eng. 30(5), 295–310 (2004)
2. Becker, S.: Coupled Model Transformations. In: Proc. 7th International Workshop on Software and Performance (WOSP 2008), ACM Sigsoft (June 2008) (to appear)
3. Becker, S., Grunske, L., Mirandola, R., Overhage, S.: Performance Prediction of Component-Based Systems: A Survey from an Engineering Perspective. In: Reussner, R., Stafford, J., Szyperski, C. (eds.) Architecting Systems with Trustworthy Components. LNCS, vol. 3938, pp. 169–192. Springer, Heidelberg (2006)
4. Becker, S., Koziolek, H., Reussner, R.: Model-based Performance Prediction with the Palladio Component Model. In: Proc. 6th International Workshop on Software and Performance (WOSP 2007), pp. 56–67. ACM Sigsoft (February 2007)
5. Bertolino, A., Mirandola, R.: CB-SPE Tool: Putting component-based performance engineering into practice. In: Crnković, I., Stafford, J.A., Schmidt, H.W., Wallnau, K. (eds.) CBSE 2004. LNCS, vol. 3054, pp. 233–248. Springer, Heidelberg (2004)
6. Bondarev, E., de With, P., Chaudron, M., Musken, J.: Modelling of Input-Parameter Dependency for Performance Predictions of Component-Based Embedded Systems. In: Proc. of the 31th EUROMICRO Conference (EUROMICRO 2005) (2005)
7. Chouambe, L., Klatt, B., Krogmann, K.: Reverse Engineering Software-Models of Component-Based Systems. In: Proc. of the 12th European Conference on Software Maintenance and Reengineering (CSMR 2008), Athens, Greece, IEEE, Los Alamitos (to appear, 2008)
8. D'Ambrogio, A.: A model transformation framework for the automated building of performance models from UML models. In: Proc. 5th International Workshop on Software and Performance (WOSP 2005), pp. 75–86. ACM Press, New York (2005)

9. Eskenazi, E., Fioukov, A., Hammer, D.: Performance Prediction for Component Compositions. In: Crnković, I., Stafford, J.A., Schmidt, H.W., Wallnau, K. (eds.) CBSE 2004. LNCS, vol. 3054. Springer, Heidelberg (2004)
10. Franks, G.: Performance Analysis of Distributed Server Systems. PhD thesis, Department of Systems and Computer Engineering, Carleton University, Ottawa, Ontario, Canada (December 1999)
11. Grassi, V., Mirandola, R., Sabetta, A.: Filling the gap between design and performance/reliability models of component-based systems: A model-driven approach. Journal on Systems and Software 80(4), 528–558 (2007)
12. Gu, G.P., Petriu, D.C.: From UML to LQN by XML algebra-based model transformations. In: Proc. 5th International workshop on Software and Performance (WOSP 2005), pp. 99–110. ACM Press, New York (2005)
13. Happe, J., Friedrichs, H., Becker, S., Reussner, R.: A Configurable Performance Completion for Message-Oriented Middleware. In: Proc. 7th International Workshop on Software and Performance (WOSP 2008). ACM Sigsoft (June 2008) (to Appear)
14. Kappler, T., Koziolek, H., Krogmann, K., Reussner, R.: Towards Automatic Construction of Reusable Prediction Models for Component-Based Performance Engineering. In: Proc. Software Engineering 2008 (SE 2008), LNI, GI (February 2008) (to appear)
15. Kounev, S.: Performance Modeling and Evaluation of Distributed Component-Based Systems Using Queueing Petri Nets. IEEE Trans. Softw. Eng. 32(7), 486–502 (2006)
16. Koziolek, H.: Parameter Dependencies for Reusable Performance Specifications of Software Components. PhD thesis, University of Oldenburg, Germany (March 2008)
17. Koziolek, H., Becker, S., Happe, J.: Predicting the Performance of Component-based Software Architectures with different Usage Profiles. In: Proc. 3rd International Conference on the Quality of Software Architectures (QoSA 2007). LNCS, vol. 4880, pp. 145–163. Springer, Heidelberg (2007)
18. Liu, Y., Fekete, A., Gorton, I.: Design-level performance prediction of component-based applications. IEEE Trans. Softw. Eng. 31(11), 928–941 (2005)
19. Object Management Group (OMG). UML Profile for Schedulability, Performance and Time (2005) (last retrieved 2008-01-13)
20. Object Management Group (OMG). MOF QVT final adopted specification (ptc/05-11-01) (2006) (last retrieved 2008-01-13)
21. Petriu, D.B., Woodside, M.: An intermediate metamodel with scenarios and resources for generating performance models from UML designs. Journal of Software and Systems Modeling 6(2), 163–184 (2006)
22. Petriu, D.C., Woodside, C.M.: Software Performance Models from System Scenarios in Use Case Maps. In: Field, T., Harrison, P.G., Bradley, J., Harder, U. (eds.) TOOLS 2002. LNCS, vol. 2324, pp. 141–158. Springer, Heidelberg (2002)
23. Petriu, D.C., Shen, H.: Applying the UML Performance Profile: Graph Grammar-Based Derivation of LQN Models from UML Specifications. In: Field, T., Harrison, P.G., Bradley, J., Harder, U. (eds.) TOOLS 2002. LNCS, vol. 2324, pp. 159–177. Springer, Heidelberg (2002)
24. Real-Time and Distributed Systems Group, Carleton University. Layered Queueing Network Documentation (last retrieved 2008-01-13)
25. Rolia, J.A., Sevcik, K.C.: The method of layers. IEEE Trans. Softw. Eng. 21(8), 689–700 (1995)

26. Smith, C.U.: Performance Engineering of Software Systems. Addision-Wesley, Reading (1990)
27. Szyperski, C., Gruntz, D., Murer, S.: Component Software: Beyond Object-Oriented Programming. Addison-Wesley, Reading (2002)
28. Ufimtsev, A., Murphy, L.: Performance modeling of a JavaEE component application using layered queuing networks: revised approach and a case study. In: Proc. International Workshop on Specification and Verification of Component-based Systems (SAVCBS 2006), pp. 11–18. ACM, New York (2006)
29. Verdickt, T., Dhoedt, B., De Turck, F., Demeester, P.: Hybrid Performance Modeling Approach for Network Intensive Distributed Software. In: Proc. 6th International Workshop on Software and Performance (WOSP 2007). ACM Sigsoft Notes, pp. 189–200 (February 2007)
30. Woodside, M., Franks, G., Petriu, D.: The Future of Software Performance Engineering. In: Future of Software Engineering (FOSE 2007), pp. 171–187. IEEE Computer Society, Los Alamitos (2007)
31. Woodside, M., Petriu, D.C., Petriu, D.B., Shen, H., Israr, T., Merseguer, J.: Performance by unified model analysis (puma). In: WOSP 2005: Proceedings of the 5th international workshop on Software and performance, pp. 1–12. ACM Press, New York (2005)
32. Wu, X., Woodside, M.: Performance Modeling from Software Components. In: Proc. 4th International Workshop on Software and Performance (WOSP 2004), vol. 29, pp. 290–301. ACM Press, New York (2004)

Model-Driven Generation of Performance Prototypes

Steffen Becker[1], Tobias Dencker[2], and Jens Happe[3],[*]

[1] FZI Forschungszentrum Informatik Karlsruhe
Haid-und-Neu-Straße 10-14, 76131 Karlsruhe, Germany
sbecker@fzi.de

[2] Chair of Software Desgin and Quality (SDQ)
Am Fassanengarten 5, University of Karlsruhe (TH), 76131 Karlsruhe, Germany
dencker@ipd.uka.de

[3] Graduate School Trustsoft, University of Oldenburg
University of Oldenburg, 26111 Oldenburg, Germany
happe@informatik.uni-oldenburg.de

Abstract. Early, model-based performance predictions help to understand the consequences of design decisions on the performance of the resulting system before the system's implementation becomes available. While this helps reducing the costs for redesigning systems not meeting their extra-functional requirements, performance prediction models have to abstract from the full complexity of modern hard- and software environments potentially leading to imprecise predictions. As a solution, the construction and execution of prototypes on the target execution environment gives early insights in the behaviour of the system under realistic conditions. In literature several approaches exist to generate prototypes from models which either generate code skeletons or require detailed models for the prototype. In this paper, we present an approach which aims at automated generation of a performance prototype based solely on a design model with performance annotations. For the concrete realisation, we used the Palladio Component Model (PCM), which is a component-based architecture modelling language supporting early performance analyses. For a typical three-tier business application, the resulting Java EE code shows how the prototype can be used to evaluate the influence of complex parts of the execution environment like memory interactions or the operating system's scheduler.

Keywords: Performance, Prototyping, Model-Driven Software Engineering, Palladio Component Model.

1 Introduction

The early evaluation of the performance of a software system can reveal bottlenecks and allows the quality assessment of different design alternatives. Recent research is directed at early, design-time performance predictions using models of the systems under study [1]. Currently, many approaches focus on automated, model-driven transformations of annotated UML models into performance models like queueing networks [2].

---

[*] This work is supported by the German Research Foundation (DFG), grants GRK 1076/1 and RE 1674/1-2.

S. Kounev, I. Gorton, and K. Sachs (Eds.): SIPEW 2008, LNCS 5119, pp. 79–98, 2008.

Solving these models results in performance metrics which reveal possible performance issues.

While model-driven performance prediction introduces an easy and cost-efficient way of early design-time performance analyses, the model assumptions and limitations can result in inaccurate predictions. For example, most approaches disregard memory consumption and realistic scheduling disciplines especially for multi-core systems. In addition, they are limited by mathematical assumptions like exponential distributions, by the amount of states solvable analytically or restricted to mean-value analysis. Because of this, we favour an approach common in other engineering disciplines where prediction model results are validated using prototypes deployed in the target hard- and software environment.

Some approaches already exist for the automatic generation of performance prototypes. Grundy et. al [3] propose a method for the automatic generation based on a detailed model of the prototype to generate. While this results in detailed performance metrics, it requires additional modelling effort. Other approaches exist which are not yet fully automated, e.g. [4,5]. In contrast to this, we aim at a fully-working prototype generated from an existing design model with performance annotations.

In this paper, we present a transformation of instances of the Palladio Component Model (PCM) [6,7] into prototypes which can be deployed, executed, and measured on the target execution environment without additional coding. The PCM is a meta-model for the specification of component-based software architectures and enables early design-time performance predictions of a system under study. Components and their interconnection model the static structure of an architecture. Behavioural specifications of the components capture the dynamic aspects of a system. They abstract from the components internal logic and focus on performance relevant aspects, i.e., they specify how a component utilises the available resources. The behavioural specification includes an abstraction of the architecture's data flow to reflect the influence of the systems usage on performance. The PCM's well-defined meta-model allows easy transformations for different kinds of performance evaluation. The generated prototype presented in this paper runs on Java EE and simulates resource demands by executing resource consuming algorithms such that the time needed on the target hardware corresponds to the time demand specified in a PCM model instance. Note that this approach requires a PCM model that actually reflects the system under study. The prediction accuracy of the performance prototype mainly depends on the quality of this model.

To demonstrate our prototype generator, we applied the prototype generation to a PCM instance of a Management Information System (MIS) introduced by [8]. Our results show the straight forward generation and deployment of the MIS's prototype. The measurements of the deployed prototype reflect the influence of the underlying execution environment that can hardly be captured by analytical or simulation based method. This includes the existing but limited speedup of multiple CPU cores, the influence of the OS scheduler, and the amount of memory accesses. These low level details are difficult to capture by analytical models since they strongly depend on the actual execution environment.

The contribution of this paper is a model-driven transformation of abstract performance models (PCM instances) to directly executable performance prototypes. The high-level performance specification includes abstract information on the control flow and demands to resources, but no information on the actual business logic of the system. A new, automated mapping of abstract resource demands specified in the PCM (e.g. 10 CPU units or 15 ms) to different load generating algorithms allows the prototype to emulate the specified processing times. The model of an industrial application called MIS validates the prototype generation.

This paper is structured as follows. Section 2 highlights related work in the area of performance prediction, measuring, and prototyping. Section 3 gives a brief introduction to model-driven performance evaluation with the PCM. The mapping of PCM instances to prototypical Java EE applications is described in section 4. Section 5 gives details on the method to generate artificial resource demands. A case study presented in section 6 demonstrates how the generated prototypes help evaluating the performance of the system under study. After discussing limitations of our current approach in section 7, we conclude the paper and highlight options for future work.

2 Related Work

The approach presented in this paper relates to (model-driven) prototype generation and model-based performance evaluation in general.

Balsamo et al. published a recent survey [2] on early-design time performance evaluations usising models of the systems under study. Ongoing research is directed at model-driven generation of performance prediction models from software design models, e.g., [9,10,6]. However, as the performance prediction models rely on simplifying assumptions, the need for prototyping arises [4].

Bardram et al. [11] highlight the importance of architectural prototyping for the evaluation of quality attributes like performance, availability, testability, modifiability, etc. They present a conceptual framework and stress the importance of architectural prototypes for doing trade-off analyses between the mentioned quality attributes. The presented arguments also motivate our work. We additionally present an automated, tool-supported approach to generate a performance prototype.

In [12], Avritzer and Weyuker present an approach to capture the resource demands caused by a running system. Based on the captured information, they generate a program issuing a synthetic workload resembling the original one. This program is placed in different execution environments. Measurements taken there reveal insights into the performance in the new environments. In contrast, our approach supports early design time decisions and therefore does not require measurements of an existing system. It uses workloads and resource demands specified in a PCM instance to generate a performance prototype, which allows early performance estimates of the system under study.

Based on the former work, Woodside and Schramm [13] propose an approach closely related to the one presented in this paper. They use layered queuing network models [14] to generate synthetic workloads which correspond to the model's specification. They aimed at capturing concurrent load and network impact on performance which is hard to predict with analytical and simulation-based methods. This paper carries on the ideas of Woodside and Schramm. It improves the generation of performance prototypes using model-driven techniques and a more sophisticated synthetic resource demand generation. Additionally, the PCM allows the performance evaluation of data dependent workloads [15].

In [4], Hu and Gorton introduce architecture prototyping for the evaluation of software architectures with a high degree of concurrency. The presented approach uses a programming language called HL. It yields performance metrics such as resource utilisation or the schedulability of tasks. However, the HL programs need manual coding and are not generated from a design model.

The model-driven benchmark generation tool MDABench [16,17] of Zhou, Gorton, and Liu semi-automatically generates Java EE applications and web service applications from abstract UML 2.0 specifications. This includes the necessary test data and a complete load driver. However, the server side of the benchmark still requires manual interaction as the tool generates only stubs for the business logic.

Denaro et al. [5] propose a method to derive application tests to do early performance prototyping. They state that middleware and database layers have a major impact on the performance of an application. As the usage of the middleware is determined by the application's business logic, their method aims at generating the stubs for the application's business logic to tests the performance of the middleware. In contrast to Denaro's approach, our prototype emphasises hardware and operating system influences, like the number of CPU cores, the OS scheduler, or the file system implementation. In addition, Denaro's approach is not yet automated.

In [3,18], Grundy, Cai et al. present an approach for the generation of fully-working implementations of client-server applications based on an architecture model of the prototype. The model contains details on the clients requests and workloads, the server's services, as well as the used database and middleware technology. As such, it defines a domain-specific language for the specification of prototypes. In contrast to this, our approach uses already existing performance models and tries to generate resource demands according to the information already available in the model.

3   Model-Driven Performance Evaluation

Model-driven performance prediction [2] allows software architects to specify performance models in a language specific to their domain. This can be UML models annotated with performance relevant information (using for instance the UML-SPT profile [19]) or architecture description languages specialised for performance predictions. To derive performance metrics, the software model is transformed into a performance model as shown in Figure 1.

Typical models for performance analysis are queueing networks, stochastic Petri nets or stochastic process algebras. The performance metrics derived from the performance model should then be translated back into the design model, to allow an easy interpretation for software architects.

The following briefly introduces the Palladio Component Model (PCM) [6,7], an architecture description language targeting software performance predictions. The PCM follows the process depicted in figure 1. Section 4 builds upon this description and provides a mapping into a performance prototype ready for deployment and execution on a Java EE server.

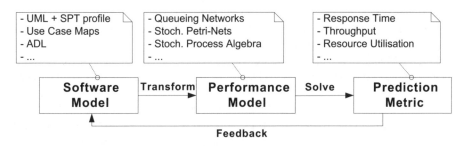

Fig. 1. Model-driven Performance Prediction

The Palladio Component Model

The Palladio Component Model (PCM) is an architecture description language supporting design time performance evaluations of component-based software systems. Based on its meta-model, different transformations can evaluate the performance of PCM instances, e.g., by mapping them to a specific simulation [6]. This paper extends the performance evaluation approach envisioned by the PCM by a model-driven transformation to performance prototypes.

The PCM is divided into several packages. The following gives a brief overview on the most important packages: the repository package, the assembly package, the allocation package, and the usage model.

Repository. Repositories store software components and/or their performance specifications, which are the core entities of the PCM. They have provided and required interfaces and can be composed to form systems.

Components exist in two types: BasicComponents are components which cannot be decomposed further while CompositeComponents are composed from other components. While disregarding the latter in the reminder of this paper, the former contain an abstract behavioural specification called Resource Demanding-Service Effect Specification (RDSEFF) for each provided service. RDSEFFs describe how component services use resources and call required services using an annotated control flow graph.
Following Szyperski's definition [20], a component is a unit of independent deployment with explicit dependencies only. As a consequence, component specifications in the PCM are parameterised for their later environment. The parameterisation of a component's performance specification covers influences of required services, different soft- and hardware environments, as well as different input parameters of provided services. Similar to UML activities, RDSEFFs consist of three types of actions: InternalActions, ExternalCallActions, and control flow nodes.

InternalActions model resource demands and abstract from computations performed inside a component. For performance prediction, component developers need to specify demands of internal actions to resources, like CPUs or hard disks. Demands can depend on parameters passed to a service or return values of external service calls.

ExternalCallActions represent invocations of a component to services of other components. For each ExternalCallAction, component developers can specify performance relevant information about the service's parameters. For example, the size of a collection passed to a service can significantly influence its execution time, while the actual values have only little effect. Modelling only the size of the collection keeps the specification understandable and the model analysable. Besides input parameters, the PCM also deals with return values of external service calls.

In the PCM, external service calls are always synchronous calls, i.e., the execution is blocked until a call returns. This is necessary for considering the effect of return values on performance.

Control flow elements allow component developers to specify branches, loops, and forks of the control flow. BranchActions represent "exclusive or" splits of the control flow, where only one of the alternatives can be taken. In the PCM, the choice can either be probabilistic or determined by a guard. In the first case, each alternative has an associated probability giving the likelihood of its execution. In the latter case, boolean expressions on the service's input parameters guard each alternative. With a stochastic specification of the input parameters provided by the caller, the guards are evaluated to probabilities. LoopActions model the repetitive execution of a part of the control flow. A probability mass function specifies the number of loop iterations. For example, a loop might execute 5 times with a probability of 0.7 and 10 times with a probability of 0.3. The number of loop iterations can depend on the service's input parameters.

Assembly. Software architects retrieve component specifications from repositories to build software systems. The assembly model specifies the interconnection of the system's components. An AssemblyConnector binds a required interface of one component to a corresponding provided interface of another component. The assembly model allows software architects to use the same component multiple times in a single software architecture. For example, a generic caching component can accelerate the access to a network data source and the file system. To reflect the different performance properties of a component in different contexts, the PCM defines the so called AssemblyContext, which holds a component's context specific information, e.g. its connection to other components. In a similar way, component developers can build CompositeComponents.

Allocation. After the creation of a component assembly, the component deployer allocates the components on executing hardware nodes. A ResourceEnvironment (similar to a UML deployment diagram) models the systems execution environment. It describes the available processing nodes and their resources like CPUs or hard disk drives. For each resource, the model contains a specification of its processing speed, e.g., the number of instructions processable by a CPU in a given time span. A specification of the networking infrastructure connects the nodes and allows communication. The component allocation establishes a link between components and executing hardware nodes. A component allocated on a specific nodes uses its resources for processing.

Usage Model. With the UsageModel, domain experts describe user interaction with a software system. A UsageModel contains several UsageScenarios each describing a different class of users, which differ, for example, in their behaviour or arrival rate. Domain experts specify the behaviour of each user class comparable to the behavioural specification of software components (RDSEFF) including Loops, Branches, and calls to the system under study. They furthermore characterise input parameters of calls to the system. The specification only contains information relevant for performance analyses, e.g., the number of elements in an array passed to a service for processing.

4   Performance Prototype Generation

This section presents a mapping of PCM instances to a prototype implementation based on Enterprise Java Beans (EJB). The prototype reflects the behaviour of the *modelled* application with code which causes the same resource demands as specified. For this, it uses the resource demand specifications in the model and generates a corresponding load on the resource. If the modelled resource demands and behavioural specifications characterise the final system correctly, the prototype's performance reflects the final system's performance.

In this paper, we assume that the PCM model reflect the behaviour of the modelled application with sufficient precision. This is a common assumption for all model-based and model-driven performance evaluation methods. If this assumption cannot be established by the software architect creating the model then both the analytical or simulation-based predictions as well as the prototype predictions will be wrong. In this paper, we additionally assume that the selection of the workload generators reflect the application's behaviour.

The mapping of PCM instances to EJBs has to deal with static structures, dynamics of the system, component allocation, and system usage. Figure 2 gives an overview on these four parts and their respective elements.

Static Structure. For the static structure, components including their provided and required interfaces have to be mapped to EJBs. Additionally, component instantiation and establishing component connections requires the generation of appropriate deployment descriptors in EJB.

	PCM Concept	ProtoCom
Static	Interfaces	Java Interface
	BasicComponents	Classes with Simulated SEFF
	CompositeComponents	Facade Class
	AssemblyContext	Instance of Component Class
	AssemblyConnector	Deployment Script
Dynamic	Internal Actions	Resource Demand Generator
	Call Actions	RMI/SOAP Call
	Control Flow	Java Control Flow
	Data Flow Annotations	Simulated Dataflow
Allocation	AllocationContext	Deployment Script
	Resources	[Uses Physical Resources]
Workload	UsageModel	Workload Driver

Fig. 2. Overview on the Prototype Mapping

Dynamics. The behaviour of single component services as specified in RDSEFFs have to be mapped to Java code emulating the resource demands of `InternalActions` and following the specified control flow (`Loops`, `Branches`, etc.). In addition, the performance relevant abstractions of the data flow have to be passed on while executing the generated code. They are needed to determine values for the resource demands, loop iteration counts, branch conditions, etc.

Allocation. To ease the execution of the generated prototype, build scripts help in building the application and deploying it on the right hardware nodes. The PCM resource environment needs no mapping, as we use the real hardware for executing the prototype instead of the PCM's hardware model.

Workload. To finally get performance metrics, the mapping generates a workload driver from the PCM's usage model. This driver is instrumented with measuring probes which collect the desired metrics.

The following subsections detail the introduced parts.

4.1 Static Structure

The mapping of PCM components to EJBs shall allow an easy definition of the connectors between the components. As a single component may be used multiple times in a given architecture each time having different connections to other components, a component has to keep its references to required components flexible. The following first describes how to map the components, how to instantiate them, and finally, how to connect them to fulfil the stated requirement.

In EJB, each component is represented by a Java class annotated with a specific set of Java annotations. Since the PCM considers components as stateless, the mapping creates a Java class for each component and annotates it as stateless session bean. The class has to offer methods which accept references to required components. This pattern is known as dependency injection [21]. It ensures that the component's implementing class remains independent of its actual communication partners.

In the PCM, `AssemblyContexts` specify the usage of a component in a `System`. For each `AssemblyContext` (referencing a component), the mapping adds an entry to the generated EJB deployment descriptor, which instructs the EJB framework to create a new instance of the referenced component. To connect the generated EJB instances, the mapping adds the necessary references for each `AssemblyConnector` to the deployment descriptor, i.e., it specifies which dependencies have to be injected into an EJB. Consider, for example, two `AssemblyContexts`, which reference components A and B and are connected by an `AssemblyConnector` so that A can call services on B. When deployed, the generated deployment descriptor instantiates bean A and B and injects a reference of B into A. For `CompositeComponents`, the mapping generates a façade class, which delegates calls to its inner components.

4.2 Dynamics

For the dynamic behaviour of the prototype, the mapping generates code for each service offered by a component based on the service's RDSEFF. The following elaborates the mapping of a RDSEFF's data flow elements and then describes the transformation of its InternalActions, ExternalCallActions and control flow.

Data Flow. To support the data flow annotations available in RDSEFFs, the generated prototype evaluates the annotations at run-time whenever the value of an annotation is needed. As annotations used in a RDSEFF may contain variables which are passed to the RDSEFF when it is called, the generated method takes a list of parameter characterisations plus their respective values. Using this list, the parameter characterisations which appear in annotations are replaced by their actual values. Based on the parameter characterisation's values, the annotation's result is determined. Annotations may contain stochastic expressions. Thus, the evaluation can involve drawing random numbers using a pseudo random number generator.

For example, an annotation array.NUMBER_OF_ELEMENTS $*$ IntPMF$[(0.5; 1)(0.5; 2)]$ would be evaluated as follows. First, the generated code looks up the actual value of the variable array.NUMBER_OF_ELEMENTS in the list of variables passed to this RDSEFFs. Afterwards, it evaluates the integer probability function literal which describes a random value having a value of 1 in 50% of all cases and 2 in all remaining cases. Finally, it multiplies both values to get the final result.

InternalActions. For InternalActions, the generated code for each InternalAction performs three steps. First, it determines the resource demand by evaluating the specification of the resource demand copied from the PCM instance as described in the previous paragraph. The result is the resource demand given in *hardware independent units*, e.g., in abstract CPU work units for a CPU processing demand.

Second, using the type of resource required, the mapping selects a resource demand generation strategy. For example, for a CPU processing load, a CPU intensive algorithm is executed. For a demand to a hard drive, another algorithm reads and writes data to/from a hard drive. Section 5 gives further details on the resource demand generators.

Third, based on the hardware independent resource demand and the type of resource used to execute the demand, a hardware dependent resource demand is determined, i.e., its processing time is computed. Therefore, a hardware independent resource demand (e.g., 10 CPU Units) is divided by a resource's ProcessingRate (e.g., 10 CPU Units per second) to determine the demands hardware dependent execution time (e.g., 1 second). The workload generator now creates an artificial workload (e.g., of 1 second) on the actual resource (e.g., the CPU) as described in section 5.

ExternalCallActions. For ExternalCallActions, the mapping generates code which calls the specified service on its required interface. The prototype uses the reference to the required component passed to the component via dependency injection as described in section 4.1. Additionally, the generated code creates a new list of variables and their values and passes it to the called service. This requires the evaluation of the respective annotations in the PCM instance.

Control Flow. For all control flow actions, a corresponding Java construct exists, e.g., a Java for-loop for the LoopAction or the if-statement for BranchActions. However, some of these control flow constructs need to evaluate data flow annotations before they can be executed. For example, to execute a loop, the generated code has to evaluate the number of loop iterations before it can actually execute the loop body for the evaluated number of iterations.

4.3 Allocation

The prototype mapping generates build scripts, which ease the task of creating deployable JAR archives. In addition, it helps in distributing the compiled binaries to the hardware nodes as specified in the PCM's Allocation model. After executing the build scripts, the system is ready to run.

4.4 Workload Driver

The PCM prototype mapping generates a workload driver from the PCM's UsageModel. The workload driver mimics the users' behaviour specified in the UsageModel. It executes Java threads each of which simulates a single user's interaction with the system. If the number of users/threads is high, it is possible to distribute the workload driver on several machines.

For each UsageScenario of the UsageModel, the workload driver simulates the arrival of users according to the specified Workload. The workload can either be open or closed. In the first case users arrive with a specified inter arrival time, execute their scenario, and finally leave the system. In the latter case, a predefined number of users execute the UsageScenario, then delay their execution for a specified think time, and start the whole process again.

The actions executable by a user are similar to the actions available in a RDSEFF. Because of this, the mapping of these concepts to Java code is analogue to the mapping of the control flow concepts in RDSEFF like Loops and Branches. However, for calls the mapping is different, as the workload driver first has to query the Java EE server running the prototypical application for a reference of the component to be called.

Finally, the PCM prototype mapping generates code to measure the performance of the prototype. The code records response times of single requests and stores them in a database to visualise the results graphically after a measurement run.

5   Resource Demand Calibration

The resource demands specified in the model need to be mapped to actual code that consumes the specified amount of processing time. Therefore, algorithms, like the Fast Fourier Transform or Fibonacci number computations, shall generate the necessary load. The prototype framework automatically determines fitting input parameters for an algorithm to meet the specified resource demands on a given platform. A calibration identifies the dependency of input parameters and processing time for an algorithm. Its results define the algorithm's input parameters during prototype execution. If, for example, a Fibonacci number generating algorithm shall approximate a resource demand of 32 ms, the calibration determines the amount of Fibonacci numbers to compute during this period, say 253. The prototype uses this value, instead of the specified time, to generate the resource demand of 32 ms. The calibration measures the execution time of an algorithm in the single-threaded case, i.e., its (almost) uninterrupted and undisturbed execution time. During the prototype's execution, the system may process multiple requests concurrently. The measured performance metrics reflect influences of the underlying platform such as resource contention and caching effects. Thus, different load generating algorithms can lead to different performance results when executed concurrently (see Section 6 for an example). The following describes the requirements and preconditions of the proposed approach and introduces the calibration as well as the execution of demands in detail. A discussion of open challenges and limitations concludes this section.

Calibration Requirements. The calibration needs to map specified processing times to input parameters of an algorithm. It shall be independent of the actual platform and algorithm, i.e., the calibration shall automatically determine the input parameter of an algorithm on a given platform to create the specified resource demands. For example, it may require 43 Fibonacci number computations on one system and 345 on another to generate a demand of 1 ms. In the scenarios considered in this paper, the times taken by the demand generating functions range from one millisecond to several seconds. Furthermore, the framework shall support multiple load generating algorithms, since the different behaviour of algorithms (e.g. memory usage) can affect a prototype's performance. Finally, the calibration of an algorithm's input parameters shall be fully automated and transparent to the software architect, to achieve a proper applicability of our approach.

Calibration Strategy. In order to fulfil the above requirements, we assume that the load of an algorithm is controlled by a single integer value as input parameter, e.g. the amount of Fibonacci numbers generated. The execution time of each algorithm needs to be minimal for 0 and increases monotonically with the input value. For the Fibonacci number generation, the computation of 0 numbers is (surprisingly) fastest and its execution time increases the more numbers it computes. Except the need for a monotonically increasing function, we do not make any further assumptions about the dependency of the input parameter's value and the algorithm's execution time. The dependency can be linear, exponential or any other monotonically increasing function.

To efficiently approximate resource demands, we first calibrate an algorithm for a given hard- and software environment. Its input parameters are determined for a set of predefined execution times. The results provide the basis for load generation during a prototype's execution. Since, in general, a prototype can issue arbitrary many different resource demands, we cannot determine the input parameters for all demands in advance. Instead, we compose requested demands of smaller, previously calibrated ones. The following explains the details of the calibration as well as the resource demand break down.

5.1 Determining the Input Value for a Specific Resource Demand

The calibration method iteratively approximates the best input value to reach a specified execution time. Therefore, it implements a variant of the bisection method [22], which is a root-finding algorithm.

We want the execution time of an algorithm $exec_{alg}(n)$ with input parameter n to match the specified target execution time t: $exec_{alg}(n) = t$. Thus, we need to solve

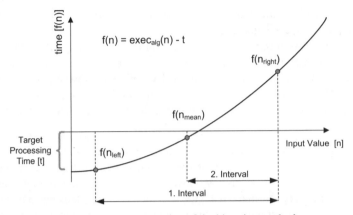

Fig. 3. Abstract illustration of the bisection method

$exec_{alg}(n) - t = 0$. If we define $f(n) = exec_{alg}(n) - t$, the problem becomes a typical root finding problem with $f(n) = 0$. Figure 3 illustrates the approximated function $f(n)$ as well as the bisection method. Provided that all implemented algorithms have strictly monotonic behaviour, each generated function has got exactly one root point representing the corresponding iteration parameter to the targeted run time.

To find function f's root, the calibration needs to identify two input values n_{left} and n_{right} that represent the borders of the first interval. The interval must contain the function's root, thus the function must be smaller than zero for the left border ($f(n_{left}) < 0$) and larger for the right one ($f(n_{right}) > 0$). For the first, the calibration selects zero ($n_{left} = 0$) as initial value, which corresponds to the smallest possible value of f. To find an value for n_{right} with $f(n_{right}) > 0$, the calibration executes the algorithm with a predefined value. If the result for f is smaller than zero, the calibration doubles the input value and re-executes the algorithm. This continues until a value with $f(n_{right}) > 0$ is found. For the above example, the interval's left border is $n_{left} = 0$. Since the generation of zero Fibonacci numbers consumes no time, the functions value is $f(n_{left}) = -32$. The initial value for the right hand side is $n_{right} = 200$. However, the functions value $f(n_{right}) = -5$ is still below zero. Thus, the calibration doubles the value ($n_{right} = 400$) and determines the new result, e.g. $f(n_{right}) = 48$ which is greater than zero. The initial interval borders are $n_{left} = 0$ and $n_{right} = 400$.

When the borders of the first interval have been determined, the execution of the bisection method starts. It repeatedly halves the interval, determines the execution time of the algorithm for the interval's mean value, and selects the subinterval which contains the function's root. The intervals mean value of the example is $n_{mean} = 200$ with a value of $f(200) = -5$. Thus, the bisection method selects $n'_{left} = n_{mean} = 200$ as left and $n'_{right} = n_{right} = 400$ as right border of the new interval. Figure 3 illustrates two iteration steps of the bisection method. The approximation terminates as soon as the distance of the interval borders is equal or less than 1 millisecond or a predefined number of iterations is exceeded.

To enable exact input value calibrations, the execution time of an algorithm needs to be determined accurately. This requires multiple executions of the algorithm during each iteration of the bisection method. The application of statistical methods removes outliers and achieves stable results over multiple executions. The next section describes how a single resource demand can be mapped to multiple pre-calibrated input values of a load generating algorithm.

5.2 Resource Demand Break Down

The bisection method allows us to determine the input value of an algorithm on a specific platform for a certain resource demand. However, the process requires several iterations including multiple executions of the algorithm with different input values. As we want to keep the calibration effort minimal, we focus on a limited number of resource demands whose input parameters are determined during the calibration period. All other resource demands are composed from the predetermined ones.

During the calibration the algorithm's input values for 2^n with $n \in \{0 \dots 10\}$ milliseconds are determined. The results of the calibration are stored in a table which contains approximated parameters associated with their individual execution times. Using the greedy strategy, an incoming demand is dived into multiple sub-demands of 2^0 ms to 2^{10} ms. To generate the workload of the whole demand, each of the sub-demands is executed sequentially. This allows us to efficiently and automatically approximate different demand types on arbitrary platforms. For example, a demand of 300 ms is approximated by the sub-demands: 256 ms + 32 ms + 8 ms + 4 ms. For each sub-demand the input value of the used algorithm is retrieved from the previous calibration. Executing the algorithm four times with the corresponding input values leads to a total time consumption of 300 ms. The overhead introduced by the break down and multiple executions is much smaller than 1 ms and can therefore be neglected. This allows an approximation of any demand for any platform and algorithm. Next, we discuss the limitations of this calibration approach.

5.3 Discussion

The accuracy of the demand calibration is limited due to disturbances of the underlying platform, like the garbage collection or operating system services. During the calibration period, multiple executions of the algorithm in combination with statistical analyses limit the influence of these disturbances. However, during the run time of a prototype, these influences can lead to deviations about 6% of requested and actual processing time. It furthermore requires to execute the prototype multiple times in order to achieve stable results. The varying execution times are a result of disturbances of the underlying platform and cannot be totally excluded from the resource demand generation. The use of longer calibration runs with more executions of the algorithm can increase accuracy, but cannot totally remove the effect.

On the other hand, it can also be desirable to capture overheads on account of life cycle activities such as garbage collection. An algorithm can for example mimic object creations, memory usage, and even trigger stress related effects such as swapping. If the load generating algorithm is chosen in the right way, it allows software architects to identify the systems load limits and evaluate the effect of memory usage on software performance. However, the amount of memory used cannot be specified within the PCM, but would be defined by the algorithm in use. This allows only vague estimations of the actual memory usage of an application.

Please note, that the algorithm itself does not model I/O or CPU bursts of a process. The RD-SEFFs of the PCM describe such behavioural aspects of an application, which software architects have to describe explicitly. The following case study demonstrates the accuracy of our approach as well as the influence of the underlying platform and the selected algorithm on performance.

It is often desirable to express the execution time of an internal action in dependency of the system's state. The PCM models such dependencies with stochastic expressions. They can for example derive the execution time of an internal action from the number of concurrently running tasks (load dependent server) or from the number of elements in an array. During execution, the performance prototype evaluates the stochastic expressions. The result of the evaluation represents the actual execution time and is passed to the calibrated resource demand, which translates the demand into parameters for the load generating algorithm.

6   Case Study

To demonstrate the usefulness of our prototype generator and the resource demand generators for the software architect in validating analytical or simulation-based predictions, we applied it in a case study to a typical three-tier business information system called the Management Information System (MIS). The system has been published initially by Wu [8] as a case study for the component extension of layered queueing networks (LQNs) [23]. The system is a reporting application which creates reports of an organisations's activities on demand. There are different types of reports having different complexities, e.g., large reports vs. short reports.

We created a PCM model instance for the MIS system loosely based on the system specification given in [8]. We focused our model on the application layer and the database. Figure 4 depicts the static structure of the application and the main use case considered in the following.

The use case generates small and larger reports. Users request small reports with a probability of 80% and large reports with a probability of 20%. Given the type of report, the use case requires different processing times on the CPU of the system. Figure 4 depicts the demands as annotations to the respective actions in the system's control flow. The demands are given in seconds, i.e., they depend on the system's hardware.

For the single user case, the execution times for creating small reports sums up to 1.53 seconds while the generation of large reports sums up to 6.47 seconds. Hence, we expect these times with the given probabilities as response times from the generated prototype in cases without resource contention.

For the measurements, we generated the prototype with the mapping described in section 4. Afterwards, we packaged the resulting EJB code and deployed it on the Glassfish Java EE application server [1] using the generated deployment scripts. For the measurements, we did not use a database server as it would have required hand-written database access code. Instead, we also used the generated resource demands for the

---

[1] https://glassfish.dev.java.net/

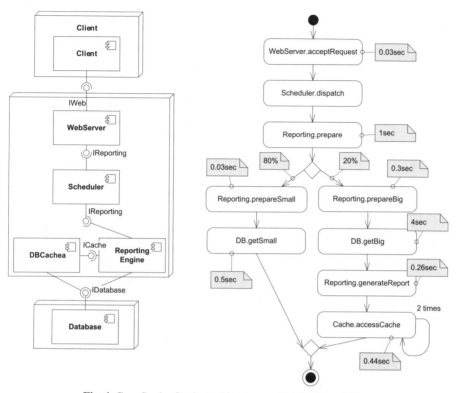

Fig. 4. Case Study: Static Architecture and Main Control Flow

database actions. The whole system executed on an Intel Centrino Core2Duo laptop running under Windows Vista. The generated client application executed 10 warm-up cycles and took 100 measurements afterwards. We used two different resource generation strategies. First, we used the calculation of Fibonacci numbers which requires only limited memory access. As second strategy, we used the sorting of an array which requires intensive memory access in contrast to the Fibonacci strategy.

Figure 5(a) shows the histogram of the measured response times for a single user generating workload. The dark grey bars show the response times for the Fibonacci strategy, the light grey bars show the response times for the sorting strategy. The mean value for small reports is 1.5 seconds and 6.1 seconds for large reports. Thus, the calibration described in section 5 works fine for both strategies as the measured response times closely match the times specified in the model (Error < 6%).

The results given in figure 5(b) show the same experiment for two concurrent users. The Fibonacci strategy shows a similar response time as in the first experiment, which was expected as the underlying hardware contains a dual core CPU so that each core executes a single thread. However, the response times are slightly more delayed (1.65 seconds for small and 6.6 seconds for large reports). This effect becomes even more significant for the sorting strategy. While the algorithm can execute on both cores, we assume that the execution has to wait for the memory bus or caches to become available.

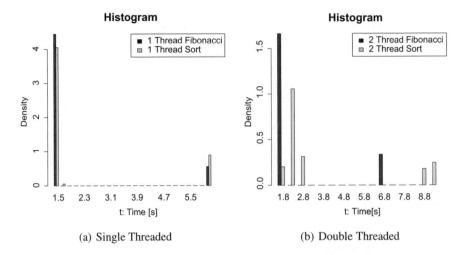

(a) Single Threaded   (b) Double Threaded

Fig. 5. Execution of Different Resource Demand Generators

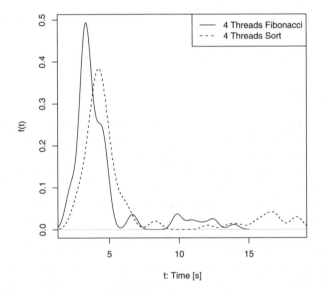

Fig. 6. Execution with 4 Threads

Hence, the results show contention effects and the response time increases. Note, for the prototype prediction to produce good results the selected algorithm for the generation of the artificial resource demand has to reflect the real system's behaviour (see also section 7). The average response time for small reports is 2.3 seconds and 9.2 seconds for long reports. Such effects are hard to predict using performance prediction methods which commonly neglect memory, and caching effects.

Finally, figure 6 depicts the probability density of the response times for four concurrent users. As there is now contention for the CPU by both demand generating strategies, the response times increase even further. In this scenario, also the scheduler realisation in the underlying operating system influences the results, which makes the response time even harder to predict.

To summarize, the case study demonstrated the prototype generation worked, the accurate calibration results of the resource demand generation strategies, and the use of the prototype revealed effects, which are hard to predict using model-driven software performance engineering. While we assume that the major effect discovered in the case study was the memory bus contention, prototypes can reveal other types of problems hard to model, like hard disks access, file system effects, caches, CPU architecture, garbage collection, etc. We plan to use the presented prototype generator to investigate these effects in future case studies.

7   Discussion

This section summarizes the assumptions and limitations for the transformation of PCM instances to ProtoCom prototypes.

Validity of the PCM Model Instance: As the ProtoCom mapping relies on its particular PCM input model, the model has to be valid with respect to the resource demands. The prototype only provides the means to execute a PCM instance in a more realistic execution environment but it cannot provide insights for the question whether the PCM instance's resource demands are valid with respect to the final application. However, this information availability by estimates or rough measurements is a common assumption of all early, design-time performance prediction approaches. If the demands cannot be provided the proposed approach is unapplicable.

Database Interaction: In many cases, the database is the bottleneck of typical three tier applications. Using only resource demands and workload strategies which execute a certain mix of database reads and writes to cause a load similar to the one specified in the PCM model might not reflect the database's internal concurrent processing adequately. This is especially true if the mix is not representative to the mix in the final application. In such cases, manual written code is needed for more precise predictions. Nevertheless, you only have to write such code if the database is the bottleneck and if the database's response behaviour is highly dependent on the application's request mix. A more detailed investigation of the database issue will be performed in the future.

Choosing the Right Load Generation Strategy: Picking the right resource demand simulation strategy is crucial for the results to be realistic as explained in the previous section. Currently, there is no guidance for the user helping him to choose the right one. Additionally, ProtoCom's implementation is limited to a global selection of a strategy per ProcessingResourceType. However, different resource demands in different InternalActions may be better reflected by different strategies. These improvements are subject to future work.

System External Calls: The code mapping generates only mock stubs for system external services. It is desirable for a prototype to exchange the stub with code calling the real service. However, this also implies specifying parameter values when needed in these calls (see next list item).

No Realistic Parameter Passing: ProtoCom relies on PCM's abstraction from the real data and uses parameter characterisations instead. However, this has several drawbacks.

First, the network load is not realistic, as ProtoCom transmits parameter characterisations instead of the parameters of the real application. In cases where both differ significantly, ProtoCom's results may be of less precision. As a remedy, in future versions of ProtoCom a network load bytesize estimation can help. If the estimation results in a larger bytesize than the size of the parameter characterisations, an additional random payload could be added to the transmitted packages. However, this does not help if the estimated bytesize is smaller than the serialised simulated stack.

Second, it is difficult to call system external services like database queries if this involves parameter passing. In this case, the stub generated for system external services needs manual adjustment and test data has to be used instead of realistic parameter values.

Costs: We assume that the PCM model used to generate the prototype has been built as part of a simulation-based or analytical analysis. We further assume that the prototype is only generated for those instances which the analyses classified as feasible keeping the additional costs low. However, a detailed study of the overall return-on-invest (ROI) is subject to future work.

8   Conclusions

This paper presented a mapping of instances of the Palladio Component Model (PCM) to a prototype implementation which is readily executable on a Java EE application server. The generated application's behaviour with respect to the resource demands needed during execution is the same as specified in the PCM instance. We gave details on a strategy to calibrate the resource demand generators to the underlying hardware. A case study demonstrates that the mapping works and the results gained demonstrate that effects hard to predict on the model level can be revealed using the generated prototype.

The mapping presented in this paper helps software architects to access the performance of created architecture designs under more realistic conditions compared to performance analysis models which have to rely on simplifying assumptions. Due to a model-driven approach, the time needed to generate and execute the prototype is reduced to a minimum. However, the drawback is the time spent to wait for real measurements to be taken.

Future work is directed at generating more realistic network and hard-disk demands. For the network demands, the prototype mapping should evaluate the PCM annotations for the bytesizes of the transferred packages and simulate this by sending packages of appropriate length. For hard disks, several different resource generation strategies are needed which generate a different mix of read and write transactions which additionally vary in size.

Acknowledgements

We like to thank the members of the Chair of Software Design and Quality (SDQ) at the University of Karlsruhe (TH) for their valuable discussions and thorough review of the contents of this paper.

References

1. Smith, C.U., Williams, L.G.: Performance Solutions: A Practical Guide to Creating Responsive, Scalable Software. Addison-Wesley, Reading (2002)
2. Balsamo, S., Di Marco, A., Inverardi, P., Simeoni, M.: Model-Based Performance Prediction in Software Development: A Survey. IEEE Transactions on Software Engineering 30(5), 295–310 (2004)
3. Grundy, J., Cai, Y., Liu, A.: Generation of Distributed System Test-beds from High-level Software Architecture Descriptions. In: Proceedings of the 2001 IEEE International Conference on Automated Software Engineering, San Diego, CA (2001)
4. Hu, L., Gorton, I.: A performance prototyping approach to designing concurrent software architectures. In: Proceedings of the 2nd International Workshop on Software Engineering for Parallel and Distributed Systems, pp. 270–276 (1997)
5. Denaro, G., Polini, A., Emmerich, W.: Early performance testing of distributed software applications. In: SIGSOFT Software Engineering Notes, vol. 29, pp. 94–103. ACM Press, New York (2004)
6. Becker, S., Koziolek, H., Reussner, R.: Model-based Performance Prediction with the Palladio Component Model. In: Proceedings of the 6th International Workshop on Software and Performance (WOSP2007), ACM Sigsoft (2007)
7. Reussner, R.H., Becker, S., Koziolek, H., Happe, J., Kuperberg, M., Krogmann, K.: The Palladio Component Model. Interner Bericht 2007-21, Universität Karlsruhe (TH), Faculty for Informatics, Karlsruhe, Germany (2007)
8. Wu, X.: An Approach to Predicting Performance for Component Based Systems. Master's thesis, Carleton University (2003)
9. Petriu, D.C., Wang, X.: From UML description of high-level software architecture to LQN performance models. In: Münch, M., Nagl, M. (eds.) AGTIVE 1999. LNCS, vol. 1779, pp. 47–63. Springer, Heidelberg (2000)
10. Cortellessa, V., Di Marco, A., Inverardi, P.: Integrating Performance and Reliability Analysis in a Non-Functional MDA Framework. In: Dwyer, M.B., Lopes, A. (eds.) FASE 2007. LNCS, vol. 4422, pp. 57–71. Springer, Heidelberg (2007)
11. Bardram, J.E., Christensen, H.B., Corry, A.V., Hansen, K.M., Ingstrup, M.: Exploring quality attributes using architectural prototyping. In: Reussner, R., Mayer, J., Stafford, J.A., Overhage, S., Becker, S., Schroeder, P.J. (eds.) QoSA 2005 and SOQUA 2005. LNCS, vol. 3712, pp. 155–170. Springer, Heidelberg (2005)
12. Avritzer, A., Weyuker, E.J.: Deriving Workloads for Performance Testing. Software–Practice and Experience 26(6), 613–633 (1996)
13. Woodside, C.M., Schramm, C.: Scalability and performance experiments using synthetic distributed server systems. Distributed Systems Engineering 3, 2–8 (1996)
14. Rolia, J.A., Sevcik, K.C.: The Method of Layers. IEEE Transactions on Software Engineering 21(8), 689–700 (1995)
15. Koziolek, H.: Parameter Dependencies for Reusable Performance Specifications of Software Components. PhD thesis, University of Oldenburg (2008)

16. Zhu, L., Liu, Y., Gorton, I., Bui, N.B.: Customized Benchmark Generation Using MDA. In: WICSA 2005: Proceedings of the 5th Working IEEE/IFIP Conference on Software Architecture, Washington, DC, USA, pp. 35–44. IEEE Computer Society, Los Alamitos (2005)
17. Zhu, L., Gorton, I., Liu, Y., Bui, N.B.: Model Driven Benchmark Generation for Web Services. In: SOSE 2006: Proceedings of the 2006 International Workshop on Service-Oriented Software Engineering, pp. 33–39. ACM, New York (2006)
18. Cai, Y., Grundy, J., Hosking, J.: Experiences Integrating and Scaling a Performance Test Bed Generator with an Open Source CASE Tool. In: ASE 2004: Proceedings of the 19th IEEE international conference on Automated software engineering, Washington, DC, USA, pp. 36–45. IEEE Computer Society, Los Alamitos (2004)
19. Object Management Group (OMG): UML Profile for Schedulability, Performance and Time (2005)
20. Szyperski, C., Gruntz, D., Murer, S.: Component Software: Beyond Object-Oriented Programming, 2nd edn. ACM Press and Addison-Wesley, New York (2002)
21. Fowler, M.: Inversion of control containers and the dependency injection pattern (2004) (Last retrieved 2008-01-06)
22. Burden, R., Faires, J.: Numerical Analysis. PWS Publishing Co., Boston (1988)
23. Wu, X., Woodside, M.: Performance Modeling from Software Components. SIGSOFT Softw. Eng. Notes 29(1), 290–301 (2004)

SCALASCA Parallel Performance Analyses of SPEC MPI2007 Applications

Zoltán Szebenyi[1,2], Brian J. N. Wylie[1], and Felix Wolf[1,2]

[1] Jülich Supercomputing Centre, Forschungszentrum Jülich GmbH, Germany
[2] Aachen Institute for Advanced Study in Computational Engineering Science,
RWTH Aachen University, Germany
{z.szebenyi,b.wylie,f.wolf}@fz-juelich.de
http://www.scalasca.org/

Abstract. The SPEC MPI2007 1.0 benchmark suite provides a rich variety of message-passing HPC application kernels to compare the performance of parallel/distributed computer systems. Its 13 applications use a representative cross-section of programming languages (C/C++/ Fortran, often combined) and MPI programming patterns (e.g., blocking vs. non-blocking vs. persistent point-to-point communication, with or without extensive collective communication). This offers a basis with which to examine the effectiveness of parallel performance tools using real-world applications that have already been extensively optimized and tuned (at least for sequential execution), but which may still have parallelization inefficiencies and scalability problems. In this context, the SCALASCA toolset for scalable performance analysis of large-scale parallel applications, which has been extended to distinguish iteration/timestep phases, is evaluated with this suite on an IBM SP2 'Regatta' system, and found to be effective at identifying significant performance improvement opportunities.

Keywords: Parallel/distributed systems; Benchmark suite; Performance measurement & analysis tools; Application tracing & profiling.

1 Introduction

Various parallel performance tools studies have considered benchmark suites, such as evaluation of the VAMPIR trace collection and visualization toolset with the 13 applications of the SPEC MPI benchmark suite [1,2,3,4] and the OMPP profiler with the 11 applications of the SPEC OpenMP benchmark suite [5]. Such tools provide in-depth analyses that offer insight into performance and scalability problems indicated by whole execution measurements [6,7]. While tools that aggregate and summarize measurements during execution readily handle long-running complex applications, those that rely on trace collection and analysis are not so fortunate, since trace sizes grow proportionately with the length of measurement (in addition to the orthogonal dimensions of the number of processes/threads, density of traced events and number of metrics associated with each event).

S. Kounev, I. Gorton, and K. Sachs (Eds.): SIPEW 2008, LNCS 5119, pp. 99–123, 2008.

The open-source SCALASCA toolset [8,17] addresses these scalability issues with a compound approach consisting of flexible measurement configuration (including filtering), runtime summarization of measurements during execution, and event trace collection matched with a replay-based trace analysis that exploits the parallelism and distributed-memory resources of the target system [9,10]. From an initial summarization measurement of a fully-instrumented application, an appropriate list of user functions to filter can be determined and specified in subsequent measurements. After verifying that the filter produces an accurate summary measurement (without undue dilation), and that a resulting trace won't be so excessively large as to require highly disruptive intermediate buffer flushing, it can be used for a tracing experiment. Without recompilation or reinstrumentation of the application, straightforward reconfiguration of the measurement runtime system allows traced events to be buffered until measurement completion, after which the trace analyzer replays them in parallel to automatically calculate a rich set of execution performance properties. Both runtime summary and postmortem trace analysis use a common report format, allowing them to be examined with the same interactive analysis report explorer. The library for reading and writing the XML reports also facilitates the development of utilities which process the reports in various ways, such as the extraction of measurements for each process or their statistical aggregation, for the generation of timeline charts and metric graphs, respectively.

This paper presents SCALASCA measurements and analyses of Version 1.0 of the SPEC MPI2007 benchmark suite application kernels on an IBM SP2 'Regatta' system, with particular attention given to the scalability of the applications and the SCALASCA toolset itself, and examination of performance variation between processes and different timesteps/iterations of the applications' executions.

2   Experiment Configuration

2.1   SPEC MPI2007 1.0 Benchmark Suite

Version 1.0 of the SPEC MPI2007 benchmark suite [1,2] was released in June 2007 to provide a standard set of MPI-based HPC application kernels for comparing the performance of parallel/distributed systems' hardware, operating system, MPI execution environment and compilers. The initial release includes 13 applications and a 'medium-sized' reference dataset (MPIm2007) for benchmarking runs requiring up to 2GB of memory per process and configurable for up to 512 processes.

Table 1 summarizes the 13 applications of the MPI2007 suite, showing that they derive from a wide variety of subject areas and are implemented using a representative cross-section of programming languages (C/C++/Fortran, often combined). From the MPI usage breakdown in the table, it can be seen that a variety of MPI functions are used at many locations ('sites') in the source code, however, performance analysis can concentrate on the smaller number of communication and synchronization functions (shown as c&s/used 'funcs')

Table 1. SPEC MPI2007 1.0 applications' coding and subject area

Application code	Program language	LOC	MPI funcs	sites	paths	Application subject area
104.milc	C	17987	9/18	51	111	Lattice quantum chromodynamics
107.leslie3d	F77,F90	10503	8/13	43	12	Combustion dynamics
113.GemsFDTD	F90	21858	9/16	237	21	Computational electrodynamics
115.fds4	F90,C	44524	8/15	239	8	Computational fluid dynamics
121.pop2	F90	69203	11/17	158	173	Oceanography
122.tachyon	C	15512	8/16	17	8	Computer graphics: ray tracing
126.lammps	C++	6796	12/25	625	41	Molecular dynamics
127.wrf2	F90,C	163462	7/23	132	62	Numerical weather prediction
128.GAPgeofem	F77,C	30935	8/18	58	13	Geophysics finite-element methods
129.tera_tf	F90	6468	9/13	42	17	Eulerian hydrodynamics
130.socorro	F90	91585	11/20	155	147	Quantum chemistry
132.zeusmp2	C,F90	44441	11/21	639	85	Astrophysical hydrodynamics
137.lu	F90	5671	10/13	72	24	Linear algebra SSOR

and the distinct program call-paths on which they are actually executed during benchmark runs ('paths').

Table 2 tallies the MPI functions used by 32-way benchmark executions, and shows that a similarly diverse range of MPI programming patterns are implemented, e.g., blocking, vs. non-blocking vs. persistent point-to-point communication, with or without extensive collective communication, etc. (SPEC rules allow only MPI parallelization, so auto-parallelization capabilities of compilers must be disabled, at least in this initial version of the benchmark suite.) The suite therefore provides a comprehensive test, both for MPI benchmarking purposes, but also for examining the effectiveness of parallel performance tools with real-world applications.

2.2   IBM SP2 Regatta p690+ System

The John von Neumann Institute for Computing 'JUMP' system [11] hosted by Jülich Supercomputing Centre consists of 41 IBM SP2 p690+ frames, each with 16 dual-core 1.7GHz Power4+ processors and 128GB of shared main memory, connected via IBM High Performance Switch. At the time measurements were made, the system was running AIX 5.3, with IBM's POE 4.2 MPI and GPFS filesystem, and use of compute nodes managed via LoadLeveler.

The available IBM XL compiler suites (versions 7.0/8.0 for C/C++ and 9.1/10.1 for Fortran) were unable to compile and/or link some of the SPEC MPI2007 applications when the build was configured using the specification provided for them with the benchmark distribution. In such cases, aggressive optimization options were progressively removed until a viable application executable was produced. Full optimization of the code and run-time environment were neither essential nor particularly desirable for our purposes, as the study

Table 2. MPI function calls used by 32-way SPEC MPIm2007 executions on JUMP

	Irecv	Isend	Recv	Send	Wait	Waitall	Waitany
104.milc	359340	359340			718680		
107.leslie3d	3201600	3201600			320160		
113.GemsFDTD			3316	3316			
115.fds4			35271	35271		151264	
121.pop2	558007700	558007700				319663712	
122.tachyon							
126.lammps	196544		9152	205696	196544		
127.wrf2	6508380		10106	6518486	6508380		
128.GAPgeofem	6099876	6099876				1404288	
129.tera_tf	1989504		360	1989864	1989504		
130.socorro	3286178			3286178			3286178
132.zeusmp2	845056	845056				249888	
137.lu	19000		7600320	7619320	19000		

	Sendrecv	Recv_init	Send_init	Start	Startall	Testsome	Scan
113.GemsFDTD	1240000						
122.tachyon		16158	16158	6536	1	223	
126.lammps							32

	Allgather	Allgatherv	Allreduce	Barrier	Bcast	Gather	Reduce
104.milc			17700	62	122		
107.leslie3d			140832	1088			64
113.GemsFDTD				160	292000		128
115.fds4	303040			320		8512	
121.pop2			26080640	8640	9664		
122.tachyon	32			32			
126.lammps			1696	64	1888		
127.wrf2					67488		
128.GAPgeofem			2016224		352		
129.tera_tf			60352	15520	1184		
130.socorro	512	7936	37536		9696		1088
132.zeusmp2			12864	96	1280		64
137.lu			224	32	288		

	Cart_create	Comm_split	Comm_create	Comm_free	Comm_dup	Comm_group	Group_range_incl
104.milc		32					
113.GemsFDTD		32					
121.pop2			96			96	96
126.lammps	32			32			
128.GAPgeofem					32		
130.socorro					224		
132.zeusmp2	32	32					
137.lu		32					

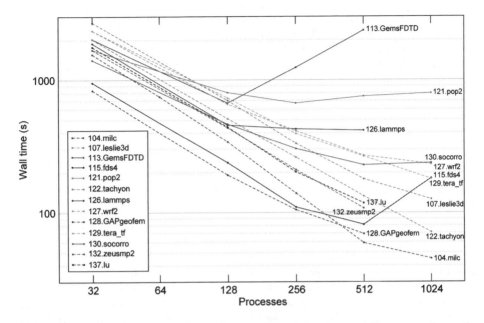

Fig. 1. SPEC MPIm2007 1.0 benchmark execution times with different numbers of processes on the IBM SP2 system 'JUMP.' Eight of the benchmarks (shown with dashed lines) have good speedup, up to 1024 processes when supported by the benchmark and 512 processes otherwise. The remaining five benchmarks (shown with solid lines) have clear scaling problems. *126.lammps* uses a maximum of 140 processes (idling any excess provided) and therefore shows no significant speedup beyond 128 processes. *130.socorro* and *115.fds4* both show good speedup to 512 processes, before respectively having small and significant slowdowns. Finally, *121.pop2* only scales to 256 processes before slowing down and *113.GemsFDTD* only to 128 processes before its dramatic performance breakdown.

is more focussed on 'typical' application performance in a representative HPC environment than benchmarking.

Figure 1 shows a graph of the benchmark execution times with different numbers of processes, on a log–log scale, from which the scalability of each benchmark can be determined. To reduce the impact of variability in run times (due to non-dedicated use of the communication switch and filesystem in the production configuration of the JUMP system), the best run time of several measurements is taken although this is contrary to the SPEC benchmark rules. (Including confidence intervals in the graphs and tables would be appropriate in a comprehensive study, however, these have been omitted to reduce unnecessary clutter and clarify the underlying behaviour.)

While around half of the benchmarks scale well, it is clear that certain others have very limited scalability, before no further speed-up is possible or performance degrades unacceptably. Although no tuning has been done for JUMP, and measurements were taken on a non-dedicated production system, from review of published benchmark results [1] the same scalability limitations are seen to be common to specially 'tuned' benchmark measurements on dedicated systems.

Of course, analyzing the performance of optimally-tuned applications that scale perfectly has much less value than identifying potential opportunities for improvement of applications with problems, and is key to producing better performing and more scalable applications.

2.3   SCALASCA Toolset

SCALASCA is an open-source toolset for scalable performance analysis of large-scale parallel applications [8,17] developed by Jülich Supercomputing Centre in conjunction with the University of Tennessee. Version 1.0 includes integrated runtime measurement summarization and selective event tracing [9] with automatic trace analysis based on parallel replay [10], to ensure scalability for long-running and highly-parallel MPI, OpenMP and hybrid applications.

When the SCALASCA instrumenter is prepended to each application compile and link command, it produces fully-instrumented executables without modifying or inhibiting compiler optimizations. This exploits capabilities for function entry and exit instrumentation provided by most (but not all) modern compilers, and the standard PMPI library interposition interface. A source preprocessor is also provided for OpenMP pragma/directive and annotated region instrumentation (though not used in this work). Manual annotation of significant code regions (e.g., initialization) can also be done with a macro-based user API, which has been extended for annotating repetitive phases (such as solver iterations or time-steps).

SCALASCA measurement collection and analysis is performed by a nexus that is also prefixed to the normal application execution command-line, whether part of a batch script or interactive run invocation. Experiments with an instrumented executable can be configured to collect runtime summaries and/or event traces (optionally including hardware counters), with the latter traces automatically analyzed with the same number of processes as used for measurement. Both summary and trace analyses are generated in the same profile format, which can be interactively explored with the SCALASCA analysis report examiner GUI (shown in Figures 10&11). Command-line tools are also provided for processing analysis reports, e.g., to produce filters containing lists of functions to ignore for improved measurement configuration, and new prototype tools are being developed for graphing and charting metrics calculated for repetitive phases.

Table 3 shows the SPEC MPIm2007 application execution characteristics determined from SCALASCA runtime summarization experiments. Application programs are seen to typically consist of hundreds to thousands of global timesteps or solver iterations, with the farming-based *122.tachyon* being an exception. Although *130.socorro* only does 20 iterations, it has by far the most complex call-tree and the deepest frame depth (with MPI communication down to depth 18, one further than *127.wrf2*): some highly recursive functions in the initialization phase of *127.wrf2* were filtered out and are not counted here. At tens of gigabytes per process rank, complete traces of either *122.tachyon* or

Table 3. SPEC MPIm2007 1.0 applications' 32-way execution characteristics

Application code	Program execution steps	depth	callpaths	RSS (MB)	Trace buffer content (MB) total	MPI	filter	residue	Filter funcs
104.milc	8+243	6/6	255/257	341	2683	1.7	2626	57	4
107.leslie3d	2000	3/3	40/40	1078	1437	15.	1422	16	6
113.GemsFDTD	1000	4/5	166/185	505	3619	5.9	3582	37	1
115.fds4	2363	1/8	149/151	209	122	2.1	117	6	6
121.pop2	9000	6/6	403/403	748	6361	2494.	2606	3841	6
122.tachyon	N/A	3/3	25/27	676	59884	0.7	59809	75	5
126.lammps	500	6/6	162/162	401	291	0.8	290	1	9
127.wrf2	1375	17/22	4951/4975	297	1109	0.4	1106	5	69
128.GAPgeofem	235	4/4	44/44	361	996	33.	971	34	2
129.tera_tf	943	3/4	57/59	74	2459	10.	1628	831	4
130.socorro	20	18/23	10350/10352	148	10703	13.	10587	120	21
132.zeusmp2	200	5/5	171/179	377	5	3.4	—	3	0
137.lu	180	4/4	48/49	384	42	28.	—	28	0

130.socorro would be prohibitively large, however, specifying a few functions to filter reduces their requirements to around 100MB/process. Many of the other applications also benefit from substantial reduction of measurement overheads when one or more of their user functions are filtered. Unfortunately, a full execution measurement of the MPI-dominated *121.pop2* remains intractible even when only MPI functions are traced, therefore it was necessary to reduce the number of steps it does from 9000 to 2000 (by modifying its input file).

Table 4 presents the SPEC MPIm2007 application execution times for uninstrumented runs and for a variety of SCALASCA measurement experiments with 32, 128 and 512 processes. When measurements are being collected, run times are naturally longer than the uninstrumented execution times, due to dilation introduced by instrumentation and measurement processing, however, this can be minimized by providing appropriate filters specifying functions to be ignored during measurement (as determined by an initial summarization measurement). When an initial full summarization measurement is not practical, as was the case with *122.tachyon*, a filter could be determined from a shorter or smaller execution. (Although the dilation remains serious, further reduction was not pursued since *122.tachyon* was ultimately not particularly interesting.) For *132.zeusmp2* and *137.lu* filtering was neither necessary nor desirable.

As well as reducing measurement dilation, filtering is also appropriate for reducing the trace buffer capacity requirements, to avoid highly disruptive intermediate flushes of trace buffers to disk during measurement: examples of catastrophic disruption from intermediate trace flushing are detailed in [4]. Furthermore, very large traces are also awkward to analyze, so judicious filtering balances what measurements are collected and analyzed with what is omitted on expediency grounds. Functions that have been filtered in this way are 'invisible' during analysis, as if they had been 'in-lined.' Even with all user functions filtered (i.e., measuring only MPI functions), the 2.5GB/rank trace buffer capacity

Table 4. SPEC MPIm2007 1.0 applications' execution times in wallclock seconds with 32, 128 and 512 processes on the p690+ cluster for a variety of instrumentation and measurement/analysis configurations. 'None' is a reference run with neither instrumentation nor measurement (beyond elapsed time), whereas the additional columns refer to measurements of fully-instrumented versions (i.e., using automatic function instrumentation by the compiler and MPI library interposition instrumentation), sometimes augmented with user-defined phase annotations (p), where measurement was configured for runtime summarization only (Sum) or runtime summarization combined with event tracing (Trace). Measurements marked (f) used filtering of selected user functions with excessive overheads. After trace collection during measurement, additional time is required to dump buffered trace event records to disk (Td) for subsequent automatic trace analysis (Ta), both done in parallel with the total trace data.

| Application code | Instrumentation/Measurement | | | | | Tracing | Trace |
	None	Sum	Sum+f	Sum+pf	Trace	Td+Ta	(GB)
32							
104.milc	1556	2140	1616	—	1611	13+50	1.587
107.leslie3d	2704	2945	2807	2892	2787	43+113	0.403
113.GemsFDTD	2028	2680	2042	2111	2102	57+144	0.634
115.fds4	951	1010	960	957	959	92+141	0.130
121.pop2	1687	2415	2176	2104	N/P	—+—	—
121.pop2 (2000)	398	N/A	514	N/A	518	124+2734	13.613
122.tachyon	2024	N/P	6016	—	6023	1+68	0.007
126.lammps	1883	1988	1899	2001	1963	41+74	0.038
127.wrf2	2352	2945	2499	2475	2550	425+907	18.138
128.GAPgeofem	833	984	879	884	874	14+182	0.670
129.tera_tf	2399	2583	2458	2390	2395	17+71	24.737
130.socorro	1411	3990	1631	1701	1703	120+373	3.420
132.zeusmp2	1683	1727	—	—	1729	28+67	0.113
137.lu	1771	1815	—	—	1910	13+159	1.100
128							
113.GemsFDTD	670	—	1033	—	1038	103+216	0.944
512							
104.milc	59	—	63	—	69	5+7	0.827
107.leslie3d	179	—	193	—	199	310+343	7.037
113.GemsFDTD	2363	—	N/A	—	N/A	—+—	—
115.fds4	81	—	86	—	88	272+743	1.050
121.pop2	752	—	1072	—	N/P	—+—	—
121.pop2 (2000)	182	—	226	—	326	1380+2627	103.646
122.tachyon	133	—	383	—	380	2+27	0.069
126.lammps	416	—	445	—	434	233+360	0.167
127.wrf2	269	—	300	—	310	1878+2535	107.929
128.GAPgeofem	69	—	82	—	87	50+333	15.216
129.tera_tf	265	—	287	—	298	163+316	72.381
130.socorro	228	—	263	—	268	635+913	25.756
132.zeusmp2	108	112	—	—	115	5+19	2.084
137.lu	118	119	—	—	119	36+126	19.493

requirements of *121.pop2* were impractical for tracing a full execution, therefore measurements were repeated with only 2000 rather than the full 9000 steps.

For applications with identifiable repetitive phases, corresponding to global timesteps or solver iterations, additional annotation instrumentation was manually inserted into the source code. This was possible for all except *122.tachyon* which is based on a task-farming parallelization, and *104.milc* which has a complex structure of nested loops and branches. The overhead of this additional instrumentation during measurement is found to be much less than the run-to-run variation of the applications themselves, and the phase markers can be exploited in subsequent analyses.

After an initial set of 32-way measurements, from which appropriate measurement filters could be determined, 128-way and 512-way measurements were then taken. (512-way measurements were skipped for *113.GemsFDTD* due to its adverse scaling.) Although the measurement times for runtime summarization and trace collection are seen to scale in proportion to the uninstrumented application execution time, trace sizes and corresponding trace handling (dumping of buffers and post-mortem analysis) generally grow more expensive. In a few cases, however, traces actually become smaller or the use of parallel I/O decreases trace handling time. For example, *121.pop2* trace sizes and writing times grew by factors of 7.6 and 11 respectively, however, parallel trace analysis time actually slightly improved with 8 times the number of processes.

3   Results and Analyses

The final automatic trace analysis reports for each SPEC MPIm2007 benchmark application execution (with 32 processes), including functions and annotated phases, were postprocessed to extract the aggregate and individual process execution behaviour of each application-specific phase (corresponding to global timesteps or solver iterations as appropriate). *104.milc* and *122.tachyon* are excluded from this analysis.

SCALASCA analyses automatically determine a variety of performance metrics for each application call-path and thread of execution, which are concisely presented in hierarchical trees (as shown in Figures 10&11). Simple *Visits* counts and MPI message-passing statistics (e.g., numbers of sends and receives or collective operations and associated *Bytes transferred*) complement metrics derived from measured times. MPI *Communication* and *Synchronization* times can be distinguished from total *Execution* time, and further split into times for *Point-to-point* and *Collective* operations. These summary metrics, which are straightforward to calculate during measurement, can be augmented by specialized metrics that can only be determined from analysis of traces searching for patterns of events indicative of inefficiencies.

Eight of the remaining 11 applications are treated collectively in Figures 2–5, whereas *107.leslie3d*, *129.tera_tf* and *132.zeusmp2* show particularly interesting execution behaviour and are examined in more detail afterwards.

The left column in Figures 2–5 graphs total *Execution* time and MPI *Communication* time for each iteration phase. The values for the process(es) with the largest times are shown red, the median shown blue, and the shortest shown green. In most cases, no significant difference is apparent in total *Execution* time between the fastest and slowest processes, and the graphs appear uniformly green. *137.lu* is one of the exceptions, consistently having an observable difference in every iteration, whereas a difference is only apparent in the first iteration of *113.GemsFDTD* and some of the iterations of *121.pop2*. Variation in MPI *Communication* time is much more pronounced, both between iterations and between processes within iterations, exemplified by *115.fds4* and *113.GemsFDTD* respectively.

Whereas most applications show a stable constant execution time for each iteration (sometimes with the first and/or last iteration being distinguished), some reveal gradually deteriorating performance (e.g., *126.lammps* and *127.wrf2*). Much larger *Execution* time of certain iterations of *126.lammps* at regular intervals are also clearly distinguished, and from further analysis found to correlate to more point-to-point communication every 20th iteration and collective communication every 100th. The execution of *127.wrf2* is clearly dominated by its 1st and 1201th iterations, however, there are also significant iterations with collective communication every 300 iterations.

The right column in Figures 2–5 shows total *Execution* time and MPI *Communication* time for each iteration phase as a timeline chart for each process. In each chart, the value for the largest time is shown in dark red, with the other values on a progressive scale down to light yellow, and white used if there is no value for a particular entry. (This colour scale is shown at the bottom of Figures 10&11.) Globally consistent behaviour is generally apparent, including variation per iteration which appears as peaks in the graphs on the left.

137.lu can again be readily distinguished by its broadly non-deterministic variation of *Execution* time across processes in any iteration, however, MPI *Communication* time reveals a more complex story. Certain processes consistently have much shorter *Communication* times than the others, indicative of load imbalance. More dramatic load imbalance is evident from the horizontal stripes in the MPI *Communication* time chart of *113.GemsFDTD*, where processes with ranks 7, 30 & 31 consistently take longer than the others: the latter are found not to participate in certain local update operations and consequently are always early when they must communicate with partners. Similar striping can also be seen in *128.GAPgeofem* and on odd-numbered process ranks of *126.lammps*. For *121.pop2* it is predominantly higher numbered process ranks that have longer MPI *Communication* times.

Note that the phase annotations do not explicitly synchronize processes, such that the time for a particular iteration on one process can vary significantly from that of its peers, however, inter-process communication results in loose synchronization in those cases where explicit collective synchronization is not used by the application itself in each iteration.

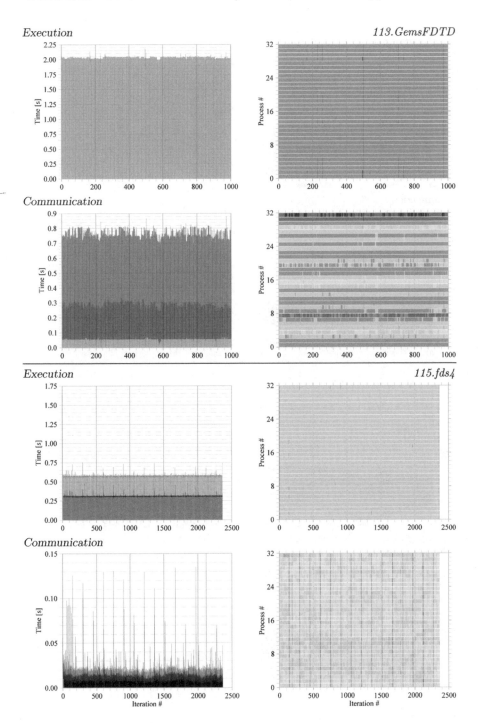

Fig. 2. SPEC MPIm2007 *113.GemsFDTD* and *115.fds4* iteration time metrics

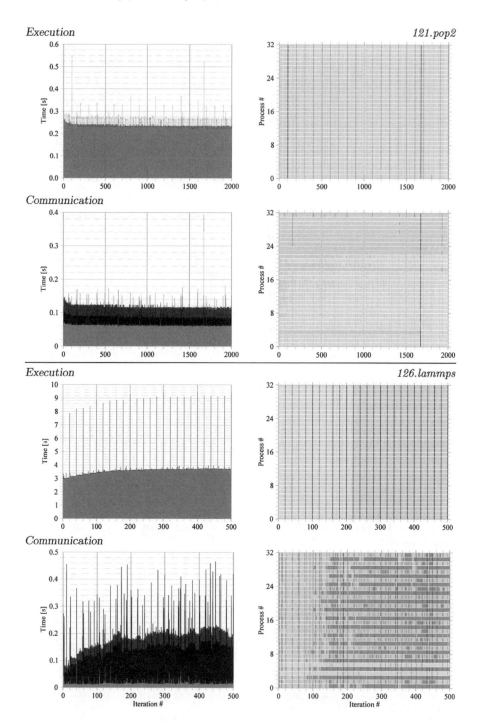

Fig. 3. SPEC MPIm2007 *121.pop2* and *126.lammps* iteration time metrics

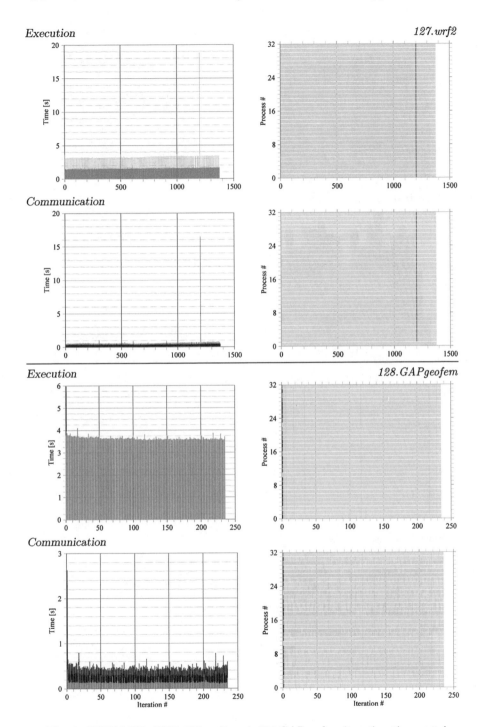

Fig. 4. SPEC MPIm2007 *127.wrf2* and *128.GAPgeofem* iteration time metrics

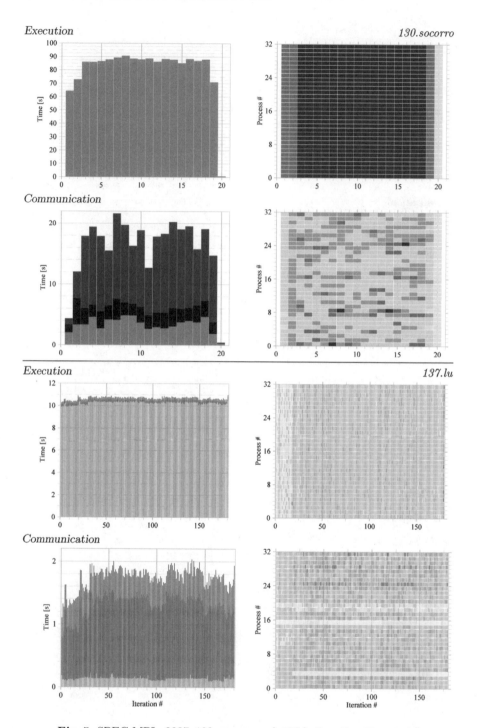

Fig. 5. SPEC MPIm2007 *130.socorro* and *137.lu* iteration time metrics

3.1   *107.leslie3d*

Iteration statistics graphs and timeline charts for a variety of performance metrics measured for *107.leslie3d* are shown in Figure 6. The *Execution* time metric shows a clear transition at iteration number 1015, with iterations taking roughly 1.35s before and 1.37s afterwards. This is seen to correlate with the median *Point-to-point Communication* time metric increasing from 0.10s to 0.13s after iteration 1015. Furthermore, the fraction of *Point-to-point Communication* time considered to be due to early receivers blocked waiting on senders to initiate communication (*Late Sender*) is clearly anti-correlated with the performance degradation and mostly restricted to processes with ranks 10 & 11. They are also found to be receiving messages in non-optimal order: *Late Sender / Wrong Message Order* during that period indicates that a message already in transit could have been received instead of waiting for another not yet initiated. The *Collective Communication* time metric doesn't show a transition, but has a prominent peak value for iteration 1015. Although there is a significant variation in the number of call-path *Visits* and *Bytes transferred* by processes, they remain constant thoughout, and therefore don't explain the dramatic transition. Additional *107.leslie3d* measurement experiments showed similar transitions, though with varying onset, severity, and affected processes, suggesting that an external influence is responsible for this significant disruption in execution performance. While other benchmarks seem less susceptible to this effect, it has also been identified in *121.pop2* and *126.lammps* measurements. One explanation could be process migration away from its local memory within the SP2 SMP node, however, an AIX API to determine processor bindings for processes has not yet been identified to be able to investigate this.

3.2   *129.tera_tf*

Iteration statistics graphs and timeline charts for a variety of performance metrics measured for *129.tera_tf* are shown in Figure 7. The *Execution* time metric shows a progressive increase from 1.2s to 2.9s for iterations, with occasional non-deterministic peaks. This increase is largely explained by the increase in maximum *Point-to-point Communication* time (0.1s growing to 1.5s) during the course of execution: the maximum *Collective Communication* time also grows to 0.4s. Both graphs show intriguing fine-scale variations from iteration to iteration amid larger-scale progressive trends

Blocking time of early receivers waiting for senders to initiate communication, considered *Late Sender* time, is seen to contribute significantly to *Point-to-point Communication* time, and found to affect different processes at different stages of execution. A 'hump' in maximum *Late Sender* time for iterations between 240 and 450 is remarkably prominent. Not shown, *Collective Synchronization* time is insignificant, with only the final iteration containing MPI_Barrier calls, and variation in the number of callpath *Visits* and *Bytes transferred* by processes is clearly evident, but constant throughout.

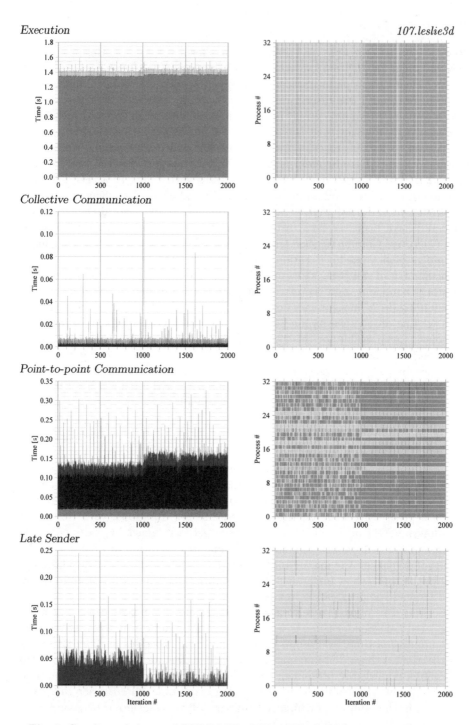

Fig. 6. Graphs and charts of SPEC MPIm2007 *107.leslie3d* iteration time metrics

3.3   132.zeusmp2

Although *132.zeusmp2* demonstrated extremely good scalability to 512 processes, SCALASCA analyses of 32-way experiments identified potentially important inefficiencies which warranted further investigation. Further experiments were therefore collected with 512 processes, to examine how these inefficiencies develop at larger scale.

Iteration statistics graphs and timeline charts for a variety of performance metrics measured for 512-way execution of *132.zeusmp2* are shown in Figures 8 and 9. The *Execution* time metric (upper left) shows a progressive increase from 0.43s to 0.49s for timesteps (after the initial timestep), with occasional outliers taking a little longer. Following down the column of metric graphs, this behaviour is explained by the median aggregate *Communication* time, which increases from 0.05s to 1.0s during the course of execution, with occasional iterations taking almost double as long. This is predominantly *Point-to-point Communication* time, with around a fifth due to *Collective Communication* time. Minimum time per iteration for the point-to-point operations fluctuates around 0.02s. Notably, while *Collective Communication* time was negligible during 32-way runs of *132.zeusmp2*, it has grown to be relatively significant in this 512-way experiment.

The bottom graphs of Figure 9 show that blocking time of early receivers waiting for senders to initiate communication, i.e., *Late Sender* time, contributes around half of the *Point-to-point Communication* time, and around half of it is for receiving messages out of order (i.e., *Late Sender / Wrong Message Order*). Multiple iterations are seen to have elevated times across most of the processes, and account for pronounced peaks in the median time, e.g., for iterations 39, 53 & 179, in both of these metrics. These higher communication times also carry through to observable delays in total *Execution* time for those iterations. Variation in the number of callpath *Visits* and *Bytes transferred* by process is clearly evident, but constant throughout, so provide no further insight into this dynamic execution behaviour.

The detailed metric charts and graphs provide a comprehensive view of the execution performance across processes and through time for annotated iterations and timesteps, which complements the profile-oriented SCALASCA analysis presentation.

From the runtime summarization report shown by the SCALASCA analysis report examiner GUI in Figure 10, MPI *Communication* time is found to be 18.4% of total execution time. 70% of this is *Point-to-point Communication time*, however, *Collective Communication time* which was insignificant with 32 processes now contributes the rest: this might be indicative of deteriorating load balance or lower efficiency of collectives using the IBM High Performance Switch when using multiple SMP nodes. MPI *Point-to-point Communication time* is largely concentrated in MPI_Waitall calls in the three routines bvalemf1, bvalemf2 and bvalemf3 on the call-path to hsmoc via ct and transprt. For these MPI_Waitall calls, there is a substantial variation across the 512 processes. with

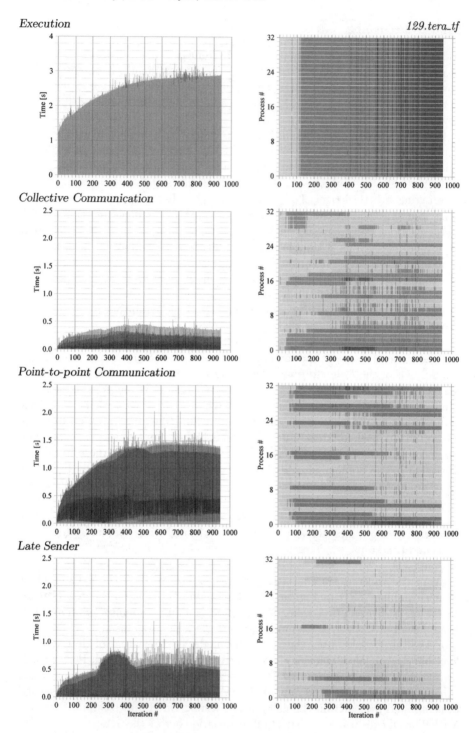

Fig. 7. Graphs and charts of SPEC MPIm2007 *129.tera_tf* iteration time metrics

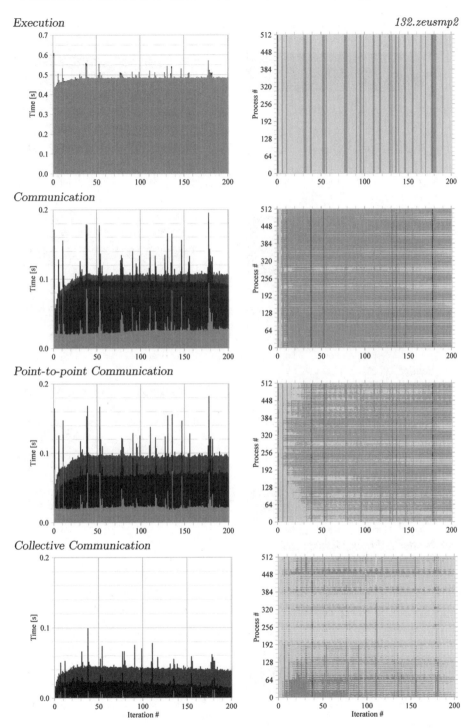

Fig. 8. Graphs and charts of SPEC MPIm2007 *132.zeusmp2* timestep metrics

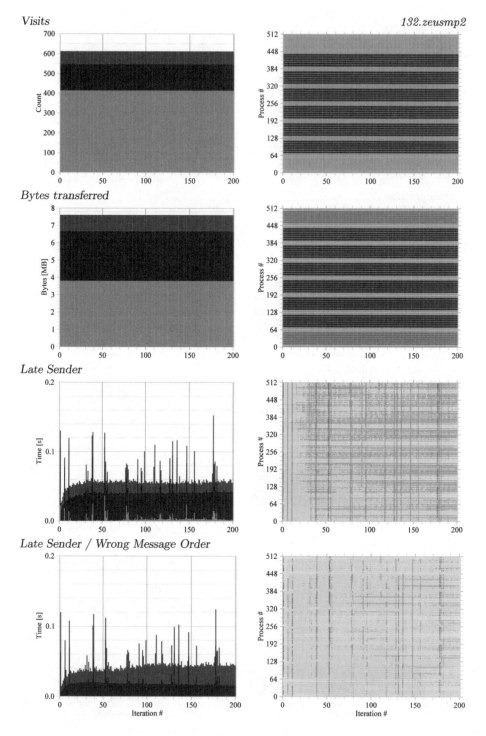

Fig. 9. Graphs and charts of SPEC MPIm2007 *132.zeusmp2* timestep metrics (cont.)

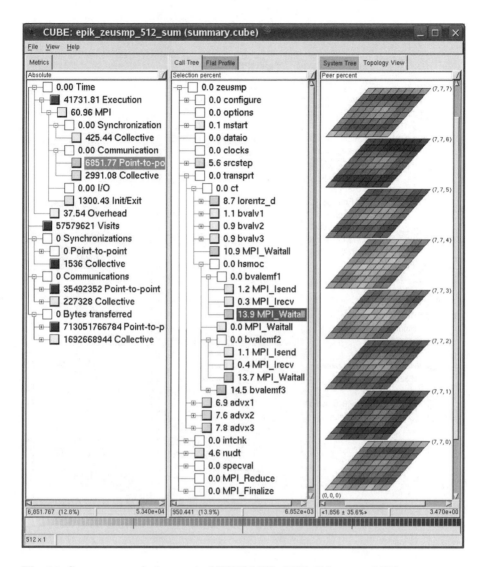

Fig. 10. SCALASCA analysis report of SPEC MPIm2007 *132.zeusmp2* 512-process execution runtime summarization experiment, showing unbalanced distribution of *Point-to-point Communication time* (left pane) on critical call-path to MPI_Waitall calls in function **bvalemf1** (central pane). Closed tree nodes show inclusive metric values (including child node values), whereas open tree nodes show exclusive metric values (excluding child values). Numerical metric values are also colour-coded according to the scale at the bottom. Values in each pane are accumulated from those in panes to the right, and selecting a metric or call-path sets that node's metric value as the focus for panes to the right. 12.8% of total execution time is MPI *Point-to-point Communication time*, 13.9% of which is in the MPI_Waitall calls from **bvalemf1**, with a 35.6% standard variation across the 512 processes, and highest values predominantly for processes in the 2nd and 7th z-planes of the application's $8 \times 8 \times 8$ Cartesian grid (right pane).

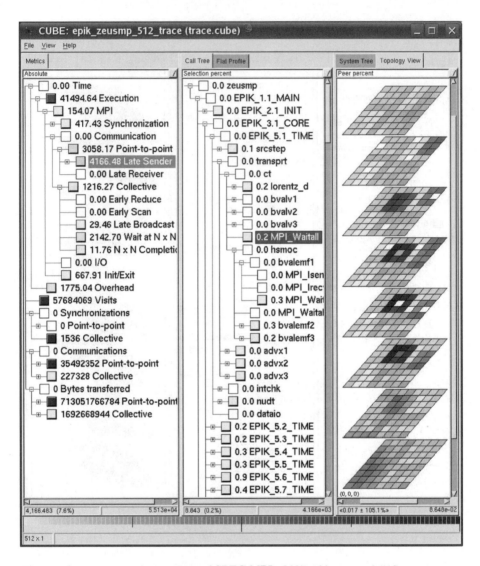

Fig. 11. SCALASCA analysis report of SPEC MPIm2007 *132.zeusmp2* 512-process execution tracing experiment, including manually inserted timestep annotations, showing unbalanced distribution of *Late Sender time* for the MPI_Waitall calls directly from function ct during the first timestep. 7.6% of total execution time is due to *Late Sender* situations, which is 57.7% of MPI *Point-to-point Communication time*. This varies considerably from timestep to timestep, and manifests as a 105.1% standard deviation in the MPI_Waitall calls in ct during the first timestep, localized to a small number of interior processes of the $8 \times 8 \times 8$ Cartesian grid.

highest values localized on certain processes, which can be determined from their locations within the $8 \times 8 \times 8$ Cartesian grid used by *132.zeusmp2*.

Additional insight into the origin of this imbalance in MPI *Point-to-point Communication* time can be derived from the automatic trace analysis report shown in Figure 11. Metrics which are only available from trace analysis show that inefficiencies are growing, e.g., *Late Sender* situations are now 57.7% of MPI *Point-to-point Communication time*. The additional timestep annotations distinguish the metric variation between timesteps, which is clearly considerable. Of more concern, however, is the huge variation between processes within each timestep, which is localized to relatively small numbers of interior processes.

3.4   Review of SCALASCA SPEC MPI2007 Benchmark Analyses

SPEC MPI2007 is a substantial suite of application kernels for testing the effectiveness of performance tools. By collecting and analyzing execution measurement experiments with 512 processes for each benchmark, the various SCALASCA measurement and analysis techniques have demonstrated that they scale well, and provide insight into significant performance problems. Annotating repetitive execution phases [12,13] and associated timeline charts of those phases [14] support deeper and clearer understanding of those performance issues, to determine which execution intervals and processes are affected. Although the analyses presented here concentrated on MPI communication and synchronization, metrics acquired from processor and network hardware counters can readily be incorporated in measurement experiments for a holistic view of execution performance [15].

Certain dubious coding constructs used in the SPEC MPI2007 applications, however, resulted in analysis problems. For example, a non-void function without an explicit return statement was incorrectly instrumented by the IBM XL compiler, such that exits were not matched with corresponding entry instrumentation. In these rare cases, the offending source code was modified and then the compiler generated correct instrumentation.

The analyses also identified oddities in some of the SPEC MPIm2007 benchmarks, e.g., *115.fds4* makes numerous calls to MPI_Waitall always with an empty list of requests. Although this is a valid test of MPI performance, simple application optimization would skip the MPI_Waitall call in such cases.

122.tachyon and *129.tera_tf* appear to scale perfectly, however, other SPEC MPI2007 applications show performance tailing off with larger numbers of processes, and the SCALASCA analyses at large scale provide crucial insight into the governing performance factors, as demonstrated with *132.zeusmp2*. For *137.lu*, *132.zeusmp2* and *126.lammps* the problem size is too small to scale to larger numbers of processes, or there are coded scalability limiters (enforced or implied). Clearly unacceptable scaling of *113.GemsFDTD* appears mainly to be due to its inefficient scheme for distributing data using broadcasts during initialization prior to the update loop.

4   Conclusions and Future Work

Applying established performance analysis techniques for phase annotation, event filtering, runtime summarization, event tracing and analysis presentation, via the SCALASCA toolset, to the SPEC MPI2007 benchmark suite applications has revealed a variety of complex execution behaviour and potential opportunities for performance improvement. Although 512 processes is a relatively modest scale for the current generation of HPC applications, the ability to collect and analyze measurements effectively from long-running, real-world applications was demonstrated.

With their limited scalability and significant process memory requirements, the SPEC MPIm2007 benchmarks are clearly not suitable for the largest 'leadership' computer systems, such as IBM BlueGene, Cray XT and Sun Constellation. When a 'large-sized' benchmark configuration becomes available, it will be interesting to repeat the SCALASCA analyses at the large-scale for which the toolset was designed and already validated with other HPC applications [16].

Automated classifications of equivalence groups of phases and processes with related behavioural characteristics are currently being investigated with the aim of making measurements and analyses more concise, and thereby more scalable. Future work will also examine how the presentation of such analyses can be scaled adequately for much larger numbers of processes (often in the tens of thousands) and integrated within the SCALASCA interactive analysis report explorer GUI.

References

1. Standard Performance Evaluation Corporation, SPEC MPI2007 benchmark suite, http://www.spec.org/mpi2007/
2. Müller, M.S., van Waveren, M., Lieberman, R., Whitney, B., Saito, H., Kalyan, K., Baron, J., Brantley, B., Parrott, C., Elken, T., Feng, H., Ponder, C.: SPEC MPI 2007 — An application benchmark for clusters and HPC systems. In: Proceedings of ISC 2007, Dresden, Germany (June 2007) (Also available as internal report ZIH-IR-0708, Technische Universität Dresden, Germany)
3. Müller, M.S.: Applying performance tools to real world applications. In: Proceedings of Seminar 07341 on Code Instrumentation for Massively Parallel Performance Analysis, Dagstuhl, Germany (September 2007)
4. Müller, M.S., Knüpfer, A., Jurenz, M., Lieber, M., Brunst, H., Mix, H., Nagel, W.E.: Developing scalable applications with Vampir, VampirServer and Vampir-Trace. In: Parallel Computing: Architectures, Algorithms and Applications, Proc. 12th ParCo Conf., Jülich/Aachen, vol. 15, pp. 637–644. IOS Press, Amsterdam (2008)
5. Fürlinger, K., Gerndt, M., Dongarra, J.: Scalability analysis of the SPEC OpenMP benchmarks on large-scale shared-memory multiprocessors. In: Shi, Y., van Albada, G.D., Dongarra, J., Sloot, P.M.A. (eds.) ICCS 2007. LNCS, vol. 4488, pp. 815–822. Springer, Heidelberg (2007)
6. Aslot, V., Eigenmann, R.: Performance characteristics of the SPEC OMP2001 benchmarks. In: Proc. 3rd European Workshop on OpenMP, EWOMP 2001, Barcelona, Spain (September 2001)

7. Saito, H., Gaertner, G., Jones, W., Eigenmann, R., Iwashita, H., Lieberman, R., van Waveren, M., Whitney, B.: Large system performance of SPEC OMP2001 benchmarks. In: Proc. Int'l Workshop on OpenMP Experiences and Implementations (WOMPEI 2002) (2002)
8. Wolf, F., Wylie, B.J.N., Ábrahám, E., Becker, D., Frings, W., Fürlinger, K., Geimer, M., Hermanns, M.-A., Mohr, B., Moore, S., Pfeifer, M., Szebenyi, Z.: Usage of the SCALASCA toolset for scalable performance analysis of large-scale parallel applications. In: Proc. 2nd Int'l Workshop on Tools for High Performance Computing, Stuttgart, Germany, Springer (July 2008) (to appear)
9. Wylie, B.J.N., Wolf, F., Mohr, B., Geimer, M.: Integrated runtime measurement summarization and selective event tracing for scalable parallel execution performance diagnosis. In: Kågström, B., Elmroth, E., Dongarra, J., Waśniewski, J. (eds.) PARA 2006. LNCS, vol. 4699, pp. 460–469. Springer, Heidelberg (2007)
10. Geimer, M., Wolf, F., Wylie, B.J.N., Mohr, B.: Scalable parallel trace-based performance analysis. In: Mohr, B., Träff, J.L., Worringen, J., Dongarra, J. (eds.) PVM/MPI 2006. LNCS, vol. 4192, pp. 303–312. Springer, Heidelberg (2006)
11. John von Neumann Institute for Computing, Jülich Multiprocessor IBM p690+ cluster, http://www.fz-juelich.de/jsc/jump
12. Wylie, B.J.N., Gove, D.J.: OMP AMMP analysis with Sun ONE Studio 8. In: Proc. 5th European Workshop on OpenMP EWOMP 2003, Aachen, Germany, September 2003, pp. 175–184. RWTH Aachen University (2003)
13. Malony, A.D., Shende, S.S., Morris, A.: Phase-based parallel performance profiling. In: Parallel Computing: Architectures, Algorithms and Applications, Proc. 11th ParCo Conf., Málaga, Spain, September 2005. NIC Series, vol. 33, pp. 203–210. John von Neumann Institute for Computing, Jülich, Germany (2005)
14. Fürlinger, K., Gerndt, M., Dongarra, J.: On using incremental profiling for the performance analysis of shared-memory parallel applications. In: Kermarrec, A.-M., Bougé, L., Priol, T. (eds.) Euro-Par 2007. LNCS, vol. 4641, pp. 62–71. Springer, Heidelberg (2007)
15. Wylie, B.J.N., Mohr, B., Wold, F.: Holistic hardware counter performance analysis of parallel programs. In: Parallel Computing: Architectures, Algorithms and Applications, Proc. 11th ParCo Conf., Málaga, Spain, September 2005. NIC Series, vol. 33, pp. 187–194. John von Neumann Institute for Computing, Jülich, Germany (2006)
16. Wylie, B.J.N., Geimer, M., Wolf, F.: Performance measurement and analysis of large-scale parallel applications on leadership computing systems. In: Scientific Programming, special issue on Large-scale Programming Tools and Environments. IOS Press, Amsterdam (to appear, 2008)
17. Jülich Supercomputing Centre, SCALASCA toolset for scalable performance analysis of large-scale parallel applications, http://www.scalasca.org/

Generating Probabilistic and Intensity-Varying Workload for Web-Based Software Systems*

André van Hoorn, Matthias Rohr, and Wilhelm Hasselbring

Software Engineering Group, University of Oldenburg, Germany
{van.Hoorn,Rohr,Hasselbring}@Informatik.Uni-Oldenburg.DE

Abstract. This paper presents an approach and a corresponding tool for generating probabilistic and intensity-varying workload for Web-based software systems. The workload to be generated is specified in two types of models. An application model specifies the possible interactions with the Web-based software system, as well as all required low-level protocol details by means of a hierarchical finite state machine. Based on the application model, the probabilistic usage is specified in corresponding user behavior models by means of Markov chains. Our tool Markov4JMeter implements our approach to probabilistic workload generation by extending the popular workload generation tool JMeter. A case study demonstrates how probabilistic workload for a sample Web application can be modeled and executed using Markov4JMeter.

1 Introduction

Web-based software systems, such as online shopping systems or auction sites, are large-scale software systems which users access through an interface provided by a Web server. These typically business-critical systems must satisfy contractually specified service level agreements, e.g., upper bounds on user-perceived response times with respect to certain load conditions. In order to systematically evaluate the performance, load tests are carried out: a software called *workload generator* mimics user behavior by submitting requests to the Web server; the performance of the software is monitored for later analysis [1]. Usually, such a workload generator either replays requests from recorded real-world workload or generates requests based on mathematical models [2]. In order to provide meaningful results, a key requirement for load tests is that the simulated user behavior is realistic, i.e., the *virtual users* behave like real users do.

The first part of this paper will present our approach for specifying and generating probabilistic workload for Web-based software systems based on mathematical models. The main elements of the workload specification are two types of models. An *application model* specifies the possible interactions with the Web-based software system, as well as all required low-level protocol details by

---

* This work is supported by the German Research Foundation (DFG), grant GRK 1076/1.

S. Kounev, I. Gorton, and K. Sachs (Eds.): SIPEW 2008, LNCS 5119, pp. 124–143, 2008.

means of a hierarchical finite state machine. By means of Markov chains, the probabilistic usage is specified in *user behavior models* corresponding to the application model. Moreover, our approach explicitly considers the specification of a varying workload intensity, i.e., the number of concurrent virtual users, within a single workload generation run. This allows to easily carry out long-term load tests with realistic workload intensity profiles. We will present the conceptual architecture of a workload generator which executes such specifications of probabilistic and intensity-varying workload. Based on our approach, we implemented the corresponding workload generation tool Markov4JMeter. Markov4JMeter extends the popular workload generator JMeter [3]. The resulting implementation and integration into JMeter are demonstrated in the second part of this paper. The case study of this paper illustrates how probabilistic workload for a sample Web application can be specified using our approach and how this specification can be executed with JMeter extended by Markov4JMeter.

The remainder of this paper starts with a summary of the background and related work in Section 2. A description of our workload generation approach including the workload specification and the conceptual workload generator is given in Section 3. Section 4 presents the implementation of Markov4JMeter and its integration into JMeter. As a case study, Section 5 demonstrates how Markov4JMeter is used to generate workload for a sample Web application. Our conclusions follow in Section 6.

2 Background and Related Work

Web-based software systems provide *services* through a Web interface using protocols like the Hypertext Transfer Protocol (HTTP) [4]. Each service can be considered a use case, e.g., signing on to the system or adding an item to the shopping cart. Invoking such a service requires submitting one or more parameterized lower-level protocol-specific *requests*. For example, in order to sign on, it is usually required to first request the corresponding HTML form and to submit the completed form including username and password in a second step. The HTTP request/response model is illustrated in Figure 1. A number of users concurrently accesses a Web-based system by submitting HTTP requests and waiting for the server response. Each user independently alternates between submitting a request and waiting for a time period called *think time* after it has received the server response. A *session* denotes the sequence of related request or service invocations issued by the same user [5].

In their workload generation approach, Barford and Crovella [2] introduced the ON/OFF model. Software processes called User Equivalents (UE) alternate between the two states ON (submit request and wait for the response) and OFF (think time period). We use the concept of UEs in our workload generation approach presented in Section 3.2. The UE concept is denoted as *user simulation thread* in this paper. A user simulation thread executes the workload model of a single virtual user.

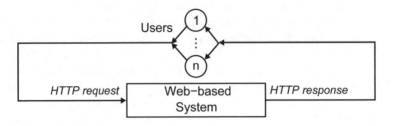

Fig. 1. Typical HTTP request/response model of a Web-based system that is concurrently accessed by n users

Markov chains are a common means for characterizing user behavior, e.g., for Web-based software systems [5] or in statistical software testing [6]. A Markov chain is a probabilistic finite state machine, i.e., each transition between two states is weighted with a probability. Menascé et al. [5] used Markov chains to model classes of user behavior within a session by so-called *Customer Behavior Model Graphs* (CBMG). The states of a CBMG represent service invocations. The CBMGs can be derived from Web server access logs using clustering algorithms [5]. Lee and Tian [7] showed that Markov chains provide fairly accurate models of Web usage. Ballocca et al. [8] derived user behavior in their workload generator from CBMGs. Based on the CBMGs by Menascé et al., Markov chains are the key elements of our user behavior models presented in Section 3.1.

According to Krishnamurthy et al. [9], we consider the class of *session-based systems*. In these systems, inter-requests dependencies exist, meaning that some requests within a session depend on requests submitted earlier during the same session. For example, a user must not submit an order without having added a single item to the shopping cart (and must not have removed all items from the cart later). Shams et al. [10] used so-called Extended Finite State Machines (EFSM) to model valid sequences of interactions with the application using conditional transitions between states and by explicitly considering the parameters to be passed with a submitted request. The application models defined in Section 3.1, specifying allowed sequences of service invocations within a session, were inspired by this work. However, they do differ from Shams et al.'s EFSMs in that the application model is separated into a logic session layer and an underlying technical protocol layer for abstraction purposes.

Peña-Ortiz et al. [11] provide an overview of outstanding and historical workload generators including an evaluation in terms of their features and capabilities. We explicitly modeled the workload generator on a conceptual level including the execution semantics and implemented the resulting tool Markov4JMeter as an extension for the popular workload generator JMeter [3].

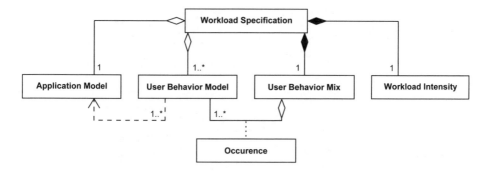

Fig. 2. Class diagram of the workload specification elements and their relations

3   Our Workload Generation Approach

Section 3.1 defines the workload specification including the probabilistic workload model. The conceptual architecture of the workload generation tool executing this workload specification is presented in Section 3.2.

3.1   Workload Specification

The workload specification for our probabilistic workload generation approach consists of the four elements listed below.

- An *application model*, specified as a hierarchical finite state machine.
- A number of corresponding *user behavior models*, each one specified as a Markov chain.
- A *user behavior mix*, specified as probabilities for the individual user behavior models to occur during workload generation.
- A definition of the *workload intensity*, specified as the (possibly varying) number of users to simulate during the experiment.

   The application model defines the *allowed* sequences of service invocations submitted within a user session and contains all protocol-level details required to generate valid requests. The actual order of service invocations is derived from probabilistic *user behavior models* corresponding to the application model. The workload generator combines the application model and the user behavior models into *probabilistic session models* based on which the requests are executed for each virtual user. This is described in Section 3.2. The *user behavior mix* defines with which probability each user behavior model occurs during workload generation. The *workload intensity* is a specification of the number of users to simulate during the experiment, given as a mathematical formula of the elapsed experiment time.

   These elements are described in detail in the remainder of this section. Figure 2 illustrates their multiplicities and relations among each other in a UML Class Diagram.

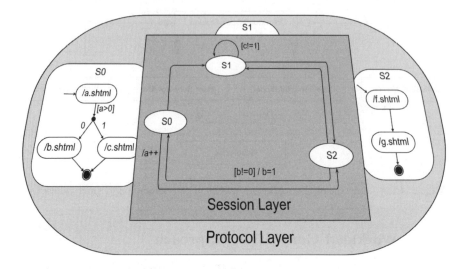

Fig. 3. Sample application model illustrating the separation into session layer and protocol layer

Application Model. An application model is a two-layered hierarchical finite state machine. It consists of a *session layer* modeling the valid sequences of service invocations within a user session and a *protocol layer* specifying the related protocol details. Figure 3 displays the illustrating example used in this section.

Session Layer. Each node on the session layer, called *application state*, corresponds to a service provided by the application. An edge between two states, called *application transition*, represents a valid sequence of service invocations within a session. Thus, our session layer corresponds to UML Protocol State Machines as they were introduced into version 2 of the UML standard [12].

Application transitions can be labeled with *guards* and *actions*. A guard is a boolean expression stating that a transition can only be taken if the expression evaluates to *true*. An action is a list of statements, such as variable assignments or function calls executed when a transition is taken.

The session layer in Figure 3 contains the states $S0$, $S1$, and $S2$ using the variables a, b, and c in the guards and actions. For example, a transition from state $S2$ to $S0$ is only possible if $b! = 0$ evaluates to true. When this transition fires, the variable b is assigned the value 1.

For the Web-based shopping system described in Section 5, we will demonstrate how variables, guards, and actions can be used in the application model to store additional state information during workload generation. For example, the session layer specifies that a customer must not submit a purchase request when no items are in the shopping cart. Whether an item has been added to the cart, is maintained in a dedicated variable.

Protocol Layer. Each application state has an associated finite state machine on the protocol layer. A state machine is executed when the related application state is entered. It models the sequence of protocol-level requests to be invoked. Analogous to the session layer, transitions may be labeled with guards and actions. Particularly, variables and functions can be used to assign request parameter values dynamically.

The state machine related to the application state $S0$ in Figure 3 contains the three protocol states *a.shtml*, *b.shtml*, and *c.shtml* which in this case correspond to URIs for HTTP requests. After the request for *a.shtml* has been submitted, the next state depends on the result of the evaluation of the expression $a > 0$ in the guard.

User Behavior Model. In addition to an application model, our workload specification requires the definition of one or more corresponding user behavior models. A user behavior model constitutes a probabilistic model of service invocation sequences within simulated user sessions, i.e., given the last application service invoked by a user, what is the probability for each service to be invoked next by this user. A class of similarly behaving users can be represented by a single user behavior model. Additionally, such model contains a specification of the *think time*, i.e., the time period between two consecutive protocol layer requests of the same user. For each virtual user, the workload generator submits requests based on a probabilistic session model which is a composition of the application model and one corresponding user behavior model. Section 3.2 explains the semantics of this composition in detail.

The key element of a user behavior model is a Markov chain, which can be considered a probabilistic finite state machine with a dedicated entry and a dedicated exit state. Each transition between two states is weighted with a probability. The sum of probabilities associated with all outgoing transitions of each state must be 1. Aside from the additional exit state, each state in our user behavior model's Markov chain corresponds to one application state on the session layer of the application model.

Formally, we define a user behavior model $\mathcal{B}_{A,i}$ for an application model A as a tuple $(S \cup \{\mathsf{Exit}\}, P, z_0, f_{tt})$. S denotes the set of states contained in the Markov chain with entry state $z_0 \in S$. The state Exit is the dedicated exit state which has no corresponding application state. P denotes the matrix containing the transition probabilities. The transition matrix of a Markov chain with n states $s_0 \ldots s_{n-1}$ is usually represented by an $n \times n$ matrix $P = [p_{i,j}]$. A value $p_{i,j}$ in the ith row and the jth column of the matrix P represents the transition probability from state s_i to s_j. The think time is specified as a probability distribution f_{tt}. For example when f_{tt} is assigned $N(300, 200^2)$, the think time is modeled according to the normal distribution $N(\mu, \sigma^2)$ with mean $\mu = 300\ ms$ and standard deviation $\sigma = 200\ ms$.

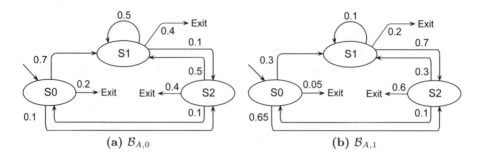

Fig. 4. Markov chains of two user behavior models corresponding to the application model in Figure 3

Figure 4 shows the Markov chains of two possible user behavior models $\mathcal{B}_{A,0}$ and $\mathcal{B}_{A,1}$ corresponding to the application model with application states $S0 \ldots S2$ shown in Figure 3. Both user behavior models $\mathcal{B}_{A,0}$ and $\mathcal{B}_{A,1}$ solely differ in their transition probabilities.

User Behavior Mix. The user behavior mix specifies with which probability each user behavior model included in the workload specification occurs during workload generation. For example, let one user behavior model represent a class of users which mainly browse through the product catalog of an online shopping store without buying anything, and let a second user behavior model represent a class of users which actually buy products during their visit. These two classes of users do not necessarily occur with the same probability in real workloads.

Formally, a user behavior mix for an application A is a set $\{(\mathcal{B}_{A,0}, p_0), \ldots, (\mathcal{B}_{A,n-1}, p_{n-1})\}$ assigning probabilities p_i to user behavior models $\mathcal{B}_{A,i}$. A tuple $(\mathcal{B}_{A,i}, p_i)$ states that user sessions based on the user behavior model $\mathcal{B}_{A,i}$ occur with the probability $p_i \in [0, 1]$ during workload generation. The sum of probabilities must be 1.

Workload Intensity. The workload intensity for an experiment is specified in terms of the number of active sessions, i.e., the number of virtual users being simulated concurrently. A generated session is considered *active* while the workload generator submits requests based on the corresponding probabilistic session model (the exit state of the Markov chain has not been reached). A function $n : \mathbb{R}_{\geq 0} \mapsto \mathbb{N}$ specifies this number $n(t)$ of active sessions relative to the elapsed experiment time t. Particularly, this allows for generating a varying workload intensity profile, e.g., based on measured workload data. Figure 5 shows the curve of a varying workload intensity specification for a workload generation experiment.

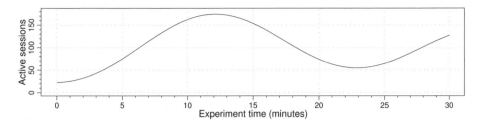

Fig. 5. Curve of a varying workload intensity specification for a workload generation experiment

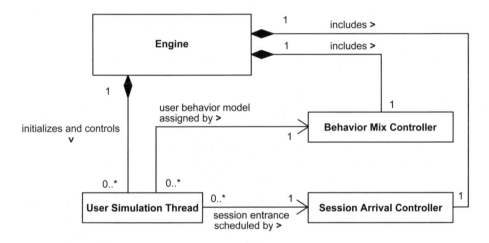

Fig. 6. Architecture of the conceptual workload generator

3.2 Workload Generation

This section describes the conceptual architecture of our workload generator. It consists of the following four components: a *workload generation engine*, a *behavior mix controller*, a *session arrival controller*, and a pool of *user simulation threads*. The workload generation engine initializes and controls the other components based on a workload specification as defined in the previous Section 3.1. Each user simulation thread periodically simulates a single user session based on probabilistic session models. The behavior mix controller assigns the user behavior models to the user simulation threads each time a new virtual user is to be simulated. The session arrival controller controls the number of active sessions according to the specified workload intensity. A more detailed description of the components, as well as the composition of the probabilistic session model and its execution, are given in the remainder of this section. Figure 6 shows the architecture including the four components and their relations as a UML Class Diagram.

User Simulation Threads. As described above, the workload generator contains a pool of user simulation threads, which are the executing entities during the workload generation. Each user simulation thread consecutively simulates users based on the specified application model and a corresponding user behavior model by executing the following steps in each iteration:

(1) Request a user behavior model from the behavior mix controller.
(2) Request the session arrival controller for a permission to execute a session.
(3) Execute the probabilistic session model which is a composition of the application model and the assigned user behavior model.

Behavior Mix Controller. The behavior mix controller controls the assignment of user behavior models to user simulation threads. Before starting the simulation of a new session, in step (1) listed above, a user simulation thread is assigned the user behavior model based on which the user simulation thread generates the workload. The probability of assigning each of the user behavior models is based on the user behavior mix which is part of the workload specification.

Session Arrival Controller. The session arrival controller controls the currently allowed number of active user sessions, i.e., the specified workload intensity, throughout the experiment. The controller provides a session entrance and exit protocol for the user simulation threads which is similar to the concept of synchronizing processes using semaphores [13].

 – The blocking operation *enterSession()* must be called by a user simulation thread when starting the simulation of a session for a new virtual user, i.e., in the above-listed step (2). The operation returns immediately if the current number of active sessions is lower than the current maximum number of active sessions specified in the workload intensity function. Otherwise, the user simulation thread gets blocked in a waiting queue until the number of active sessions falls below the specified number.
 – The non-blocking operation *exitSession()* must be called by a user simulation threads when the simulation of the probabilistic session model ends, i.e., after step (3). Thus, the number of active sessions is decremented by 1.

Probabilistic Session Model. As explained in Section 3.1, the application model defines the *allowed* sequences of service invocations submitted within a user session and contains all protocol-level details required to generate valid requests; the actual order of service invocations and the think times between two consecutive requests are specified in the *user behavior models* corresponding to the application model. An application model and a corresponding user behavior model are directly related by the application states and the states of the Markov chain. We mentioned, that the actual requests to the Web-based software system are generated by the user simulation threads which periodically execute a composition of the application model and a corresponding user behavior model – denoted a *probabilistic session model*. Now, we will define the semantics of this composition.

The composition of the application model and a user behavior model into a single probabilistic session model executed by a user simulation thread is performed straightforward by enriching the application transitions with the probabilities contained in the Markov chain of the user behavior model. Starting with the entry state z_0 defined in the user behavior model, a probabilistic session model is executed as follows. Given a current state, the next state is determined by first evaluating the guards of the outgoing transitions related to the current state. One of the transitions whose guards evaluate to *true* is randomly selected based on their assigned probabilities. The action of the selected transition is executed and the requests towards the application are submitted by traversing the deterministic state machine of the state within the protocol layer of the application model. A session ends when the determined transition leads to the Exit state of the user behavior model.

4 Tool for Generating Probabilistic and Intensity-Varying Workload

Based on the conceptual approach for generating probabilistic and intensity-varying workload presented in Section 3, we implemented a workload generation tool. Implementing such a tool from scratch would have required us to implement a bunch of low-level functionalities which do already exist in a number of workload generation tools (cf. [11] for an overview of existing tools). Instead, we integrated our approach into the popular open source workload generator Apache JMeter [3], and could thus focus on the implementation of those functionalities specific to our approach. Our extension, called Markov4JMeter, is freely available [14] under an open source license. The following Section 4.1 gives an overview of JMeter including relevant parts of its architecture. Section 4.2 describes the implementation of Markov4JMeter and the integration into JMeter. It is demonstrated how the sample workload specification used as the running example in Section 3 is defined in our workload generation tool.

4.1 Apache JMeter

Apache JMeter [3] is a Java-implemented workload generation tool for testing Web applications particularly in terms of performance. The workload is specified graphically in a so-called *Test Plan* which is a tree of *Test Elements*. The core Test Elements are *Logic Controllers* and *Samplers*. Logic Controllers, e.g., *If* and *While Controllers*, group Test Elements and define the control flow of a Test Plan when being executed. Samplers, such as *HTTP Request* or *FTP Request*, are located at the leafs of the tree and send the actual protocol-level requests. A test run can both be started by means of the graphical user interface (GUI) and from the command line using the non-GUI mode.

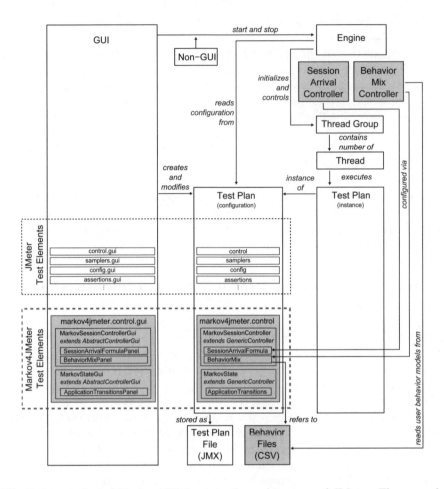

Fig. 7. Integration of Markov4JMeter into the architecture of JMeter. The gray elements are Markov4JMeter components.

The internal architecture of JMeter including the core components and their relations is illustrated in Figure 7 (the non-gray elements). The *Engine* is responsible for controlling the workload generation run. It initializes the *Thread Group* including the specified number of *Threads* (Java threads). Each Thread, represents a virtual user and executes an instance of the Test Plan. A Test Plan is internally represented by a tree of Test Element classes (Java classes) corresponding to the respective Test Elements in the Test Plan. Each Test Element class contains the implementation of the Test Element's behavior. Also, it has a corresponding GUI class providing the configuration dialog for the Test Element. Moreover, the GUI class is responsible for creating and modifying the Test Element classes. Test Plans including the configuration of the Test Elements are stored in JMX files, a JMeter-specific XML format.

4.2   Markov4JMeter

This section presents our JMeter extension called Markov4JMeter which allows for using JMeter to define and execute a workload specification according to the approach described in Section 3. A probabilistic workload specification as defined in Section 3.1 can be integrated into a JMeter Test Plan using the two additional Logic Controllers, *Markov Session Controller* and *Markov State*, added by Markov4JMeter. Moreover, Markov4JMeter includes a Session Arrival Controller and a Behavior Mix Controller corresponding to the components of the conceptual workload generator presented in Section 3.2. The remaining two components, workload generation engine and the pool of user simulation threads, could be mapped to the JMeter components Engine and Thread Group including the JMeter Threads. The Markov chains of the user behavior models are read from external comma-separated value (CSV) files. Figure 7 illustrates how the Markov4JMeter components are integrated into JMeter.

Session Controller. This Logic Controller constitutes the root of a probabilistic session model within a Test Plan. According to the JMeter Test Elements, the Markov Session Controller is divided into a Test Element class and a GUI class including the configuration dialog.

The Test Element class contains the implementation of the session model composition and execution as described in Section 3.2. In each iteration, i.e., each time a new session is to be simulated, the Markov Session Controller requests a behavior from the Behavior Mix Controller and requests the Session Arrival Controller to start the execution of this session. An iteration ends when the exit state of the behavior model is reached. The configuration dialog allows the definition of the behavior mix and the configuration of the Session Arrival Controller. A screenshot is shown in Figure 8(a). The behavior mix is defined by selecting the respective behavior files and specifying the desired probabilities. The formula defining the number of allowed active sessions during the test execution must evaluate to a positive integer.

Markov State. Markov State Test Elements are added directly underneath the Markov Session Controller. Each of these Logic Controllers represents an application state. Any subtree of JMeter Test Elements can be added to a Markov State representing the related deterministic state machine on the protocol layer of the application model. As the implementation of the Markov Session Controller, the Markov State is divided into a Test Element class and a GUI class.

The application transitions are configured within the configuration dialogs of the Markov States. Figure 8(b) shows the configuration of the application transitions starting in state $S2$ of the application model in Figure 3. The configuration dialog of the Test Element allows the definition of the state transitions with guards and actions using JMeter's variables and functions. The Markov State $S2$ in Figure 8(b) contains the HTTP Samplers *f.shtml* and *g.shtml* which are executed in this order according to the application model in Figure 3.

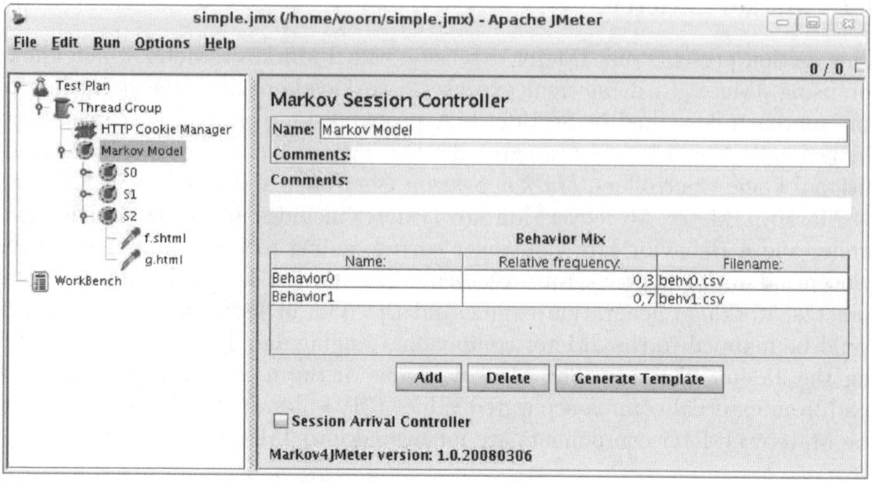

(a) Probabilistic Test Plan and configuration dialog of the Markov Session Controller including the definition of the user behavior mix

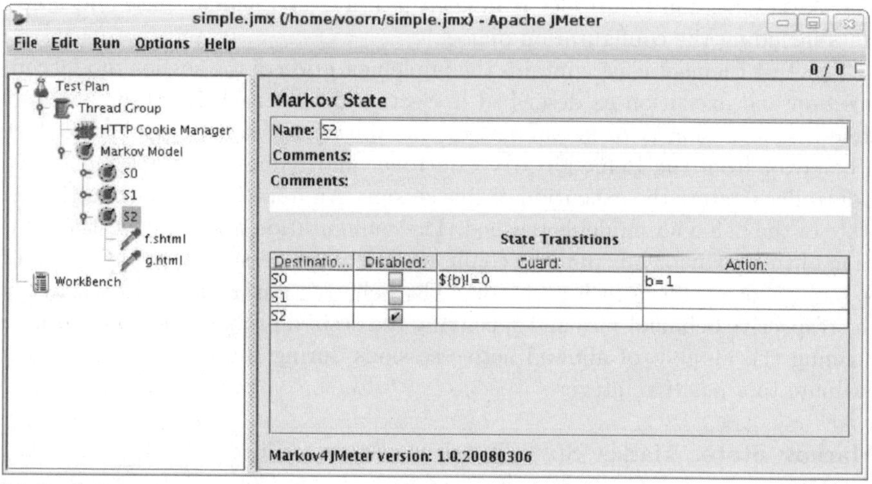

(b) Probabilistic Test Plan and configuration dialog of the Markov State $S2$. Disabling a transition is equivalent to a non-existing transition or to assigning a guard the value *false*.

Fig. 8. Screenshots showing the probabilistic Test Plan and configuration dialogs of the Markov Session Controller and a Markov State. The Test Plan corresponds to the example from Section 3.

Session Arrival Controller. According to Section 3.2, the Session Arrival Controller provides the methods *enterSession()* and *exitSession()* which are called by the Markov Session Controller before starting to execute a new session. Depending on the current number of active sessions and the configured workload intensity, a thread might get blocked until the session entrance is granted. The active sessions function is specified as a Java expression (using BeanShell[1]) which evaluates to an integer value. Markov4JMeter provides a variable for the elapsed experiment time. BeanShell scripts in external files can be used as well.

Behavior Mix Controller. As mentioned above, the Behavior Mix Controller assigns user behavior models to the Markov Session Controller based on the configured behavior mix. The models are read from the behavior files and converted into an internal representation which is passed to the Markov Session Controller. Figure 8(a) show a Behavior Mix Controller configuration with two user behavior models.

Behavior Files. The Markov chain of each user behavior model is stored in a comma-separated value (CSV) file which can be edited with any spreadsheet application. It contains the names of all Markov States underneath a Markov Session Controller. The configuration dialog of the Markov Session Controller allows to generate valid behavior templates for the current Test Plan. Figure 9 shows the behavior file of the user behavior model in Figure 4(a). Valid behavior file templates can be generated through the Markov Session Controller configuration dialog (see Figure 8(a)).

```
        ,   S0   ,   S1   ,   S2   ,    $
S0* ,  0.00  ,  0.70  ,  0.10  ,   0.20
S1   ,  0.00  ,  0.50  ,  0.10  ,   0.40
S2   ,  0.10  ,  0.50  ,  0.00  ,   0.40
```

Fig. 9. User behavior model of Figure 4(a) stored in CSV file format. The entry state of the model is marked with an asterisk (at most one). The column labeled with **$** represents the transition probability towards the exit state.

5   Case Study

This section demonstrates how probabilistic and intensity-varying workload for the iBATIS[2] JPetStore Web application can be specified using our approach and the corresponding tool Markov4JMeter, which have been presented in the previous Sections 3 and 4. Section 5.1 provides a basic overview of the JPetStore application. The workload specification following our approach presented in Section 3.1 is described in Section 5.2. Section 5.3 demonstrates how

---

[1] http://www.beanshell.org/
[2] http://ibatis.apache.org/

Markov4JMeter is used to create a JMeter Test Plan corresponding to this specification. Section 5.4 provides some interesting measurement results of workload generation runs which demonstrate the usefulness of our approach.

5.1   JPetStore

The iBATIS JPetStore is a Java Web application which represents an online shopping store that offers pets. An HTML Web interface provides access to the application. The product catalog is hierarchically structured into *categories*, e.g., "Dogs" and "Cats". Categories contain *products* such as a "Bulldog". Products contain the actual *items*, e.g., "Male Adult Bulldog", which can be added to the virtual shopping cart, the content of which can later be ordered after having signed on to the application and having provided the required personal data, such as the shipping address and the credit card number.

5.2   Workload Specification

In order to define an application model including the session layer and the protocol layer underneath (cf. Section 3.1), we identified 29 protocol request types provided by JPetStore on the HTTP protocol level. These request types were categorized into 15 application services. We selected a subset of 9 services and the corresponding 13 request types considered part of a "typical" user session. The application transitions of the application model's session layer were defined based on the hyperlinks being present on the Web pages of the JPetStore. For example, by entering the application state *Home*, the server would return the JPetStore index page. This page provides hyperlinks to the product categories, to the shopping cart, to the index page itself, and allows to sign on or off.

Figure 10(a) shows the session layer of the application model which contains the 9 application states. The variables *signedOn* and *itemInCart* are used to store additional state information. A user can only sign on and sign off if the value of the variable *signedOn* is *false* or *true*, respectively. The variable *itemInCart* is assigned the value *true* when an item is added to the shopping cart. A transition to the state *Purchase* can only be selected when a user has signed on and has added at least one item in the shopping cart.

The protocol layer is specified based on the 13 considered HTTP request types. For each request type we determined its required HTTP request method, the URI, and parameters to be passed on an invocation. The protocol state machines corresponding to the application states *Sign On* and *Purchase* are shown in Figure 10(b). In order to sign on, a user first invokes an HTTP request of type *signonForm* using the HTTP protocol method GET. The server returns a form asking for a username and a password. In a subsequent invocation, the user passes the filled in data of the completed form by invoking the HTTP request type *signon*. The variables *userId* and *password* are used as placeholders for the username and password. The protocol state machine of the application state *Purchase* shows the sequence of HTTP requests to be executed when purchasing. We omitted the HTTP protocol details for this state.

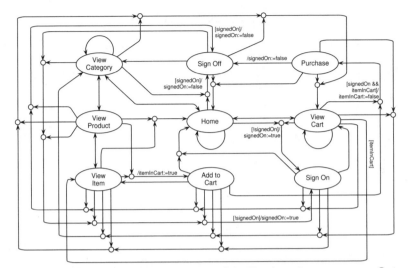

(a) Session layer of the application model. The junction connector ◯ is used to combine a set of transitions from multiple states to the same destination state (label considered label of all transitions in this set).

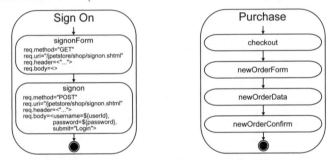

(b) Protocol state machines for two application states

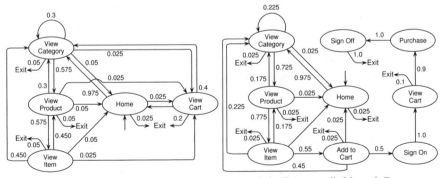

(c) Markov chains of the user behavior models *Browser* (left) and *Buyer*

Fig. 10. The application model (the session layer displayed in (a); two of the nine protocol-layer state machines displayed in (b)) and the two user behavior models (c) specified for the JPetStore

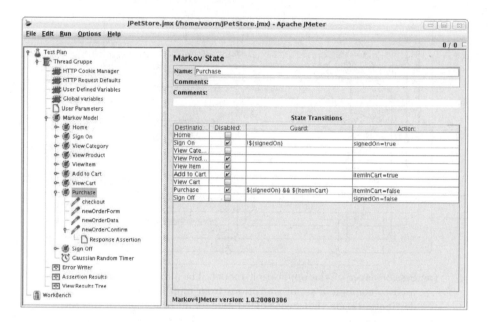

Fig. 11. Probabilistic Test Plan for the JPetStore (corresponding to the underlying formal workload specification displayed in Figure 10) and the transition configuration of the Markov State *Purchase*

We defined one user behavior model representing users solely browsing through the JPetStore and a second one where users tend to actually buy items from the store. The Markov chains of both models are displayed in Figure 10(c). For both models we specified a think time distribution $f_{tt} = N(300, 200^2)$ which is a parameterized normal distribution with mean $\mu = 300$ and standard deviation $\sigma = 200$, both values given in milliseconds.

5.3　Test Plan

As explained in Section 4.2, we created a probabilistic Test Plan for the JPetStore application model and the two user behavior models presented in the previous Section 5.2 using the additional Markov4JMeter Logic Controllers, Markov Session Controller and Session Arrival Controller. The Test Plan, as well as the configuration dialog of the Markov State *Purchase* including the definition of the application transitions, are shown in Figure 11. The active sessions function is configured to be read from an external BeanShell script. A Random Timer Test Element provides the think time.

Identifiers for categories, products, and items are randomly selected using a dedicated Markov4JMeter function before the respective request is submitted. Assertions are inserted to detect application errors which are not reflected in HTTP error codes. The server response of some requests is parsed for specific text strings in order to make sure that the requests have been processed correctly

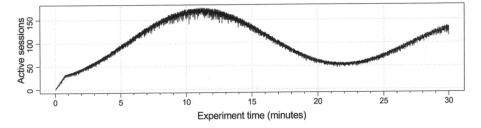

Fig. 12. Measured number of active sessions during a probabilistic and intensity-varying workload generation run. The workload intensity was specified according to the curve shown in Figure 5.

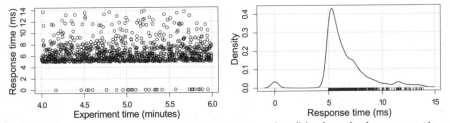

Fig. 13. Scatter plot (a) and probability density plot (b) of method response times measured during a workload generation run with probabilistic workload and a constant workload intensity

by the JPetStore. For example, after having signed on, the returned Web page must contain the string "Welcome" as well as a hyperlink labeled "Sign Out". "Thank you, your order has been submitted" must appear after having confirmed the order.

5.4 Measurement Results

Markov4JMeter has been used in a large number of workload generation experiments with the JPetStore and the workload specification described in the previous sections for the experimental evaluation of our research in the domains of performance evaluation [15], anomaly detection and automatic fault localization [16], as well as runtime reconfiguration of component-based software systems [17]. In this section we give two interesting measurement results of separate workload generation runs to demonstrate the usefulness of our approach.

Figure 12 displays a curve of the measured number of active sessions during a 30-minute workload generation run. The workload intensity was specified according to the curve shown in Figure 5. The number of active sessions was extracted from the Web server access logs. Markov4JMeter shows the expected behavior and varies the workload intensity following the input specification. The jitter is caused by the measurement granularity (1 ms) and the queueing implementation in the Session Arrival Controller.

For another experiment, Figure 13 shows the response time scatter plot and the corresponding probability density plots of the Java method *addItemToCart*. A constant workload intensity of 55 active sessions was specified for the entire run. As indicated by its name, the method *addItemToCart* is always executed when a users adds an item to the virtual shopping cart. The plots show that sporadically significantly lower response times for method executions occur. We found out that these low response times occur when a user adds an item with the same identifier to the cart more than once within the same session. This only requires a counter to be incremented. It is very likely that these low response times would not have been uncovered without our probabilistic workload and the random selection of item identifiers as described in Section 5.3.

6   Conclusions

This paper demonstrated our approach for specifying and generating probabilistic and intensity-varying workload for Web-based software systems. The workload specification provides a clean separation between application-specific details including the specification of allowed sequences of service invocations and all protocol-level details required to generate valid requests with the required technical details, as well as the corresponding models of probabilistic usage based on Markov chains. We presented a conceptual workload generator which generates workload based on the described specification. By including the specification of the (possibly varying) workload intensity, long-term load tests with realistic workload intensity profiles can be performed.

The corresponding workload generation tool Markov4JMeter has been implemented as an extension for the popular workload generator Apache JMeter. By being based on JMeter, probabilistic workload specifications for any protocol supported by JMeter can be executed. In a case study, we applied the workload generation technique to the JPetStore Web application by first specifying the underlying workload model and then creating the Test Plan executable by JMeter extended by Markov4JMeter.

Markov4JMeter is freely available at [14]. It is being used to generate probabilistic and intensity-varying workload for the evaluation of research in the domain of software timing behavior evaluation, anomaly detection and automatic fault localization, as well as runtime reconfiguration of component-based software systems.

References

1. Menascé, D.A.: Load testing of web sites. IEEE Internet Computing 6(4), 70–74 (2002)
2. Barford, P., Crovella, M.: Generating representative web workloads for network and server performance evaluation. In: Proceedings of the ACM SIGMETRICS, pp. 151–160. ACM, New York (1998)
3. Apache Software Foundation: JMeter, http://jakarta.apache.org/jmeter/

4. Fielding, R., Gettys, J., Mogul, J., Frystyk, H., Masinter, L., Leach, P., Berners-Lee, T.: Request for comment (RFC) 2616: Hypertext Transfer Protocol – HTTP (1999)
5. Menascé, D.A., Almeida, V.A.F., Fonseca, R., Mendes, M.A.: A methodology for workload characterization of e-commerce sites. In: Proceedings of the ACM Conference on Electronic Commerce (EC 1999), pp. 119–128. ACM, New York (1999)
6. Whittaker, J.A., Thomason, M.G.: A markov chain model for statistical software testing. IEEE Transactions on Software Engineering 20(10), 812–824 (1994)
7. Li, Z., Tian, J.: Testing the suitability of markov chains as web usage models. In: Proceedings of the 27th International Conference on Computer Software and Applications (COMPSAC 2003), pp. 356–361. IEEE, Los Alamitos (2003)
8. Ballocca, G., Politi, R., Ruffo, G., Russo, V.: Benchmarking a site with realistic workload. In: Proceedings of the 5th IEEE International Workshop on Workload Characterization (WWC-5), pp. 14–22. IEEE, Los Alamitos (2002)
9. Krishnamurthy, D., Rolia, J.A., Majumdar, S.: A synthetic workload generation technique for stress testing session-based systems. IEEE Transactions on Software Engineering 32(11), 868–882 (2006)
10. Shams, M., Krishnamurthy, D., Far, B.: A model-based approach for testing the performance of web applications. In: Proceedings of the International Workshop on Software Quality Assurance (SOQUA 2006), pp. 54–61. ACM, New York (2006)
11. Peña-Ortiz, R., Sahuquillo, J., Pont, A., Gil, J.A.: Modeling continuous changes of the user's dynamic behavior in the WWW. In: Proceedings of the 5th International Workshop on Software and Performance (WOSP 2005), pp. 175–180. ACM, New York (2005)
12. Arlow, J., Neustadt, I.: UML 2 and the Unified Process: Practical Object-Oriented Analysis and Design, 2nd edn. Addison-Wesley, Reading (2005)
13. Dijkstra, E.W.: Cooperating sequential processes. In: Genuys, F. (ed.) Programming Languages, Academic Press, London (1965)
14. van Hoorn, A.: Markov4JMeter, http://markov4jmeter.sourceforge.net/
15. van Hoorn, A.: Workload-sensitive timing behavior anomaly detection in large software systems (September 2007), Master's thesis (Diplomarbeit), Department of Computing Science, University of Oldenburg, Germany
16. Rohr, M.: Workload-sensitive Timing Behavior Anomaly Detection for Automatic Software Fault Localization. PhD thesis, Department for Computing Science, University of Oldenburg, Oldenburg, Germany (2008) (work in progress)
17. Matevska, J., Hasselbring, W.: A scenario-based approach to increasing service availability at runtime reconfiguration of component-based systems. In: Proceedings of the 33rd Euromicro Conference on Software Engineering and Advanced Applications (SEAA), pp. 137–144. IEEE, Los Alamitos (2007)

Comparison of the SPEC CPU Benchmarks with 499 Other Workloads Using Hardware Counters

Lodewijk Bonebakker

Sun Microsystems Laboratories,
Menlo Park, CA, USA
lodewijk.bonebakker@sun.com
http://research.sun.com

Abstract. This work extends an existing workload comparison approach used for simulation based metrics to computer system based metrics. We apply this approach using processor hardware counters and compare characterizations of SPEC CPU2000 and SPEC CPU2006, against real (commercial) workloads and other benchmarks collected on the same computer system architecture. Using Independent Component analysis we reduce the many dimensional workload characterization space into a lesser dimensional representative space prior to comparing the distribution of workloads. We find that the SPEC CPU benchmarks are for the most part representative on the identified principal components, with notable exceptions.

Keywords: SPEC CPU2000, SPEC CPU2006, workload characterization, workloads, benchmark, comparison.

1 Introduction and Outline

The SPEC CPU benchmark suites are one of the most successful and authoritative benchmark suites available. Nearly every vendor of computer systems and processors publishes results on SPEC CPU. SPEC is a collaboration of industry and academia, and benchmarks are selected from candidates submitted by industry, academia and other interested parties. For each revision of the SPEC CPU benchmark, interested parties are asked to submit candidate workloads. During the selection process the SPEC workgroup has to balance competing commercial interests to retain a broad set of benchmarks thought to be broadly representative of the computing space. SPEC maintains as goal SPEC CPU's relevance as a trusted means of comparing processor performance on compute intensive applications [1].

While the representativeness of SPEC CPU is assumed, given the involved process of selecting component benchmarks, there is little evidence in the scientific literature to either support or challenge it. A few comparisons have been made evaluating SPEC CPU and other benchmark representativeness for specific areas like mobile computing or multi-media applications [2,3] and (for an older version of SPEC CPU) with commercial applications [4]. Much of this earlier

S. Kounev, I. Gorton, and K. Sachs (Eds.): SIPEW 2008, LNCS 5119, pp. 144–153, 2008.
© Springer-Verlag Berlin Heidelberg 2008

work concentrates on specific workload characteristics like cycles per instruction, branch mis-prediction rates and cache hit-ratios. The popularity of SPEC CPU and its position as *de facto* standard raises concerns regarding its use and abuse in computer system architecture evaluation [5].

In this work we extend an existing method for determining similarity between simulated workloads to use system data. This approach was first introduced in [6], and adopted and extended since, see for example [7,8,9]. This approach was applied to the question of benchmark subsetting, with the aim of reducing the number of benchmarks under consideration without losing generality [10]. [8,9] examine similarity within SPEC CPU2000 and their results indicate that there exists considerable redundancy within SPEC CPU2000. Novel in our approach is that we rely exclusively on processor hardware counters to provide the information with which we perform our comparison and similarity analysis.

Modern computer processors have a rich set of on-chip registers that can be used to track processor events. We concentrate on workloads characterized on the UltraSPARC III+^{TM} processor, running at 900 MHz. We compare SPEC CPU2000 and SPEC CPU2006 against a set of 447 commercial workloads and 52 common benchmarks. These workloads include databases, web-servers, high-performance computing, and span the diversity of customers of Sun Microsystems, Inc. Workload characterization was performed by collecting processor hardware counter and operating system statistics made available through the Solaris^{TM} operating system on UltraSPARC III+ based computer systems.

The outline is as follows; In Section 2 we describe our workload set, both SPEC CPU2000, SPEC CPU2006 and the commercial workloads and benchmarks. In Section 3 we describe our data collection and reduction process. Section 4 describes dimensionality reduction of our data-set, constructs the workload space for comparison and presents the data. In Section 5 we discuss observations made during evaluation. In Section 6 we summarize and make recommendations for future research.

2 Workload Set Composition

Our set of 1089 workloads consists of 260 SPEC CPU2000 and 330 SPEC CPU2006 characterizations, combined with a further 447 collected commercial workloads and 52 other benchmarks. For both SPEC CPU2000 and SPEC CPU2006 a full set of workload characterizations of SPEC CPU *rate* were collected for 1,2,4,8 and 12 processors. The system used was an Sun Fire^{TM}4800, with 12 UltraSPARC III+ processors at 900MHz, with 8MB of cache and 24GB of total memory. The system has three processor memory boards, each with 4 processors and 8 GB of RAM. During runs with fewer than 12 processors the unneeded processors were deactivated.

We used the Sun Studio^{TM}11 compilers, the recommended compiler options and optimizations and compared our achieved SPEC numbers, both base, peak and rate, with those posted for the same processor type and clock speed on the SPEC website [1]. We found that our results, with our workload characterization instrumentation included, differed by less than 1% from the published results.

The commercial workloads and other benchmarks were collected in the benchmark centers at Sun Microsystems, Inc. These commercial workloads reflect a cross-section of workloads common to customers of Sun Microsystems, Inc. Workloads include, SAP, ORACLE, PeopleSoft and Siebel database and application server workloads; data warehouse and decision support workloads like SAS, supply chain management suites like Manugistics, high performance computing applications like Fluent and Linpeak as well as Java, cryptography and message broker applications. The other benchmarks are for example SPECweb{99, 99SSL, 2005}, SPECjAppServer{2001, 2002, 2004}, TPC-C and TPC-W. Overall the collected commercial workloads and other benchmarks cover a large segment of the workload space. An even larger number of workloads were collected on a range of UltraSPARC III+ processors with clock speeds of either 900MHz, 1050MHz, or 1200MHz, but we limit ourselves to only workloads collected on systems with 900MHz processors.

While processing the collected workloads, we encountered many iterations, up to 12 in one case, of the same application. During subsequent analysis we found that in many cases the iterations differed not only by role (application server, database server, client), system composition (number of processors) and tuning, but also by data-set. Based on results from [11], we consider the combination of an application with a data-set to be a distinct workload. Subsequently, the 447 collected workloads are based on 97 unique applications and 248 distinct data-set combinations.

3   Data Collection and Reduction

To collect data in a standardized manner from all systems involved, we used a measurement script WCSTAT [12], which is internal to Sun Microsystems, Inc. This script standardizes data collection by specifying the sequence and duration in which data collection utilities are run. WCSTAT performs data collection in two phases, first the standard system utilities for 600 seconds, followed by 900 seconds of hardware counter sampling. These two phases are designed to minimize measurement tool impact on the collected workload data. The disadvantage of this two phase approach is that the workload under study must be stable for the full 1500 seconds of measurement [11]. This defines our stability criterion, since the workload cannot have significant deviations of behavior during measurement, otherwise we risk misrepresenting workload behavior. [13] provides an analysis of expected sampling accuracy.

Within WCSTAT the operating system utilities vmstat, iostat, mpstat, and netstat are used to characterize workload at the operating system level. The hardware counters are sampled using cpustat, and for convenience all (with the exception of two user defined) hardware counters are sampled. The UltraSPARC III+ has two hardware counter registers, so only two hardware counters can be sampled at any given time. To sample the full set of available hardware counters, the registers are set to a specific hardware counter context and sampled for one second. After reading the registers, cpustat selects the next hardware counter context. This allows us to sample all hardware counters in about 32 seconds of measurement. Overall the 900 second measurement interval gives us circa 28 measurements per hardware counter context. This further emphasizes why workload stability is an essential requirement for this work. In order to achieve this workload stability while measuring the SPEC CPU2000 benchmarks, we repeated the benchmark throughout the full 1500 seconds of measurement. We made sure that no start-up effects impacted data collection on the SPEC CPU benchmarks. The longer duration of the SPEC CPU2006 benchmarks usually did not require repeated runs. Based on prior observations of the SPEC CPU2006 component benchmarks, we chose to use the first 1800 seconds as representative of the whole benchmark. In a prior effort we fully characterized SPEC CPU2006 for the duration of each component benchmark, but corruption of the data-set prior to processing necessitated this shortcut.

For each workload, the measured data are stored in a collection of text files, each with their own specific format. We use a JAVA based application to parse each data file and upload the results into tables of a database. Each column of measured data maps to a table in the database. The database preserves the original measured values and their timestamps relative to start of measurement, allowing cross-referencing of any anomalous events.

Measured data are not ready for analysis. From our raw data-set of 1292 collected workloads we removed those cases where either the workload was not in steady state or we suspected interference from our measurements. A full discussion of the rejection criteria and their validation is beyond the scope of this paper, but we follow the procedure discussed in [11]. In short: steady state verification is based on statistical trend analysis. If there is sufficient evidence of a trend, the workload is rejected. We proceed with the remaining workloads. We standardize the collected data to a single processor and scale to a cycle count of one billion cycles per second. After scaling we standardize on instruction count. The reduced data are now ready for analysis. In total 1292 workloads were measured but the stability requirement rejected 203, leaving a data-set of 1089 workloads. Of these accepted workloads, 260 are SPEC CPU2000, 330 are SPEC CPU2006, 447 are commercial workloads and 52 are other benchmarks.

4   Dimensionality Reduction and Workload Comparison

We have 1089 workloads with each 72 metrics. These 72 metrics include system metrics from `iostat`, `vmstat`, `netstat`, and `mpstat`. Since we want to understand SPEC CPU representativeness, we accept only `cpustat` based metrics from our data-set. This reduces the total number of metrics under consideration to 46. As mentioned before, these metrics reflect the hardware counters available on the UltraSPARC III+ processor. For example [14], CYCLECNT, DCRD, DCRDMISS, DCWR, DCWRMISS, DISPATCH02NDBR, ..., ECICMISS, ECMISSES, ECRDMISS, ..., FAPIPECOMPLETION, FMPIPECOMPLETION, ICMISS, ICMISSCANCELLED, ICREF, INSTRCNT, ... , PCSNOOPINV, ..., SISNOOP, WCMISS, WCSCRUBBED, WCSNOOPCB, WCWBWOREAD. It is our goal to make qualitative statements regarding the similarity of these workloads based on the hardware counters, and we define similarity to be the same as proximity in a N-dimensional workload space. We now need to construct such a workload space. The first step is to normalize the metrics used and then apply dimensionality reduction.

We use a log-based standardization to accommodate the large differences in magnitude within the data-set. We standardize using $x' = \log(x + 1)$ and then normalize, $\mathbf{x'} = \frac{\mathbf{x} - \mu_{\mathbf{x}}}{\sigma_{\mathbf{x}}}$, following [15]. The latter step normalizes the log-standardized data around the origin. We note that the hardware counters rarely measured less than 100 events over the 1-second sample interval, thus the error introduced by $x + 1$ is small.

The large number of measured metrics and the presence of strong correlations between some of these metrics, make the use of dimensionality reduction techniques a practical necessity. Dimensionality reduction techniques reduce the number of dimensions under consideration with little or no loss of information. From the literature [8,9,10,16], we expect our set of 46 metrics to contain a significant amount of redundancy. The same literature uses either *Principal Component Analysis* [8,9,10] or *Independent Component Analysis* [16] as their primary means of reducing the many-dimensional data-set into a lesser dimensional set without throwing away information.

Principal Component Analysis (PCA) [17] is the common choice. PCA reduces dimensionality through a linear transformation that transforms the data to a new coordinate system such that the variance projections of the data comes to lie along coordinates [17]. The greatest variance is projected on the first coordinate and is named the first principal component, the second greatest variance

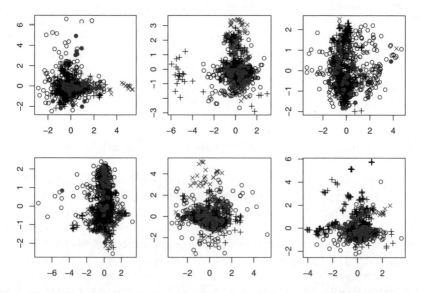

Fig. 1. The 12 Independent Components, normalized for instructions, plotted pairwise. Legend: ○ workloads, ● benchmarks, × SPEC CPU2000, + SPEC CPU2006).

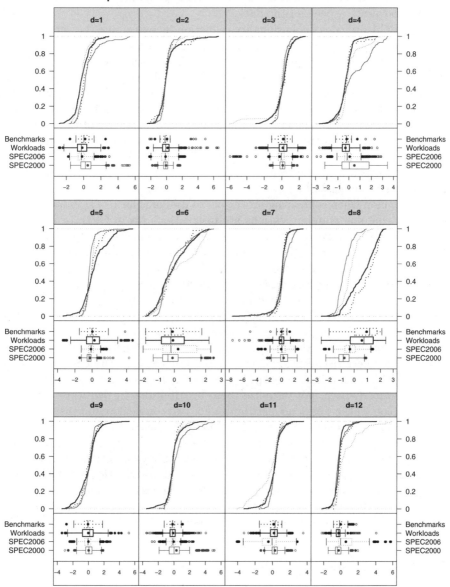

Fig. 2. Cumulative distribution plot along each dimension of the reduced data-set for SPEC CPU2000, SPEC CPU2006, the real workloads and the other benchmarks. Metrics standardized per processor instruction.

on the second coordinate, and so on. PCA can be used for dimensionality reduction in a data-set while retaining those characteristics of the data-set that contribute most to its variance, by keeping lower-order principal components and ignoring higher-order ones. Such low-order components often contain the "most important" aspects of the data.

While PCA provides dimensionality reduction by explaining the variance, *Independent Component Analysis* [17,18,19], uncovers the underlying data components. Independent component analysis (ICA) is a method for finding underlying factors or components from multivariate (multidimensional) statistical data. What distinguishes ICA from other methods is that it looks for components that are both statistically independent, and nongaussian [19]. The method finds the independent components by maximizing the independence of the estimated components. Based on the work in [11] we select ICA to reduce the dimensionality of our data-set, specifically we use *FastICA* [20] as implemented in **R** [21]. We use PCA as a heuristic to determine the likely number of ICA dimensions, a pre-requisite for *FastICA*.

It is common when comparing processors to use some form of standardization. The most common standardizations are instructions (as in CPI), or cycles (as in IPC). For brevity we evaluate only for per instruction standardization (CPI). After applying standardization, normalization and dimension reduction, we are left with a reduced, 12 dimensional workload space.

We present the collected data and evaluate the degree to which the SPEC CPU2000 and SPEC CPU2006 benchmark collections represent the other workloads. SPEC CPU aims to be representative of compute intensive workloads that stress the processor and memory hierarchy. Since many of the collected workloads and benchmarks exhibit significant I/O and coherence traffic, we expect to find differences between SPEC CPU and the collected workloads and other benchmarks. These differences will be visible in the coverage and distribution in the workload space. We visualize these distributions in two ways - first we make 2D plots of the workload distribution for two consecutive dimensions in the workload space, plotted in Figure 1. Anomalies in the distribution are visible as differences in locality. Second we compare the cumulative distribution functions for SPEC CPU2000, SPEC CPU2006 and the remaining workload and benchmarks with each other, plotted in Figure 2. Differences in distribution will be emphasized in the cumulative distributions and their respective barplots, allowing us to see where differences in distribution are most pronounced. This approach was inspired by the two-sided Kolmogorov-Smirnov test [22].

5   Observations

We show that in the reduced workload space SPEC CPU does not provide full representativeness. This result should not be unexpected. The workloads and other benchmarks, *e.g.*, TPC-C, SPECjAppServer, contain significantly more I/O and coherence traffic than the single threaded, processor centric SPEC CPU benchmarks. Next we investigate if any of the observed effects are due to data artifacts and workload selection effects.

The collection of real workloads runs the gamut from database workloads and web-servers to the high performance workloads found on today's largest clusters.

We believe that while we may not have fully captured the correct quantitative distribution of all workloads in our data-set, we have captured their diversity. Looking at the distributions, specifically the barplots for the different standardizations, it is clear that dynamic range is also a good indicator of population differences. Both distribution and dynamic range cannot easily be argued away as just a population artifact, since 447 is considered an adequate sample for many populations. What is clear from Figure 2 is that the set of collected benchmarks more accurately represents the collected workloads than SPEC CPU. We use this as a bootstrap validation to show that this approach can make sufficient distinction.

The next issue is that of data transformation, why did we chose ICA instead of the more commonly used and easier to understand PCA? Where PCA explains variance with each principal component, ICA reveals the hidden factors that underlie the structure of the data. PCA would have given the maximum correlations between the different processor hardware counters. Based on the evaluation in [11] showing that ICA has better distinctive properties when used on hardware counter data, we chose ICA to extract the hidden factors explaining the structure of the data. The downside of using ICA is that it is much harder to relate the independent components back to physical artifacts in the original system. A related issue is the use of dimensionality reduction in the first place. We believe that the many dimensions of our original data-set and the multitude of hidden, non-linear relations between the underlying metrics, make it impossible to do any meaningful research *without* dimensionality reduction.

We note that there are also considerable differences between SPEC CPU2006 and SPEC CPU2000, see for example $d = 1, 4, 5, 8$ in Figure 2. Relating this back to the remarks by Citron in [5], we can see how cherry picking workloads from SPEC CPU, instead of using the whole set, can greatly impact coverage and subsequently representativeness on the important characteristics. Inversely, if we have workload characterization data on the workloads SPEC CPU aims to represent, we can quantitatively determine a representative sets for each processor under consideration. The approach followed in this work can easily be ported to different platforms, requiring only a mechanism for sampling the hardware counter registers during benchmark execution. Taking the cross-section of these sets could then be used to construct a new SPEC CPU benchmark. The representativeness of the chosen cross-section can then immediately be quantitatively evaluated for all contributing processors and metrics of interest.

6   Summary and Conclusions

In this work we have presented an approach that uses metrics readily obtainable from real computer systems to provide a quantitative evaluation of representativeness between chosen sets of workloads. Using a standardized measurement setup, we characterized a total of 1089 workloads, 260 characterizations of SPEC CPU2000 component benchmarks, 330 characterizations of SPEC CPU2006 component benchmarks, and a set of 447 real workloads and 52 other benchmarks.

The workloads run the gamut from database and web-server workloads to popular high performance computing workloads, while the other benchmarks contain benchmarks like TPC-C, TPC-W and SPECjAppServer{2001,2002,2004}. Each workload is described using 72 metrics, of which 46 are hardware counters. Before comparison, the metrics are standardized by instructions, and then log-normalized. The dimensionality of the data-set is reduced using Independent Component Analysis and evaluation takes place in this reduced workload space by examining the distribution properties for the different workload sets.

We have applied the approach to a set of 1089 workloads and evaluated the representativeness of SPEC CPU and the benchmarks relative to the other 499 workloads using only the hardware counters. We showed that for most independent components in the reduced workload space SPEC CPU is representative, but that there are distinct cases were SPEC CPU is not representative. We believe that the I/O and coherency behavior of the workload population explains the difference. The included sample of other benchmarks is found to be more representative of the workload sample.

This approach is efficient and may be used to evaluate representativeness of a subset of workloads or benchmarks relative to a larger population. Inversely, this approach can be used to quantitatively select a representative set of benchmarks for a given population of workloads. Future research should evaluate if and how this approach can be adapted for use in the creation of the next generation SPEC CPU.

References

1. Standard Performance Evaluation Corporation, http://www.spec.org/
2. Diefendorff, K., Dubey, P.: How multimedia workloads will change processor design. Computer 30(9), 43–45 (1997)
3. Antochi, I., Juurlink, B., Vassiliadis, S., Liuha, P.: GraalBench: a 3D graphics benchmark suite for mobile phones. In: LCTES 2004: Proceedings of the 2004 ACM SIGPLAN/SIGBED conference on Languages, compilers, and tools for embedded systems, pp. 1–9. ACM Press, New York (2004)
4. Maynard, A.M.G., Donnelly, C.M., Olszewski, B.R.: Contrasting characteristics and cache performance of technical and multi-user commercial workloads. In: ASPLOS-VI: Proceedings of the sixth international conference on Architectural support for programming languages and operating systems, pp. 145–156. ACM Press, New York (1994)
5. Citron, D.: MisSPECulation: partial and misleading use of SPEC CPU2000 in computer architecture conferences. In: ISCA 2003: Proceedings of the 30th annual international symposium on Computer architecture, pp. 52–61. ACM Press, New York (2003)
6. Eeckhout, L., Vandierendonck, H., De Bosschere, K.: Workload design: selecting representative program-input pairs. In: Proceedings of the International Conference on Parallel Architectures and Compilation Techniques, pp. 83–94. IEEE Computer Society, Washington (2002)

7. Vandierendonck, H., De Bosschere, K.: Eccentric and fragile benchmarks. In: IS-PASS 2004: Proceedings of the 2004 IEEE International Symposium on Performance Analysis of Systems and Software, pp. 2–11. IEEE Computer Society, Washington (2004)
8. Joshi, A., Phansalkar, A., Eeckhout, L., John, L.K.: Measuring benchmark similarity using inherent program characteristics. IEEE Transactions on Computers 55(6), 769–782 (2006)
9. Phansalkar, A., Joshi, A., Eeckhout, L., John, L.K.: Measuring program similarity: Experiments with SPEC CPU benchmark suites. In: ISPASS 2005: IEEE International Symposium on Performance Analysis of Systems and Software, pp. 10–20. IEEE Computer Society, Washington (2005)
10. Vandierendonck, H., De Bosschere, K.: Experiments with subsetting benchmark suites. In: WWC-7: IEEE International Workshop on Workload Characterization, pp. 55–62. IEEE Computer Society, Washington (2004)
11. Bonebakker, L.: Finding representative workloads for computer system design. PhD thesis, Technische Universiteit Delft (2007) ISBN/EAN 978-90-5638-187-5
12. Sun Microsystems Inc.: Collecting high quality data to characterize strategic workloads. Sun Microsystems Inc. Internal (2004)
13. Bonebakker, L.: Quantifying hardware counter sampling error in computer system workload characterization. Technical report, Sun Microsystems Laboratories (2007)
14. Sun Microsystems, Inc.: UltraSPARC III Cu Users Manual. Sun Microsystems, Inc. 1.0 edn. (2002)
15. Raatikainen, K.E.E.: Cluster analysis and workload classication. SIGMETRICS Performance Evaluation Review 20(4), 24–30 (1993)
16. Eeckhout, L., Sundareswara, R., Yi, J.J., Lilja, D., Schrater, P.: Accurate statistical approaches for generating representative workload compositions. In: Proceedings of the IEEE International Workload Characterization Symposium, pp. 56–66. IEEE Computer Society, Washington (2005)
17. Jolliffe, I.: Principal Component Analysis. Springer Series in Statistics. Springer, New York (2002)
18. Hyvärinen, A., Oja, E.: Independent component analysis: Algorithms and applications. Neural Networks 13(4-5), 411–430 (2000)
19. Hyvärinen, A., Karhunen, J., Oja, E.: Independent Component Analysis, 1st edn. Adaptive and learning systems for signal processing, communications and control. Wiley Interscience, John Wiley & Sons, Inc, New York (2001)
20. Hyvärinen, A.: FastICA (2006),
    http://cran.r-project.org/src/contrib/Descriptions/fastICA.html
21. R Development Core Team: R: A Language and Environment for Statistical Computing. R Foundation for Statistical Computing, Vienna, Austria (2006) ISBN 3-900051-07-0
22. Sheskin, D.: Handbook of parametric and nonparametric statistical procedures, 3rd edn. Chapman & Hall/CRC, Boca Raton (2004)

Tuning Topology Generators Using Spectral Distributions

Hamed Haddadi[1], Damien Fay[2], Steve Uhlig[3], Andrew Moore[2],
Richard Mortier[4], Almerima Jamakovic[3], and Miguel Rio[1]

[1] University College London
[2] University of Cambridge
[3] Delft University of Technology
[4] Vipadia Ltd

Abstract. An increasing number of synthetic topology generators are available, each claiming to produce representative Internet topologies. Every generator has its own parameters, allowing the user to generate topologies with different characteristics. However, there exist no clear guidelines on tuning the value of these parameters in order to obtain a topology with specific characteristics.

In this paper we optimize the parameters of several topology generators to match a given Internet topology. The optimization is performed either with respect to the link density, or to the spectrum of the normalized Laplacian matrix. Contrary to approaches in the literature that rely only on the largest eigenvalues, we take into account the set of all eigenvalues. However, we show that on their own the eigenvalues cannot be used to construct a metric for optimizing parameters. Instead we present a weighted spectral method which simultaneously takes into account all the properties of the graph.

Keywords: Internet Topology, Graph Spectrum.

1 Introduction

Today's Internet is formed from more than 25,000 Autonomous Systems (ASes), each of which can contain tens or hundreds of routers. Constant evolution and change in the Internet, due to failures and bugs in the short term, and growth and death of networks in the long term, has made it difficult for scientists to produce representative Internet topologies at either AS or router level. However, such maps are essential for the simulation and analysis of ideas including new and improved routing protocols, and peer-to-peer, media-streaming applications. Since obtaining accurate, timely maps of the Internet topology is difficult, and development of new protocols and systems requires understanding their performance over a range of scenarios, researchers use synthetic topology generators.

There are many such generators, each of which is parameterized, often with multiple parameters, giving rise to a plethora of potential synthetic graphs. Understanding and generating those graphs, useful because they accurately

S. Kounev, I. Gorton, and K. Sachs (Eds.): SIPEW 2008, LNCS 5119, pp. 154–173, 2008.

represent features of the true underlying Internet graph, is difficult. Existing approaches to tuning the generator parameters range from selection of particular metrics of interest, e.g., link count, and tuning to match that particular metric, to simply using the default parameters encoded in the particular release of the generator package in use!

The core problem is to select an appropriate cost function which reflects those aspects of the graph that are important to the user and weights those aspects accordingly. Such a selection process is inherently subjective: there is no "best" cost function in general. Once a suitable cost function is selected, it is a simple matter to tune the available parameters of the topology generator to produce output that optimally matches said cost function.

In the light of this, our contributions in this paper are as follows:

- We propose a new cost function, the *weighted spectrum*, constructed from the eigenvalues of the normalized Laplacian matrix, or graph spectrum;
- We demonstrate that the graph spectrum alone is unsatisfactory as a cost function;
- We provide an efficient approximation of the weighted spectrum;
- We use this approximation to tune parameters for a set of Internet topology generators, enabling us to use these generators to effectively match a particular measured Internet topology.

The graph spectrum is a useful starting point for such a cost function as it yields a set of invariants about a graph that encode all the properties of that graph [8]. Our proposed cost function improves on the simple graph spectrum because it incorporates the knowledge that not all eigenvalues are equally important, and weights toward those that are considered to encode more significant aspects of the graph's structure. The basis of our algorithm is to provide a way to measure the difference between two graphs with respect to a common reference, a suitable regular graph.[1]

After reviewing related work in Section 2, we outline background theory in Section 3 before introducing the topology generators we use in Section 4. In Section 5 we present the results of our analysis and in Section 6 we compare topologies generated at optimal values of the parameters with an observed dataset. Finally, we conclude the paper in Section 7 and discuss future work.

2   Related Work

Zegura *et al.* [27] analyze topologies of 100 nodes generated using pure random, Waxman [25], exponential and several locality based models of topology such as Transit-Stub [6]. They use metrics such as average node degree, network diameter, and number of paths between nodes, and use the number of edges as the metric of choice for optimization of the tuning parameter. However as we show in this paper, the number of links is not an ideal choice particularly in random

---

[1] A regular graph is one where all nodes have the same degree.

networks, due to the network structure only resembling the observed Internet topology at link counts much higher than those suggested by the optimization process.

Tangmunarunkit *et al.* [23] provide a first point of comparison of the underlying characteristics of degree-based models against structural models. A major conclusion is that the degree-based model in its simplest form performs better than random or structural models at representing all the studied parameters. They compare three categories of model generators: the Waxman model of random graphs, the TIERS [10] and Transit-Stub structural models, and the simplest degree based generator, called the Power-Law Random Graph [1]. They compare under three metrics: expansion, resilience and distortion and conclude that the hierarchy present in the measured networks is stricter than in degree-based generators. However, they leave many questions unanswered about the accuracy of degree-based generators and their choice of metrics and parameter values.

Heckmann *et al.* [15] discuss different types of topologies and present a collection of real-world topologies that can be used for simulation. They then define several similarity metrics, such as the shortest path distributions, node degree distributions and node rank exponents, to compare artificially generated topologies with real world topologies from AT&T's network. They use these to determine the input parameter range of the topology generators of BRITE [19], TIERS and GT-ITM [6] to create realistic topologies.

Gkantsidis *et al.* [13] perform a comparison of clustering coefficients using the eigenvectors of the k largest eigenvalues of the adjacency matrices of BGP topology graphs. However, the choice of k is somewhat arbitrary, and further, the selected eigenvectors are all given equal importance. They consider the rest of the spectrum as noise, although it has been shown that the eigenvalues of either the adjacency matrix or the normalized Laplacian matrix can be used to accurately represent a topology and some specific eigenvalues provide a measure of properties such as robustness of a network to failures [5,16].

Vukadinovic *et al.* [24] used the normalized Laplacian spectrum for analysis of AS graphs. They propose that the normalized Laplacian spectrum can be used as a fingerprint for Internet-like graphs. Using the Inet [26] generator and AS graphs from BGP data, they obtain eigenvalues of the normalized Laplacian matrix. The differences between synthetic and observed topologies indicate that the structural properties of the Internet should be included in an Internet AS model alongside power law relationships. They believe that the graph spectrum should be considered an essential metric when comparing graphs. We expand on this work by demonstrating how an appropriate weighting of the eigenvalues can be used to reveal structural differences between two topologies.

Use of spectrum for graph comparison is not limited to Internet research. Hanna [14] uses graph spectra for numerical comparison of architectural space in large building plans. By defining space as a graph, he shows that the spectra of two plan types can be used effectively to judge the effects of global vs. local changes to, and hence the edit distances between, the plans. Hanna believes spectra give a reliable metric for capturing the local relationships and can be used to guide optimization algorithms for reproducing plans.

3   Graph Spectra

In this section we introduce a brief overview of graph and establish the techniques used later in the paper. Here we define the spectrum, the associated normalized Laplacian matrix, and several relevant facts relating to this matrix. Given an undirected graph $G = (V, E)$, V is the set of vertices (nodes), E is the set of edges (links) and d_v is the degree of node v.

Definition 1. *For a connected graph the normalized Laplacian of the graph G is the matrix $L(G)$ defined as:*

$$L(G)(u, v) = \begin{cases} 1, & \text{if } u = v \text{ and } d_v \neq 0 \\ -\dfrac{1}{\sqrt{d_u d_v}}, & \text{if } u \text{ and } v \text{ are adjacent} \\ 0, & \text{otherwise} \end{cases} \tag{1}$$

The associated spectrum is the set of ordered eigenvalues of L denoted by $\lambda_1, \lambda_2, \ldots, \lambda_{N-1}$ where N is the number of vertices and the eigenvalues are ordered such that $0 \leq \lambda_1 \leq \cdots \leq \lambda_i \leq \lambda_{i+1} \leq \cdots \leq \lambda_{N-1} \leq 2$. The normalized Laplacian has some very interesting properties, the relevant ones of which we list here:

1. For a connected graph the spectrum is symmetrical around 1 i.e., $\lambda_i = \lambda_{N-i-1}$;
2. If D is the diameter of the graph (the maximum number of steps between all pairs of nodes) and $vol(G)$ denotes the volume of G which is the sum of the node degrees d_v:

$$\lambda_1 \geq \frac{1}{Dvol(G)} = \frac{1}{D\sum_{v}(d_v)} \tag{2}$$

Thus, the first eigenvalue is bounded by the node degrees of the vertices.

3. For a connected graph

$$2h_G \geq \lambda_1 \geq \frac{h_g^2}{2} \tag{3}$$

where h_G is the Cheeger constant and is a measure of the minimum cut-set of a graph, see e.g. [8] for a full explanation. The Cheeger constant is closely related to flow problems in graphs and is thus of obvious importance to network designers.

For these and other reasons, e.g. as presented in [8,5,24,13], the spectrum of a graph is often called the *footprint* of a graph. More specifically, in this paper we evaluate the use of the spectrum as a measure of the deviation of a graph, explained below. A random graph is defined as one for which all but $o(N)$ vertices almost certainly have degree [7]:

$$d_v = \frac{N}{2} + o(N) \tag{4}$$

where $o(N)$ denotes of the order of N. For random graphs there exists a large set of properties which form an equivalence class of properties such that if one of the properties is proven then all are proven, see e.g. [7] for an initial list. There also exist non-random graphs which satisfy the equivalence class of properties. These are known as quasi-random graphs. One of the most tractable properties of the equivalence class of properties is the 4-cycle. A 4-cycle is a route starting and ending at one vertex which passes through 4 points in total, where these may be repeated points:

$$N_G(C_4) \leq (1 + o(1))(\frac{N}{2})^4 \tag{5}$$

where C_4 denotes a 4 cycle and $N_G(C_4)$ denotes the number of such cycles. However, in this paper our interest does not lie in random graphs (those examined here are not random but structured) but in a measure called the deviation of a graph, $dev(G)$, which is a measure of a graph's deviation from pseudo-randomness. For a regular graph, in which each vertex has the same degree, this is defined as the number of 4-cycles. However, this can also be related to the spectrum: in a given graph G with N eigenvalues $\lambda_1, \ldots, \lambda_N$, the deviation is calculated as follows. For a regular graph:

$$dev(G) = \sum_i (1 - \lambda_i)^4 \tag{6}$$

and for a general graph:

$$dev(G) = \sum_i (1 - \lambda_i)^4 + 20\sqrt{Irr(G)} \tag{7}$$

where $Irr(G)$ is the irregularity of the graph [8]. The deviation of a graph may be used as a measure of the structure in a graph, i.e., its distance away from randomness. It is the first term on the right hand side of the bound above which forms the metric proposed in this paper. This term expresses the appropriate weighting, i.e., a power of 4, of the eigenvalues that sum to form the bound on the deviation of a graph.

Next we consider the interpretation of the eigenvalues of the normalized Laplacian matrix. In the following only eigenvalues less than or equal to 1 are considered, as the spectrum is symmetrical for connected graphs. Spectral clustering is a technique which uses the eigenvalues of the normalised Laplacian matrix to perform clustering of a dataset [20]. The first (smallest) eigenvalue and associated eigenvector are associated with the main clusters of data. Subsequent eigenvalues and eigenvectors can be associated with cluster splitting and also identification of smaller clusters [22]. Typically, there exists what is called a spectral gap in which for some k, $\lambda_k \ll \lambda_{k+1} \approx 1$. That is, eigenvalues $\lambda_{k+1}, \ldots, \lambda_N$ are approximately equal to one and are likely to represent noise in the original dataset. It is then typical to reduce the dimensionality of the data using an approximation based on the spectral decomposition. It is interesting to note that while the normalized Laplacian has well behaved convergence properties with regards to clustering, this is not true for other matrices derived from the adjacency matrix [17]. However, with regards to topological graphs, while the first eigenvalue may be associated, as above, with the optimal cut, which can be considered the optimal cluster, interpretation of subsequent eigenvalues cannot be associated with specific graph properties other than the distribution of cluster information within a graph.

Having established the background material necessary for our method we now examine the construction of a metric for graph comparison. Given two graphs, G_1 and G_2 say we wish to determine at what points their structure vary. As a first attempt one might try to construct a metric based on the differences between the eigenvalues as:

$$C = \sum_i \lambda_{i,G_1} - \lambda_{i,G_2} \tag{8}$$

However, pairwise comparison of the eigenvalues as above leads to comparing eigenvalues which represent different structures in the graph, i.e., it is more appropriate to compare eigenvalues of similar size. In order to achieve this, the distribution of eigenvalues is used to construct our metric as:

$$C = \int_i (1-i)^4 (P(\lambda_{i,G_1} = i) - P(\lambda_{i,G_2} = i)) d_i \tag{9}$$

In this paper the distribution of eigenvalues $P(\lambda_i = i)$ is estimated by using pivoting and Sylvester's Law of Inertia to compute the number of eigenvalues that fall in a given interval.

While the primary motivation for using a power of four in the equation above is the number of 4-cycles, and thus the deviation from random behaviour of a graph as discussed above, an interesting link can also be made with the well known clustering coefficient, as will now be shown. First however, some background must be established. Consider the adjacency matrix for a graph, A, in which:

$$A_{i,j} = 1 \text{ if } i \rightarrow j$$

where $A_{i,j}$ is the ith and jth entry of A. The number of paths of length 2 between nodes i and j, t, can easily be found by squaring the adjacency matrix as:

$$A_{i,j}^2 = t \text{ if } i \rightarrow k \rightarrow j$$

for some intermediate node(s) k. In general the t paths of length N between nodes i and j can be found by taking the Nth power of A as:

$$A_{i,j}^N = t \text{ if } i \rightarrow j \text{ via } N \text{ steps.}$$

noting that for a cycle a path must start and finish at the same point gives:

$$A_{i,i}^N = t \text{ if } i \to i \text{ via an } N \text{ cycle.}$$

Now consider the spectral decomposition of the matrix A:

$$A = \sum_i \gamma_i \epsilon_i \epsilon_i^T \tag{10}$$

where γ_i and ϵ_i are the ith eigenpair of A. These form an orthonormal basis for A (i.e. ortogonal $\epsilon_i \epsilon_j^T = 0$ and normal $\epsilon_i \epsilon_i^T = \mathbf{1}$), and so:

$$A^N = \left(\sum_i \gamma_i \epsilon_i \epsilon_i^T \right)^N \tag{11}$$

Here we are interested in the number of N-cycles which is the trace of A^N:

$$tr(A^N) = \sum_i \gamma_i^N \tag{12}$$

Thus, for an adjacency matrix the number of N-cycles in the graphs is the sum of the eigenvalues. Next consider the normalised Laplacian which can be related to the adjacency matrix as:

$$L(G) = I - D^{-1/2} A D^{-1/2} \tag{13}$$

where D is a diagonal matrix whose ith entry is the degree of node i. Taking the identity matrix to the left and taking the trace gives:

$$tr(I - L(G)) = tr(D^{-1/2} A D^{-1/2}) \tag{14}$$

However, $tr(I - L(G))$ is also related to the eigenvalues of $L(G)$ as:

$$tr(I - L(G)) = \sum_i 1 - \lambda_i \tag{15}$$

Putting the two results together and taking a power of N results in:

$$tr((I - L(G))^N) = tr((D^{-1/2} A D^{-1/2})^N) = \sum_i (1 - \lambda_i)^N \tag{16}$$

The right hand side of this equation is the weighted spectrum but it is the terms on the left hand side we will now examine. Noting that the i,jth entry of $D^{-1/2} A D^{-1/2}$ is:

$$(D^{-1/2} A D^{-1/2}))_{i,j} = \frac{A_{i,j}}{\sqrt{d_i}\sqrt{d_j}} \tag{17}$$

then an N-path passing through a set of nodes, S say, will consist of a product of $\#S$ such terms:

$$\prod_S \frac{A_{i,j}}{\sqrt{d_i}\sqrt{d_j}} \tag{18}$$

If node i has K N-*cycles*, consisting of the sets $S_{1,...,K}$ then the ith diagonal element of $(I - L(G))^N$ is:

$$(D^{-1/2}AD^{-1/2}))^N_{i,i} = \sum_{k=1}^{K} \prod_{i,j \in S_k} \frac{1}{d_j} \tag{19}$$

Next we consider the clustering coefficient of a graph, G. The cluster coefficient, $\gamma(G)$, is defined as the average number of 3-cycles divided by the total number of possible 3-cycles:

$$\gamma(G) = 1/N \sum_i \frac{T_i}{d_i(d_i - 1)/2}, d_i \geq 2 \tag{20}$$

where T_i is the number of 3-cycles for node i, d_i is the degree of node i. Now consider a specific 3-cycle between nodes a, b and c. For the cluster coefficient the contribution to the average is (noting that the 3-cycle will be considered three times, once from each node):

$$\frac{1}{d_a(d_a - 1)/2} + \frac{1}{d_b(d_b - 1)/2} + \frac{1}{d_c(d_c - 1)/2} \tag{21}$$

However, for the weighted spectrum and taking the number of 3-cycles (Note: 4-cycles are the main focus of this research for reasons explained above), this particular 3-cycle makes the following contribution to the overall sum (i.e. using $K=1$, $S_k = a, b, c$ for node a then likewise for nodes b and c):

$$\frac{3}{d_a d_b d_c} \tag{22}$$

So it can be seen that the clustering coefficient normalises each 3-cycle according to the total number of possible 3-cycles while the 3-cycle weighted spectrum instead normalises using a product of the degrees. Thus the two metrics can be considered to be similar but not equal. Note also that in contrast to the clustering coefficient (one number) the weighted spectrum results in many terms which represent sucessively finer and finer clusters.

4   Available Topologies

4.1   Synthetic Topologies

There are many models available that claim to describe the Internet AS topology. Several of these are embodied in tools built by the community for generating simulated topologies. In this section we describe the particular models whose output we compare in this paper. The first are produced from the Waxman model [25], derived from the Erdös-Rényi random graphs [11], where the probability of two nodes being connected is proportional to the Euclidean distance between them. The second come from the Barabasi and Albert (BA) [3] model, following measurements of various power laws in degree distributions and rank exponents by Faloutsos *et al.* [12]. These incorporate common beliefs about preferential attachment and incremental growth. The third are from the Generalized Linear Preference model [4] which additionally model clustering coefficients. Finally, Inet [26] and PFP [28] focus on alternative characteristics of AS topology: the existence of a meshed core, and the phenomenon of preferential attachment respectively. Each model focuses only on particular metrics and parameters, and has only been compared with selected AS topology observations.

4.2 Waxman

The Waxman model of random graphs is based on a probability model for interconnecting nodes of the topology given by:

$$P(u, v) = \alpha e^{-d/(\beta L)} \tag{23}$$

where $0 < \alpha, \beta \leq 1$, d is the Euclidean distance between two nodes u and v, and L is the network diameter, i.e., the largest distance between two nodes. Note that d and L are not parameters for the Waxman model. The Internet is known not to be a random network but we include the Waxman model as a baseline for comparison purposes.

4.3 BA

The BA [2] model was inspired by the idea of preferentially attaching new nodes to existing well-connected nodes, leading to the incremental growth of nodes and the links between them. Starting with a network of m_0 isolated nodes, $m \leq m_0$ new links are added with probability p. One end of each link is attached to a random node, while the other end is attached to a node selected by preferring the more popular, i.e., well-connected, nodes with probability

$$\Pi(k_i) = \frac{k_i + 1}{\sum_j k_j + 1} \tag{24}$$

where k_j is the degree of node j, with probability q, m links are rewired and new nodes are added with probability $1 - p - q$. A new node m has m new links that, with probability $\Pi(k_i)$, are connected to nodes i already present in the system. We use the BRITE [19] implementation of this model in this paper.

4.4 GLP

Our third model is the Generalized Linear Preference model (GLP) [4]. It focuses on matching characteristic path length and clustering coefficients. It uses a probabilistic method for adding nodes and links recursively while preserving selected power law properties. In the GLP model, when starting with m_0 links, the probability of adding new links is defined as p where $p \in [0, 1]$. Let $\Pi(d_i)$ be the probability of choosing node i. For each end of each link, node i is chosen with probability $\Pi(d_i)$ defined as:

$$\Pi(d_i) = (d_i - \beta) / \sum_j (d_j - \beta) \qquad (25)$$

where $\beta \in (-\infty, 1)$ is a tunable parameter indicating the preference of nodes to connect to existing popular nodes. We use the BRITE implementation of this model in this paper.

4.5 Inet

Inet [26] produces random networks using a preferential linear weight for the connection probability of nodes after modeling the core of the generated topology as a full mesh network. Inet sets the minimum number of nodes at 3037, the number of ASes on the Internet at the time of Inet's development. By default, the fraction of degree 1 nodes α is set to 0.3, based on measurements from Routeviews[2] and NLANR[3] BGP table data in 2002.

4.6 PFP

In the Positive Feedback Preference (PFP) model [28], the AS topology of the Internet is considered to grow by interactive probabilistic addition of new nodes and links. It uses a nonlinear preferential attachment probability when choosing older nodes for the interactive growth of the network, inserting edges between existing and newly added nodes. As the PFP generator does not have any user-tunable parameters we include it only in the last part of Section 5 for completeness.

4.7 Observed Topology

Our observed topology dataset comes from the CAIDA Skitter project.[4] CAIDA computes the adjacency matrix of the AS topology from the daily Skitter measurements. These are obtained by running traceroutes over a large range of IP addresses and mapping the prefixes to AS numbers using RouteViews BGP data. Since the Skitter data represents paths that have actually been traversed by packets to their destinations, rather than paths calculated and propagated by BGP system, it is more likely to faithfully represent the IP topology than the BGP data alone. For our study, we used the graphs for March 2004 as used by Mahadevan et al. [18]. This dataset reports 9,204 unique ASes across the Internet.

---

[2] http://www.routeviews.org/

[3] http://www.nlanr.net/

[4] http://www.caida.org/tools/measurement/Skitter/

5   Results

The aim of this section is to examine how well the topology generators match the Skitter topology for different values of their parameters. To facilitate this comparison, grids are constructed over the possible values of the parameter spaces and various cost functions are evaluated as follows:

1. A cost function measuring the matching between the number of links in skitter and the generated topologies:

$$C_1(\theta) = (l_t(\theta) - l_{skitter})^2 \qquad (26)$$

   where C_1 is the first cost function, θ are the model parameters (which differ for each topology generator), l_t is the number of links (which is a function of the parameters) and $l_{skitter}$ is the number of links in the Skitter dataset.
2. A cost function measuring the matching between the spectra of the Skitter network and of the generated topologies:

$$C_2(\theta) = \sum_i (P(\Lambda \leq \lambda_{t,i}) - P(\Lambda \leq \lambda_{skitter,i}))^2 \qquad (27)$$

   where $\lambda_{t,i}$ is the ith eigenvalue for topology t.
3. A cost function measuring the matching of the weighted spectra:

$$C_3(\theta) = \sum_i ((w * P(\Lambda = \lambda_{t,i}) - w * P(\Lambda = \lambda_{skitter,i}))^2 \qquad (28)$$

   where weight $w = (1 - i)^4$.

In addition to examining different parameter values across a grid, the optimum parameters with respect to $C_3(\theta)$ are estimated using the Nelder Meade simplex search algorithm [21,9]. Note that the topologies generated by the topology generators are random in a statistical sense, due to differing random seeds for each run. Ten topologies are generated for each value of θ and the average spectral distribution is calculated. We found that the variance of the spectral distributions was sufficiently low to allow reasonable estimates of the minima in each case.

5.1   Link Densities

Figure 1 displays the value of the cost function $C_1(\theta)$ as a function of the topology generator parameters. On the upper and lower left graphs, the grayscale color indicates the value of the cost function. For Inet (lower right) there is only one parameter, p, so it is plotted as a curve in Figure 1(d). Figure 1 shows that a minimum exists for each topology in approximately the same regions as the default values of each generator.[5] For the BA generator it is known that for

---

[5] Some of these default values are listed in table 1.

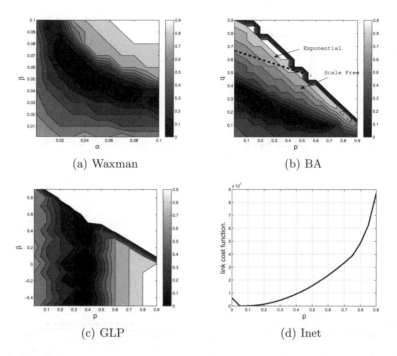

Fig. 1. Topology generator parameter grid for sum squared error from number of links

values of p and q above the line shown in Figure 1(b), the topologies generated
follow an exponential node degree distribution while those below follow a scale-free distribution. It is encouraging to note that the values of $C_1(\theta)$ are large in
the exponential region and the minimum is in the scale-free region as the node
degree distribution of the Internet is known to be approximately scale free [2].
Overall the results obtained by tuning the parameters based on $C_1(\theta)$ appear
reasonable. For link density matching it is possible to obtain parameter values
which match the link densities exactly. Indeed, there is a ridge of parameters for
BA, GLP and Waxman for which the link densities can be matched. However,
as noted in the introduction, there is no control over any other characteristic of
the graph using this method.

5.2 Spectra PDF

Figure 2 shows the spectral PDF of the Skitter dataset and the four topology
generators calculated at three parameters values in each grid (the parameter
values are indicated in brackets in the legends). The aim is to illustrate how
much the spectral PDFs change with the values of the parameters. The spectral
PDFs of Waxman (Figure 2(a)) vary significantly for different values of α and β.
Furthermore, none of the Waxman PDFs match well the spectral PDF of the

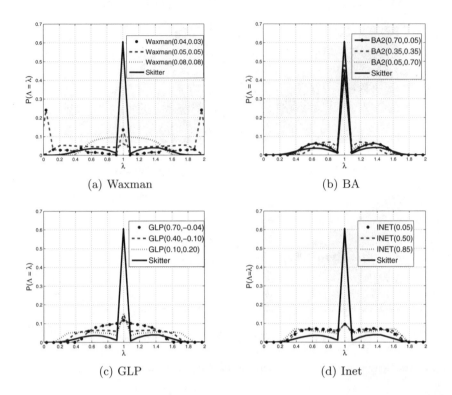

Fig. 2. PDF of Spectra

Skitter graph. The BA PDFs vary to a lesser extent (Figure 2(b)) and appear to give a much better match than the Waxman model, especially around eigenvalue 1 ($\lambda = 1$). This better match of BA is not surprising as the Waxman model is not a good model for the Internet as noted in Section 4. GLP (Figure 2(c)) and Inet (Figure 2(d)) give similar results to BA, with a poor match outside eigenvalue 1. The better match of the BA model around eigenvalue 1 is interesting. As noted in Section 3 the regions away from eigenvalue 1 are far more important than the region around $\lambda = 1$. However, what is required is a technique that reveals the differences with distance from one as these are more important. Thus it would appear difficult to evaluate which model, or even which parameter, is better based on the PDFs alone. This point is now further explored by analysis of the grids calculated with respect to $C_2(\theta)$.

5.3 Limitations of Spectra CDF

Figure 3 shows the value of the second cost function $C_2(\theta)$ as a function of the topology generator parameters, in the same way as Figure 1. As can be seen

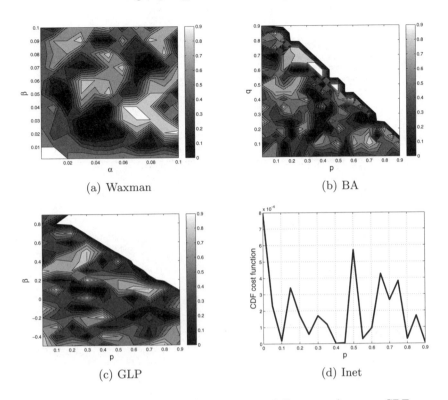

Fig. 3. Parameter grid for sum of absolute differences of spectra CDFs

in Figure 3, there are many islands corresponding to local minima, creating a rugged landscape. The variance in the PDFs referred to in this section is actually greater than any gradient that might exist in the grid. This means that it is not possible to estimate the minimum with respect to $C_2(\theta)$. Figure 3 shows that the spectrum on its own is not sufficient to identify the optimum parameters of any of the topology generators. This is because each eigenvalue in $C_2(\theta)$ is weighted equally. As noted in Section 3, the eigenvalues close to 1 are more likely to be affected by the random seeds for each topology generator and are the source of the noise on the grid.

5.4   Weighted Spectra

The previous section illustrated the limitations of using the raw eigenvalues to find optimal topology generator parameters to match the Skitter topology. Figure 4 shows a plot of the weighted spectra of the same topologies as those shown on Figure 2. As can be seen the results are quite different from those shown in Figure 2. The Waxman weighted spectra still shows a bad fit with respect to the Skitter data (mainly around 0 and 2) compared to the other generators.

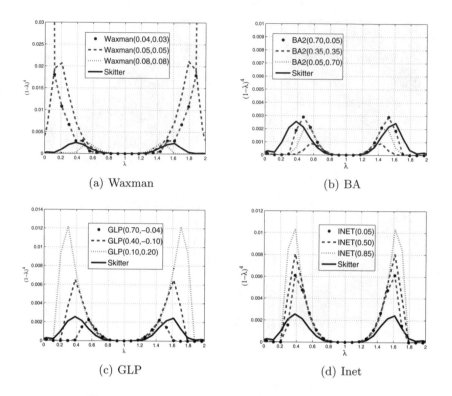

Fig. 4. Weighted spectra grid for generator parameters

The other generators (BA, GLP and Inet) now show that they are capable of matching the weighted spectra of the Skitter topology, especially around the point of greatest weight ($\lambda = 0.4$ or 1.6). The difference between the weighted spectra around 1 is no longer of importance (in contrast to Figure 2), reflecting that the weights here approach zero as we approach eigenvalue 1. In the next section the optimum values and the resulting weighted spectra will be compared.

5.5 Weighted Spectra Comparison

Figure 5 shows the grids associated with $C_3(\theta)$. As can be seen the grids show that there is a region with a minima in each case and in addition, comparing Figure 5 and Figure 1 it can be seen that these minima lie in a region close to those for $C_1(\theta)$. However, it should be noted that the weighted spectra will try to fit more than just the number of links in a topology. This demonstrates the inherent trade-off. Also of note is that the region of interest for the BA model lies inside the region of scale-free behaviour as shown in Figure 5(b).

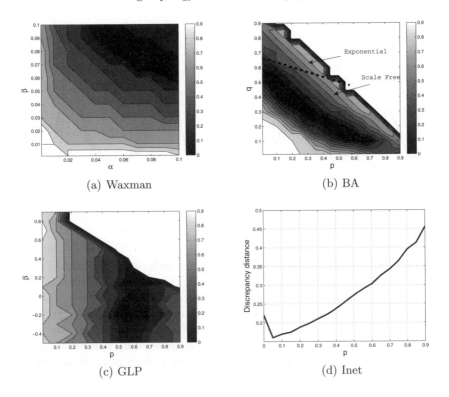

(a) Waxman   (b) BA

(c) GLP   (d) Inet

Fig. 5. Grid of sum squared error of weighted spectra for topology generators

6   Generating Topologies with Optimum Value Parameters

Table 1 displays the optimum values for the topology generators for generating networks that are close to the Skitter graph. In addition, we give the values for $C_3(\theta)$, which show that PFP gives the closest fit followed by BA, GLP, Waxman and finally Inet. While these results are mostly expected, the ranking of Inet as the worst topology generator is surprising. We have also listed some of the default parameters used in certain generators such as BRITE [19]. While many of the optimised parameters are close to the default values, which is encouraging,

Table 1. Optimum parameter values for matching Skitter topology

Waxman	$\alpha = 0.08$ (default= 0.15)	$\beta = 0.08$ (default= −0.2)	$C_3(\theta) = 0.0026$	$\overline{C_3}(\theta) = 0.0797$
BA	$p = 0.2865$ (default= 0.6)	$q = 0.3145$ (default= 0.3)	$C_3(\theta) = 0.0014$	$\overline{C_3}(\theta) = 0.0300$
GLP	$p = 0.5972$ (default= 0.45)	$\beta = 0.1004$ (default= 0.64)	$C_3(\theta) = 0.0021$	$\overline{C_3}(\theta) = 0.0446$
Inet	$\alpha = 0.1013$ (default= 0.3)	−	$C_3(\theta) = 0.0064$	$\overline{C_3}(\theta) = 0.0150$
PFP	−	−	$C_3(\theta) = 0.0014$	$\overline{C_3}(\theta) = 0.0371$

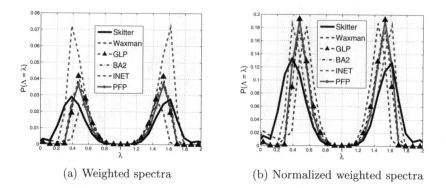

(a) Weighted spectra   (b) Normalized weighted spectra

Fig. 6. Comparison of the weighted spectra

it should be noted that the default parameters are for a *typical* graph and are not selected for any particular situation. Thus a direct comparison is meaningless.

Figure 6(a) shows the weighted spectra for each of the topology generators and inspection of this figure goes some way to explaining the discrepancy in the results. As can be seen the main peak in the weighted spectra for the Skitter data occurs at a value of $\lambda = 0.4$. The Waxman generator peak occurs at $\lambda = 0.6$ which is closer to 1 demonstrating the greater amount of random structure

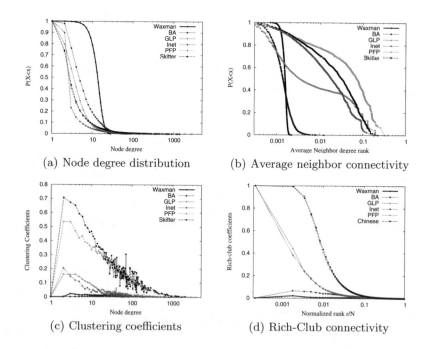

(a) Node degree distribution   (b) Average neighbor connectivity

(c) Clustering coefficients   (d) Rich-Club connectivity

Fig. 7. Comparison of topology generators and Skitter topology

in the Waxman topologies. However, for the Inet generator the peak occurs at the correct point (λ =0.4) but the weighted power at this point is far greater than in the skitter topology. By normalizing the weighted spectrum this point becomes clear:

$$\overline{C_3}(\theta) = \sum_i \frac{((w_i * P(\Lambda = \lambda_{t,i}))}{\sum_i ((w_i * P(\Lambda = \lambda_{t,i}))} - \frac{((w_i * P(\Lambda = \lambda_{skitter}))}{\sum_i ((w_i * P(\Lambda = \lambda_{skitter}))} \tag{29}$$

Using the normalised weighted spectrum the results in Figure 6(b) show that Inet is the best match for the Skitter data while the Waxman model still performs worse than the other models. Further research is required before stating which version of C_3 is superior.

Figure 7 shows a comparison of the optimized topologies with respect to four typical network metrics: the node degree distribution, the average neighbor connectivity, the clustering coefficient and the rich-club connectivity [28]. As can be seen PFP gives the best match for these metrics in agreement with our proposed metric $C_3(\theta)$. The performance of the other topologies is mixed showing that while one topology is able to match one metric it fails to match another. For example, the GLP generator achieves a reasonable match for the node degree distribution but fails to match the average neighbor connectivity. It is interesting to note that BA does not match the rich club connectivity which is not evident in our metric.

7   Conclusions

Comparison of graph structures is a frequently encountered problem across a number of problem domains. To perform a useful comparison requires definition of a cost function that encodes which features of the graphs are considered important. Although the spectrum of a graph is often claimed to be a way to encode a graph's features, the raw spectrum contains too much noise to be useful on its own. In this paper we have introduced a new cost function, the *weighted graph spectrum*, that improves on the graph spectrum by discounting those eigenvalues that are believed to be unimportant and emphasising the contribution of those believed to be important.

We use this cost function to optimise the selection of parameter values within the particular problem domain of Internet topology generation. The weighted spectrum was shown to be a useful cost function in that it leads to parameter choices that appear sensible given prior knowledge of the problem domain, i.e., are close to the default values and, in the case of the BA generator, fall within the expected region. In addition, as the metric is formed from a summation, it is possible to go further and identify which particular eigenvalues are responsible for significant differences. Although it is currently difficult to assign specific features to specific eigenvalues, it is hoped that this feature of our cost function will be useful in the future.

Acknowledgments

We would like to thank Andrew Thomason of Cambridge University for advice on comparison techniques and insight on use of graph deviation. We greatly acknowledge encouragement and advice of Richard Gibbens for pursuing this research. We also appreciate the comments and constructive feedback by anonymous reviewers. This work is conducted as part of the EPSRC UKLIGHT/ MASTS project under grants GR/T10503/01 and GR/T10510/03.

References

1. Aiello, W., Chung, F., Lu, L.: A random graph model for massive graphs. In: STOC 2000: Proceedings of the 32nd Annual ACM Symposium on Theory of Computing, Portland, OR, May 2000, pp. 171–180 (2000)
2. Albert, R., Barabasi, A.-L.: Topology of evolving networks: local events and universality. Physical Review Letters 85, 5234 (2000)
3. Barabasi, A.L., Albert, R.: Emergence of scaling in random networks. Science 286(5439), 509–512 (1999)
4. Bu, T., Towsley, D.: On distinguishing between Internet power law topology generators. In: Proceedings of IEEE Infocom 2002, New York, NY (June 2002)
5. Butler, S.: Lecture notes for spectral graph theory. Lectures in Nankai University, Tianjin, China. (2006)
6. Calvert, K.L., Doar, M.B., Zegura, E.W.: Modeling Internet topology. IEEE Communications Magazine 35(6), 160–163 (1997)
7. Chung, F., Graham, R.: Quasi-random graphs with given degree sequences. Random Struct. Algorithms 32(1), 1–19 (2008)
8. Chung, F.R.K.: Spectral Graph Theory. CBMS Regional Conference Series in Mathematics. American Mathematical Society (1997)
9. Dennis, J., Woods, D.: Optimization in microcomputers: The nelder-meade simplex algorithm. In: Wouk, A. (ed.) New Computing Environments: Microcomputers in Large-Scale Computing, pp. 116–122. SIAM (1987)
10. Doar, M.B.: A better model for generating test networks. In: IEEE GLOBECOM 1996, London, UK (November 1996)
11. Erdös, P., Rényi, A.: On random graphs. In: Mathematical Institute Hungarian Academy, 196, London, (1985)
12. Faloutsos, M., Faloutsos, P., Faloutsos, C.: On power-law relationships of the Internet topology. In: Proceedings of ACM SIGCOMM 1999, Cambridge, Massachusetts, United States, pp. 251–262 (1999)
13. Gkantsidis, C., Mihail, M., Zegura, E.: Spectral analysis of Internet topologies. In: Proceedings of IEEE Infocom 2003, San Francisco, CA (April 2003)
14. Hanna, S.: Representation and generation of plans using graph spectra. In: 6th International Space Syntax Symposium, Istanbul (2007)
15. Heckmann, O., Piringer, M., Schmitt, J., Steinmetz, R.: On realistic network topologies for simulation. In: MoMeTools 2003: Proceedings of the ACM SIGCOMM workshop on Models, methods and tools for reproducible network research, New York, NY, USA, pp. 28–32 (2003)
16. Jamakovic, A., Uhlig, S.: On the relationship between the algebraic connectivity and graph's robustness to node and link failures. In: Next Generation Internet Networks, 3rd EuroNGI Conference on, Trondheim, Norway (2007)

17. Luxburg, U., Bousquet, O., Belkin, M.: Limits of spectral clustering. In: Advances in Neural Information Processing Systems. MIT Press, Cambridge (2005)
18. Mahadevan, P., Krioukov, D., Fomenkov, M., Dimitropoulos, X., Claffy, K.C., Vahdat, A.: The Internet AS-level topology: three data sources and one definitive metric. SIGCOMM Computer Communication Review 36(1), 17–26 (2006)
19. Medina, A., Lakhina, A., Matta, I., Byers, J.: BRITE: an approach to universal topology generation. In: IEEE MASCOTS, Cincinnati, OH, USA, August 2001, pp. 346–353 (2001)
20. Nadler, B., Lafon, S., Coifman, R., Kevrekidis, I.: Diffusion maps, spectral clustering and eigenfunctions of fokker-planck operators. In: Neural Information Processing Systems (NIPS) (2005)
21. Nelder, J., Mead, R.: A simplex method for function minimization. Comput. J. 7, 308–313 (1965)
22. Ng, A., Jordan, M., Weiss, Y.: On spectral clustering: analysis and an algorithm. In: Dietterich, T., Becker, S., Ghahramani, Z. (eds.) Advances in Neural Information Processing Systems 14. MIT Press, Cambridge (2002)
23. Tangmunarunkit, H., Govindan, R., Jamin, S., Shenker, S., Willinger, W.: Network topology generators: degree-based vs. structural. In: Proceedings of ACM SIGCOMM 2002, Pittsburgh, PA, pp. 147–159 (2002)
24. Vukadinovic, D., Huang, P., Erlebach, T.: On the spectrum and structure of Internet topology graphs. In: Unger, H., Böhme, T., Mikler, A.R. (eds.) IICS 2002. LNCS, vol. 2346, Springer, Heidelberg (2002)
25. Waxman, B.M.: Routing of multipoint connections. IEEE Journal on Selected Areas in Communications (JSAC) 6(9), 1617–1622 (1988)
26. Winick, J., Jamin, S.: Inet-3.0: Internet topology generator. Technical Report CSE-TR-456-02, University of Michigan Technical Report CSE-TR-456-02 (2002)
27. Zegura, E.W., Calvert, K.L., Donahoo, M.J.: A quantitative comparison of graph-based models for Internet topology. IEEE/ACM Transactions on Networking (TON) 5(6), 770–783 (1997)
28. Zhou, S.: Characterising and modelling the Internet topology, the rich-club phenomenon and the PFP model. BT Technology Journal 24 (2006)

Performance, Benchmarking and Sizing in Developing Highly Scalable Enterprise Software

Xiaoqing Cheng

Performance, Data Management & Scalability, SAP AG
xiaoqing.cheng@sap.com

Abstract. Performance and scalability are essential characteristics of large-scale enterprise software. This paper presents the technologies behind the processes implemented at SAP. During the specification, design and implementation phases, *Performance Design Patterns* are used as guidelines, which also define the Key Performance Indicators (KPI) for performance and scalability tests. With proven scalability of software applications, SAP's *Sizing Process* enables the transformation of business requirements into hardware requirements. It also allows SAP's customers to flexibly configure their specific applications, on operating system (OS), database (DB), and hardware platforms of their choice. The *SAP Standard Application Benchmarks* are developed and executed to test the scalability in extremely high load situations and to verify the sizing statements from the sizing process. They are also used for SAP internal regression tests across releases, and by SAP's hardware partners for platform tests. Besides the response time centric performance testing, analysis and optimization, SAP follows a KPI-focused approach which permits potential performance problems to be reliably predicted already in simple and easy-to-execute tests. The SAP NetWeaver Portal Benchmark is used to demonstrate how to conduct performance and scalability tests using single user tests and load tests. We will introduce the KPIs used for Java memory analysis and optimization. Finally, this paper shows how the results of these tests can be used in hardware sizing in customer implementation projects.

1 Introduction

SAP's enterprise software applications support companies of all sizes and in all industries in executing mission-critical business processes. In these highly integrated software applications, complex business processes are mapped onto the software systems. In large global companies, tenths of thousands of concurrent users, distributed over continents and time zones, may work collaboratively in a system landscape connected by a wide area network (WAN). In all the application areas, performance and scalability are the essential characteristics that ensure the success and return of investment (ROI) of software solutions.

Performance Expectations. Performance can be considered both from a system point of view, and a user point of view. While system administrators are

S. Kounev, I. Gorton, and K. Sachs (Eds.): SIPEW 2008, LNCS 5119, pp. 174–190, 2008.

interested in achieving required system throughput with a limited IT budget, the end users are seeking reasonable response time when interacting with software systems. Acceptable response times are related to the content of business processing. For example, to save an Internet Sales order (business-to-customer) with only a few line items, sub second response time is expected, while a business-to-business order including several thousands of line items needs highly complex pricing calculations and availability checks, and thus a significant longer response time will be accepted.

The Importance of Scalability. Scalability refers to the predictable resource consumption of a software application under different system load, while the response time remains in the reasonable range. A system load, in a simple case, can be specified by the average number of user interaction steps per unit of time (e.g. hits per second). Scalability is a multi-dimensional behavior, related to varying system load in different categories including data volume, hardware adaptivity, and geographical distribution of data centers.

Within the life cycle of a software application, which also includes the phases of operation and maintenance, and retirement, the performance and scalability aspects need to be considered differently. This paper focuses on efficient and effective processes for reliable performance assessment and optimization in the development phase, comprising activities in the areas of performance, benchmarking and sizing.

2 A KPI-Focused Approach for Performance Testing, Analysis and Optimization

2.1 Performance Design Patterns

Many performance issues cannot be solved by fixing a simple bug in the software code alone. They are caused by inappropriate design decisions made in the software architecture. Performance design patterns specify target behaviors and design rules for software components and interfaces while at the same time allowing a high degree of freedom for the implementation.

A SAP business application generally consists of 3 layers: the persistence layer, the application layer, and the front end layer. Relational database systems are typically used in the persistence layer, and the data accesses are executed by so-called SQL statements [3]. While the persistence layer has to ensure the data consistency under highly concurrent data accesses, the application layer carries out CPU intensive processing of business logic. The application layer of a large software system is typically built up by a load-balanced cluster of application servers, which scale in CPU and memory and provide high availability at the same time. The front end layer represents the user interface (UI), typically running on PCs, connected by a LAN or WAN to the application servers, providing high usability and productivity to the end users. SAP's performance design patterns cover these major software layers and their interactions. They prescribe the following:

Major Database Accesses should be Supported by Appropriate Indexes. Indexes of a database table accelerate the data access and ensure a data read time nearly independent of the length of the database table. Since data need to be read in many different ways using different keys and selection criteria, many indexes can be necessary to provide the best selectivity. On the other hand, too many indexes of a database table would slow down the modification of a database table, because of updates of these indexes. When designing a database table, data reads and updates must be carefully analyzed for major business processes. Based on the data access patterns identified, appropriate indexes are designed and used to support major data accesses.

Complete WHERE Clauses of SELECT Statements. The performance when reading data from a database is impacted by the size of the result set of a SELECT statement. The intention of this design pattern is to restrict the size of result sets to the minimum of data which is required for processing.

Using Buffers and Caches at the Application Server Layer. In the application layer, data representing intermediate results are accessed very frequently. Caching or buffering this kind of data on application servers can speed up performance by a factor of 10 to 100. In the design phase, the type and amount of data for caching and buffering needs to be analyzed very carefully. The most important considerations are cache key design, scope of sharing, invalidation mechanism, and read/write ratio. The cache key helps to find the cached entities quickly. Cached data can be shared in different contexts: only within a user session, by different sessions of a user, or by all users. In most cases, when the original data are modified, it is not necessary to reload the cache; instead it is enough to mark the cached copies as invalid. The life time of the cached data is of particularly high importance. The synchronization overhead of too frequent updates, both between application servers and against the database, could eliminate the benefit of caching.

No Identical Accesses to Persistence Layer. For data consistency reasons, the persistence layer represents a central resource in SAP applications. Data accesses to this central instance must be reduced to a necessary minimum. During user interaction steps within a transaction (i.e. between two successive data commits) the same data needs to be read from the persistence layer only once and should be cached for reuse. This design pattern represents a simple and efficient criterion in the data and architecture design and can be easily verified in testing.

Parallel Processing Enabled. As long as the data consistency is ensured, business objects should be processed in parallel, to be able to utilize the parallel processing capabilities of modern hardware. However, under highly concurrent usage, some processing procedures need to be explicitly protected by critical sections. These critical sections should be designed as long as is necessary to guarantee consistency, and as short as possible so as to enable parallel processing. This requirement also applies to the behavior of the interface for mass data processing.

Linear Dependency. The scalability of a large application can only be achieved when the resource consumption depends maximally linearly on the number and size of processed business objects. Otherwise, the resource requirements will exceed any possible limits quickly, and result in unpredictably increasing response times. To ensure linear dependency, models of business processing must be adjusted and optimized. Later on in this paper, we will present a simple procedure to test the linear dependency and to locate the software components causing the non-linearity.

One Network Round Trip per User Interaction Step. A user interaction step has at least one synchronous communication cycle, which is a network round trip, between the front end and the application server. It is triggered by a user action, e.g. clicking a button in the UI screen, and typically results in a new UI screen. Since network performance is mainly defined by the latency time and bandwidth, minimal number of network round trips and minimal transferred data volume will optimize the network time.

Average End-to-End Response Time Below One Second. End-to-end response time includes the server response time, the network time and front end rendering time. The user interaction steps to complete a business process could have different response times, depending on the content of business processing. Certain average limits are necessary to fulfill usability and end user productivity requirements.

Sizing Procedure Available. A sizing procedure, or sizing guideline, helps to determine the hardware resource consumption behavior of a software application depending on the parameters of the business processes. It is the responsibility of the development team to provide clear architectural concepts for predictable resource consumption, and to verify them by testing.

2.2 Key Performance Indicators Reliably Predict Possible Performance Issues

The traditional response time centric approach of performance testing, analysis and optimization tries to break down end-to-end response time into times spent in individual software components, and to identify the causes of the hotspot times. The optimization activities will then try to reduce or even eliminate the identified hotspot times. The major advantages of this approach are easy to understand and most effective in performance related customer support cases.

Although SAP enterprise applications are delivered as standard business applications, they are customized and modified in nearly every customer installation, thus adapting them to the individual business processes of SAP customers. In addition, they can be personalized by each individual end user. Moreover, these applications support different operating systems, databases and hardware platforms, so that SAP customers can choose their favorite platforms. Under these circumstances, it is impossible to construct and run a set of test cases that weed out all possible performance issues on all possible hardware configurations.

The goal of development testing therefore is to find as many as possible functional and performance issues by executing a limited set of specified test cases. This is one of the most important motivations to use KPIs over and above the tried and tested response time, since these KPIs can help to predict possible issues even when they don't actually occur in the test cases being measured.

Requirements for KPIs. Firstly, good KPIs should reflect the performance both from a user and system point of view. Secondly, good KPIs should be measured accurately. Accuracy supports the optimization process: If a KPI can be measured with an accuracy of 5%, then this KPI can only verify optimizations providing more than 5% improvement. Otherwise, it is impossible to know whether an optimization really improves the performance. Thirdly, only reproducible measurement results can be used for performance evaluation. If the measurement results of a KPI cannot be reproduced, there must be some unknown factors with significant performance impacts. To identify the unknown factors is the next step in the performance analysis and optimization process. And last but not least, good KPIs should give indications for possible optimizations.

The Importance of Defining the Right KPIs. In the KPI-focused approach, the question which performance characteristics should be defined as KPIs is much more important than meeting concrete KPI values. Let's consider our network KPIs as examples to discuss the importance of good KPIs. Network time has a highly indeterministic behavior, since the network resources are shared by many unpredictable consumers, and depend highly on the network topology. This means that the measurement results significantly depend on when and where you measure. In addition, different installations of a software application may use different network transport protocols and could have different quality of services. For this reason, instead of the network time, SAP uses the number of network round trips and transferred date volume, in the application layer of a protocol stack, as KPIs for network performance. These two KPIs can be measured very accurately, and they give clear guidelines to developers on how to improve network performance: one network round trip per user interaction step and minimal transferred data volume. When testing in today's LAN with maximal 10 ms latency time and giga bit per second bandwidth, network performance issues hardly ever occur. But in a WAN, an intercontinental network connection could have a latency time higher than 300 ms, and 100 kilo byte per second as a typical bandwidth. Using measured network KPIs, the real network time can be reliably predicted for different given latency times and bandwidths. In case of sequential network round trips, as a simple example, $network\ time = number\ of\ network\ round\ trips \cdot latency\ time + \frac{data\ volume}{bandwidth}$.

Derived from the performance design patterns, SAP uses the following KPIs in performance tests carried out by developers themselves, and for quality check points and regression tests run by quality teams.

Number of Accesses to the Persistence Layer. In the case of relational databases, this is the number of executed SQL statements. This number indicates the performance and scalability impact of data accesses to the persistence layer which typically represents a central system resource in a SAP system. Achieving this KPI depends on applying the performance design patterns "Using buffers and caches at application server layer" and "No identical accesses to persistence layer".

Data Volume Transferred to and from the Persistence Layer (KB). All databases provide main memory caches to speed up repetitive data accesses. Unnecessary high data volume could cause higher eviction rate and reduce the effectiveness of the database caching. Another aspect covered by this KPI is the limited bandwidth of data transfer between the persistence and the application layer. This KPI is related to the performance design pattern "Complete WHERE clauses of SELECT statements".

CPU Consumption (msec). CPU time represents central system resources shared by many concurrent computing processes and users, thus it could easily become a bottleneck for performance and scalability. In general, CPU time is close to, but not necessarily equal to the response time, depending on whether a request is processed sequentially or in parallel, and on the wait time during the request processing. The CPU time measurement results can be reproduced much easier than the response time, because they largely depend on the test case and the CPU speed, whereas the response time is influenced additionally by many different wait times.

Peak Memory Consumption (MB). Like the CPU, the physical main memory is another central system resource, but it is more critical than CPU. When the CPU resource becomes a bottleneck, it will result in increased system response time. That means, the requests are waiting longer in some system queues and their processing will be postponed (CPU bound). However, when the system resource memory is exhausted, applications cannot continue to run, resulting in a system crash like the Java out of memory error (memory bound).

In modern programming languages like Java, with automatic memory management based on Garbage Collection (GC), the memory consumption behavior cannot be described by a single KPI. The topic of Java memory KPIs and GC tuning will be discussed in the next section.

Number of Network Round Trips and Data Volume Transferred Between Front End and Application Layer (KB). These two KPIs for network performance have already been discussed in detail earlier in this paper.

2.3 Java Memory KPIs and GC Tuning

The Java runtime takes over the responsibility of memory management; the Java programmer only decides when to create objects, which can be used through references, and deletes all references to the object after usage. Once an object has no more references, it will be automatically detected and removed by the Java garbage collector. This automatic memory management enhances the productivity in software development and improves the quality of software code. Memory

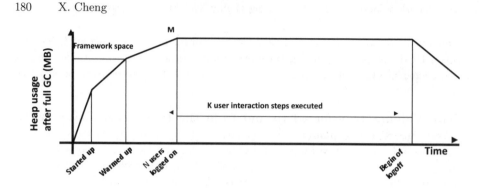

Fig. 1. Measurement procedures of Java memory KPIs in a load test

analysis in Java thus is not only a matter about how to provide enough space; it is complicated by the dynamic aspect of Java garbage collection, which impacts the Java performance and scalability significantly [5].

In Java, we distinguish between memory utilization and memory consumption. Memory utilization is the allocation of physical memory by a Java Virtual Machine (JVM). On the one hand it is necessary to make sufficient Java heap and stack configuration to ensure that available physical memory is really utilized, on the other hand, Java heap and stack must fit completely into the physical memory to avoid paging. While the memory utilization is a matter of configuration, memory consumption is the memory requirement or behavior of a Java application under certain usage, which is independent of the JVM configuration. For a complete observance of Java memory behavior, we propose the following three Java memory KPIs:

Framework Space (MB). This is the memory footprint of a JVM after start up and warm up. This KPI value depends on the number of Java applications which are deployed, started and used on the JVM, and indicates, for a given JVM heap configuration, how much memory is still available to run the applications.

User Session Space (MB). This is the amount of memory allocated by a logged-on, but inactive user, and which cannot be shared by other users. This corresponds to the static, traditional memory KPI of a user session.

Processing Space (MB per User Interaction Step). This is the dynamic part of the Java memory consumption, it is defined as the average garbage colleted memory per user interaction step.

Figure 1 illustrates the measurement procedures of the three Java memory KPIs, when using a multi-user load test. For high reproducibility of the measurement results, we always consider the heap usage after explicitly triggered full GCs. The framework space is determined after system warm-up. The user session space = (M – framework space) / N, and the processing space = total garbage collected bytes during the execution of K user interaction steps / K.

It is important to mention that these three Java memory KPIs are independent from JVM configuration and system load. They reflect the memory requirement of a Java application itself. Thus, these KPIs can be used to support the Java memory optimization.

In principle, each GC cycle runs through three sequential phases: Mark, Sweep and Compact, which all consume system resources such as CPU time. More critical is the fact that, despite different parallel and concurrent GC algorithms, the "stop the world pause" where all the Java application threads are held down cannot be omitted completely. This can result in poor response time and poor CPU utilization [6]. Also, because there is no locality of memory access during GCs, memory paging becomes very dangerous for Java applications. And in the worst case, so-called Java resonance may occur, where the CPU utilization oscillates between 0% and 100%. To evaluate the impact of GC, we propose the following two GC KPIs, which can be calculated as average counters from a GC log:

- **GC Duration,** i.e. the average elapsed time required to complete a GC cycle. This GC KPI represents the negative impact.
- **GC Interval,** i.e. the average elapsed time between two successive GC occurrences.

GC duration should always be considered in relation to GC interval. Assuming that the average object life time remains constant, the higher the GC interval is, the more efficient the GC cycle, i.e. able to recycle more garbage and to copy fewer objects for compaction.

Using these GC KPIs, it is possible to evaluate the efficiency of different Java heap configurations and the GC algorithms used, when putting the same load on a system. In a productive installation with given heap configuration and GC algorithm, the GC KPIs indicate whether the performance impact of GC activities is acceptable. As rules of thumb, we recommend a minor GC duration of less than 0.2 seconds and a minor GC interval of more than 1 second, and a full GC duration of less than 10 seconds and a full GC interval of more than 10 minutes.

In summary, whenever possible, it is best to first try to optimize the Java memory consumption using the memory KPIs, and then start with GC tuning via the GC KPIs. The influencing factors and programming guidelines are shown in the following table.

Table 1. Guidelines for Java memory optimization

The influencing factor	*Programming Guideline*
Volume of temporary objects	Reuse objects as long as possible
Life time of intermediate objects	Release unneeded objects as early as possible
Volume of long time objects	Use well designed and balanced caches in Java

2.4   KPI-Focused Performance Testing, Analysis and Optimization

Single User Tests. Single user tests can check important business processes already in the early phases of development projects. They focus on the end-to-end response time and system resource consumption, and are able to break them down into the system components. Single user tests provide baseline performance figures which can serve as starting points for multi-user load tests. An important aspect of single user tests is that the test system can be shared by many users for different implementation and testing activities, when the test system is running at moderate load. The another advantage of single user test is that they can be easily repeated for accurate and reproducible measurement results.

To deliver relevant measurement results, possible caching and JIT (Just In Time) compilation effects should be taken into consideration. Therefore, test cases should first be executed to warm up the system, before measurements start.

Let's look at a simple procedure to check the linear dependency in resource consumption using a single user test. Let's suppose the linear dependency of number of line items of a sales order should be checked, and a performance trace is available which can measure the total response time and CPU time, as well as the response time and CPU time of the methods and routines called. In a first test run, you create a sales order with 5 line items, and in a second test run, you create a sales order with 20 line items. When comparing the total response times and CPU times, the increasing factor should be below 4. Otherwise a non-linear dependency exists. To identify possible non-linear methods and subroutines, you can compare the sorted hotspot lists of methods and subroutines in the performance trace: they should stay in the same order. If the order is changed, those methods and subroutines that have moved towards the top of the hotspot lists are the candidates for a further detailed analysis.

Multi-user Load Testing. Multi-user load testing is used to generate a system load by simulating a specified number of concurrent users, who execute defined critical business processes. In addition to solving the functional issues which occur under load and were not detected by single user tests, a much more important task of multi-user load testing is to monitor and understand the system behavior under load. While the first part is to ensure the accurate simulation of a specified system load, the second part is to analyze how the measured KPIs react to the increasing system load. A system load is not only represented by the number of concurrent users and the average think time, which is the elapsed time between two successive user interaction step, but also impacted by the system data used in the multi-user load tests [2].

Before starting with load tests, single user tests must be conducted. Based on the single user measurement results, a prediction of the results of the load test should be made assuming linear dependency of resource consumption, or scalability. This is what we call a sizing procedure and will be described in section 4. The extrapolated test results are verified in the multi-user load test, thus they represent the success criteria of a multi-user load test project.

Custom load tests are often conducted in large, highly modified and mission-critical software implementation projects at customer sites, shortly before going live. A successful custom load test can ultimately ensure that the performance requirements of a complex software application, including the hardware platform, the system landscape and the communication network infrastructure, have been met.

Within the development of standard application software, the major goals of multi-user load testing are to analyze the scalability behavior regarding highly concurrent usage of the software and to solve potential scalability issues before release. The mathematical queuing theory [1] provides queuing models, for example, the Markov Chain model M/M/n for a symmetric multiprocessor system with n processors/cores, to enable the study of system response time behaviors related to system utilization. The example below shows how to prove the CPU scalability regarding number of concurrent users.

After carefully analyzing critical business processes, a representative sequence of user interaction steps is determined. We simulate increasing numbers of concurrent users executing this sequence of user interaction steps with constant think time and measure the KPIs of CPU time per user interaction step, CPU utilization, and the corresponding response time. Putting these measurement results together in a chart, as shown in Fig. 2, we can then exam the CPU scalability:

- CPU time per user interaction step remains constant over increasing numbers of concurrent users. This corresponds to the fundamental assertion in the queuing theory models, that the service time of a specific request is independent of the current system utilization. Otherwise, if the CPU time per user interaction step increases, this would cause an over linear increase of CPU utilization and a non-linear increase of response time, which we call a "busy waiting" issue regarding the CPU scalability.
- CPU utilization increases linearly with the number of concurrent users. This behavior demonstrates especially that the software is able to utilize available CPU resource in an efficient way. If the CPU utilization doesn't increase linearly with the number of concurrent users, then the response time would increase rapidly, something we call a "serialization" issue of the CPU scalability.
- Response time behaviors as expected by the queuing theory model. According to the M/M/n model, the response time should start with a constant section, followed by a linearly increasing section, and finally ending in an exponentially increasing section, where the CPU utilization is close to 100%.

Performance Optimization. Don't start with any performance optimization before you can measure the impact. This recommendation emphasizes that any performance optimization should always be documented by measurements before and after the optimization to validate the improvement gained. Otherwise, you don't really know the effect of your optimization effort. All performance optimization concepts should be derived by analyzing the current measured KPIs,

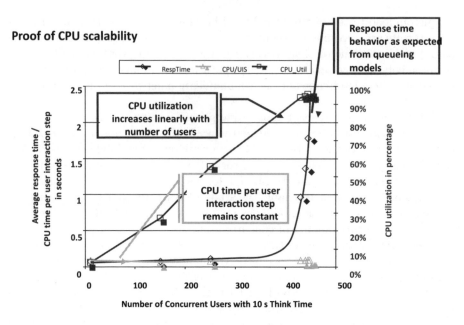

Fig. 2. Multi-user load tests of SAP NetWeaver Portal benchmark EP-ESS to prove the CPU scalability

and by making forecasts of possible performance improvements. This forecasting can be supported by additional prototyping and measurements efforts. Based on realistic forecasts, many possible performance optimization concepts can then be correctly prioritized. This helps in project planning and ensures maximum success of a performance optimization project, also taking into consideration all possible constraints of time, budget, development resources, and high-level strategies.

Although good KPIs can give an indication of possible optimizations, developing optimization concepts remains a creative procedure, highly dependent on the expertise and creativity of the software architects and developers involved. Below we will discuss possible levels at which to implement performance optimizations, by going backwards in the software life cycle, from operation and maintenance to requirement specification.

– **Performance optimization by software configuration tuning.** The most effective and cost-efficient way of performance optimization is to solve performance and scalability issues, identified during the productive usage of a software application, by applying proper configurations. For this reason, SAP provides its customers with a variety of configuration guidelines based on the experiences made in our internal testing, to cover advanced landscaping and high availability requirements and different usage types.
– **Performance optimization by utilizing additional hardware resources.** If the software application is scalable regarding hardware

utilization, then any performance issues can be solved by adding more hardware resources. This is a relatively cost-efficient way to solve the problem, since today's hardware purchase prices don't play a dominating role in the total cost of ownership (TCO). To proactively support the reliable estimation of hardware requirements, SAP provides its customers with specific sizing guidelines for all delivered software applications (http://service.sap.com/sizing). The sizing aspect is discussed in section 4 of this paper.

- **Performance optimization by bug fixing in the code.** When violations against performance design patterns are identified in analyzing measured KPIs, and the issues can be fixed by changing the code, then this is the most suitable performance optimization. As a disadvantage of this kind of performance optimization, additional testing effort is necessary to avoid functional destabilization. The necessary testing effort will depend on how critical the code modification is.
- **Performance optimization by improving the software architecture.** When the identified performance and scalability issues cannot be fixed by simple code modification, and redesign of interfaces or fundamental changes in underlying algorithms are necessary, then expensive effort for design, implementation and testing is needed for performance optimization at this level.
- **Performance optimization by redesign of the business process and its mapping onto the software solution.** If no optimization potential can be identified in the software application, the next step is to go a level higher to consider the business process. Most solutions at this level are achieved by optimizing the mapping of the business process into software concepts.

3   Benchmarking

SAP Standard Application Benchmarks are based on enterprise applications used productively in customer environments. Thus they are eminently suitable for helping customers make decisions for appropriate hardware platforms used in their IT landscape. They are also used by hardware partners to conduct platform tests. The benchmark certification procedure is monitored by the SAP Benchmark Council made up of representatives of SAP and its hardware and technology partners. A description of all SAP Standard Application Benchmarks including the certified results can be found at SAP's Benchmark Web site [7].

In SAP benchmarking, we use a measurement unit called SAPS (SAP Application Performance Standard), for processing power related to business processes. 100 SAPS is defined as the processing power required to complete 2000 fully business-processed order line items within one hour. Fully business-processed means the complete business process of an order line item: creating the order, creating a delivering note for the order, displaying the order, changing the delivery, posting a goods issue, listing orders, and creating an invoice. This business process is represented by the Sales and Distribution (SD) benchmark, which is the most established benchmark in the SAP Standard Application Benchmark suite.

Table 2. KPI values of a certified EP-ESS benchmark with SAP NetWeaver Portal 7.0, SP12, running on a 2 processors / 4 cores / 8 threads machine with approximately 10,000 SAPS

Number of concurrent users with 10 seconds think time	2600
CPU utilization	99%
Average response time	1.811 s
CPU time per user interaction step	0.018 s
Framework space	325 MB
User session space	< 1 MB
Processing space	8.714 MB
GC interval	2.390 s
GC duration	0.424 s

In the course of the benchmarking process, the hardware partners execute the SD benchmark or any other benchmark in the suite of specific SAP releases on their hardware platforms to demonstrate their scalability and processing power. The benchmark results, especially the SAPS numbers of specific hardware configurations, are certified by SAP on behalf of the SAP Benchmark Council and published at SAP's Benchmark Web site. Using this information, SAP customers are able to search the available hardware platforms for configurations that best meet their business needs.

Among SAP Standard Application Benchmarks, there are currently two major Java benchmarks: the EP-ESS (SAP NetWeaver Portal Employee Self-Service Benchmark) and EP-PCC (SAP NetWeaver Portal People Centric CRM Benchmark) benchmarks. Employee self-service represents business scenarios for the "employee" role, e.g. to record working time, to create leave requests, to display overview of leave requests, to maintain personal data, address, bank information and to request paycheck inquiries. The EP-ESS benchmark simulates a huge number of concurrent users executing SAP NetWeaver Portal top level navigations. These navigation steps launch stateful business transactions in the back end which are Single-Sign-On (SSO) supported, role-based and personalized.

The EP-ESS benchmark has been used as a tool by SAP and the JVM vendors to improve the performance and scalability of application software and the JVM platforms on different operating systems and different databases. Tab. 2 shows the KPI values of a certified EP-ESS benchmark.

4   Sizing

The performance of customer production systems depends both on the performance behavior of the software applications including OS, DB and JVM, and on the hardware configurations. Following on from the performance assurance processes during development and the benchmarking process used to prove the scalability, the sizing process "delivers" the performance and scalability to customer production systems by enabling correct prediction of hardware resource requirements depending on the business processes. The sizing process consists of two major parts: 1. Creation of sizing guidelines based on the results of performance tests and analysis in the development phase. 2. Using these sizing guidelines in customer sizing projects. [4] provides an in-depth description of the SAP sizing process.

Sizing guidelines represent hardware resource consumption behavior of a software application related to the influencing factors of the business process. Identifying the influencing factors is a creative process which requires good understanding of the business process, the software architecture and the implementation techniques. In general, it is an iterative process of experimental measurements and analysis. The results of this process are a set of influencing factors and a related set of test cases. For these test cases, SAP measures the following sizing KPIs to derive sizing formulas:

CPU Consumption. SAP typically measures CPU time per user interaction step. For example, for the SAP NetWeaver Portal sizing, SAP measures the CPU time of a portal navigation step. The influencing factors of a portal navigation step, are the number and types of the iViews displayed on the target portal page of a portal navigation step. An iView is an iFrame-like region of a portal page, which hosts the UI of a back end application. Once an average CPU time per user interaction step has been determined, the CPU sizing formula can be expressed as:

$$numberOfCPUs = \frac{CPU_{UIS} \cdot noUsers}{(thinkTime + responseTime) \cdot CPU_{Utilization}} \quad (1)$$

Where

$$noUsers = \text{number of concurrent Users}$$
$$CPU_{UIS} = \text{CPU time per user interaction step}$$

In term of SAPS, the formula can be rewritten to read:

$$totalSAPS = \frac{SAPSpCPU_{UIT} \cdot CPU_{UIS} \cdot noUsers}{(thinkTime + responseTime) \cdot CPU_{Utilization}} \quad (2)$$

Where

$$SAPSpCPU_{UIT} = \text{SAPS per CPU used in test}$$

Memory. SAP also measures the peak memory consumption of a user session. In case of Java applications, the three Java memory KPIs introduced in section 2.3 are measured. If the user session space dominates the memory consumption, the memory sizing formula could be:

$$totalRequiredMemory = userSessionSpace \cdot noUsers \quad (3)$$

If the processing space dominates, a possible memory sizing model could couple the memory sizing to the CPU sizing. For example, in sizing the SAP NetWeaver Portal, SAP recommends 1 GB physical memory for every 300 SAPS CPU power.

Front End Network Requirement. As introduced early, SAP measures two network KPIs: the number of network round trips and the data volume transferred per user interaction step. For a bandwidth sizing, the following formula can be applied:

$$totalBandwidth = sf \cdot \frac{transferredData_{UIS} \cdot noUsers}{thinkTime + responseTime} \qquad (4)$$

Where

$$sf = \text{Saftey factor}$$
$$transferredData_{UIS} = \text{Transferred data volume per user interaction step}$$

where the *safetyFactor* can be determined by taking account of the protocol overhead and the possible utilization of a network connection.

Database Space. This is the space of the database tables needed during the execution of the application.

Using the application specific sizing guidelines, technical consultants work together with business department, implementation project team and hardware vendor, to determine for the business process to be implemented:

– **the application usage profile**, e.g. the concrete values of the influencing factors,
– **the user activity profile**, e.g. the number of concurrent users and average think time.

The application usage profile and user activity profile are the required sizing inputs. As a next step the formulas from the sizing guidelines can be applied to calculate the required hardware resources. Different hardware vendors can provide their proposals for the target hardware configurations, taking into consideration system landscaping requirements like high availability, etc.

As a simple example, let's consider the CPU sizing of SAP NetWeaver Portal. To determine the application usage profile, we need to find out the typical average portal page in terms of number and types of iViews displayed on that page. With this information, a corresponding value of the term "$SAPSPerCPUUsedInTest \cdot CPUTimePerUserInteractionStep$" can be found in the sizing guideline and the CPU sizing formula (2) can be applied. Note that SAP assumes an average CPU utilization of 65% for production systems.

As a second example, let's look at how to predict load test results based on single user measurement results, by using the CPU sizing formula (1). Using *CPUTimePerUserInteractionStep* from a single user test, *thinkTime* reflecting the typical user behavior, and *NumberOfCPUs* of the test system, the formula (1) represents the relationship between *numberOfConcurrentUsers*, *responseTime* and *CPUUtilization*. In a first use case when you want to stress the application at *CPUUtilization*, and based on the experiences made in single user tests, you expect a *responseTime* (since *thinkTime* $>>$ *responseTime* holds in general, the estimated *responseTime* would have negligible impact on the term *"thinkTime + responseTime"*), then the *numberOfConcurrentUsers* to be simulated can be determined. In a second use case when you want to simulate *numberOfConcurrentUsers* and use estimated *responseTime*, the resulting *CPUUtilization* can be predicted.

[4] describes further sizing approaches used in customer sizing projects. The *Initial Sizing* provides sizing statements related to SAP standard delivery of software application. It is supported by a tool, the *Quick Sizer* which is available for SAP customers at http://service.sap.com/sizing. During *Expert Sizing*, sizing measurements for highly modified software applications are conducted at the customer site, to adjust the standard sizing guidelines accordingly. SAP provides *Delta Sizing* and *Upgrade Sizing* to help customers when extending business scenarios and upgrading to SAP new releases. *User-Based Sizing* and *Throughput-Based Sizing* can be applied to help determine more accurate sizing inputs. These depend on whether an application has user interaction or works as background batch jobs.

5   Conclusion

SAP performance design patterns define the target behavior of software components and interfaces and guide the performance considerations in the design and implementation phases. SAP follows a KPI-focused approach for performance testing, analysis and optimization. It enables the reliable detection of potential performance issues by testing a limited set of specified test cases. A set of comprehensive performance KPIs ist used both in single user tests and multi-user load tests to support the performance optimization processes by predicting and documenting the performance improvements quantitatively, and to verify scalability.

SAP introduces three Java memory KPIs. They are application-specific and independent on the JVM configurations, thus they are used to support the Java memory optimization. We also use GC KPIs indicating the performance impact of Java garbage collection which are used for JVM configuration tuning.

SAP Standard Application Benchmarks enable a standardized comparison of different hardware platforms and help SAP customers to make decisions for their IT landscape. They are also used within SAP as a tool for performance optimization and for verification of sizing statements. The SAP NetWeaver Portal Employee Self Service benchmark EP-ESS is presented to illustrate the introduced KPIs and the methodology of scalability tests.

With proven scalability, SAP's sizing process reliably predicts the hardware resource requirements depending on the influencing factors of the business processes to be implemented, for ensuring appropriate performance of customer productive systems. As an example of this sizing process, we discussed the CPU and Java memory sizing for SAP NetWeaver Portal.

References

1. Bolch, G., et al.: Queuing Networks and Markov Chains: Modeling and Performance Evaluation with Computer Science Applications. John Wiley & Sons, New York (1998)
2. Cheng, X.: Demystify Java-Based Load Tests and Their Results. SAP Insider, Wellesley Information Services, October-November-December (2006),
   https://www.sdn.sap.com/irj/servlet/prt/portal/prtroot/docs/library/
   uuid/c1c8a123-0e01-0010-f8bf-a2d8ea8ec5b7
3. Tow, D.: SQL Tuning. O'Reilly Media (December 2004)
4. Janssen, S., Marquard, U.: Sizing SAP Systems. Galileo Press GmbH, Bonn (2007)
5. Meier, R.: Techniques for minimizing the performance impact of Java garbage collection across your system landscape. SAP Professional Journal 9(3), Wellesley Information Services (May/June 2007)
6. Sun Microsystems: Java SE 6 HotSpot^{TM} Virtual Machine Garbage Collection Tuning. Sun Microsystems, SDN, http://java.sun.com/javase/technologies/
   hotspot/gc/gc_tuning_6.html
7. SAP Standard Application Benchmarks, http://www.sap.com/benchmark

Phase-Type Approximations for Message Transmission Times in Web Services Reliable Messaging

Philipp Reinecke and Katinka Wolter

Humboldt-Universität zu Berlin
Unter den Linden 6,
10099 Berlin
{preineck,wolter}@informatik.hu-berlin.de

Abstract. Web-Services based Service-Oriented Architectures (SOAs) become ever more important. The Web Services Reliable Messaging standard (WSRM) provides a reliable messaging layer to these systems. In this work we present parameters for acyclic continuous phase-type (ACPH) approximations for message transmission times in a WSRM implementation confronted with several different levels of IP packet loss. These parameters illustrate how large data sets may be represented by just a few parameters. The ACPH approximations presented here can be used for the stochastic modelling of SOA systems. We demonstrate application of the models using an M/PH/1 queue.

Keywords: Phase-Type Distributions, WSRM, Modelling, Distribution Fitting, Response Time Analysis, Queueing Model.

1 Introduction

Web-Services-based Service-Oriented Architectures (SOAs) play an increasing role in private and commercial activities on the Internet. These systems require reliable transmissions of SOAP messages over possibly unreliable links.

The Web Services Reliable Messaging (WSRM) standard provides an interface for reliable message transmissions [1] over arbitrary SOAP transports. WSRM operates on top of the existing network stack (e.g. using HTTP on top of TCP/IP). From the application's point of view, a WSRM implementation guarantees several properties (e.g. INORDER, EXACTLY-ONCE) for message transmissions.

WSRM employs an acknowledgement-based restart mechanism. The transmission of SOAP messages is ensured by retransmitting messages whose arrival has not been acknowledged within a certain timeout. As observed in [2], a restart mechanism at this high level in the network stack is necessary even though the TCP already provides reliable connections: High fault levels in the IP may result in stalling of TCP connections, which in turn translate into message loss due to

S. Kounev, I. Gorton, and K. Sachs (Eds.): SIPEW 2008, LNCS 5119, pp. 191–207, 2008.

timeouts in the upper layers. Furthermore, it should be noted that the WSRM handles a wide variety of faults which are not addressed by the TCP at all, e.g. failures of intermediary SOAP nodes or failures in DNS resolution.

The timeout after which the message transmission task is restarted strongly influences the timing characteristics of the WSRM as perceived by the application. In previous work we studied the effect of different restart strategies [2], and the adaptivity of restart strategies in the WSRM area [3].

In this work we provide phase-type approximations for the effective transmission times encountered in a WSRM implementation where messages are transmitted over a link with IP packet loss. We consider three scenarios with different loss levels and derive acyclic continuous phase-type (ACPH) approximations for the transmission time distribution. We present three different approximations for each data set: First, we use a simple ACPH(2) model fitted by matching the first three moments [4]. The second model is a Hyper-Erlang distribution (HErD), fitted using the G-FIT tool [5, 6]. Third, we approximate the trace distributions with general ACPH distributions using the PhFit tool [7].

We provide several contributions. First, we show how a large data set can be represented in just a few model parameters and can hence be stored in a very efficient and compact way. Second, we provide a model of a lossy communication network using WSRM that can be inserted into a larger model of e.g. a web services scenario. We present a simple M/PH/1 queue as an example of how to use our fitted models. In that sense, we provide benchmarks to evaluate web services performance and reliability. Third, we compare different models as well as different fitting tools on a large data set of measurements in an intricate scenario. The shape of the empirical distribution is unlike any known probability distribution, therefore a compromise must be found between matching the heavy tail well, based on extremely few observations, and providing a good fit for the bulk of the data.

The remainder of this paper is structured as follows: The next section briefly introduces the basic formalisms employed throughout the paper. Section 3 presents the experiments. In Section 4 we discuss important properties of the data sets and present the ACPH models. We evaluate our approximations in Section 5. The paper concludes with an application of the models in an M/PH/1 queue.

2   Acyclic Phase-Type Distributions (ACPH)

Phase-type distributions represent the time to absorption in a Markov chain with one absorbing state. Acyclic Phase-type distributions (APH) form an important subclass of PH distributions. In this paper we focus on acyclic continuous phase-type distributions (ACPH).

An ACPH model with N transient states is described by the tuple $(\mathbf{Q}, \boldsymbol{\alpha})$, where $\boldsymbol{\alpha} = (\alpha_1, \alpha_2, \ldots, \alpha_N)$ is the vector of initial probabilities, and $\mathbf{Q}$ is the transition matrix for the transient states. The underlying CTMC is specified by [8]:

$$\hat{Q} := \begin{bmatrix} Q & q \\ 0 & 0 \end{bmatrix}.$$

The column vector q can be easily derived from Q: $q = -Q\mathbb{1}$. The vector of initial probabilities is

$$\hat{\alpha} = (\alpha, \alpha_{N+1}) \text{ with } \sum_{i=1}^{N+1} \alpha_i = 1.$$

Note that $\alpha_{N+1} = 0$ for all distributions we consider here.

The probability density function (PDF) and the cumulative density function (CDF) of an ACPH distribution are given by, respectively [7],

$$f(x) = \alpha e^{Qx} q$$
$$F(x) = 1 - \alpha e^{Qx} \mathbb{1}.$$

The ith non-central moment of an ACPH can be computed as [4]

$$E[X^i] = i! \alpha (-Q)^{-i} \mathbb{1}.$$

In this work we present ACPH approximations of WSRM message transmission times. We consider models from the general ACPH class and models from two subclasses, viz. second-order ACPH models (ACPH(2)) and Hyper-Erlang distributions (HErD). The next two paragraphs discuss properties of these special cases.

Second-Order ACPH. ACPH(2) models are comprised of only two transient states, i.e.

$$\alpha = (\alpha, 1 - \alpha)$$
$$Q = \begin{bmatrix} -\lambda_1 & \lambda_1 \\ 0 & -\lambda_2 \end{bmatrix}.$$

ACPH(2) models are attractive due to their low number of states, which allows for efficient models. Furthermore, using moment-matching [4], parameters for these models can often be obtained directly from the first three moments.

However, precise matching of the first three moments with ACPH(2) is limited by tight bounds on the second and third moment of the data. For data sets whose moments are outside of these bounds, one must either employ a higher-order ACPH or settle on a model that only approximates the second and/or third moment [4].

Hyper-Erlang Distributions. Hyper-Erlang distributions (HErDs) consist of a mixture of M Erlang distributions with parameters $(\lambda_r, k_r), r = 1, \ldots, M$, where λ_r and k_r give the rate and number of phases (or the shape), respectively, of the rth Erlang distribution in the HErD.

The transition matrix for the underlying CTMC has the following general structure $(r = 1, \ldots, M)$:

$$
Q = \begin{bmatrix}
\ddots & & & & & & & \\
& -\lambda_{r-1} & 0 & 0 & & & & \\
& 0 & -\lambda_r & \lambda_r & 0 & & & \\
& & 0 & -\lambda_r & \lambda_r & 0 & & \\
& & & & \ddots & & & \\
& & & & 0 & -\lambda_r & 0 & 0 \\
& & & & & 0 & -\lambda_{r+1} & \lambda_{r+1} \\
& & & & & & & \ddots
\end{bmatrix}.
$$

For a HErD, the vector of initial probabilities (α) specifies the probabilities of entering each Erlang branch (or the *weights* of the branches). Accordingly, in α each weight α_r is followed by $k_r - 1$ zeros:

$$
\alpha = (\alpha_1, 0, \ldots, 0, \alpha_2, 0, \ldots, 0, \alpha_M, 0, \ldots, 0).
$$

Hyper-Erlang distributions allow us to approximate the distribution of the data more closely than is possible with moment matching using second-order acyclic PH distributions. Moreover, any ACPH can be approximated by a HErD of sufficiently high order, although this may require a HErD with an infinite number of states. On the other hand, typical HErD models have an order higher than two and thus may become computationally expensive. However, HErD matching can be performed more efficiently than general ACPH matching. See e.g. [5, 6] for more detail on Hyper-Erlang distributions.

3   Experiments

Web Services Reliable Messaging provides reliable SOAP message transmissions to Web Services by re-sending messages for which no acknowledgement has been received before a timeout elapsed. Every message can thus be transmitted several times. In particular, a retransmission may arrive earlier than the original transmission. Our data sets present the time between the first attempt at sending the message and the first time the message arrived at the destination. This Effective Transmission Time (ETT) determines the effect of the WSRM on the application [2, 3]. The current section describes the experiment setup and measurement preparation procedures.

3.1   Experiment Setup

In our setup a Web Services client transmits one-way messages asynchronously to a server, using WSRM. An enhanced version of Sandesha1/Axis1 [9, 10] provides the WSRM implementation for the experiments. The modifications add support for asynchronous message transmissions (implemented similarly to [11]) and improve Sandesha's stability and performance.[1] The operation environment consists of a 10 Mbit LAN connection, emulated on top of the physical 100 Mbit Ethernet, using the Linux traffic control facilities [12]. Fault injection occurs in the 10 Mbit connection on a dedicated host. We inject packet loss at the IP layer.

In each experiment run the client transmits 20000 messages with a payload of 256 bytes and a message inter-arrival time of 100 ms. Experiment runs that take longer than one hour to complete are discarded. In order to avoid the effects of software aging, client and server are restarted between runs.

Packet Loss Model. IP Packet loss is generated according to a simplified continuous-time Gilbert loss model with one loss-free and one lossy state. Gilbert loss models generate sequences of alternating loss episodes and loss-free periods of exponentially-distributed length, which capture characteristics of packet-loss on Internet links quite well [13, 14, 15, 16, 17]. We consider three scenarios with different mean loss episode and loss-free period lengths, presented in Tab. 1.

Table 1. Loss model scenarios

	S_1	S_2	S_3
Loss episode length	0.05 s	1 s	1 s
Loss-free period length	120 s	30 s	8 s

WSRM Restart Algorithms. We provide results for three different algorithms to compute the restart timeout: The *Fixed Intervals* algorithm uses a constant timeout of 4 s. The well-known Jacobson/Karn algorithm adjusts the timeout based on the mean and variance of round-trip time observations [18, 19]. We set the parameters for the Jacobson/Karn algorithm as follows: $k = 4, \alpha = 1/8, \beta = 1/4$, and initial timeout $RTO_{initial} = 4$ s. Third, we use the QEST algorithm presented in [20], which observes the distribution of completion times and computes a timeout that minimises the expected completion time. The parameters for QEST are: Number of buckets $H = 1000$, maximum timeout $t_{max} = 60$ s and initial timeout $RTO_{initial} = 4$ s.

In order to reduce load on the medium, both Jacobson/Karn and QEST perform exponential back-off upon timeout, i.e. they double the restart timeout for the next transmission.

3.2   Measurement Preparation

Measurements were obtained by off-line analysis of message send/receive events recorded during the experiments.

---

[1] The current branch of Sandesha development, Sandesha2/Axis2, supports asynchronous invocations natively, but was not stable enough for the experiments. However, the basic operation of different WSRM implementations can be considered comparable.

Accuracy. Since measurements were computed from time-stamps recorded on two different machines, both system clocks needed to be synchronised. System clocks were synchronised using NTP. Clock synchronisation in the test-bed was assessed based on NTP log files. System clocks stayed within +/- 2 ms of each other during the experiments, which we consider sufficiently accurate so as to not necessitate the use of skew removal procedures such as presented in e.g. [21, 22, 23].

Artifacts. Many runs exhibited a transient increase of ETTs shortly after the start of the experiment, whose root cause could not be identified. Since this phenomenon affected experiments irrespective of the scenario or the restart strategy used, we consider this an artifact introduced by the test-bed itself. We only include message numbers $1000, \ldots, 20000$ in our data sets.

Furthermore, all data sets for Fixed Intervals have minimum values of 8–9 ms (median 9–13 ms), whereas in the S_1 and S_2 data sets minima for Jacobson/Karn and QEST are in the range of 12–13 ms (median 10–18 ms). In the S_3 data sets, all strategies have similar minima and median (7–9 ms and 11 ms, respectively).

All experiments whose measurements have lower minima were performed some time after the experiments with higher minima. The decrease indicates a change in network characteristics in the time in between. The nature and cause of this change is unknown. We consider this difference negligible for the approximations presented in the next section.

4   Phase-Type Approximations

We approximate the data using different classes of acyclic phase-type distributions. For each scenario/algorithm combination we aggregate observations from four runs into one data set (76004 samples) for the approximation, and keep one run (19001 samples) for cross-evaluation of the models. We employ the R statistics package [24] in the statistical evaluation of the data.

4.1   Data Set Characteristics

Table 2 presents some statistical properties of the data sets. S_{iFI}, S_{iJK} and S_{iQ} denote data sets for Fixed Intervals, Jacobson/Karn and QEST algorithm, respectively, obtained in the ith scenario. Note that all data sets exhibit a coefficient of variation (CoV) above one, which points at possible heavy-tailed behaviour of the distribution underlying the data.

Visual inspection of the empirical complementary cumulative density function (CCDF) for S_{1FI}, S_{2FI} and S_{3FI} (Figures 1–3) reveals that the bulk of the samples is small, with large values centred around 3 s and 6 s and few observations between the bulk and the extreme values. The 'steps' in the CCDF become more pronounced with higher loss levels, e.g. in S_{3FI}. The accumulation of extreme values at 3 s and 6 s as well as the gaps in between are due to the way TCP

Table 2. Statistical properties of the data sets (in ms)

	S_{1FI}	S_{1JK}	S_{1Q}	S_{2FI}	S_{2JK}	S_{2Q}	S_{3FI}	S_{3JK}	S_{3Q}
Mean	17.24	21.32	22.44	124.71	106.51	104.60	386.29	334.91	313.76
Std. Dev.	59.54	46.57	26.98	542.27	441.05	426.03	995.20	903.30	955.51
Minimum	8	12	12	8	12	12	8	9	7
Median	11	16	18	11	17	17	11	11	11
95% quantile	19	24	27	213	179	449	3011	2404	1986
99% quantile	152	162	160	3014	2883	2674	4051	3031	3140
Maximum	3017	2226	562	6280	6562	9260	9900	12499	21056
CoV	11.91	4.79	1.45	18.91	17.15	16.59	6.64	7.23	9.27

detects packet loss during the three-way handshake on connection setup: The TCP starts with a fixed retransmission timeout (RTO) of 3 s, which is doubled on every expiration [19]. This means that any SOAP message transmission for which the TCP connection setup experiences packet loss will be delayed by at least 3 s. Since the Fixed Intervals algorithm restarts the transmission only if the message has not been acknowledged after 4 s, it will not resend messages for which only one packet loss happened during connection setup. These message will have effective transmission times between 3 and 4 s. Messages whose connection setup suffers from more than one packet loss are delayed by more than 4 s and will thus be resent. If the retransmission does not experience packet loss, it will succeed earlier than the first one. In this case, instead of a large ETT of 3 s we observe a small ETT from the bulk of the distribution. On the other hand, some retransmissions will also be delayed by packet loss. Since these messages were restarted after at least 4 s and experience a minimum delay of 3 s, their ETT is above 7 s. Then, the first transmission, which was delayed by only 6 s, will finish earlier, which explains the accumulation of samples around 6 s.

In the interest of brevity we omit the empirical CCDFs of the data sets from the experiments with Jacobson/Karn and QEST. These differ from the observations for the Fixed Intervals algorithm in that they gather more samples in the bulk. In particular, in the S_1 data set, Jacobson/Karn has fewer observations around 3 s, while for QEST the tail of the observations breaks down even below 1 s. With higher loss levels, however, both start to show peaks around 3 s and 6 s similar to observations from Fixed Intervals. This can be explained by the way in which these algorithms adjust the restart timeout: Message transmissions that are not delayed by packet loss finish very fast. Based on observations of these low completion times, both algorithms compute low timeout values (with Jacobson/Karn being more conservative), typically much lower than the 4 s of the Fixed Intervals algorithm. These lower timeouts allow the algorithms to detect (and restart) delayed transmissions early, which results in low completion times. On the other hand, Jacobson/Karn and QEST perform exponential back-off when the timeout elapses. With higher loss levels, it is likely that several timeouts elapse successively. Then, the timeout grows quickly, eventually allowing

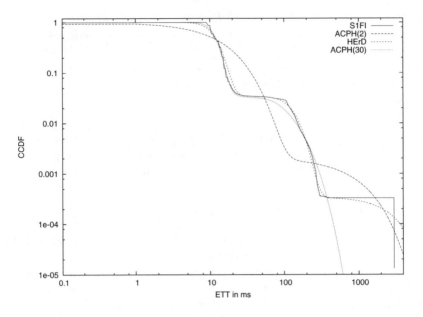

Fig. 1. Empirical CCDF and CCDFs of the approximations for $\mathcal{S}_{1\mathrm{FI}}$

even very slow transmissions to finish without restart. When the first transmission completes without restart, the timeout is recomputed from the observations. The algorithm will then again trigger restarts of slow transmissions.

Table 3. Parameters for the ACPH(2) models, obtained by moment matching

	$\mathcal{S}_{1\mathrm{FI}}$	$\mathcal{S}_{1\mathrm{JK}}$	$\mathcal{S}_{1\mathrm{Q}}$	$\mathcal{S}_{2\mathrm{FI}}$	$\mathcal{S}_{2\mathrm{JK}}$	$\mathcal{S}_{2\mathrm{Q}}$	$\mathcal{S}_{3\mathrm{FI}}$	$\mathcal{S}_{3\mathrm{JK}}$	$\mathcal{S}_{3\mathrm{Q}}$
α_1	2.05e-03	2.46e-03	9.07e-03	1.00e-01	1.10e-01	7.86e-02	2.62e-01	2.29e-01	5.70e-02
λ_1	1.11e-03	1.66e-03	8.13e-03	8.06e-04	1.04e-03	9.13e-04	6.78e-04	7.05e-04	3.53e-04
λ_2	6.49e-02	5.04e-02	4.69e-02	7.21e+01	8.36e+01	5.40e-02	1.91e+01	8.80e-02	6.57e-03

4.2   ACPH(2)-Approximation

Table 3 presents the ACPH(2) models obtained by moment-matching [4] for the first three moments. Note that the third moment could not be matched exactly by an ACPH(2) in data sets $\mathcal{S}_{2\mathrm{FI}}$, $\mathcal{S}_{2\mathrm{JK}}$ and $\mathcal{S}_{3\mathrm{FI}}$. In these cases we approximate the third moment as suggested in [4].

4.3   Hyper-Erlang Approximation

We employ the G-FIT tool [5], which implements an EM-algorithm for fitting the parameters of a HErD to a data set. In order to improve the quality of the fitting, we initialise the parameters λ_r and $\boldsymbol{\alpha}$ using the logarithmic aggregation method presented in [6]. We then fit the parameters using the EM algorithm and the whole (i.e. non-aggregated) data set.

We found that using a Hyper-Erlang distribution with 15 branches and shape parameters $k_r = r$ for the rth branch provided good approximation of the data. Table 4 shows the parameters for the data set $\mathcal{S}_{2\mathrm{FI}}$. Parameters for the other data sets can be downloaded from [25].

Table 4. HErD parameters for $\mathcal{S}_{2\mathrm{FI}}$. The shape parameter k_r of the rth Erlang branch is $k_r = r$.

r	α_r	λ_r	α_{r+1}	λ_{r+1}	α_{r+2}	λ_{r+2}	α_{r+3}	λ_{r+3}
1	1.11e-09	2.20e-03	2.35e-05	4.77e-03	1.03e-04	3.631e-02	4.05e-03	9.47e-03
5	1.87e-03	9.22e-02	1.26e-03	7.10e-03	8.05e-14	2.71e-03	4.98e-03	3.36e-02
9	6.26e-03	8.430e-03	6.69e-03	6.92e-02	1.46e-02	7.70e-02	7.64e-03	4.47e-01
13	3.44e-02	4.48e-03	3.42e-02	1.14e+00	8.84e-01	1.24e+00		

4.4 ACPH Parameters

We use the PhFit tool [7] to fit general ACPH distributions to the data. In order to reduce the time needed for fitting the data, we used logarithmic aggregation [6] to reduce the size of the data sets before applying PhFit. We compared approximations using the full data sets to those obtained using the aggregated representation and found that the aggregation procedure had no detrimental effect on the quality of the models.

We present here approximations with 30 phases in the body and no special treatment for the tail, with an upper limit of body fitting at the 0.001 quantile. It should be noted that one of the strengths of PhFit lies in fitting the body and the tail of the data separately, which provides for better approximations (at the cost of losing the convenient closed-form phase-type representation). However, with our data sets we were not able to obtain feasible parameters for the tail

Table 5. General ACPH(30) parameters for $\mathcal{S}_{2\mathrm{FI}}$

i	α_i	λ_i	α_{i+1}	λ_{i+1}	α_{i+2}	λ_{i+2}	α_{i+3}	λ_{i+3}
1	4.36e-02	1.38e-04	6.51e-03	1.82e-02	7.36e-04	2.28e-02	1.80e-02	6.43e-02
5	1.80e-04	6.56e-02	8.85e-06	6.94e-02	4.09e-05	7.10e-02	1.54e-03	8.28e-02
9	4.83e-04	9.55e-02	1.76e-05	1.16e-01	5.85e-07	1.44e-01	9.30e-05	1.55e-01
13	2.91e-03	1.93e-01	9.45e-05	1.94e-01	2.83e-06	1.98e-01	1.33e-05	2.91e-01
17	1.34e-05	3.89e-01	1.41e-05	5.60e-01	5.18e-06	5.82e-01	4.90e-02	8.03e-01
21	7.08e-01	8.14e-01	1.66e-01	8.14e-01	2.15e-03	8.15e-01	2.44e-04	8.15e-01
25	6.06e-05	8.15e-01	1.59e-05	8.15e-01	2.11e-06	8.15e-01	9.31e-06	8.15e-01
29	1.86e-05	8.15e-01	4.42e-06	8.15e-01				

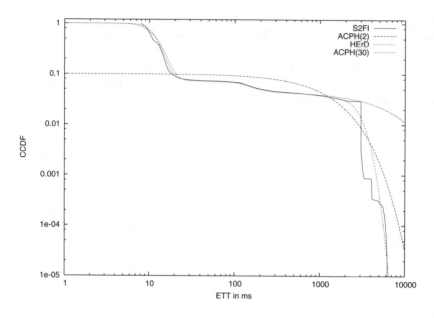

Fig. 2. Empirical CCDF and CCDFs of the approximations for $\mathcal{S}_{2FI}$

fitting. For this reason, we expect our ACPH(30) models to not represent the tail behaviour correctly. Table 5 presents the ACPH(30) model for the $\mathcal{S}_{2FI}$ data set. As with the HErD models, general ACPH(30) models for the other data sets are available from [25].

5   Evaluation

In the previous section we presented three models for each data set. In order to facilitate appropriate application of the models, we will now evaluate the quality of these approximations.

Visual inspection of the ACPH models for e.g. the Fixed Intervals data sets (Figures 1–3) shows that the models approximate the CCDF of the data quite differently. The ACPH(2) models tend to follow the general shape of the empirical CCDF only roughly. In Fig. 1 the CCDF of the ACPH(2) fluctuates around the empirical CCDF, while in $\mathcal{S}_{2FI}$ and $\mathcal{S}_{3FI}$ the ACPH(2) overestimates the portion of samples below 10 ms. In contrast, the more complex HErD and the ACPH(30) models provide good approximations of the CCDF for all three scenarios. Both follow the general shape of the CCDF closely.

Note that the ACPH(30) model underestimates the length of the tail in the model for $\mathcal{S}_{1FI}$, and overestimates it in $\mathcal{S}_{2FI}$ and $\mathcal{S}_{3FI}$. This behaviour may be avoided by appending a special tail to the distribution. However, one cannot easily derive the actual shape of the tail from the data. In fact, one may argue that extreme values are rare events, and that thus the breakdown observed in

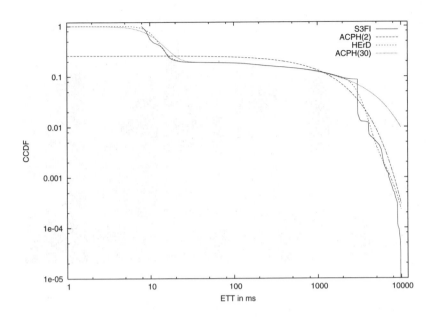

Fig. 3. Empirical CCDF and CCDFs of the approximations for $\mathcal{S}_{3\text{FI}}$

the data sets is simply an artifact of the limited observation period. On the other hand, restart aims to reduce effective transmission times by replacing slow transmissions with fast ones (cf. (4.1)), which makes an abrupt tail breakdown appear likely.

While the similarity of the shape of the CCDFs offers some measure of the goodness of the approximation, other quality measures may be of more interest in particular applications. In [26, 27], several quality measures were proposed.

Table 6. Quality measures employed in the evaluation

Measure	Definition
Rel. Err. in the first moment (c_1 is the mean)	$e_1 = \frac{|c_1(\hat{F}) - c_1(F)|}{c_1(F)}$
Rel. Err. in the second moment (c_2 is the variance)	$e_2 = \frac{|c_2(\hat{F}) - c_2(F)|}{c_2(F)}$
Rel. Err. in the third moment (c_3 is the centred third moment)	$e_3 = \frac{|c_3(\hat{F}) - c_3(F)|}{c_3(F)}$
Absolute PDF area distance	$\text{PDFAD} = \int_0^\infty |\hat{f}(t) - f(t)| dt$
Absolute CDF area distance	$\text{CDFAD} = \int_0^\infty |\hat{F}(t) - F(t)| dt$

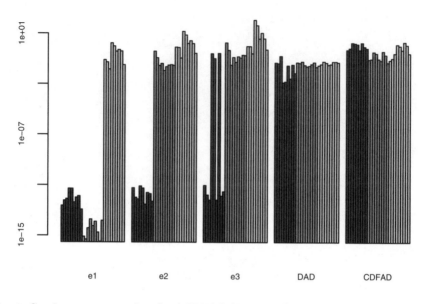

Fig. 4. Goodness measures for the ACPH(2) (dark grey), HErD (medium grey) and ACPH(30) (light grey) models

Our quality measures are summarised in Tab. 6. Note that area distances have been computed up to the maximum of the observations for each data set.

Figure 4 presents an overview of the relative error in the first three moments $(c_1, \ldots, e_3)$, absolute PDF area distance (PDFAD) and absolute CDF area distance (CDFAD). The figure shows values for the measures for the nine models we obtained using each approach, e.g. the first nine bars (dark grey) of every measure represent the quality of the ACPH(2) models for $\mathcal{S}_{1\mathrm{FI}}$, $\mathcal{S}_{1\mathrm{JK}}$, $\mathcal{S}_{1\mathrm{Q}}$ and so on.

We note that the ACPH(2) models (dark grey) provide the best approximations of the first three moments. Only in $\mathcal{S}_{2\mathrm{FI}}$, $\mathcal{S}_{2\mathrm{JK}}$ and $\mathcal{S}_{3\mathrm{FI}}$ do we observe a significant relative error in the third moment. Recall that for these data sets, no exact matching of the third moment was possible, and thus this error is to be expected. The Hyper-Erlang models match the first moment precisely, but exhibit much larger relative errors in the second and third moments. Finally, our ACPH(30) models have large relative errors in the first three moments. According to the area distance measures, all models approximate the data similarly well.

Cross-Evaluation. Recall that we used only four runs from each scenario for fitting the models. Table 7 lists statistical properties of the fifth run for each scenario and restart algorithm. We observe subtle differences between the data sets used for the fitting procedure and the evaluation data sets, however, the data sets obviously exhibit the same general characteristics.

Table 7. Statistical properties of the data sets used for cross-evaluation

	$\mathcal{S}_{1\text{FI}}$	$\mathcal{S}_{1\text{JK}}$	$\mathcal{S}_{1\text{Q}}$	$\mathcal{S}_{2\text{FI}}$	$\mathcal{S}_{2\text{JK}}$	$\mathcal{S}_{2\text{Q}}$	$\mathcal{S}_{3\text{FI}}$	$\mathcal{S}_{3\text{JK}}$	$\mathcal{S}_{3\text{Q}}$
Mean	19.38	20.32	19.22	120.68	117.10	105.37	403.33	275.83	260.86
Std. Dev.	63.41	49.96	22.86	538.25	466.86	399.14	1021.36	692.76	654.60
Minimum	9	12	12	9	12	12	8	9	9
Median	13	16	15	10	16	15	10	13	13
95% quantile	25	23	23	161	267	495	3009	1879	1803
99% quantile	149	160	162	3013	2551	2516	4059	3017	3013
Maximum	3017	2106	328	4465	3863	3366	9018	5467	6011
CoV	10.71	6.04	1.41	19.89	15.90	14.35	6.41	6.31	6.30

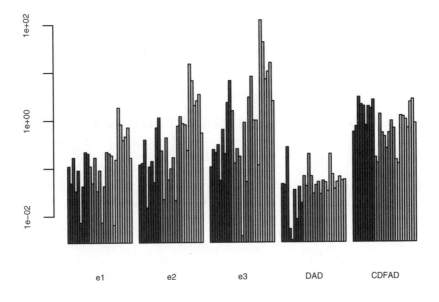

Fig. 5. Goodness measures with cross-evaluation

Using these data sets, we can assess how well the models capture the typical characteristics of the data. Figure 5 presents the goodness measures for this case. As expected, the goodness of the fit decreases. In particular, the first moments are not matched exactly by any of the models. However, the models still fit the data quite well.

6   Application

The models presented here can be easily employed in performance modelling of Web Services that rely on WSRM as the transport between different components.

To illustrate this potential application we set up a simple M/PH/1 queueing model [8] using the ACPH models for the $\mathcal{S}_{2FI}$ data set. In this example, the phase-type distributed service process models the transmission of SOAP messages over a WSRM implementation that uses the Fixed Intervals algorithm to send messages over a link with IP packet loss characteristics according to a Gilbert model. The stream of SOAP messages generated by the Web Service application is modelled by a Markovian arrival process. We are interested in the mean queue length versus the utilisation of the system, from which the reader may easily compute other standard measures in queueing systems such as response time, waiting time, etc.

The mean service time, that is the mean of the models fitted to our data, equals $E[S] = 124.71$ ms for both the ACPH(2) and the HErD model, and $E[S] = 341.85$ ms for the ACPH(30) model. Note that the ACPH(30) model overestimates the mean service time.

We vary the arrival rate λ to obtain different values of the utilisation ρ of the queue. The M/PH/1 queueing system then has the following matrix-geometric solution for the mean queue length [8]:

$$E[N] = \mathbf{z}_1 \left(\mathbf{I} - \mathbf{R}\right)^{-2} \mathbb{1}, \tag{1}$$

where $\mathbf{I}$ is the identity matrix. For the M/PH/1 queue the matrix $\mathbf{R}$ evaluates to

$$\mathbf{R} = \lambda \left(\lambda \mathbf{I} - \lambda \tilde{\mathbf{B}} - \mathbf{Q}\right)^{-1},$$

where the matrix $\tilde{\mathbf{B}}$ is the cross-product of the unit vector $\mathbb{1}$ and the vector of initial probabilities $\boldsymbol{\alpha}$, i.e. $\tilde{\mathbf{B}} = \mathbb{1}.\boldsymbol{\alpha}$. The steady-state boundary probability vector can then be computed as (cf. [8], (8.37))

$$\mathbf{z}_1 = (1 - \rho)\boldsymbol{\alpha}\mathbf{R}.$$

Similar in structure to a DTMC the steady-state probability vectors can be computed as $\mathbf{z}_i = \mathbf{z}_1.\mathbf{R}^{i-1}, i = 1, 2, \ldots$.

Figure 6(a) shows the mean queue length of an M/PH/1 on a log-scale where the three curves differ in the service process represented by the three models we fit to our data, the ACPH(2), the HErD and the ACPH(30) model. Interestingly, both the ACPH(2) and the HErD service distributions not only have the same mean value but also a fairly similar development of the mean queue length. When looking at those two curves one may decide that there is not much gain in the huge HErD model, as compared to the conveniently small two-state ACPH(2) model. We will see that this conclusion is justified in other respects as well.

The caudal curve, shown in Fig. 6(b), represents the tail behaviour of a matrix-geometric queue [28]. The caudal curve is constructed using the largest real eigenvalue of the matrix $\mathbf{R}$ versus the utilisation ρ of the queue. Equation (17) in [28] defines the blocking probability in a matrix-geometric queue, showing that if the caudal curve is above the bisector the queue length distribution has a heavy tail, while if the caudal curve is below the bisector there is little probability mass in the tail.

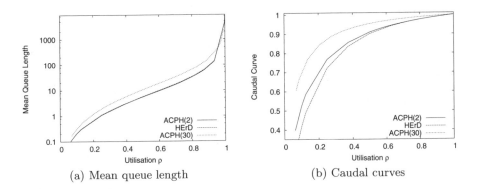

(a) Mean queue length (b) Caudal curves

Fig. 6. Mean queue length and caudal curves for all three models in $\mathcal{S}_{2\mathrm{FI}}$

As were the expected queue lengths, also the caudal curves using the ACPH(2) and the HErD service time distribution are very similar. More precisely, for low load the ACPH(2) service time distribution has the heavier tail, while for high load the curves cross and the HErD model leads to the heavier tail.

Since the ACPH(30) model overestimates the tail of the data set, the tail of the queue length distribution is overestimated as well. Furthermore, the large mean value of the ACPH(30) model can be traced back to the overestimated tail.

One may summarise, that for low load the ACPH(2) model gives a conveniently small model that leads to reasonably good results. For high load one might rather resort to the large HErD model, while the ACPH(30) model should be applied with care.

7   Conclusion and Future Work

In this work we presented phase-type models for the distributions of the effective message transmission times in a WSRM implementation under various levels of packet loss. We evaluated the goodness of fit of these models and demonstrated the use of ACPH models in an M/PH/1 queueing model. We conclude that the convenient ACPH(2) class may be sufficient to model the observed transmission times, while there is little gain with large HErD models. Furthermore, general ACPH(30) models perform rather poorly without special treatment for the tail of the distributions.

In this paper we limited ourselves to continuous phase-type distributions. According to [29], discrete phase-type (DPH) models may be preferable for fitting distributions with abrupt changes in the CDF. Since our data exhibits such changes, future work will include trying to fit DPH distributions with appropriate scale factors to these data sets.

Acknowledgements. Philipp Reinecke is supported by the German Science Foundation (DFG), grant number Wo-898/2-1. We also thank Miklós Telek for his help with the PhFit tool.

References

[1] BEA Systems, IBM, Microsoft Corporation Inc, TIBCO Software, Inc.: Web Services Reliable Messaging Protocol (WS-ReliableMessaging) (February 2005)

[2] Reinecke, P., van Moorsel, A.P.A., Wolter, K.: The Fast and the Fair: A Fault-Injection-Driven Comparison of Restart Oracles for Reliable Web Services. In: QEST 2006: Proceedings of the 3rd International Conference on the Quantitative Evaluation of Systems, Washington, DC, USA, pp. 375–384. IEEE Computer Society, Los Alamitos (2006)

[3] Reinecke, P., Wolter, K.: Adaptivity Metric and Performance for Restart Strategies in Web Services Reliable Messaging. In: WOSP 2008 (2008) (accepted for publication)

[4] Telek, M., Heindl, A.: Matching Moments for Acyclic Discrete and Continous Phase-Type Distributions of second order. International Journal of Simulation Systems, Science & Technology 3(3–4), 47–57 (2002)

[5] Thümmler, A., Buchholz, P., Telek, M.: A Novel Approach for Phase-Type Fitting with the EM Algorithm. IEEE Trans. Dependable Secur. Comput. 3(3), 245–258 (2006)

[6] Panchenko, A., Thümmler, A.: Efficient phase-type fitting with aggregated traffic traces. Perform. Eval. 64(7-8), 629–645 (2007)

[7] Horváth, A., Telek, M.: PhFit: A General Phase-Type Fitting Tool. In: Field, T., Harrison, P.G., Bradley, J., Harder, U. (eds.) TOOLS 2002. LNCS, vol. 2324, pp. 82–91. Springer, Heidelberg (2002)

[8] Haverkort, B.R.: Performance of Computer Communication Systems: A Model-Based Approach. John Wiley & Sons, Chichester (1998)

[9] The Apache Software Foundation: Apache Sandesha, http://ws.apache.org/sandesha/

[10] The Apache Software Foundation: Apache Axis, http://ws.apache.org/axis/

[11] Zdun, U., Völter, M., Kircher, M.: Pattern-Based Design of an Asynchronous Invocation Framework for Web Services. Int. J. Web Service Res. 1(3), 42–62 (2004)

[12] Various authors: NetEm – LinuxNet (Last visited October 8th, 2007), http://linux-net.osdl.org/index.php/Netem

[13] Zhang, Y., Paxson, V., Shenker, S.: The Stationarity of Internet Path Properties: Routing, Loss, and Throughput. ACIRI Technical Report (2000)

[14] Zhang, Y., Du, N., Paxson, V., Shenker, S.: On the Constancy of Internet Path Properties. In: Proceedings of the ACM SIGCOMM Internet Measurement Workshop (2001)

[15] Varela, M., Marsh, I., Grönvall, B.: A systematic study of PESQ's behavior (from a networking perspective). In: Proceedings of the 5th International Conference MESAQIN 2006: Measurement of Audio and Video Quality in Networks (2006)

[16] Sanneck, H., Carle, G., Koodli, R.: A framework model for packet loss metrics based on loss runlengths. In: Proceedings of the SPIE/ACM SIGMM Multimedia Computing and Networking Conference 2000, San Jose, CA, SPIE/ACM SIGMM (January 2000)

[17] Jiang, W., Schulzrinne, H.: Modeling of Packet Loss and Delay and Their Effect on Real-Time Multimedia Service Quality. In: Proc. NOSSDAV (2000)

[18] Karn, P., Partridge, C.: Improving Round-Trip Time Estimates in Reliable Transport Protocols. ACM Transactions on Computer Systems 9(4), 364–373 (1991)

[19] Krishnamurthy, B., Rexford, J.: Web Protocols and Practice. Addison Wesley, Reading (2001)

[20] van Moorsel, A., Wolter, K.: Analysis and Algorithms for Restart. In: Proc. 1st International Conference on the Quantitative Evaluation of Systems (QEST), Twente, The Netherlands, September 2004, pp. 195–204 (2004)

[21] Paxson, V.: End-to-End Internet Packet Dynamics. In: Proceedings of the ACM SIGCOMM 1997 conference on Applications, Technologies, Architectures, and Protocols for Computer Communication, Cannes, France. Computer Communication Review, vol. 27(4), pp. 139–154. ACM Press (1997)

[22] Moon, S.B., Skelly, P., Towsley, D.: Estimation and Removal of Clock Skew from Network Delay Measurements. Technical report, University of Massachusetts, Amherst, MA, USA (1998)

[23] Khlifi, H., Grégoire, J.C.: Low-complexity offline and online clock skew estimation and removal. Computer Networks: The International Journal of Computer and Telecommunications Networking 50(11), 1872–1884 (2006)

[24] R Development Core Team: R: A Language and Environment for Statistical Computing. R Foundation for Statistical Computing, Vienna, Austria (2006) ISBN 3-900051-07-0

[25] Reinecke, P., Wolter, K.: ACPH models for WSRM (2008), http://www.informatik.hu-berlin.de/~preineck/acphmodels/

[26] Bobbio, A., Telek, M.: A Benchmark for PH Estimation Algorithm: Results for Acyclic-PH (1994)

[27] Horváth, A., Telek, M.: Approximating heavy tailed behaviour with Phase type distributions. In: 3rd International Conference on Matrix-Analytic Methods in Stochastic models (MAM 2003) (2000)

[28] Haverkort, B.R., van Moorsel, A.P., Dijkstra, A.: MGMtool: A Performance Modelling Tool based on Matrix Geometric Techniques. In: Pooley, R., Hillston, J. (eds.) Computer Performance Evaluation 1992, Modelling Techniques and Tools, Antony Rowe Ltd, pp. 397–401 (1992)

[29] Bobbio, A., Horváth, A., Telek, M.: The scale factor: a new degree of freedom in phase-type approximation. Perform. Eval. 56(1-4), 121–144 (2004)

A Framework for Simulation Models of Service-Oriented Architectures*

Falko Bause, Peter Buchholz, Jan Kriege, and Sebastian Vastag

Informatik IV, TU Dortmund
D-44221 Dortmund, Germany
{falko.bause,peter.buchholz,jan.kriege,sebastian.vastag}@udo.edu

Abstract. Service-Oriented Architectures (SOA) are one of the main paradigms for future software systems. Since these software systems are composed of a large number of different components it is non trivial to assure an adequate Quality of Service (QoS) of the overall system and performance analysis becomes an important issue. To consider performance issues early in the development process, a model based approach becomes necessary which has to be embedded into the development process of SOA to avoid overhead and assure consistency. In particular the specification of the software system should be used as a base for the resulting performance model. However, since common specification techniques for SOA are very high level, many details have to be added to come to an executable simulation model which is often needed for a detailed analysis of performance or dependability. This paper presents an approach which combines an extended version of process chains to describe the SOA components and some quantitative specifications at the higher levels. For the modelling of the detailed architecture and protocols the simulation tool *OMNeT++* is used. Both modelling levels are combined resulting in an executable simulation model for the whole architecture.

Keywords: Service-Oriented Architectures, Simulation, Process Chains, *OMNeT++*.

1 Introduction

Service-Oriented Architectures (SOA) are one of the major paradigms to describe and realize complex software systems as they are required in todays IT-infrastructure. The description level of SOA is very high such that several details are hidden in the description and a loose coupling between different processes is assumed for a functioning system. Nevertheless, quantitative aspects like performance or dependability are major issues of SOA which are only partially addressed up to now. In general Service Level Agreements (SLAs) are negotiated between service provider (i.e. the SOA component) and the user which could be some business process or another component in a hierarchical SOA.

---

* This research was supported by the Deutsche Forschungsgemeinschaft as part of the Collaborative Research Center "Modelling of Large Logistics Networks" (559).

S. Kounev, I. Gorton, and K. Sachs (Eds.): SIPEW 2008, LNCS 5119, pp. 208–227, 2008.

This implies that the non-functional properties of SOA components are known and are considered during orchestration [11]. Both tasks are non trivial. Since performance and dependability issues should be considered during the whole software design process [9], modeling is often the method of choice. However, the common description level of SOA is too high to allow a direct derivation of performance models. Thus, a common way is to manually derive an abstract performance model from a SOA specification and solve this model analytically [10,13]. Although the use of simple analytically tractable models is often a good choice, in particular in the early design phases, these models reach their limits when detailed design decisions have to be made. In those situations simulation models are more adequate. However, it is known that the realization of simulation models is cumbersome and error prone. To obtain more reliable simulation models, the description language has to consider the specifics of the application domain [14] and predefined standard components have to be used whenever possible. For SOA this is a problem, if apart from the high level orchestration of services also details of the communication between services have to be described in the model. At the higher level, processes have to be described using the same graphical notation like process chains or one of the description languages like BPEL. Lower levels consisting of the protocols and resources required by the different operations cannot be adequately specified with these approaches. More appropriate at this level is the model world of some network simulator which on the other hand cannot be applied for the specification of SOA.

In this paper we propose a hybrid specification approach that combines the best of both worlds. On the one hand we use *ProC/B* [2] for the specification of SOA. *ProC/B* is a modeling paradigm to specify process chain models at a high level using a graphical interface. On the other hand we apply *OMNeT++* [12] for the specification of network resources used by the components of SOA for communication. The resulting model is mapped onto a C++ simulation model using the simulation kernel of *OMNeT++*. The approach has several advantages since it allows one to use the high level graphical description format of *ProC/B* and the predefined network components of *OMNeT++*. Furthermore, it results in relatively efficient simulation models (see also [3]) based on the simulation functionality of *OMNeT++*. Despite from an in principle very efficient simulator, the problem of large models and different time scales in large models remains and can only be resolved by choosing an appropriate abstraction level.

The combination of the high level view of *ProC/B* and the low level view of *OMNeT++* is not straightforward, especially if the models at the different levels should be kept as they are. In this paper, we propose an approach to combine both models by assigning remote service calls in *ProC/B* to message transfers in *OMNeT++*. This can be done extending existing models only slightly. One part of the extension involves annotations of the ProC/B model, similar to annotations of UML models for performance analysis [1,16]. The other part of the extension concerns the network resources which are adapted to account for the annotations of the ProC/B model.

The paper is structured as follows. In the next two sections *ProC/B* and *OMNeT++* are briefly introduced. Section 4 presents the new concepts and constructs to combine both worlds. Then, in section 5, the approach is clarified by means of an example. The paper ends with the conclusions.

2   Process Chain Models

Various versions of process chains exist in the literature. Our work is based on a variant introduced by Kuhn ([7,8]) which is used within the collaborative research center "Modelling of Large Logistics Networks" 559 (CRC 559;[5]) for modelling and performance evaluation of logistics networks. Since process chains are a descriptive tool they do not allow one to derive simulation models automatically. In former times simulation models had to be build on their own without any formal relation to the process chain model, implying well-known problems of additional modelling effort or inconsistencies between the models. *ProC/B* [2] is an approach to diminish these problems by enhancing and stating the informal process chain description more precisely (cf. [4]). *ProC/B* captures the structure of a system in form of function units (FUs) and the behaviour by process chains (PCs). In *ProC/B*, FUs might offer services, which can be used by activities of process chains. Each service is again described by a process chain and can use services of internal or imported FUs, thus resulting in a hierarchical model description.

Fig. 1 shows the top level of an example of a *ProC/B* model. The model consists of a single PC, named `customer` and a single user-defined FU `Travel_agency`, which offers several services. In this example all services, except `submit_form`, require no input parameters and give no result values. A process chain element (PCE) of a PC might call a service of a FU by specifying the name of FU and service together with the necessary parameters. The mechanism is similar to most programming languages, e.g. the activity `submit_form` calls service `submit_form` of FU `Travel_agency` setting the formal parameter `travel_info` to `data.travel_info`[1].

The *ProC/B* model of Fig. 1 represents a use case of the "Web Services Architecture Usage Scenarios"[15] where customers contact a travel agency's Web site and ask for information on flights and hotel rooms, select a specific combination, which is then booked by the travel agency. PC `customer` in Fig. 1 directly visualises a customer's behaviour: First the customer requests a Web form, completes it and submits the filled form to the agency's Web site. The travel agent sends back a list of available flights from which the customer makes a choice. After submitting the option, the travel agent responds with a list of available accommodations, so that the customer again can make his choice. The travel agent finalises the transaction by booking flight and hotel room and charging the customer's credit card, which all is done by service `submit_accommodation_choice`

---

[1] Access notations to parameters and variables of processes are prefixed with keyword *data* for technical reasons in order to distinguish them from global variables. Global variables are not shown in Fig. 1.

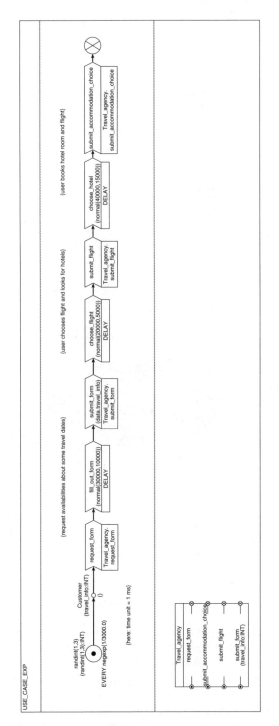

Fig. 1. Example of a *ProC/B* model

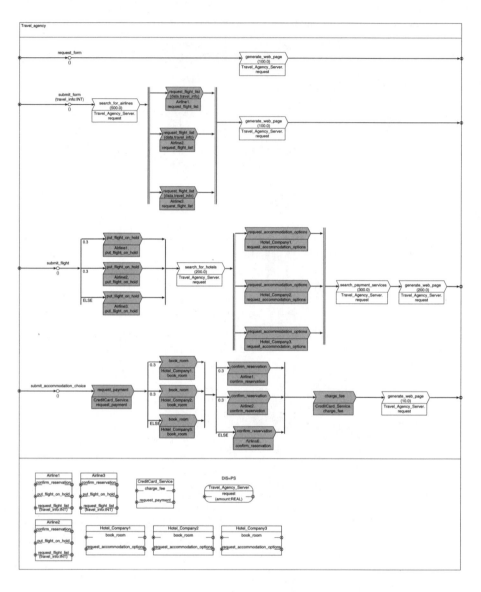

Fig. 2. FU Travel_agency

within FU Travel_agency. The shown model describes the customer's activities at an abstract level and we only specified those parameters, which we thought of being relevant for performance evaluation. E.g., responses of the travel agent are not modelled, since we assume that replies are of similar size; the customer's request is classified into 3 categories (attribute travel_info) and initially set by random (see "randint(1,3):INT") and the customer activities at her local PC (filling out the form, choosing a flight etc.) are modelled by delays with a randomly chosen duration. Customers determine the load of the model specified

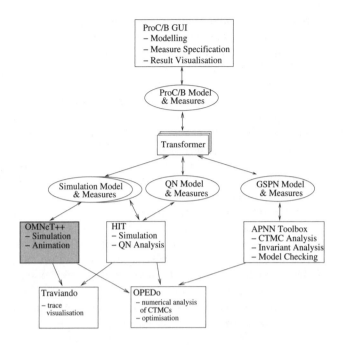

Fig. 3. *ProC/B* toolset

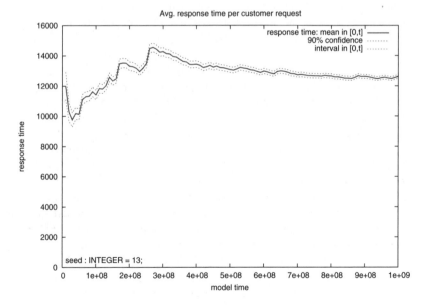

Fig. 4. A possible simulation result

according to exponentially distributed inter-arrival times with a mean of 3000 time units and might arrive single or in bulks of at most 3 (see "randint(1,3)"). We consider a time unit to be equal to 1 ms in our example.

The internals of FU Travel_agency are shown in Fig. 2. Each service is described by a PC and several other FUs offer services being used in activities of the travel agency. All FUs except FU Travel_Agency_Server are user-defined FUs and their internals can be specified analogously to FU Travel_agency (cf. Fig. 6). It is a matter of choice whether these FUs are modelled within or on the same level as FU Travel_agency using *ProC/B*'s capability of importing services (cf. [2]). The hierarchical model description ends at standard FUs which have a pre-defined behaviour, like Travel_Agency_Server. *ProC/B* offers two kinds of standard FUs: servers act as traditional queues, and so-called counters support the manipulation of passive resources.

It is possible to specify *ProC/B* models precisely enough to obtain a simulation model for a performance analysis. In the course of the CRC 559 we developed a toolset which provides a graphical user interface to specify *ProC/B* models and transformer modules which map *ProC/B* models to the input languages of existing analysis tools, so that *ProC/B* models can be analysed automatically (cf. [2] and Fig. 3). Fig. 4 shows a possible result from a simulation run. The diagram shows the average response time of a customer request to FU Travel_agency. The *ProC/B* toolset also offers the possibility to get similar results for each specific activity of PC customer. We do not want to go into those details of the model now and refer the reader to [2]. Instead we consider refinements of *ProC/B* and the model in order to capture the system's behaviour more accurately.

In many practically relevant applications timers and timeouts are used, e.g. in operating systems or network protocols. Timers can also be used to model system characteristics on higher levels, like e.g. for the behaviour specification of a customer. Up to now timeouts were not considered in process chain models. Recently we extended *ProC/B* by a timer construct as follows.

In Fig. 5 we use the specification of timeouts for modelling the impatience of Web customers. When requesting a form calling service request_form of FU Travel_agency, a customer sets his individual timer with a timeout value of 3000 time units. At latest after 3000 time units he will receive a boolean value stored here in variable data.in_time as the answer. The (informal) semantics of this syntactical construct is that at the same time as the timer has been set the specified service is called. If the service call returns on time, the timer is deleted and the process proceeds with a true boolean value for the specified variable, i.e. with data.in_time = TRUE in the example. If the timer expires before the service call returns, the specified variable is set to FALSE and the process proceeds immediately. Other possibly user-defined result values are set to default values. A service call returning after the timer has elapsed will be ignored. In the example, the behaviour of a customer depends on the value of the variable data.in_time and possible other result values of the service call. In Fig. 5 an expired timer implies counting this incident in the user-defined result measure lost_customers and it implies the termination of the customer process.

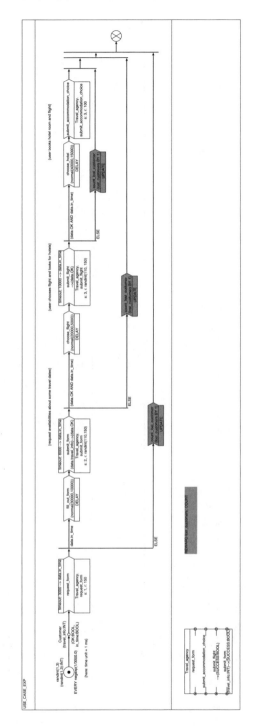

Fig. 5. *ProC/B* model with timeout definitions

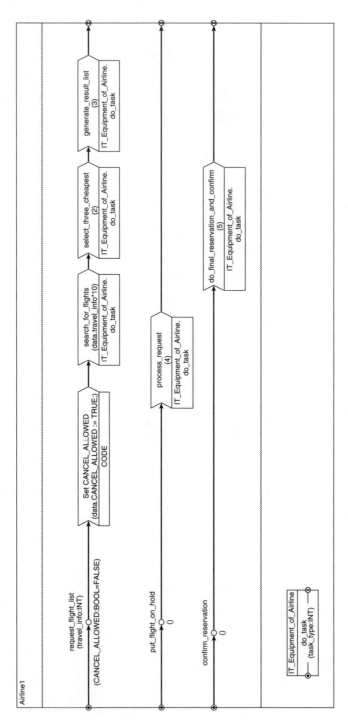

Fig. 6. Supporting cancellation of "expired" processes

Normally, an initiated service call will be executed until it ends, as specified by the PC. The user can have influence on this behaviour by setting the pre-defined process local variable CANCEL_ALLOWED, see Fig. 6. After executing the activity specified by a PCE, a process checks whether the corresponding timer, if available, has expired and whether its boolean variable CANCEL_ALLOWED is true. If both conditions are met, the process terminates immediately. This construct allows also the modelling of lower level network mechanisms at an abstract level including the saving of resource capacities.

In Sect. 5 we will revisit this example and show some more details.

As indicated by Fig. 3 we also integrated a mapping to *OMNeT++* [3] into the *ProC/B* toolset. This does not only allow us to benefit from the features of a modern object-oriented simulator but also offers the possibility to use existing *OMNeT++* frameworks for modelling communication aspects. Sect. 4 describes the use of the INET framework for considering network aspects in performance models of service-oriented architectures.

3   Modelling Networks and Protocol Stacks

OMNeT++ [6] is a public-source discrete event simulation environment, that has been developed and used extensively for the modelling of communication protocols. Additionally, it has been proved suitable in other application areas as well (cf. [3]). *OMNeT++* models are composed of modules which can be simple or compound. The module interfaces and their relationships are described with *OMNeT++*'s NED language. While simple modules are implemented as a combination of NED files and C++ classes, compound modules, that may consist of other simple and compound modules, are only described by NED files. Modules are connected via gates and can communicate by messages either sent along connections or sent directly to the destination module.

There are several simulation model frameworks available for *OMNeT++* es-pecially for building network models. One of these frameworks is the INET Framework including (among others) protocol implementations of IPv4, IPv6, TCP, UDP, Ethernet and 802.11. These protocols are represented by simple modules and can be combined to compound modules to form network hosts. Several assembled compound modules that implement routers, switches etc. are already included. Additionally, modules for network interfaces, routing tables or the auto-configuration of a network are provided. Some of those modules are part of almost every host like *RoutingTable*, which can be used for querying, adding or deleting routes, or *InterfaceTable*, which contains a list of all inter-faces of a host. Other modules are only instantiated once, like for example the *FlatNetworkConfigurator*, that can be used to assign IP addresses to hosts.

The communication between network layers is realized by messages between the modules representing those layers. An upper layer protocol may send a message representing a data packet to the next lower layer (linked with some additional information to determine the destination of the packet like an IP address), which will encapsulate and forward the data. Receiving packets works in a similar way.

In the next section we describe how *ProC/B* and the INET Framework can be combined to simulate service-oriented architectures. This approach uses an INET model of the network topology, while a *ProC/B* model is used to specify the activities and the process flow.

4   Combining Both Worlds

In *ProC/B* calls from PCEs to FUs are instantaneous. No model time is consumed between the start of a service call and the start of its execution. In the *ProC/B* paradigm this is a reasonable assumption, since process chains and function units are used to separate behaviour from structure descriptions and it is implicitly assumed that services run on the same hardware or communication needs negligible time. In the Web services example of Sect. 2 some PCEs represent access to some remote component, e.g., the query of airline databases for availability of passenger tickets. Typically, a service call to a remote component requires apart from the processing time at the remote component also time for communication which, depending on the communication medium and the distance, might take a large percentage of the overall time and in particular can have some jitter. In Fig. 2 all calls to remote sites are indicated in blue.

Communication between remote sides is usually realized via network components that can be adequately modelled using the modules from the INET framework. Typical INET models represent some network and specify the load generation in host modules employing different pre-defined modules of the INET framework. The main idea to combine *ProC/B* and INET is to define a mapping between all FUs and some hosts of an INET model. PCEs are implicitly related to the hosts of their surrounding constructed FU. The mapping need neither be injective nor surjective. Whenever a PCE specified within an FU A calls a service of an FU B mapped to a different host, messages between the two hosts associated with A and B are exchanged in the INET model. E.g., one can define that all activities of FU `Travel_agency` are performed on host 1, those of FU `Airline1` on host 2, those of FU `CreditCard_Service` on host 3 etc. (cf. Fig. 7) or one can define a mapping onto 3 hosts as we have done in Sect. 5. Surely, the INET model has to be prepared appropriately in order to be simulated in conjunction with the *ProC/B* model. In principle this means that we keep two models, the *ProC/B* model and the INET model. Both are enhanced by some constructs to realize the combination into a single simulation model.

In order to account for network traffic, we enhanced the *ProC/B* description by some information on the amount of data, which needs to be sent. Fig. 8 shows a part of FU `Travel_agency` with additional attributes for PCEs doing a remote service call. Since a service call in *ProC/B* has two directions, calling the service and receiving the result, also two attributes are specified, one for the send direction (`s:`) indicating the amount of data being sent to the FU/host and

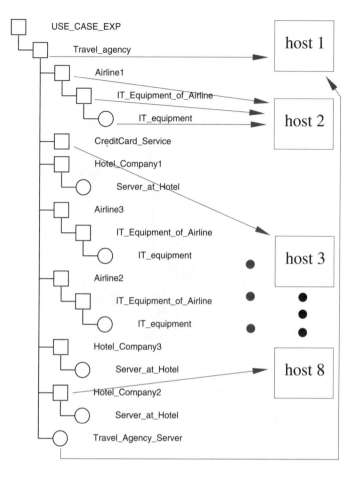

Fig. 7. Mapping FUs to hosts

one for the receive direction (r:) indicating the amount of data being sent back from the FU/host. As mentioned, whenever a remote service call is initiated a message from the *ProC/B* part is sent to the INET part of the *OMNeT++* model and received by modified host modules. They replace similar host models in the INET model to interface with the *ProC/B* model part and lack the random traffic generators for TCP and UDP. Instead they include a new module on application layer called **ProCBApp** which interfaces the process model and the INET network part by translating messages with set s: or r: parameters into TCP data transmissions with requested bytelength.

The TCP transmission delay for a *ProC/B* remote service call is determined as follows: The initial *ProC/B*-message indicating a PCE → FU call is suspended at the PCE, instead a message is sent to the corresponding modified host module (see red arrows in Fig. 9). The host will initiate a TCP connection and transmit the amount of data specified for the request. The called peer will close the connection after the transmission. When the connection reset packet arrives at

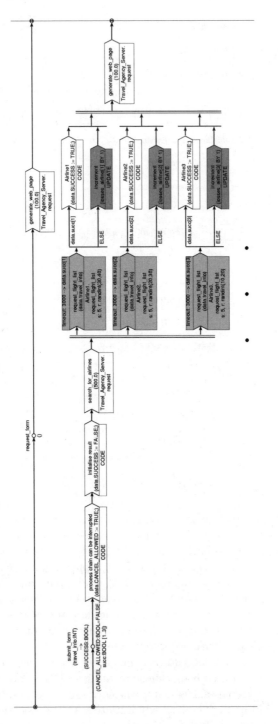

Fig. 8. Part of FU Travel_agency with send/receive attributes (here in KB) for INET

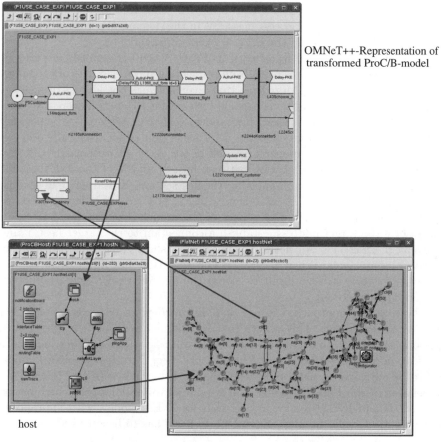

Fig. 9. Message flow to an FU when calling a service

the first host, the simulation clock has progressed for the amount of time a data transmission including connection handling would take. A signal message is directly sent back to the PCE and the waiting call is released to continue to the target FU in zero time. Similarly the result of a service call is returned: After the last activity of a service call has been performed, a message is sent to the host module of the corresponding FU and the message is transferred to the INET part of the *OMNeT++* model. Once the message arrived back at the originally sending host, it is sent to the calling PCE, so that activities within the *ProC/B* part of the model can proceed.

Holding the service call message back and using a replacement message in the INET model has two important advantages: First, the INET does not transmit information, it transmits the bytelength of the information. Transmitting the original service call with INET's simulated IP stack would require more complex input or output parameters at the service call. Second, there is no interference with process statistics, since a *ProC/B* process is still either in the PCE or in the called FU. By suspending process messages in the domain of a *ProC/B* element for the time of transmission statistics are kept consistent.

By including the INET framework in *ProC/B* models service calls can be delayed by realistic values resulting from connection speed and network topology given by the INET model. More than that, even network bottlenecks or message losses due to overload conditions become relevant for FU calls if there are many calls at the same time. As described above, each FU is bound to a network host. In contrast to network elements, FUs are organised hierarchically and can include each other as components. A call in FU A to an included FU B thus induces a network communication between host X and Y of the INET model, provided the FUs have been mapped to the hosts X and Y. Rather than sending messages from PCEs to FUs as service calls, a TCP transmission is prepared in host X and given to the INET part of the model. The simulated IP-Stack will resolve the target address, establish a connection to the target host Y and transmit the message. All network activities consume some time, typically in range of milliseconds. When the called Function Unit has finished the service call, the network is used again to signal the end of service and again some network latency occurs.

Following this approach, the use of INET models as network topology for *ProC/B* is supported. This allows the modeller to work with a fine-grained network description to evaluate effects of network hardware and bottlenecks to application processes specified as *ProC/B* activities. Currently the INET model has to be adjusted by hand in order to be used together with the *OMNeT++* translation of the *ProC/B* model. But we intend to automate the combination of *ProC/B* and INET in such a form that for INET models with appropriate host definitions only the mapping of FUs to hosts has to be specified.

5 Application Example

In the following we present the model from Sect. 2 in more detail and show some additional modelling constructs that enable the use of *OMNeT++* and the INET framework for *ProC/B* models.

As already mentioned, our model addresses a Web service usage scenario described informally in [15]. It consists of several FUs representing servers that offer Web services and PCs that are used to model the behaviour of those Web services and the behaviour of customers accessing the travel agency Web service.

To reduce complexity we did not include some directory service like UDDI in our model and assume that the Web service discovery has already taken place beforehand. However, from a modelling point of view also those services could be integrated.

In this scenario Web services are offered by a travel agency, three airlines, three hotel companies and a credit card service. The FU Travel_agency offers four services that can be used by the PC Customer to request the availability of hotel rooms and flights and to book them eventually. The PC Customer and the

FU `Travel_agency` are shown in Fig. 5. The behaviour of the PC has already been described in Sect. 2. For the use of the model with *OMNeT++* and the INET framework additional attributes can be specified for service calls that comprise messages sent over a network. We use the timeout mechanism described in Sect. 2 to model the customer behaviour. We assume that a customer will wait 3 seconds for the input form of the travel agency to show up. In later steps of the process he or she accepts to wait 6 and 10 seconds for the availability of his travel dates and the list of hotels, respectively. Additionally, the modeller can specify the amount of data that has to be transmitted and that will be received when sending over a network. These amounts may be a fixed number or drawn from a probability distribution. For example for the call of PC `Customer` to the service `submit_form` of `Travel_agency` a fixed number of 2 KB has to be transmitted. The data returned may vary between 110 and 150 KB, since in reality it will depend on the number of available flights that the travel agency has found. The amounts of data are summarised in table 1. At this abstract level the modeller does not have to specify the actual contents of the messages, only a message size is required to model the delay for sending the message over a network. In fact the messages sent in this model may even be of different types: While the communication between the customer and the travel agency is made up of simple HTTP requests and responses for accessing several websites, the travel agency and the airlines exchange SOAP messages. However, when calling a service additional parameters may be passed, so that activities of that service may depend on these parameters. While the network latency only depends on the message size and not on the actual content, additional delay may be caused by processing the messages, e.g. marshalling and unmarshalling of XML-based messages may take up some CPU resources. The latter delay has been omitted in our example, though it can easily be modeled by additional servers, that are accessed whenever a message needs to be processed.

The inner view of the FU `Travel_agency` is shown in Fig. 2. The FU has been extended by some additional modelling constructs for the simulation with *OMNeT++* as one can see in Fig. 8 and as described in the following.

Each of the four services is modelled by a PC. Additionally, it contains further FUs for hotel companies, airlines and the credit card service and a server that is accessed when generating the websites that are delivered to the customer.

The simplest service, `request_form`, will just generate the initial website for a customer by an access to the server. Service `submit_form` (see Fig. 8) is invoked after a customer has entered date and destination of his travel and returns a list of possible flights to the customer. It makes use of the variable `CANCEL_ALLOWED` that has already been explained in Sect. 2, and thus the PC can be interrupted when a timeout has occurred. The service looks up eligible airlines in its local directory, sends messages to the airlines and receives flight dates afterwards. We assume that `Airline1` is a large airline and returns a longer list of flights than the other airlines as one can see from table 1. All calls to the airlines make use of the timeout mechanism again. If all three airlines fail to deliver any flight information within 3 seconds the travel agency cannot serve the customer's request and will

Table 1. Amount of data sent between different hosts of the model

Source	Destination	Data (KB)	
		send	receive
Customer	Travel_agency.request_form	1	150
	Travel_agency.submit_form	2	110-150
	Travel_agency.submit_flight	3	110-150
	Travel_agency. submit_accommodation_choice	3	100
Travel_agency. submit_form	Airline1.request_flight_list	5	30-40
	Airline2.request_flight_list	5	20-30
	Airline3.request_flight_list	5	10-20
Travel_agency. submit_flight	Airline1.put_flight_on_hold	2	1
	Airline2.put_flight_on_hold	2	1
	Airline3.put_flight_on_hold	2	1
	Hotel_Company1. request_accommodation_options	5	10
	Hotel_Company2. request_accommodation_options	5	10
	Hotel_Company3. request_accommodation_options	5	10
Travel_agency. submit_accommodation_choice	CreditCard_Service.request_payment	2	3
	Hotel_Company1.book_room	2	2
	Hotel_Company2.book_room	2	2
	Hotel_Company3.book_room	2	2
	Airline1.confirm_reservation	2	2
	Airline2.confirm_reservation	2	2
	Airline3.confirm_reservation	2	2
	CreditCard_Service.charge_fee	2	2

return the boolean variable SUCCESS set to false finally resulting in a loss of
the customer. If at least one of the airlines returns the flight options in time this
variable is set to true and the PC Customer will continue with the next step.
The service submit_flight is invoked after a customer has chosen his flight.
The service needs to contact an airline to put the flight on hold and request
accommodation options from the hotel companies. The former is done by sending
a message to one of the airlines, while the latter is modelled in a similar manner
as the compilation of possible flights in the service submit_form. First the hotel
companies are looked up in a local database and after that messages are sent
to them (again using the timeout mechanism). For the final step in the booking
process the service submit_accommodation_choice is invoked. This service first
contacts the credit card service to negotiate payment options. After that a hotel
company is contacted again to book a specific hotel, the reservation of the flight is
confirmed and finally the credit card service is contacted again to charge the fee.
The booking process is completed after a website is generated for the customer
summarising the travel plan.

Modelling of the FUs for the airlines, hotel companies and the credit card service is less complex, since no further remote services are invoked from there. Each of the FUs for the airlines contains a server with discipline processor sharing, that is used for modelling the IT equipment of the airline. Most of the tasks like searching for flights, generating result lists and reserving flights are performed by an access to the server. The three airlines only differ in the capacity of the server. The inner view of one of the FUs for the airlines is shown in Fig. 6. A similar situation holds for the FUs that represent the hotel companies: Their services are modelled by one or more accesses to processor sharing servers (that have a different speed for each of the hotel companies) as well. Finally requests to the services of the credit card company are only delayed for an uniformly distributed duration.

As already mentioned, customers might leave the website of the travel agency when the time they are willing to wait for a response is exceeded. Additionally, the results from some hotel companies and airlines might be ignored when the travel agency service assembles the result list, if those results are not delivered before a timeout has occurred. *ProC/B* offers the possibility to specify measurements [2], called rewards, at any FU. When simulating *OMNeT++* will estimate results for those rewards [3]. Apart from standard rewards like throughput, response time or the population, *ProC/B* allows for the specification of user-defined rewards. As one can see in Fig. 5 a reward has been defined to estimate the mean number of lost customers. Further rewards are used to estimate the mean number of hotel companies and airlines that did not respond in time (see Fig. 8).

For simulation the *ProC/B* model has been combined with the FlatNet model (cf. Fig. 9), which is one of the standard models that are part of the INET Framework. Next to the host for customers, travel agencies and airlines share a server in our mapping. Hotel companies where separated from the booking process to a dedicated server. Locating services to different machines in the INET network model requires data communication for each service call between PCEs and distant FUs.

Results of some simulation runs are shown in table 2. Two model parameters are varied here: inter-arrival times of new customers and the transmission delay on cable lines between two routers of the INET model. Remember that customers might arrive in bulks.

The first value of each block is the number of lost customers per second from which we calculated the relative loss. The effects of intense customer arrivals are clearly visible in increased response times of the travel agencies booking system resulting in higher customer losses. Surely, the reason is that the database systems inside the model are slowed down by the increasing number of simultaneous requests. If communication network latencies are increased, many user requests that have been in time before become late. The two rightmost columns indicate the line between significant loss of customers and the complete failure of service.

Table 2. Lost customers per second (10000 seconds model time)

mean inter-arrival time (sec.)	network delay	0.001s	0.01s	0.05s	0.075s	0.1s
4	lost customers per sec.	0.0650	0.0687	0.1318	0.1879	0.4976
	standard deviation	0.3517	0.3560	0.4982	0.5538	0.7371
	confidence 90%	20.00%	13.21%	16.63%	11,27%	9.76%
	relative loss	13.0%	13.7%	26.4%	37.6%	99.5%
3	lost customers per sec.	0.2007	0.1965	0.2768	0.3754	0.6708
	standard deviation	0.6110	0.6040	0.7003	0.7922	0.8965
	confidence 90%	10.25%	6.30%	10.27%	8.39%	4.47%
	relative loss	30.1%	29.5%	41.5%	56.3%	100%
2	lost customers per sec.	0.5903	0.6245	0.6795	0.7432	0.9856
	standard deviation	1.0100	1.0693	1.1395	1.1632	1.2273
	confidence 90%	10.00%	10.88%	5.19%	10.24%	3.69%
	relative loss	59.0%	62.5%	68.0%	74.3%	98.6%

6   Conclusions

In this paper we presented an approach supporting modelling of service-oriented architectures also accounting for lower level network operations. Web services and their orchestration are described on a higher level using a process chain-like description (*ProC/B*) and lower network activities are modelled using (possibly available models of) the INET framework. As a matter of course the combination of *ProC/B* models for Web services and INET models for networks seems not always appropriate due to the different time scales, but the presented approach gives at least the principal possibility to validate this assumption.

Currently we have to adjust INET models by hand for being used together with *ProC/B* models, but we head for an automated support for appropriate INET models.

So far only synchronous communication has been considered. Future research is directed to support also asynchronous communication by extension of *ProC/B*.

References

1. Balsamo, S., Marzolla, M.: Performance evaluation of UML software architectures with multiclass Queueing Network models. In: WOSP 2005: Proceedings of the 5th international workshop on Software and performance, pp. 37–42. ACM, New York (2005)
2. Bause, F., Beilner, H., Fischer, M., Kemper, P., Völker, M.: The ProC/B Toolset for the Modelling and Analysis of Process Chains. In: Field, T., Harrison, P.G., Bradley, J., Harder, U. (eds.) TOOLS 2002. LNCS, vol. 2324, pp. 51–70. Springer, Heidelberg (2002)
3. Bause, F., Buchholz, P., Kriege, J., Vastag, S.: Simulating Process Chain Models with OMNeT++. In: Proc. of 1st International Conference on Simulation Tools and Techniques for Communications, Networks and Systems (SIMUTools) (2008)

4. Bause, F., Buchholz, P., Tepper, C.: The ProC/B-approach: From Informal Descriptions to Formal Models. In: ISoLA - 1st International Symposium on Leveraging Applications of Formal Method, Paphos, Cyprus (2004)
5. Collaborative Research Center 559 Modelling of Large Logistics Networks, http://www.sfb559.uni-dortmund.de
6. Hornig, R., Varga, A.: An Overview of the OMNeT++ Simulation Environment. In: Proc. of 1st International Conference on Simulation Tools and Techniques for Communications, Networks and Systems (SIMUTools) (2008)
7. Kuhn, A.: Prozessketten in der Logistik - Entwicklungstrends und Umsetzungsstrategien. Verlag Praxiswissen, Dortmund (1995)
8. Kuhn, A.: Prozesskettenmanagement - Erfolgsbeispiele aus der Praxis. Verlag Praxiswissen, Dortmund (1999)
9. Menascé, D.A., Almeida, V.A.F., Dowdy, L.W.: Performance by Design. Prentice Hall, Englewood Cliffs (2004)
10. Menascé, D.A., Ruan, H., Gomaa, H.: QoS Management in Service-oriented Architectures. Perform. Eval. 64(7-8), 646–663 (2007)
11. Muthusamy, V., Jacobsen, H.A., Coulthard, P., Chan, A., Waterhouse, J., Litani, E.: SLA-driven Business Process Management in SOA. In: Lyons, K.A., Couturier, C. (eds.) CASCON, pp. 264–267. IBM (2007)
12. OMNeT++ Community Side, http://www.omnetpp.org/
13. Rud, D., Schmietendorf, A., Dumke, R.R.: Performance Modeling of WS-BPEL-Based Web Service Compositions. In: SCW, pp. 140–147. IEEE Computer Society, Los Alamitos (2006)
14. Tsai, W.T., Cao, Z., Wei, X., Paul, R., Huang, Q., Sun, X.: Modeling and Simulation in Service-Oriented Software Development. Simulation 83(1), 7–32 (2007)
15. Web Services Architecture Usage Scenarios (2004), http://www.w3.org/TR/2004/NOTE-ws-arch-scenarios-20040211/
16. Woodside, C.M.: From Annotated Software Designs (UML SPT/MARTE) to Model Formalisms. In: Bernardo, M., Hillston, J. (eds.) SFM 2007. LNCS, vol. 4486, pp. 429–467. Springer, Heidelberg (2007)

Model-Driven Performability Analysis
of Composite Web Services

Paolo Bocciarelli and Andrea D'Ambrogio

Dept. Computer Science, Systems and Production
University of Roma "Tor Vergata"
Roma, Italy
{bocciarelli,dambro}@info.uniroma2.it

Abstract. Web services are the building blocks of the emerging computing paradigm based on service-oriented architectures (SOAs). A web service is a self-describing, open component that supports rapid composition of distributed applications. In a SOA context, service providers are strategically interested both to predict and describe the QoS of the offered services. This paper introduces a model-driven approach to automatically predict and describe the QoS of composite web services specified by use of the Business Process Execution Language for Web Services. The paper is founded on a lightweight QoS-oriented extension of the WSDL and specifically addresses the QoS in terms of the performability attribute, which defines a combined measure of performance and reliability. The proposed approach is illustrated by use of an example application that shows how the performability analysis may lead to predictions that do not correspond to those obtained by approaches that only consider the performance attribute.

Keywords: model-driven development, composite web services, performability, performance, reliability.

1 Introduction

Service-oriented computing is becoming the prominent paradigm for distributed computing and e-commerce. Web services are the building blocks for the application of service-oriented computing on the Web [1]. A web service is a self-describing, open component that supports rapid composition of distributed applications. In a service-oriented architecture (SOA), the service provider creates a service description by use of WSDL (Web Service Description Language) and publishes it to one or more discovery registries (such as UDDI), so that service consumers can find the service using a wide variety of search criteria and then use the WSDL description to develop or configure a client that will interact with the service.

A WSDL description is an XML document that contains all the information about service capabilities and invocation mechanisms [2]. Unfortunately, a WSDL document only addresses the functional aspects of a web service without containing any useful description of non-functional or quality of service (QoS) characteristics.

S. Kounev, I. Gorton, and K. Sachs (Eds.): SIPEW 2008, LNCS 5119, pp. 228–246, 2008.

Different web services may provide similar functionality, but with distinct quality of service properties. In the selection of a web service, it is important to consider both functional and QoS properties in order to fully satisfy the needs of a service consumer [3][4].

This is even more important when dealing with composite web services, or services resulting from the composition of a set of services in execution on networked server hosts. In a composite web service the component services cooperate to execute a process that defines the interaction workflow. The service-oriented architecture provides the necessary support for the consolidation of multiple services into a single composite service corresponding to the overall process.

Several terms have been proposed in literature to describe different styles of collaboration between services, the most relevant ones being orchestration and choreography [5].

These terms represent two different patterns of interactions between component services. *Orchestration* represents the control from the perspective of one party, which is the central authority (or *coordinator*) that controls the execution of component web services. Orchestration refers to an executable process where a coordinator is in charge of controlling the execution flow by explicitly invoking the component services, which only respond to the coordinator requests. *Choreography* is instead much more collaborative and does not rely on a central coordinator.

Several languages have been developed for web service composition [6]. Composite web services addressed in this paper refer to orchestration-based patterns of interaction described by use of the *BPEL* (Business Process Execution Language for Web Services) [7].

A BPEL process is an XML document typically generated with graphical design tools by business analysts rather than programmers. A BPEL process is executed by an orchestration engine that coordinates all of the activities and publishes the process through a standard web service interface.

In a BPEL context, service providers are strategically interested both to describe the QoS characteristics of the offered services, to better qualify their offer and gain a significant advantage in the global marketplace, and to predict the level of QoS that can be offered to service consumers when building composite web services that make use of services managed by various service providers.

In this respect in our past work [8] we introduced a model-driven approach for predicting at composition time, and managing at execution time, the *performance* of composite services.

In such an approach, a composite service is initially described in terms of its abstract model, i.e., a BPEL-oriented UML model representing the abstract workflow of the process. The annotation of performance data onto BPEL-oriented UML models is carried out by use of P-WSDL (Performance-enabled WSDL) [9], a lightweight WSDL extension that is based on the UML Profile for Scheduling, Performance and Time (SPT) [10] and that specifically addresses the performance-related attributes of QoS. The performance-enabled UML description of the resulting composite service is finally translated into a LQN (Layered Queueing Network) performance model.

In this paper we propose an extension of such an approach by introducing a *reliability* prediction method that, combined with the performance-related one, gives the basis for obtaining a joint prediction measured in terms of *performability* [11][12].

The proposed approach is founded on Q-WSDL [13], a lightweight WSDL extension for the description of QoS characteristics of a web service, such as performance, reliability, availability or security. Q-WSDL is inspired both to the aforementioned SPT Profile and to the UML Profile for Quality of Service and Fault Tolerance (QoS Profile) [14].

The rest of paper is structured as follows. Section 0 briefly recalls the Q-WSDL notation. Section 3 illustrates the proposed model-driven approach to predict the performability of a composite service and finally Section 4 gives an example application that shows how the performability analysis may lead to predictions that do not correspond to those obtained by approaches that only consider the performance attribute.

2   QoS-Enabled WSDL (Q-WSDL)

A WSDL description is an XML document that contains all the information about service capabilities and invocation mechanisms. The capabilities are described in terms of the operations of the service and the input and output messages for each operation. What is needed to invoke the service is provided by a binding implementation description that describes how messages are sent through the network to reach the service location, where the hosting environment executes the service implementation.

Unfortunately, a WSDL document only addresses the functional aspects of a web service without containing any useful description of non-functional or QoS characteristics. Different web services may provide similar functionality, but with distinct quality of service properties. In the selection of a web service, it is important to consider both functional and QoS properties in order to fully satisfy the needs of a service consumer [15]. To this purpose a lightweight WSDL extension has been proposed in [13] for the description of QoS characteristics of a web service, such as performance, reliability, availability, security, etc.

The Q-WSDL metamodel, expressed in terms of MOF (Meta Object Facility) [16] is shown in Figure 1. Such definitions are specified in the WSDL XML Schema, which has been used to identify the classes and associations of the WSDL metamodel, illustrated in the portion of Figure 1 bounded by a dashed line shape. Classes and associations outside the dashed line shape in Figure 1 extend the WSDL metamodel to include the description of the QoS characteristics of a web service. The complete set of classes and association in Figure 1 (both inside and outside the dashed line shape) identifies the Q-WSDL metamodel.

The extension is inspired both to the SPT Profile and to the QoS Profile, which extend the UML metamodel to specify UML models with QoS-oriented annotations. A complete description of Q-WSDL and the related MOF-based metamodel transformation is out of the scope of this paper.

For a detailed description of the model-driven WSDL extension the reader is referred to [13].

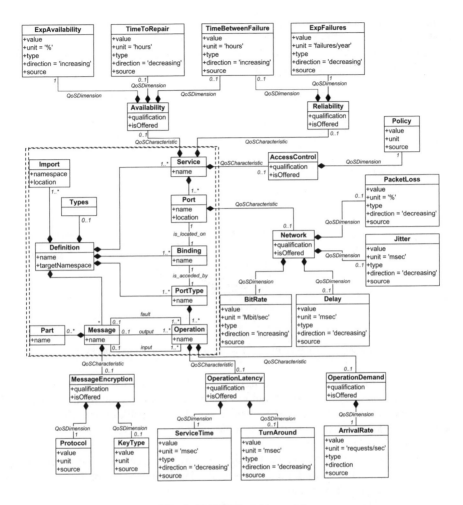

Fig. 1. Q-WSDL metamodel

3   Model-Driven Performability Prediction of Composite Services

The proposed approach to predict the performability of composite web services is based on the one proposed in [8]. The approach, illustrated in Figure 2, is integrated into a complete model-driven service composition process, which consists of activities (squared rectangles) that take as input and/or produce as output XML documents (rounded rectangles) representing various types of WSDL and BPEL documents. Straight lines represent control flow, while dashed lines represent flow of XML documents.

The use of model-driven approaches for predicting the performance of software systems is also well recognized in literature (see, e.g., the contribution in [17], which extends MDA to integrate performance validation).

In our approach the composite service is initially specified in terms of its abstract model, that is a workflow of abstract services, described by means of an UML Activity Diagram (AD) [18]. A service discovery is then carried out in order to bind the abstract services to a set of concrete services.

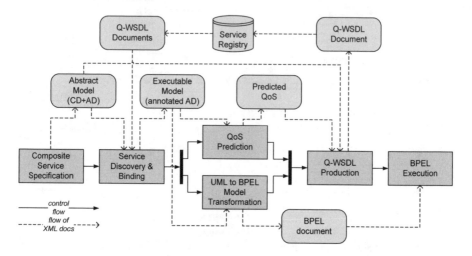

Fig. 2. QoS-enabled model-driven service composition process

Once a set of candidate services has been gathered for each abstract service, a service selection activity is carried out to identify the configuration of the composite service: each abstract service in the abstract model is mapped to a specific concrete service, in order to satisfy both the functional and non-functional requirements of the overall distributed application.

At this step, the abstract model is transformed into an executable model, consisting of an AD annotated with binding and QoS data obtained from the Q-WSDL descriptions of concrete services.

The use of QoS annotations to define the QoS parameters of component services may prove hard to carry out in practical use cases, due to the fact that component services are part of an "open world" that is typically not known to the orchestration coordinator. To this purpose, Q-WSDL provides the capability to define QoS values in terms of probability distributions, rather than of fixed, hard values, to take into explicit account the significant variations that may occur to QoS parameters of component web services [19].

A model-driven transformation is then carried out to obtain the QoS prediction (specifically related to the performability attribute in the paper case), and then to check if the evaluated configuration is able to satisfy the offered or negotiated level of QoS.

Finally, the service interface of the BPEL process and the QoS predictions are used to produce the Q-WSDL document of the composite web service, to be published in a web service registry.

As above mentioned, the QoS prediction in Figure 2 is carried out in terms of performability, which refers to the joint analysis of performance and reliability. The former is defined in terms of, e.g., throughput or service time, while the latter is defined as the probability of failure-free operation of a web service for a specified amount of time.

The following two sections describe the model-driven methods for performance and reliability prediction. Then the approach that combines the two methods into a performability prediction method is illustrated.

3.1 Performance Prediction

The performance prediction is carried out by first translating the annotated AD representing the BPEL executable process into a LQN model and then by solving such a model in order to obtain the performance indices of the composite web service, such as throughput, utilization, or response time. The use of UML to LQN model transformations for predicting the performance of software systems has been widely investigated, and several contributions are available in literature [20][21][22].

The AD to LQN model transformation, described in [8], is specified by use of a pattern-based approach that describes how basic BPEL structures are transformed into the corresponding LQN structures. In this section we briefly recall the rationale of such a transformation.

The main element of a BPEL process is called activity. An activity is either primitive or structured. The main primitive types are: *invoke*, to invoke an operation of a web service described in WSDL, *receive*, to wait for a message from an external source and *reply*, to reply to an external source. The main structured activities are: *sequence*, to define an execution order, *flow*, for parallel execution, *switch*, for conditional executions and *while*, for looping.

Additional BPEL constructs, such as *pick*, *wait*, *repeatUntil*, etc., are not considered in this paper, but can be easily addressed by a straightforward extension of the proposed approach. The BPEL-oriented extensions are introduced to model the BPEL constructs and are annotated according to the UML Profile for Automated Business Processes [23], while QoS-oriented extensions are obtained from the Q-WSDL documents of component services and are annotated onto the AD according to the Q-WSDL notation.

Table 1 summarizes the main stereotypes that extend UML metaclasses to specify BPEL models of composite services. Each stereotype can be applied to the instances of the base metaclasses that the stereotype extends. The stereotypes applied to the `Action` metaclass represent the main primitive BPEL types, i.e., *invoke*, to invoke an operation of a web service, *receive*, to wait for a message from an external source and *reply*, to reply to an external source.

Table 1. BPEL stereotypes

Stereotype	Base Metaclass	Description
«process»	ActivityPartition	BPEL process coordinator
«partner»	ActivityPartition	BPEL partner (component web service)
«receive»	Action	BPEL receive activity
«invoke»	Action	BPEL invoke activity
«reply»	Action	BPEL reply activity

The mapping of BPEL primitives to LQN structures is shown in Figure 3. The interested reader may refer to [8] for a detailed illustration of the model transformation.

The transformations are based on the following general rules:

- An `ActivityPartition` instance stereotyped as «process» or «partner» is mapped to LQN `Task` instance.
- An `Action` instance stereotyped as «receive» or «invoke» is mapped to a LQN `Entry` instance. An `Action` instance stereotyped as «reply» is instead mapped to a LQN `Activity` instance of the LQN task associated to the coordinator of the composite service.
- The `ActivityEdge` instance between two actions stereotyped respectively as «receive» andr «invoke» is mapped to a `Call` instance in the LQN model.
- `Fork` and `Join` nodes are mapped to `AND-Fork` and `AND-Join` activities. Note that, as shown in the Figure 3, in case of concurrent flows executed on different partititions, a *fork handler* LQN activity is introduced to model the corresponding entry call.
- The BPEL `switch` and `while` primitives are not mapped to specific LQN constructs. They are dealt by associating `PAprob`/`PArep` tagged values to Action instances stereotyped as «PAstep» in the switch/while constructs (according to the SPT profile) and then using such tagged values to compute the number of calls to LQN entries.
- A message exchanged between BPEL partners is modeled as an `ObjectNode` instances and transformed to LQN `Call` instances from the entry of the LQN task associated to the sending partner, to the entry of virtual LQN task (Net) that models the network connecting the two BPEL partners. The virtual task has a single entry whose execution demand (*dem*) attribute is derived from performance properties described in the Q-WSDL. The number of calls (*n_req* and *n_resp*) to such an entry can be derived by the Q-WSDL description as well. Specifically, the values of *dem*, *n_req* and *n_resp* are obtained as follows:

$$dem = \frac{ebs}{min\{B_S, B_r\}} \qquad n\_req = \frac{m_{req}}{ebs} \qquad n\_resp = \frac{m_{resp}}{ebs}$$

where *ebs* is the size of the elementary block transferred on the network, B_s and B_r are the throughput (in terms of bit/seconds) specified in the Q-WSDL description of the sending and the receiving partner, respectively, and m_{req} and m_{resp} are the sizes of the request and the response messages specified in the Q-WSDL description, respectively.

The so-obtained LQN model is given as input to a LQN solver, which carries out the model evaluation step and yields as output the predictions about the performance of the composite web service.

In the proposed approach, the BPEL engine overhead due to the events related to processing coordination activities of the orchestration is not taken into consideration and thus the performance prediction cannot be regarded as representative of a real orchestration engine.

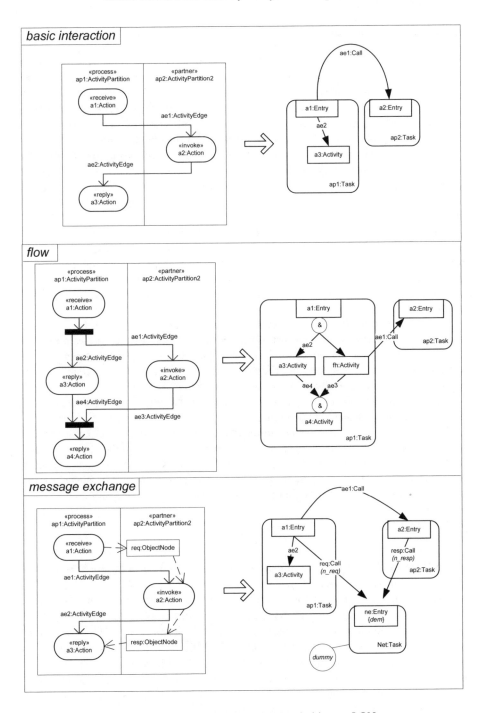

Fig. 3. Example mapping of UML-based BPEL primitives to LQN structures

3.2 Reliability Prediction

Reliability-oriented extensions are annotated onto the AD by introducing a «reliability» stereotype associated with the reliability QoS characteristics specified in Q-WSDL. Specifically, the «reliability» stereotype is introduced to specify the reliability characteristics of ActivityPartition instances that represent both the BPEL coordinator and the component web services. The stererotype is described by simple tags that specify the attributes of the characteristic and structured tags that specify the QoS dimensions associated to the characteristic. In particular, the «reliability» stereotype is described by the qualification and isOffered simple tags and by the TimeToFailure and ExpFailures structured tags, which in turn are both specified in terms of value, unit, source, type and direction elements, as illustrated in Figure 1.

Let us assume that the mean value of the time to failure, shortly denoted as MTTF, is specified for each service provided by BPEL partners in the composite web service process. The MTTF value includes both failures of the partner network link connection, that is responsible of the correct call and correct return of operation invocation from the partner side, and failures of the body code for each operation provided by the BPEL partner service.

Similarly, the reliability value specified for each operation of the BPEL coordinator includes both failures of the coordinator network connection and the software failures. The reliability of the network link can be obtained from the SLA (service level agreement) signed with the network provider, while the reliability of software executed at coordinator side can be obtained from statistical testing [18].

The nodes of the AD corresponding to instances of the ControlNode metaclass and the AD edges are considered to be failure free.

According to a widely accepted assumption [25], the failures of the different services, and of their relevant operations, are independent. By assuming an exponential distribution probability for the failures in the BPEL process, the reliability associated to each AD node a, corresponding to an instance of the Action UML metaclass that represents a BPEL basic activity, can be computed as:

$$R_a(t) = e^{-\frac{1}{MTTF_a}t}$$

(1)

where $R_a(t)$ and $MTTF_a$ are the reliability and the mean time to failure associated to the node a of the AD, respectively.

The reliability of the composite web service described by the annotated AD is predicted by use of an algorithm that iteratively applies a set of reduction rules until only a single atomic node remains. The algorithm, inspired by [26], proceeds by iteratively applying the reduction rules to the basic BPEL structures shown in Figure 4.

The structure of the annotated AD changes at each iteration and after a number of iterations it is reduced to a single node. When this state is reached, the reliability associated to the remaining node specifies the reliability of the composite web service corresponding to the annotated AD under analysis.

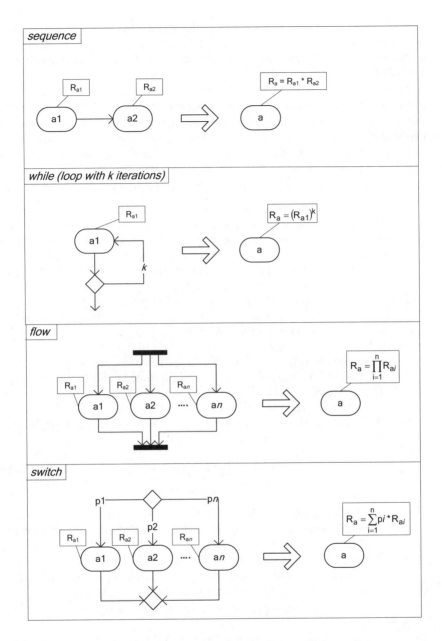

Fig. 4. Reduction rules for reliability prediction

3.3 Performability Prediction

Let us consider n different candidate configurations CS_i (i=1..n) of a composite service CS, resulting from a service discovery activity that finds more than one concrete service to be bound to the services of the abstract model. Each configuration may be analyzed by use of the methods illustrated in the previous sections in order to obtain the prediction that leads to an optimal choice of the initial configuration in terms of either performance or reliability.

At this time, it is quite usual to find conflicting predictions, in other words the optimal configuration estimated in terms of performance is not the optimal one in terms of reliability and vice versa. This claims for a joint analysis of performance and reliability so that the comparison of different design alternatives, such as which one to adopt as initial configuration, may be then based on predictions of the combined QoS attribute known as performability.

The performability prediction is carried out by use of the following algorithm:

1. Generate the state transition diagram STD associated with the Markov chain that represents the possible configurations which the composite web service may undergo before experimenting a failure (this implies that when a service fails and a working service providing the same functionality is available, the composite web service switch to a new configuration that includes the working service);
2. Select a candidate configuration as the initial configuration;
3. Use the reliability prediction method illustrated in Section 3.2 to obtain the transition probabilities of the STD;
4. Calculate the absorbing probabilities $P(CS_i)$ of being in a given working configuration (i=1..n) starting from the initial configuration;
5. Use the performance prediction method illustrated in Section 3.1 to obtain the performance associated to each configuration, e.g., in terms of its throughput $T(CS_i)$, and assign it as a reward to the configuration;
6. Obtain the performability prediction in terms of the expected reward rate of the composite web service CS given by:

$$RW(CS) = \sum_{i=1}^{n} P(CS_i)T(CS_i) \qquad (2)$$

where:

- RW (CS) is the expected reward rate of the composite service, i.e., an overall attribute that combines both the throughput and the reliability of the composite service;
- P (CS_i) is the probability of the system to be in the i-th working configuration starting from the initial configuration, as computed by means of the state transition diagram (STD);
- T (CS_i) is the throughput of the i-th candidate configuration.

The comparison among the so obtained reward rates for each candidate initial configuration allows to carry out a choice that takes into account both the performance and the reliability of the composite service.

The above described algorithm can be seen as a preliminary approach to performability analysis, due to the fact that it is built upon the following assumptions:

- the failures of services are independent, i.e. they only affect the reliability of the overall composite service;
- the failure of a service is unrecoverable;
- services fail one at a time;
- failed services may be replaced by a working service that offers the same functionality, in case it is found by the discovery activity;
- the cost of service replacement (i.e., the time needed to switch the composite service to a new configuration) is negligible.

The following section illustrates an example case study that describes the application of the proposed algorithm.

4   Example Application

In order to give an example application of the proposed model-driven methodology for the performability prediction, let us consider a composite web service that provides an operation for creating travel plans. This example has already been taken into consideration in [8], where the performance of the composite web service is predicted in terms of both the response time and the utilization by use of the method illustrated in Section 3.1.

In this section we extend such a case study, in order to show how the performability analysis that combines the prediction of performance and reliability attributes can lead to results unexpected if such attributes are dealt with separately.

A travel plan is built by first looking for flight and hotel room availability, according to the service consumer request, and then obtaining information about car renting. The travel plan should also include information about transportation from the airport to the hotel. According to user preferences, the plan may thus include either a timetable of airport shuttles or an estimated cab fare. The travel plan is finally presented to the customer for approval and booking. It is assumed that an average 70% of customers prefer a cab rather than an airport shuttle

The following component web services are required to implement the `travelPlanning` operation of the composite web service:

- a service providing information about flight availability and reservation, denoted as *flights manager (FM)* service;
- a service providing information about hotel reservation and airport services (e.g., timetables of airport shuttles), denoted as *accommodation manager (AM)* service;
- a service providing information about car renting and cab fare estimates, denoted as *transportation manager (TM)* service.

A service discovery activity is carried out to bind each abstract service to a specific concrete service matching the abstract service interface. The executable model (annotated AD) is shown in Figure 5.

Let us now suppose that two different candidate services are available for binding the TM service. Table 2 summarizes the QoS data extracted from the Q-WSDL documents of the two alternative services, namely TM_A and TM_B.

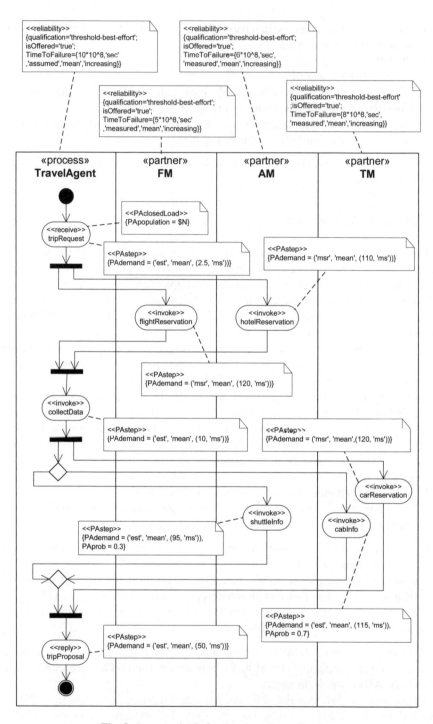

Fig. 5. Annotated AD for the example application

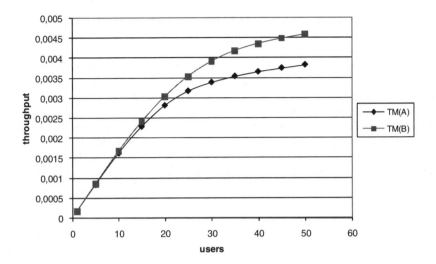

Fig. 6. Performance prediction (throughput) for the example application

Table 2. QoS data obtained from Q-WSDL documents

Parameter		TM$_A$	TM$_B$
Performance	`CarReservation` time demand	120 ms	90 ms
	`CabInfo` time demand	115 ms	84 ms
	Network bit rate	10 Mb	100 Mb
Reliability	MTTF	10*10^8	7.2*10^7
	R(1year)	0.961	0.645

If the prediction activity is limited to performance-related attributes, the choice of the initial configuration can be performed by use of the model-driven method described in Section 3.1.

The results of such a prediction activity for the example case study are summarized in the graph depicted in the Figure 6. The diagram shows the throughput of both the composite service with TM$_A$ and the composite service with TM$_B$, for different numbers of composite service consumers. It is easy to be convinced that if we focus the attention on the performance attribute only, the choice of the alternative denoted as TM$_B$ is to be preferred. This means that the composite service will be initially configured by binding the `carReservation` and the `cabInfo` operations with those provided by service TM$_B$.

As stated in section 3, a performability prediction is instead carried out in order to understand which initial configuration of the composite web service would lead to a better expected reward rate.

The *first step* of the algorithm carries out the generation of the STD that represents the possible configurations which the composite service may undergo before experimenting a failure. The states of the STD represent the working configurations of a composite service, while the transitions represent the probabilities to remain in a configuration or move to a different configuration, in case of failure of one service.

An additional state is introduced in the STD to represent the failed composite service, i.e., the state reached when a service fails in a given configuration and no services are available to replace it.

Figure 7 represents the STD for the example case study. The state CS_1 represents the composite service in the configuration that includes TM_A, while the state CS_2 represents the composite service in the configuration that includes TM_B. The state CS_0 represents the composite service in the failed state.

At the *second step* of the algorithm, a candidate initial configuration is selected. In the example case, two different alternative may be considered for the initial configuration: the first (denoted as STD_A) assumes CS_1 as the initial configuration and CS_2 as a backup configuration in case of TM_A failure, while the second (denoted as STD_B) assumes CS_2 as the initial configuration and CS_1 as a backup configuration in case of TM_B failure.

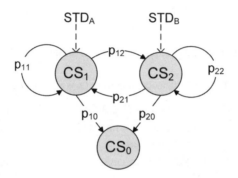

Fig. 7. STD for the example application, with two alternative initial states (STD_A and STD_B)

In the STD_A case, the composite service is initially in the configuration state CS_1, that includes TM_A. In case of TM_A failure, the composite service switches to the configuration state CS_2 in which TM_A is replaced by TM_B. In case of failure of either the composite service coordinator or of other component services the composite service fails. In case of a failure in the configuration state CS_2 no service replacements are available and thus the overall composite service fails.

In the STD_B case, the composite service is initially in the configuration state CS_2, that includes TM_B. In case of TM_B failure, composite service switches to the configuration state CS_1, in which TM_B is replaced by TM_A. In case of failure of either the composite service coordinator or of other component services the composite service fails. In case of a failure in the configuration state CS_1 no service replacements are available and thus the overall composite service fails.

At the *third step*, the transition probabilities in the STD are obtained both by carrying out the reliability prediction method described in Section 3.2 and from the reliability data extracted from the Q-WSDL documents of TM_A and TM_B (see Table 2).

Specifically, the reliability prediction gives the probability of remaining in a given working configuration state of the composite service, while the transition probabilities between working configuration states represent the probability of having a failure of

TM_A (for STD_A) and TM_B (for STD_B). Such probabilities are obtained by subtracting the reliability of TM_A and TM_B from 1. The transition probabilities between a working state and the failed state are instead obtained by subtraction from the previous transition probabilities, so that their sum equals 1.

Table 3 gives the transition probabilities for STD_A and STD_B. The reliabilities used to obtain such probabilities are computed by use of equation (1) from the MTTF over a time interval (mission time) of one year.

Table 3. Transition Probabilities for STD_A and STD_B

Transition Probability	STD_A	STD_B
p_{11}	0.746	0.746
p_{22}	0.385	0.385
p_{12}	0.039	0
p_{21}	0	0.355
p_{10}	0.215	0.254
p_{20}	0.615	0.260

The *fourth step* of the algorithm calculates the absorbing probabilities P(CSi) of being in a given working configuration starting from the initial configuration CS_1 (in the STD_A case) or from the initial configuration CS_2 (in the STD_B case), as illustrated in Table 4.

Table 4. Absorbing probabilities of states CS_1, CS_2 and CS_0 from initial state

Alternative	Description	Value
	$P(CS_1) = p_{11}$	0.746
STD_A	$P(CS_2) = p_{12}{}^* p_{22}$	0.015
	$P(CS_0) = p_{12}{}^* p_{20} + p_{10}$	0.239
	$P(CS_1) = p_{21}{}^* p_{11}$	0.265
STD_B	$P(CS_2) = p_{22}$	0.385
	$P(CS_0) = p_{21}{}^* p_{10} + p_{20}$	0.350

The *fifth step* introduces the reward to be associated to each configuration state of the STD. This step is carried out by use of the performance prediction method illustrated in Section 3.1, which yields the performance associated to each configuration in terms of the throughput $T(CS_i)$, as illustrated in Figure 6 for the composite service in the configurations with TM_A and TM_B.

Specifically, line denoted as TM(A) in Figure 6 is the throughput to be assigned as reward to the configuration state CS_1, while line denoted as TM(B) in Figure 6 is the throughput to be assigned as reward to configuration state CS_2.

Finally, at the *sixth and last step* of the algorithm, the expected reward rate is obtained for the two alternatives by use of equation (2). The results are graphically shown in Figure 8 for different numbers of composite service users.

The performability prediction in Figure 8 shows that an initial configuration with TM_A is to be preferred, in contrast with what obtained from the performance prediction in Figure 6.

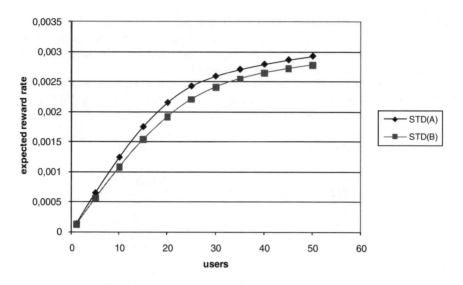

Fig. 8. Expected reward rate for the example application

This simple but effective case gives an example of the importance of combining the analysis of performance and reliability attributes. Even though the proposed algorithm undergoes some restricting limitations it can thus be considered as a first step towards the adoption of performability-oriented QoS management of composite web services.

5 Conclusions

The adoption of service-oriented architectures for software development is gaining momentum due to the increasing availability of services, or customized units of software that run in a network and that can be rapidly composed to yield distributed applications that can respond quickly to changing requirements.

In this context, service providers are strategically interested both to predict and describe the QoS of the offered services.

This paper has introduced a model-driven approach for predicting the performability of composite services specified by use of BPEL. The approach is founded on Q-WSDL, a lightweight QoS-oriented extension of the Web Service Definition Language (WSDL) and exploits an already available method for performance prediction.

The paper has introduced a model-driven method for the reliability prediction of composite services, which has then combined to the performance-related one to eventually obtain a combined prediction quantified in terms of performability.

The proposed approach has been applied to a simple case study that has shown how the performability analysis may lead to predictions that do not correspond to those obtained by approaches that only consider the performance attribute.

Work is in progress to implement the proposed method by use of existing performability evaluation tools (e.g., [27][28]) and to remove some of the existing limitations, e.g., by taking into account both multiple failures of services in a given configuration and the cost of composite service reconfiguration as a negative reward.

Acknowledgements

This work was partially supported by funds from the University of Roma TorVergata research on "Performance Validation of Complex Systems" and by the CERTIA Research Center.

References

1. Alonso, G., Casati, F., Kuno, H., Machiraju, V.: Web Services. Springer, Heidelberg (2004)
2. WWW Consortium, Web Services Description language (WSDL) Version 2.0, W3C Working Draft (January 2006), http://www.w3.org/TR/wsdl20
3. Ludwig, H.: Web Services QoS: External SLAs and Internal Policies - Or: How do we deliver what we promise? In: Proceedings of the 4th IEEE International Conference on Web Information Systems Engineering, WISE 2003 Workshops, Italy (2003)
4. Menascé, D.A.: QoS Issues in Web Services. IEEE Internet Computing, 72–75 (November/December 2002)
5. Peltz, C.: Web Services Orchestration and Choreography. IEEE Computer 36, 46–52 (2003)
6. Wohed, P., Van Der Aalst, M.P.W., Dumas, M., Ter Hofstede, A.H.M.: Analysis of Web Services Composition Languages, The Case of BPEL4WS. In: Song, I.-Y., Liddle, S.W., Ling, T.-W., Scheuermann, P. (eds.) ER 2003. LNCS, vol. 2813, pp. 200–215. Springer, Heidelberg (2003)
7. IBM, BPEL – Business Process Execution Language for Web Services, version 1.1 (2003)
8. D'Ambrogio, A., Bocciarelli, P.: A Model-driven Approach to Describe and Predict the Performance of Composite Services. In: Proceedings of the 6th Int. Workshop on Software and Performance (WOSP), Buenos Aires, Argentina (2007)
9. D'Ambrogio, A.: A WSDL Extension for Performance-enabled Description of Web Services. In: Yolum, p., Güngör, T., Gürgen, F., Özturan, C. (eds.) ISCIS 2005. LNCS, vol. 3733. Springer, Heidelberg (2005)
10. Object Management Group, UML Profile for Scheduling, Performance and Time, version 1.1 (January 2005)
11. Meyer, J.F.: On evaluating performability of degradable computing systems. IEEE Transactions on Computers C-29(8), 720–731 (1980)
12. Smith, R.M., Trivedi Kishor, S., Ramesh, A.V.: Performability Analysis: Measures, an Algorithm, and a Case Study. IEEE Transactions on Computers 37(4), 406–417 (1988)
13. D'Ambrogio, A.: A Model-driven WSDL Extension for Describing the QoS of Web Services. In: Proceedings of the IEEE International Conference on Web Services (ICWS), Chicago, USA (2006)
14. Object Management Group, UML Profile for Modeling Quality of Service and Fault Tolerance Characteristics and Mechanisms, Adopted Specification
15. Menascé, M.A.: QoS Issues in Web Services. IEEE Internet Computing, 72–75 (November/December 2002)
16. Object Management Group, Meta Object Facility (MOF) Specification, version 1.4 (2002)

17. Cortellessa, V., Di Marco, A., Inverardi, P.: Software Performance Model-Driven Architecture. In: Proceedings of the ACM Symposium on Applied Computing, Dijon, France (2006)
18. Object Management Group, Unified Modeling Language (UML): Superstructure, version 2.0
19. Rosario, S., Benveniste, A., Haar, S., Jard, C.: Probabilistic QoS and soft contracts for transaction based Web services orchestrations. In: Proceedings of the International Conference on Web Services (ICWS 2007), Salt Lake City, Utah, USA (2007)
20. Xu, J., Oufimtsev, A., Woodside, M., Murphy, L.: Performance modeling and prediction of enterprise JavaBeans with layered queuing network templates. ACM SIGSOFT Software Engineering 31(2) (2006)
21. Gu, G.P., Petriu, D.B.: From UML to LQN by XML algebra-based model transformations. In: Proceedings of the ACM Fifth International Workshop on Software and Performance (WOSP 2005), Palma de Mallorca, Spain (2005)
22. D'Ambrogio, A.: A Model Transformation Framework for the Automated Building of Performance Models from UML Models. In: Proceedings of the ACM Fifth International Workshop on Software and Performance (WOSP 2005), Palma de Mallorca, Spain (2005)
23. Gardner, T.: UML Modelling of Automated Business Processes with a Mapping to BPEL. In: Proceedings of the First European Workshop on Object Orientation and Web Services (in conjunction with ECOOP 2003), Darmstadt, Germany (2003), http://www.ibm.com/developerworks/webservices/library/ws-uml2bpel/
24. Lyu, M.R.: Handbook of Software Reliability Engineering. McGraw-Hill, New York (1995)
25. Whittaker, J.A., Thomason, M.G.: A Markov Chain Model for Statistical Software Testing. IEEE Transactions on Software Engineering 20(10), 812–824 (1994)
26. Cardoso, J., Sheth, A.P., Miller, J.A., Arnold, J., Kochut, K.: Quality of service for workflows and web service processes. Journal of Web Semantics 1(3), 281–308 (2004)
27. Das, O., Woodside, C.M.: Dependable-LQNS: A Performability Modeling Tool for Layered Systems. In: Kemper, P., Sanders, W.H. (eds.) TOOLS 2003. LNCS, vol. 2794. Springer, Heidelberg (2003)
28. Deavours, D.D., Clark, G., Courtney, T., Daly, D., Derisavi, S., Doyle, J.M., Sanders, W.H., Webster, P.G.: The Möbius Framework and Its Implementation. IEEE Transactions on Software Engineering 28(10), 956–969 (2002)

Dynamic Server Allocation for Power and Performance

Joris Slegers, Nigel Thomas, and Isi Mitrani

School of Computing Science,
Newcastle University, NE1 7RU
{j.a.l.slegers,nigel.thomas,isi.mitrani}@ncl.ac.uk

Abstract. We consider a system of servers that process incoming requests. These requests experience periods of high and low arrival rate. Servers can be powered down dynamically to conserve power. We examine this system with a view to balancing the need between processing incoming requests quickly and reducing power consumption. The system is modeled formally and heuristics are presented to decide when servers should be powered down or up. Preliminary results of the performance of these heuristics are also included.

Keywords: Resource allocation, dynamic optimization, power conservation.

1 Introduction

The vast amount of power that servers and data centres consume are starting to become a major concern, both from an economic (see e.g. [4]) and an environmental point of view. Consequently a lot of work has focussed towards reducing power consumption of individual servers and their components. Much less attention seems to have been paid to the possibility of dynamically powering servers on and off as demand fluctuates (see [1] for an overview). Previous work that does consider this possibility seems to take its inspiration mostly from work on load balancing and control theory (e.g. [9]). Another interesting approach is found in [2], where resource allocation is done through a (mock) bidding system.

This paper is based on previous work by the authors ([10] and [11]), where reallocation of servers between different job types was considered. The optimization goal there was purely to improve the response time of the system. This model has been adapted here to allow the optimization goal to include the energy consumption of a system.

The novelty of this paper lies in the explicit modelling of a system with a view to making a trade off between performance of the system and its power consumption, by dynamically powering down servers and powering them up again according to demand. Furthermore, we also present several heuristic policies that try to optimize the behaviour of this system, given this trade off. Finally we also present some initial results regarding their performance.

S. Kounev, I. Gorton, and K. Sachs (Eds.): SIPEW 2008, LNCS 5119, pp. 247–261, 2008.

2   Modeling the System

We consider a model where there are N homogeneous servers. These can be in one of two states: power up or power down. When a server is in power up, it can service incoming requests. When a server is in power down, it can't process any requests, but will consume less (or no) power. The details of the power down state are expressly left ambiguous. It can mean the server is completely shutdown, in some sleep state or any other state, as long as it is less power consuming. We will refer to 'powering up' to denote the decision to switch a server from the power down state to the power up state and 'powering down' for the converse.

The service time of a request is assumed to be exponentially distributed with rate μ. The requests themselves arrive according to a two-phase Poisson process, i.e. there are 'high' and 'low' arrival periods. During a high period, denoted by $l = 1$, requests arrive as a Poisson process with rate λ_{high}. During a low period, notation $l = 0$, fewer requests arrive, with rate λ_{low}. The high and low periods themselves have durations that are distributed exponentially with mean $1/\xi$ and $1/\eta$ respectively. We consider the servers that are currently powered up to be part of one (logical) pool, called the powered servers pool, with an unbounded queue which holds the incoming requests. We denote the number of powered up servers by k_{up}. The number of jobs in the queue (including jobs currently being processed) will be denoted by j. The other servers, which are powered down, are in a pool as well, which we will call the powered down pool. We will denote their amount by k_{down}. Since all the servers are homogeneous, we do not distinguish between individual servers in each pool, but rather focus on the number of servers powered up or down.

We assign a cost, c_{job}, to keeping a job in the system for one unit of time. These 'holding costs' reflect the relative value of completing a job quickly. Conversely we assign a negative cost (i.e. profit) c_{pow} to keep a server powered down for a unit of time. This should reflect the relative energy savings of not powering up a server.

A server can be switched from the pool of powered servers to that of powered down servers. This will take an amount of time, assumed to be exponentially distributed with rate ζ_{down}. We will denote the number of servers powering down by m_{down}. Conversely they can be powered up again. The number of servers powering up will denoted m_{up}. The time this will take is again assumed to be exponentially distributed, now with rate ζ_{up}. During a switch a server cannot serve jobs but it does consume power, i.e. it doesn't accumulate a profit from energy savings. Furthermore, the powering up and down of machines can incur additional costs, e.g. through peak power consumption, which we will denote by C_{up} and C_{down} for powering up and powering down respectively.

This means we can describe a state S of the system by:

$$S = (j, l, k_{up}, k_{down}, m_{up}, m_{down}). \qquad (1)$$

There is some redundancy in the notation since the total number of servers in the system should be constant, i.e. $k_{up} + k_{down} + m_{up} + m_{down} = N$. This is done because of convenience and has no further impact. The system behaviour is further characterized by the following transition probabilities (when no switching decision is made):

$$r(S, S') = \begin{cases} l\lambda_{high} + (1-l)\lambda_{low} & \text{if } j' = j+1 \\ \min(k_{up}, j)\mu & \text{if } j' = j-1 \\ m_{down}\zeta_{down} & \text{if } k'_{down} = k_{down} + 1 \text{ and } m'_{down} = m_{down} - 1 \\ m_{up}\zeta_{up} & \text{if } k'_{up} = k_{up} + 1 \text{ and } m'_{up} = m_{up} - 1 \\ l\xi & \text{if } l' = 0 \\ (1-l)\eta & \text{if } l' = 1 \end{cases}.$$

$$(2)$$

This characterizes a continuous time Markov chain. We can convert this into a Markov decision process by associating a set of allowed actions $\{a\}$ with each state S. Here we consider these actions to be:

- doing nothing, denoted by $a = 0$
- powering down i servers, with $0 < i \leq k_{up}$, denoted by $a = -i$
- powering up i servers, with $0 < i \leq k_{down}$, denoted by $a = i$.

These delays and costs will make the decision of when to power a server up or down non-trivial, especially in an environment with bursty arrivals. Our overall optimization goal is now to minimize the cost of the system, i.e. to find a policy of powering up/down that minimizes the average cost of the system per unit time. Here the relative value of the holding cost c_{job} versus the profit from keeping a server powered down are implicitly traded off.

Please note that the model given here is a (continuous time) Markov decision process (MDP). In principle these can be solved, i.e. we can find the policy that minimizes the long-term mean operating cost of the system, but for practical reasons this is often infeasible since the size of the state space involved quickly explodes. Amongst other things, a proper solution requires truncation of the maximum allowed queue length. For example we could consider a system with 25 servers and a maximum allowed queue length of 50. This number includes the jobs currently being processed, so it allows for roughly 25 waiting jobs. Such an MDP has 334152 states. This might seem a manageable number, but this would give rise to a system of 334152 simultaneous equations in as many different variables. These equations would then have to be repeatedly solved to find the optimal power-policy, in effect requiring the use of a (admittedly very sparse) matrix with over 111 billion elements. For a system of 26 servers, this rise to 372708 states and a matrix of just under 139 billion elements. To make matters worse, the calculated policy is non-trivially dependent on every single parameter of the system, making even the most clever precalculation infeasible.

3   Policies

In this section we consider some policies we can implement to balance the performance of the system with its power consumption. We will consider several different policies. The first is the optimal static policy, i.e. an initial allocation of servers that will not be changed for the duration. We also look at several dynamic policies.

Conspicuously absent in this section will be the optimal (dynamic) policy. As we have shown in previous work [11] it is very difficult to calculate the optimal policy. It is prohibitively expensive in computational effort for all but the simplest cases and also requires us to make some non-trivial modelling choices. For these reasons, this paper will not include the optimal dynamic policy.

3.1   Optimal Static Allocation

It is possible to get the optimal static allocation although this is not wholly trivial. We will do this by examining a single queue with n servers and a high/low arrival process. It is possible to calculate the mean queue length L_n for that queue. Since we can repeat this process for any number of servers n, we can easily determine the optimal number n^* that minimizes $c_{job}L_{n^*} + c_{pow}(N - n^*)$. This is then the optimal static allocation. In the rest of the paragraph we will outline the method for getting the mean queue length L_n. The details are rather technical and not included in this paper.

We can use the spectral expansion method to derive a solution for this queue. Details about this method can be found in the original paper [8]. The spectral expansion method enables the solution of certain two-dimensional Markov processes on a semi-infinite lattice strip. In the case considered here, the infinite dimension of the Markov process represents the different queue lengths a queue can attain. The finite dimension represents the high/low state of the arrival stream. The requirement for the technique to work is that from a certain threshold K the possible transitions out of a state no longer depend on the state in the infinite dimension. Here this is satisfied, since if there are at least as many jobs in the system as servers, i.e. N, the completion rate is then $N\mu$, regardless of the number of jobs in the system.

The spectral expansion method can be applied, giving an explicit, closed form, expression for the probability of being in each possible state. Although it is straightforward to calculate this for any given set of parameters, the expressions involved are very complex when expressed in abstract parameters. Therefore these expressions are not given in this paper.

3.2   Idle Heuristic

This heuristic policy follows the naïve policy of powering down any server that is idle and powering up a server, if possible, when there are jobs in the queue that are not currently being served by any server. It does not take account of switching times. Because in general the switching times are non-zero, we have to be slightly more precise. That is, we power up a server, if possible, when the number of jobs in the queue is bigger than the number of servers currently servicing a job and the number of servers being switched on, i.e. when: $j > k_{up} + m_{up}$. This assumes there are no batch arrivals, but we can easily extend the heuristic for that case by saying we power up $j - k_{up} - m_{up}$ servers.

It is worth noticing that even when switching is both instantaneous and free, this idle heuristic is not necessarily optimal. Consider the slightly odd situation where $i \cdot c_{job} < -c_{pow}$, i.e. the savings per unit time of having a single server powered down outweigh the penalties of having $i \geq 1$ jobs waiting. Then clearly the optimal policy is to only power up a server when there are more than i jobs waiting to be served. Although this is a somewhat artificial situation, it does show how, even when the model is vastly simplified, finding the optimal policy is not completely trivial.

3.3   Threshold Heuristic

The Threshold Heuristic is a generalization of the Idle Heuristic. For this heuristic we choose some threshold, j_{thresh}. Servers are then powered down when there are less than j_{thresh} jobs waiting to be served. In terms of our model, this means we power down a server if $j < j_{thresh} + k_{up} + m_{up}$. Conversely we power up a server if $j > j_{thresh} + k_{up} + m_{up}$, i.e. if there are more than j_{thresh} jobs waiting to be served.

Choosing the right threshold j_{thresh} is not straightforward and should, in general, depend on both the differential between the holding cost and the power savings, and the switching times. The Idle Heuristic is equivalent to setting $j_{thresh} = 0$.

3.4   Semi-static Heuristic

In this heuristic we detect whether the arrival process is in the low or in the high state. Depending on what arrival state the system is in, the optimal number of servers is allocates, assuming the high/low period lasts an infinite amount of time, i.e. we allocate as many servers as would be optimal if the arrival behaves as a standard Poisson process.

Since there are N servers in the system, we can consider any distribution of n powered up servers, serving the queue, and $N - n$ powered down servers. The queue has a certain load $\rho = \frac{\lambda}{n\mu}$, where we use the appropriate λ_{high} or λ_{low} depending on whether we are in a high or low arrival phase. The formula for the mean response time, $\bar{R}$, for this $M/M/n$ queue is quite well known (see e.g. [6]) and uses the famous Erlang C formula for the probability that all the servers in the queue are busy, which we will denote by Q here. The mean response time is:

$$\bar{R}_n = \frac{1}{\mu}[1 + \frac{Q}{n(1 - \rho)}] \, . \tag{3}$$

So that we can easily find the n that minimizes:

$$c_{job}\bar{R}_n + c_{pow}(N - n) \, , \tag{4}$$

where we assume that the queue is stable, i.e. $\lambda < n\mu$ for the appropriate $\lambda_{high/low}$.

3.5   High/Low Heuristic

The High/Low Heuristic is a modified version of the On/Off heuristic introduced by the present authors in [10]. It treats the queue of jobs as a deterministic fluid and assumes high/low periods last an infinite time. This means jobs arrive at rate

$$\gamma = \begin{cases} \lambda_{high} & \text{if } l = 1 \\ \lambda_{low} & \text{if } l = 0 \end{cases}, \tag{5}$$

where we recall that $l = 1$ denotes that the arrival stream is high and $l = 0$ denotes that it is low. Jobs are served at rate $k_{up}\mu$. We will use this approximation to calculate the cost of a decision until the queue empties. Since the system is (assumed to be) stable, this fluid approximation guarantees the queue will empty in finite time. We assume that switching servers complete their switches deterministically in the mean time indicated by the exponential distribution, i.e. when there are m_{up} servers being powered up, the first one completes its power up after $\frac{m_{up}}{\zeta_{up}}$ units of time, the second $\frac{m_{up}-1}{\zeta_{up}}$ units of time after that, etc.

Suppose there are k_{up} servers serving the queue, no servers currently being powered up or down and no powering up or down decision is made at this time. Then the queue decreases at constant rate $k_{up}\mu - \gamma$ and empties at time $\frac{j}{k_{up}\mu-\gamma}$. So the expected cost under these approximations can be shown to be the area of a triangle (see Figure 1, left) with as its length the time to empty the queue and as its height the queue size j at the start. More formally we get:

$$C_0 = \frac{c_{job}j^2}{2(k_{up}\mu - \gamma)} + \frac{c_{pow}k_{down}j}{k_{up}\mu - \gamma}. \tag{6}$$

The first part of equation 6 represents the the holding costs until the queue empties and the second part represents the power savings, again until the queue empties.

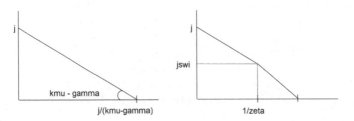

Fig. 1. The triangle whose area represents the holding cost (left) and the cost when there is a switch present (right)

When there is already a server being powered up (see Figure 1, right), assuming that the queue does not empty during the switch, its size at the point when the switch is completed, i.e. after $1/\zeta_{up}$, would be equal to j_{swi}, where

$$j_{swi} = j - (k_{up}\mu - \gamma)/\zeta_{up}. \tag{7}$$

This means that the total cost is:

$$C_1 = \frac{c_{job} j_{swi}}{\zeta_{up}} + \frac{c_{job}(j - j_{swi})}{2\zeta_{up}} + \frac{c_{job} j_{swi}^2}{2((k_{up} + 1)\mu - \gamma)} \\ + c_{pow}k_{down}\left(\frac{1}{\zeta_{up}} + \frac{j_{swi}}{(k_{up} + 1)\mu - \gamma}\right)$$

(8)

Here the first two terms represent the cost of the queue until the switch is expected to be completed, the third the cost of the queue after that moment until the switch is completed and the last terms again represents the savings from powered down servers. Extending (8) to multiple switches is straight-forward, although the formulae become increasingly convoluted. It should further be noted that when the *decision* is taken to power up i servers, (8) should be increased with the term iC_{up}.

Finally, can consider the case where a server is already being powered down. The cost then becomes:

$$C_{-1} = \frac{c_{job} j^2}{2((k_{up} - 1)\mu - \gamma)} + \frac{c_{pow}k_{down}}{\zeta_{down}} + c_{pow}k_{down}\left(\frac{j}{(k_{up} - 1)\mu - \gamma} - \frac{1}{\zeta_{down}}\right).$$

(9)

This too can be easily extended when multiple servers are powering down and should be increased with the term iC_{down} when it is a current decision to power i down servers, rather than an existing situation.

This heuristic now chooses the switching decision that minimizes the expected cost, at every state change. This calculation may seem prohibitively expensive, however note that we have to consider at most $N+1$ possible decisions, assuming all our decisions will result in stable systems. Furthermore, it is entirely feasible to precalculate a table of decisions, or even to recalculate one on a very regular basis to deal with changing parameters.

3.6 Average Flow Heuristic

The average flow heuristic is again an adaptation of a heuristic introduced in [10]. It is very similar to the High/Low heuristic. The entire analysis of the previous paragraph is applicable, with one change. For this heuristic we average out the high and low periods. This can be thought of as assuming that they are very short. This means we can use equations 6, 8 and 9, but have to substitute:

$$\gamma = \frac{\lambda_{high}\eta + \lambda_{low}\xi}{\xi + \eta}.$$

(10)

The rest of the analysis is entirely the same. It should be noted that with this heuristic we can restrict ourselves to just considering 3 possible decisions: powering 1 server up, powering 1 server down or doing nothing. This is because there are no wholesale changes in state (like the arrival stream turning on or off) and we can thus expect the proposed switches to be much more modest.

4 Results

In this section we will present some preliminary results. The heuristics in the previous section will be compared in performance under two different scenarios. We will also examine the effect of asymmetry in powering up and powering down times. And finally we will also take a separate look at the performance of the threshold heuristic.

4.1 Increased Bursts

For this experiment the system contains $N = 35$ servers, which process requests at a mean rate of $\mu = 1$. The arrival rate in the low period is $\lambda_{low} = 10$ throughout the experiment, so that if all the servers is powered up, utilization is $\frac{10}{35} \approx 29\%$. The arrival rate in the high period is plotted on the x-axis and varies from $\lambda_{high} = 10$ to $\lambda_{high} = 30$. This means that if the system is a high-arrival period and all the servers are powered up, utilization varies from 29% up to 86%. Here the high arrival periods last a mean time of $\xi^{-1} = 10$ and the low arrival periods last a mean time of $\eta^{-1} = 100$. This means the highest *average* utilization is just 34%, but the peak demands mean this number is very misleading. Powering up or down is free, but takes $\zeta_{up}^{-1} = \zeta_{down}^{-1} = 1$, or the equivalent of one completion time in the mean. Finally we consider the holding cost of a job to be $c_{job} = 1$ and the benefit of powering down $c_{pow} = -0.5$ half that. These numbers are of course relative and it just signifies that having a job in the queue is twice as expensive as having a server powered up.

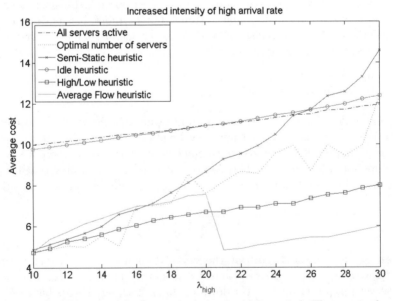

Fig. 2. Increasingly more intensive arrivals in the high period. The x-axis shows the high arrival rate λ_{high} and the y-axis the mean cost.

In Figure 2 we show the performance of the system under several heuristics. The costs were obtained from simulating the system for $T = 10000$ units of time and the displayed results form the averages from 50 runs. The 95 percentile of the relative error for each of these is small, typically within 5%, although the static allocations are a lot more susceptible to stochastic noise in the simulation and here the 95 percentile relative error can be higher.

The dash-dotted line represents the cost when all the servers are powered up all the time. This can be considered a baseline cost of sorts. As we can see the idle heuristic, an obvious choice for a heuristic, does not manage to improve on this. If we calculate the cost of a system that just has the optimal number of servers powered up, the dashed line, we find a significant improvement when the peak arrival rate is relatively low. When it increases, the optimal server allocation decides more and more servers have to be powered up so it can cope with these peak arrivals, eventually converging on the case where all the servers are powered up. Please note that this is also a static heuristic so its good performance is quite remarkable. The semi-static heuristic performs similarly at lower peak arrival rates, but its performance degrades more steeply.

The two fluid-approximation heuristics perform very well, even when the peak load is high. They seem to strike a good balance between the relatively high time needed to power up/down servers and the advantages of powering down servers when the system is quiet. There is a notable drop in average cost for the average flow heuristic from $\lambda_{high} = 20$ to $\lambda_{high} = 21$. In Figure 3 we can see this is related to the amount of switches the average flow heuristic makes. When $\lambda_{high} = 21$,

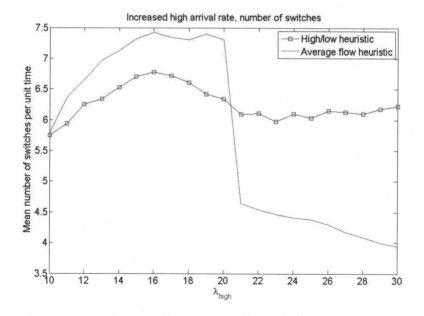

Fig. 3. Increasingly more intensive arrivals in the high period. The x-axis shows the high arrival rate λ_{high} and the y-axis the mean number of switches per unit time.

the mean arrival rate γ increases to just over 11 and this seems to make the heuristic a lot less prone to switching.

4.2   Increasing Cost Differential

For this experiment we focus on the effect of the cost differential between the power costs and the holding costs. Please recall that the system is modeled in such a way that the (negative) power cost c_{pow} of a powered down server is the difference between being (fully) powered up and powered down. This means we can add an arbitrary constant to any cost we find. This will explain the negative overall cost in the following results, since we have fixed the cost of the system when all the servers are permanently powered up at 0. We can do this, since this cost is obviously independent of the benefit we gain from any powered down server.

Here the low arrival rate is $\lambda_{low} = 10$ and the high arrival rate is $\lambda_{high} = 25$. Again, the mean duration of a high period is $\xi^{-1} = 10$ and the mean duration of a low period is $\eta^{-1} = 100$. Powering up or down is free but lasts $\zeta_{up}^{-1} = \zeta_{down}^{-1} = 1$ unit time, which is also the mean time for a job completion $\mu^{-1} = 1$, of one of the $N = 35$ available servers.

In Figure 4 we show the cost for a relative power cost of $c_{pow} = -2$ up to $c_{pow} = -0.1$. For the latter case it makes almost no sense to ever power a server

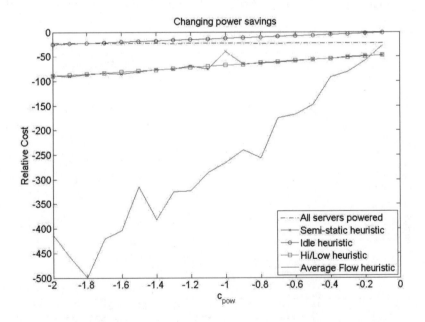

Fig. 4. The effect of increasing cost differential between holding and power costs. The x-axis shows the (negative) power cost of a powered down server. The y-axis shows the cost savings relative to having all the servers powered up.

down, as the power savings will be minimal. But for the first case we will rather have 2 more jobs waiting in the queue than power up a server. Again the results are averages of 50 runs for $T = 10000$ units of time.

Here we see that the cost improvement we can get by using the Average Flow heuristic is large. The High/Low heuristic also significantly improves over having no servers powered down, especially when the cost differential between holding and power costs increases. Surprisingly the semi-static heuristic follow the High/Low heuristic very closely in this scenario. This would suggest that they behave very similarly in this scenario. Indeed, Figure 5 seems to indicate this is true, at least for the amount of switching both heuristics do. Finally we note that the Idle heuristic continues to perform poorly.

4.3   Asymmetrical Switching Times

It can be noted that there is often a significant asymmetry between the time required to power up and that to power down. This depends on the mechanism used for this powering up and down. E.g. the time required to hibernate a normal desktop is much longer than the time needed to wake it from hibernation. In contrast, complete shutdown of a computer is often a lot quicker than boot up. The first asymmetry seems more attractive since we can then power up servers quickly when needed, whereas the powering down occurs when the system is under used. But we could also argue that the total time required to go through the cycle of powering up and down is the determining factor, since that determines

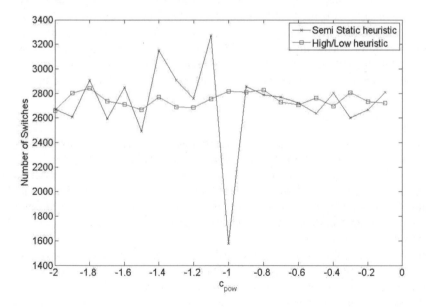

Fig. 5. The number of switches made by the Semi Static and High/Low heuristics. The x-axis shows the (negative) power cost of a powered down server. The y-axis shows the number of switches.

the overall responsiveness of the system. In this subsection we show the results of an experiment where we vary the asymmetry between the powering up and down but not the total time required to power a server up and then down.

Table 1. The impact of different asymmetry between powering up and powering down times on some heuristics

	Slow up	Even	Fast up
Idle Heuristic	35.5	35.4	35.6
Average Flow Heuristic	25.9	25.8	25.7
High/Low Heuristic	26.5	26.8	26.4

In Table 1 we see the result of differing asymmetry on the performance of three heuristics. The system under consideration here has $N = 35$ servers, which complete jobs at a rate $\mu = 1$ each. High arrival periods last a mean time of $\xi^{-1} = 100$ and have an arrival rate of $\lambda_{high} = 30$. Low arrival periods last a mean time of $\eta^{-1} = 100$ and have an arrival rate of $\lambda_{low} = 20$. The holding cost for jobs is $c_{job} = 1$ and the negative powering down cost is $c_{pow} = -0.5$. Powering up or down is not free but costs $C_{up} = C_{down} = 0.5$. The total powering time is fixed at $\zeta_{up}^{-1} + \zeta_{down}^{-1} = 2$. But for the first column the powering up time $\zeta_{up}^{-1} = 1.5$ and $\zeta_{down}^{-1} = 0.5$, implying that we have slow powering up but quick powering down. For the second column both the powering up and down time is $\zeta_{up}^{-1} = 1 = \zeta_{down}^{-1}$, meaning both powering up and down take the same amount of time. Finally the third column has quick powering up, $\zeta_{up}^{-1} = 0.5$ but slower powering down $\zeta_{down}^{-1} = 1.5$. It is clear from Table 1 that the impact of the asymmetry in powering up and down times on the performance of the heuristics is negligible. This means it is the overall time it takes to complete a power up and power down cycle that matters, not just the time taken to power up.

4.4   The Threshold Policy

We now consider the performance of the previously described threshold heuristic. This heuristics need a parameter denoting the acceptable threshold. In Figure 6 we show the average cost of the threshold heuristic, given a queue length parameter from 0, i.e. it will behave as the idle heuristic, to 10, i.e. it will view a queue of at most 10 jobs as a sign to power down a server. On the other axis in the plane, the different λ_{high} are displayed, just as in the subsection 4.1. On the z-axis we have the average cost.

Here the cost is almost linearly increasing in the selected value of the threshold but with a minimum at 0. This implies that the threshold policy does no better than the Idle heuristic, which we now know to be poor. A similar result holds for the threshold policy under the experiment in 4.2. This means we can consider the threshold policy to be a poor choice for a heuristic.

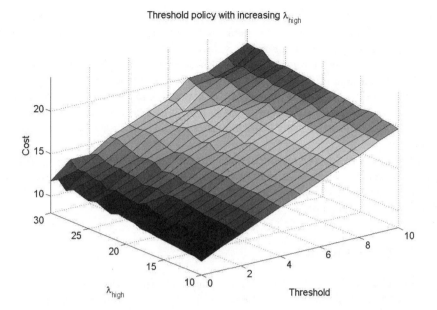

Fig. 6. Increasingly more intensive arrivals in the high period. The x-axis shows the high arrival rate λ_{high} and the y-axis the selected threshold. The z-axis shows the mean cost per unit time.

5   Conclusions and Future Work

We have presented a model with the view to balancing performance and power consumption of servers. The work here is in a preliminary stage, but the performance of several of the heuristics, in particular the average flow heuristic, is very encouraging. More work will be needed in examining this performance.

It is possible to relax the restriction on homogeneity of servers, as in [5] at the cost of increasing the complexity of the model. We can do this by introducing multiple job types with different service rates. The problem is that they do service the same arrival stream, so some sort of load balancing is now required.

A further limitation of the current work, is that it does not consider the mechanisms by which the powering down of servers take place. Certain long lasting applications can make this a bit problematic and there has been research into this problem, see e.g. [3].

The location of the servers here is not taken into account. It could be practical to select the servers to be powered down in a clever way, such as to minimize cooling costs. This is not really a limitation of the current work, since the exact server powered down is not considered here. But it does mean future work could produce significant further improvements. More generally, the gains from powering down servers are represented in a very linear fashion and really only reflect the direct impact on the power consumption of the servers themselves, rather than including additional benefits from reduced cooling costs etc. This too offers significant scope for future work.

We can also consider arrival processes that are not Markovian. Although the formal modelling of these systems is more problematic, it is straightforward to examine the performance of the heuristics presented here under these non-Markovian arrival processes using simulation. The exception would be the optimal static allocation; this is not readily calculated for non-Markovian arrival processes.

A final, and rather obvious, extension would be to include different job types for the servers to service. As well as allowing different power down states. These would reflect the various power down modes in systems, e.g. hibernate, system shutdown and disk shutdown.

Acknowledgements

The authors would like to thank the organizers of the SPEC International Performance Evaluation Workshop 2008, for the opportunity to present this work. We would also like to thank the anonymous reviewers for their helpful comments.

This work was carried out as part of the EPSRC funded project *Dynamic Operating Policies in Commercial Hosting Environments*.

References

1. Bianchini, R., Rajamony, R.: Power and Energy Management for Server Systems. Computer 37, 68–74 (2004)
2. Chase, J., Anderson, D., Thakar, P., Vahdat, A., Doyle, R.: Managing Energy and Server Resources in Hosting Centers. ACM SIGOPS Operating Systems Review 35(5), 103–116 (2001)
3. Chen, G., He, W., Liu, J., Nath, S., Rigas, L., Xiao, L., Zhao, F.: Energy-Aware Server Provisioning and Load Dispatching for Connection Intensive Internet Services, Microsoft Research Technical Report, MSR-TR-2007-130, ftp://ftp.research.microsoft.com/pub/tr/TR-2007-130.pdf
4. Fan, X., Weber, W., Barroso, L.: Power Provisioning for a Warehouse-sized Computer. In: Proceedings of the 34th Annual International Symposium on Computer Architecture, San Diego CA, June 2007, pp. 13–23 (2007)
5. Heath, T., Diniz, B., Carrera, E., Meira Jr., W., Bianchini, R.: Self-Configuring Heterogeneous Server Clusters. In: Workshop on Compilers and Operating Systems for Low Power (2003)
6. Kleinrock, L.: Queueing systems, vol. 1. Wiley Interscience, New York (1975)
7. Mastroleon, L., Bambos, N., Kozyrakis, C., Economou, D.: Autonomic Power Management Schemes for Internet Servers and Data Centers. In: Global Telecommunications Conference, GLOBECOM 2005, pp. 943–947. IEEE (2005)
8. Mitrani, I., Chakka, R.: Spectral Expension Solution for a Class of Markov Models: Application and Comparison with the Matrix-Geometric Method. Performance Evaluation 23, 241–260 (1995)

9. Pinheiro, E., Bianchini, R., Carrera, E., Heath, T.: Dynamic Cluster Reconfiguration for Power and Performance. In: Benini, L., Kandemir, M., Ramanujam, J. (eds.) Compilers and Operating Systems for Low Power, pp. 75–91 (2003)

10. Slegers, J., Mitrani, I., Thomas, N.: Static and Dynamic Server Allocation in Systems with On/Off Sources (to appear in special issue of Annals of Operations Research, entitled "Stochastic Performance Models for Resource Allocation in Communication Systems")

11. Slegers, J., Mitrani, I., Thomas, N.: Optimal Dynamic Server Allocation in Systems with On/Off Sources. In: Wolter, K. (ed.) EPEW 2007. LNCS, vol. 4748, pp. 186–199. Springer, Heidelberg (2007)

Workload Characterization of the SPECpower_ssj2008 Benchmark

Larry D. Gray, Anil Kumar, and Harry H. Li

Intel Corporation

Abstract. SPEC has recently released SPECpower_ssj2008, the first industry benchmark which measures performance and power of volume server class computers using graduated load levels. In this paper, we present a brief overview and an initial characterization of this benchmark by measuring the system resource utilization with the aid of processor monitoring events at graduated load levels and by comparing the sensitivity of final metric and other related data between various configurations consisting of hardware changes as well as software changes on Quad Core Intel Xeon processor based servers. Even though this is early data from a specific platform and OS, it still validates many expected patterns and opens exciting new opportunities for researchers to investigate specific areas as well as in-depth characterization as a next step.[1]

1 Introduction

December of 2007 brought a significant milestone for SPEC, the Standard Performance Evaluation Corporation, with the release of the industry's first benchmark to measure the power and performance of volume server platforms with an innovative graduated workload. Formally named SPECpower_ssj2008, this new benchmark measures eleven levels of server loads from zero to 100% of a given platform's full capacity to process business transactions with a server side Java application. Full disclosure reports using this benchmark provide an unprecedented amount of new information on the power consumption and performance of the tested platform.

In this paper we strive to provide some insights into workload behavior and server resource utilization characteristics of this benchmark above and beyond the wealth of information included in the now available SPEC provided documentation cataloged on the SPEC public website [2,3].

The authors have been active members of the SPECpower benchmark development team from the outset and therefore are capable of providing valuable insights on the workload, the rationale for design decisions, and the strengths and inevitable weaknesses inherent in any such product. We share this information to enhance the understanding of the benchmark and its intended usage. Our intent is that others will benefit and therefore be more interested in using the benchmark as an evaluation tool across the wide array of studies to which it can apply.

---

[1] This paper is a revised and extended edition of a paper presented on the SPEC Benchmark workshop in San Francisco 2008 [1].

S. Kounev, I. Gorton, and K. Sachs (Eds.): SIPEW 2008, LNCS 5119, pp. 262–282, 2008.

1.1 A Little History

The SPECpower committee was chartered in January of 2006 to create a benchmark that would address the emerging need to measure power consumption and performance of server class computer systems under application-like loads. The intersection of performance and power has become an important attribute of computer systems, sometimes labeled efficiency. A standard method of measuring and reporting both would require a disciplined approach beyond what was then available on the open market.

The fact that one workload or benchmark could not represent the spectrum of server usage was generally accepted and therefore the SPECpower committee was determined to create more than one "benchmark" in more than one application segment. The committee is and was staffed by engineers and managers from these companies: AMD, Dell, Fujitsu Siemens Computers, HP, IBM, Intel, and Sun Microsystems. The manufacturers were assisted by representatives from academia including the University of California Berkeley, Virginia Polytechnic Institute and State University, and Lawrence Berkeley National Laboratory. After two years of constant collaboration, design, coding and extensive testing efforts, the SPECpower committee released its first benchmark named SPECpower_ssj2008 on December 11, 2007 to very positive reviews from industry and trade press [14].

2 SPECpower_ssj2008 Overview

2.1 Measuring Power with Performance

This section provides a brief overview of the SPECpower measurement framework described in more detail in the set of documents freely available at the SPEC public web site on the SPECpower_ssj2008 page [3,4,5,6,7,9,10].

For deeper understanding of the design of the benchmark and its essential elements, refer first the to the *SPEC Power and Performance Design Overview* [9,10,11,12,13]. Several challenges are presented by the requirement to measure power consumption with performance, in particular at multiple load levels.

A *measurement methodology* was established and then realized by implementing a measurement framework that requires a separate platform to which power and temperature measurement devices are attached, with the necessary logging and reporting functions.

The two systems required are the system under test (SUT) and the Control and Collection System (CCS) [10]. Communications between the two systems is enabled by a standard Ethernet local area network (LAN).

The addition of a *measurement server* enables a host of benefits that include but are not limited to:

1. independence from the workload to enable quick integration of new workloads,
2. multiples measurements; the ability to manage a number of SUTs and multiple measurement devices. multiple JVM instances are also supported.
3. low impact to the loads on the SUT for the data consolidation and logging.

Altogether, the design permits extending the framework from the current capability to measure a stand-alone server with a single OS, to environments or topologies with multiple OS images, for instance blade servers and virtualized servers with workloads appropriate to those environments.

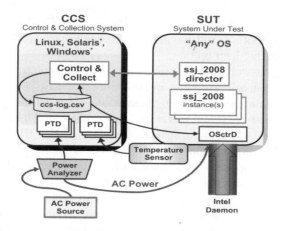

Fig. 1. Elements of the SPECpower Framework

2.2   The Measurement Framework

To better understand the terminology and characterization data later in this paper, a brief overview of the SPECpower framework software elements is provided. Figure 1 is a graphic representation of the framework with the interconnections.

On the left side of Figure 1, is the Control and Collect system (or measurement server). On the right is the SUT where the workload runs. The *up arrow* on the right, under the SUT, points to a non-standard element (not provided by SPEC), the OS counters daemon (OSctrD). Created by Intel, this software implements the capability to collect resource utilization data from a Windows OS platform, passing a configurable set of counter data to the CCS for logging, second by second, along side the power, performance and other essential data items. It is this additional element of the framework that enables producing the data shown later in this report.

The ssj_2008 workload runs on a SUT plugged into a power analyzer plugged into the building's power infrastructure, measuring power of the entire SUT platform. This is sometimes described as "watts at the wall". The power analyzer is connected to the CCS machine via a data cable where purpose built software, the PTD (Power and Temperature Daemon) records electrical activity from a power analyzer, and ambient temperature from a temperature sensor device placed at the air in-flow to the SUT.

The SPECpower_ssj2008 workload uses TCP/IP protocol to pass time, performance and status data to the CCS system which then consolidates that with power and temperature, and in this case the OS counters, logging all together into one record in a comma separated file.

2.3   A Graduated Workload

The notion of a graduated workload was inspired by the advent of processor power management technologies on volume server platforms, which are most effective at low loads and usually required to operate without a negative performance impact.

All this is driven by the global need to conserve energy, reduce carbon footprints, and the general movement to be more green. Platform power consumption has become a competitive differentiator for the system manufacturers. Add then that it has become widely recognized that most (commercial) data-center servers generally run at low loads with resources underutilized except during periods of peak business activity – which will vary widely for various types of businesses and geographies. Since there is no "typical" load level, the graduated load was conceived to assess power management across what has come to be known as the *load line*. The benchmark reports the power consumption and the performance at each load level, allowing the reader to reasonably match their usage and determine power usage for that platform.

Platform Capacity Adjustment. Systems of widely different capacity must be fairly measured, so a method was conceived to determine the full transaction throughput capacity of a given system, and then increment the workload gradations accordingly. A benchmark run begins with 3 or more *calibration levels* where an ungated stream of transactions is presented to the application. The calibration workloads are unrealistic but they serve to determine the full performance potential of the system – with the SPECpower_ssj2008 application and transaction mix.

The calibration throughput is used to set a *throughput target* for the 100% load level. The other load levels are then graduated percentages of the calibrated target load. In the normal case, the levels are increments of 10%. Fewer or more levels are configurable.

It is important, when interpreting data in this paper and from the disclosure reports of SPECpower_ssj2008 that the load levels labeled as percentages are a percent of *target calibrated throughput*. It is a common misconception that gradations are governed by processor utilization. Processor (or CPU) utilization is an outcome of the benchmark and considered to be unique to a given platform. Since there are a number of vagaries and sometimes gross differences to the meaning of CPU utilization from one architecture to another, this point is emphasized. (We encourage someone to use this as a topic a future paper).

Measurement Intervals. The graduated method loads the system with a given throughput for a fixed amount of time during which power is measured every second along with the effective transaction rate at that second. Figure 2 provides a graphic example of second by second transaction throughput across five levels of transaction load. A compliant run of SPECpower_ssj2008 executes 10 load levels plus the state known as *active idle*.

Active Idle. Idle is generally the state when the system is running no applications nor performing any operating system management tasks. CPU utilization

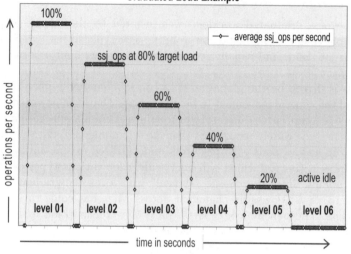

Fig. 2. Graduated Load Example

is zero. We could label this state *OS idle*. The duration of idle states can vary from fractions of seconds to minutes. Modern operating systems run many asynchronous background tasks and therefore most servers are never totally idle for long periods. *Active idle* is a SPEC defined state where an application is running and no transactions are incoming or in process; the system is ready to quickly respond to any incoming transactions. Given that servers are usually operating 24 x 7 they are also ready to accept transactions therefore active idle is the most common operating state. In this benchmark, active idle is handled and measured virtually the same as the other 10 load levels, except no transactions are scheduled.

Workload States and State Changes. Accurate, consistent and repeatable measurement of performance and power together requires that there be mechanisms to assure that a period known as the measurement interval is carefully defined, delineated and controlled. This control is implemented through the definition of *states* which identify the various phases of the workload in the detailed CCS log file. In the case of a graduated workload, the load type and level number is included. These states and the change rules are built in to the ssj2008 code and passed to the director along with the per second average performance, time stamps and other meta data.

There are four distinct phases of any given load level:

1. *Inter* is a period between load levels. This method creates a break between load levels that eases post run visual analysis.
2. *Ramp up* (pre-measurement) is a period of time that allows the application to reach a level of processing that will continue for the duration.

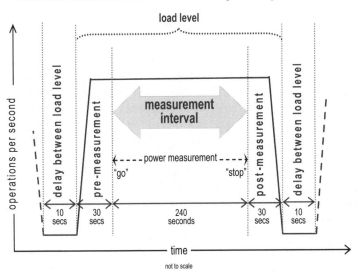

Fig. 3. State Changes in a Load Level

3. *Recording* is where data is collected and summarized in post-processing steps. This is the "measurement interval".
4. *Ramp down* (post-measurement) is a period of time where the application will continue to process transactions till the very end of the load level.

Following ramp down, the cycle begins again with another inter level or if all configured levels have been completed, the workload can terminate normally. State changes for one workload level are illustrated in the chart in Figure 3. Note that power is measured continuously to enable detailed analysis. For reporting purpose in benchmark disclosures, only the average power in the measurement interval is used. Also all these intervals are long enough to provide sufficient settle time for consistent power and performance measurements.

3   Server Resource Utilization

3.1   Overview

The SPECpower_ssj2008 benchmark emulates a server side Java transaction processing application. It exercises processors, processor caches, the memory hierarchy, implementations of the JVM (Java Virtual Machine), JIT (Just-In-Time) compiler, garbage collection, threads and some aspects of the operating system. A Java application was chosen for the very important advantage of cross operating system portability. The opportunity to leverage existing code from the SPECjbb2005 benchmark was irresistible.

Base code and transaction types [16] are from SPECjbb2005, but many substantive changes make the two not comparable. Some notable differences are a modified transaction mix, transaction scheduling and arrival method, calibration to seek the platform peak transaction capacity, altered throughput accounting, data collection via a network with TCP/IP, additional logging that increases disk I/O, plus other less significant changes. Overall, even though ssj2008 is derived from SPECjbb2005, it is very different. While running, the application makes some use of the network and does minimal disk I/O. Actual data rates are shown in a later section. With the arrival of multi-core processors in symmetric multi-processor systems, a high degree of scalability was a top benchmark design goal. It is expected that the benchmark will be run on a very wide range of low end and mid-range servers which span the space from a single socket single processor core (uni-processor servers) up to servers that support multiple processors (SMP or symmetric multiprocessor) where each processor can incorporate 1, 2, 4 and likely more processing cores – then some implementations will support SMT (Simultaneous Multi-threading).

Conscious design decisions were made such that additional disks or network interfaces would not be necessary with increases in available processing capacity. The scalability of the benchmark is an incredibly positive attribute when setting out to measure power and the performance of basic system infrastructure (processors, chipset, memory, fans, power supply, etc.) across platforms with a very broad range of transaction processing capacity.

3.2   Resource Usage and Platform Power Consumption

To the above that we also understand that platform power consumption under varied loads is largely driven by the power requirements of the processors (a generalization that applies to most platforms available today) which changes with the applied load. This may seem counter-intuitive since memory and disks are both subject to dynamic and random access.

Memory power consumption does change with load, however, as a percentage of total platform power, the range from idle to full load might be only 1-2% of platform power. Use this information only as a guide since memory designs, types, and densities can be quite different in their behavior from one to another. Modern high density disk drives show similar behavior. Once spun up, power changes are small with usage, again relative to total platform power. Network interface cards (NICs) follow the same pattern that when enabled, with a LAN cable plugged in, a NIC is consuming power very near its maximum and very small power increase is seen with higher traffic, again on the order of 1% or less of total platform power. As a caveat, it is important to note that the observations above apply to the types of memory, disks and NICs found in high volume platforms common to x86 servers. Exhaustive studies of peripheral and component power consumption are yet to be completed.

4   SPECpower_ssj2008 Metric Definition

4.1   The Primary Metric

The primary metric for SPECpower_ssj2008 is *overall ssj_ops/watt* which is ratio of aggregated ssj_ops at all 11 load level and aggregated average watts at all 11 load levels which includes active idle also.

4.2   Unprecedented Data in Full Disclosure Report

The SPECpower_ssj2008 Full Disclosure Report (FDR) presents and abundance of data on performance, power as well as detailed configuration data. Table 1 has been copied from FDR of SPECpower_ssj2008 publication [15] and highlights important data fields [8] and values.

In Table 1 above, the ssj_ops column, first row, is ssj_ops@100%. The fourth and fifth columns contain average power (in watts) and a performance to power ratio at each level. The "primary" metric is highlighted in the last row. Following page one of the FDR, are several more pages with important configuration, environment and electrical data from the benchmark run.

Table 1. Performance and Power Data

Performance			Power	Performance to Power Ratio
Target Load	Actual Load	ssj_ops	Average Power (W)	
100%	99,10%	220.306	276	799
90%	90,40%	200.860	269	746
80%	79,50%	176.684	261	677
70%	70,30%	156.344	254	616
60%	59,60%	132.525	245	541
50%	49,60%	110.222	237	465
40%	40,20%	89.388	229	390
30%	30,10%	66.875	221	302
20%	19,90%	44.157	213	207
10%	10,20%	22.649	206	110
Active Idle		0	198	0
$\sum$ssj_ops / $\sum$power =				*468*

5   Platform Hardware and Software Details

5.1   Platform Configuration Details

To understand and characterize this benchmark, we used an Intel Xeon based, 2 socket Intel "White Box" server with the following configuration described in Table 2.

Load levels of 120 seconds were used to reduce total run time as we have observed that measurements from shorter load levels are reasonably consistent with that of 240 sec load levels. Also note that we do not use SPECPower_ssj2008 metrics, since the measurements in this report are largely non-compliant; that is, they can not be published along side full disclosure reports. Data herein is intended for academic use only. The measurements and observations in the following sections are in large part exclusive to the Microsoft Windows Server operating environment. Disk write frequency and rates are largely governed by policies of the OS used. Platforms other than those used in this study may also affect the resource utilization characteristics.

Table 2. Platform Hardware and Software Details

SUT	Intel "White Box"
HW	Dual and Quad Core Intel Xeon 2.0 & 3.0 GHz
	Supermicro X7DB8/ Main Board, Super Micro 5000P
	4x 2GB FBDIMMs
	1x 700W PSU
	5U Tower Platform
OS	Microsoft Windows Server 2003 64 bit
- Power Options	Server Balanced Processor Power and Performance
JVM	JVM: BEA JRockit P27.4.0 64 bit
- Options	JVM Command Line similar to published results
Sampling Rates	Power: 1 second (average from meter)
SPECpower_ssj2008 setup	
	SSJ Director on SUT
	Load levels 120 seconds

6 SPECpower_ssj2008 Characterization Data

6.1 SSJ_2008– per JVM Instance

Code Footprint Size: Each SSJ (JVM) instance has a code size of ~1.5 MByte; when totaling the size of all methods that have been JITed and optimized.

Data Footprint Size: Each warehouse thread has ~50 MBytes of long lived *database* objects and produces ~8Kbytes of short lived transient objects per SSJ transaction. The overall data footprint depends on the number of threads (warehouses) and maximum throughput produced.

Java Heap Size and Sizing: The Java heap size is user configurable where the best size is dependent upon available memory and the number of JVMs chosen for a particular run. An optimal heap size is necessary for optimal performance. A heap size too big could cause memory swapping (total heap size > RAM). Too small a heap will incur a performance penalty due to frequent Garbage Collections (GC). Overall, due to the nature of the Java heap, an application can exercise any amount of memory and a user could measure the energy consumption impact, but the performance component only benefits to a certain extent. The optimal physical memory size is throughput capacity - processing capability - dependent and does vary by platform and its hardware expandability. As an example, for Quad-Core Intel Xeon based Dual Processor systems, ~8GB RAM is optimal when running SPECpower_ssj_2008.

6.2 Processor Utilization

Figure 4 show CPU % utilization tracking closely with the transaction loads on the Intel Core 2 architecture. On other micro-architectures it will vary (SMT etc.). Load level targets are set to be percentages of ssj_ops@calibrated. Users must be aware that CPU utilization is no part of the benchmark.

Average second by second ssj_ops are exhibiting the expected variability within a load level because the inter-arrival time of transactions is modeled with a negative exponential distribution to better simulate random arrival of work.

6.3   Power and Processor Utilization

Figure 5 shows that Power consumption varies with load. Also the variability of transaction throughput is being reflected in power consumption changes (watts).

6.4   Power, ssj_ops, and Processor Utilization

Plotted points in Figure 6 shows that ssj_ops, Power and CPU % utilization are changing together – showing a distinc relationship one to the other.

6.5   % Time in C1 State

Figure 7 shows that % time in C1 state is the inverse of CPU % utilization at all load levels. Time in C1 state contributes to power saving which varies with architecture, OS and policies. For example Intel EIST enabled in BIOS will result in more power saving at lower utilizations. C states are lower processor power states. Their specific definition is architecture and implementation dependent.

6.6   Memory Utilization

Data in Figure 8 has been collected using typical tuning (Xmx==Xms) where Java heap allocated remains same throughout the run. As a result committed memory in use remains constant at all load levels including active idle.

6.7   Network I/O

Data in Figure 9 indicates ∼1500 Bytes/sec of network I/O at all load levels including active idle. As expected network traffic is similar at all load levels and does not track load. Most of the Network I/O is from per sec request/response between Control & Collect (CCS) and SSJ_2008 Director.

6.8   Disk I/O

Disk I/O in Figure 10 shows regular bursts of ∼140Kbyte writes. On an average there is ∼3.3Kbytes/sec of Disk I/O at all load levels. Most disk writes are related to SSJ_2008 logging. Disk reads average is zero.

6.9   Basic System Events

Figure 11 shows interrupts rates of ∼700 per second at all load levels including active idle. Context switches are ∼800 /sec at higher utilization levels and decline at lower utilization while dropping to ∼400 at active idle. These events are OS and platform dependent. Since these events are showing strange patterns, more investigation is needed.

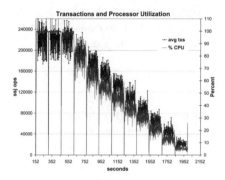

Fig. 4. CPU % Utilization

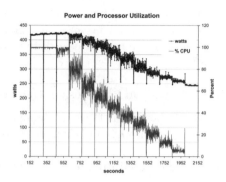

Fig. 5. Power and CPU % Utilization

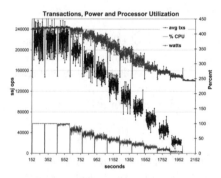

Fig. 6. Power, ssj_ops, and CPU % Utilization

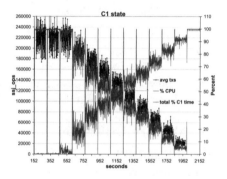

Fig. 7. % of Time in C1 State

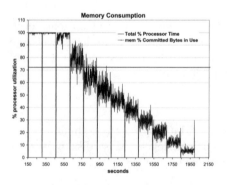

Fig. 8. Memory Utilization

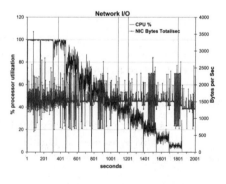

Fig. 9. Network I/O

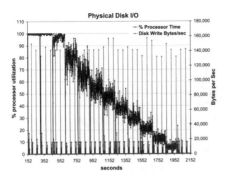

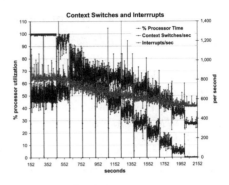

Fig. 10. Disk I/O

Fig. 11. Basic System Events

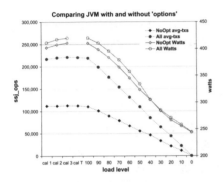

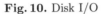

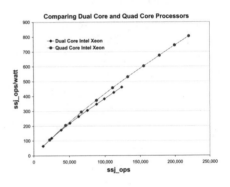

Fig. 12. Impact of JVM Options

Fig. 13. Processor Scaling

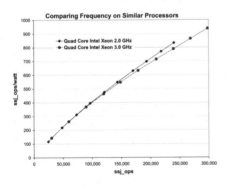

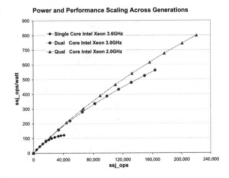

Fig. 14. Frequency Scaling

Fig. 15. Platform Generation Scaling

6.10   Impact of JVM Optimizations

Selection of JVM options can have significant impact on performance. In this experiment, we compared "no options" to the set of "best known JVM options". Figure 12 shows the difference in performance and power. When using no JVM options (default options), performance dropped by ~50% while power reduced by 0 to 3%. Please note that any findings from these experiments are dependent on the JVM and its options. JAVAOPTIONS_SSJ="" *(None, default heap and optimizations)*
JAVAOPTIONS_SSJ="-Xms3000m -Xmx3000m -Xns2400m –XXlazyUnlocking -Xgc:genpar -XXcallprofiling -XXaggressive -XXlargePages -XXtlasize:min=12k,preferred=1024k"

6.11   Processor Scaling

Figure 13 shows that when ssj_ops are plotted on the x-axis, the additional capacity of Quad Core Intel Xeon 2.0GHz/2x4MB L2 compared to Dual Core Intel Xeon 2.0GHz/4MB L2 is clearly evident.

Table 3. Processor Scaling

Dual Core to Quad Corescaling Intel Xeon processors	%increase
ssj_ops@100%	77%
Power@100%	1%

Table 3 shows that when comparing these two types of processors, performance improves drastically - ssj_ops@100% increased by ~77% while power consumption@100% increases by only ~1%.

6.12   Frequency Scaling

To view the impact of frequency scaling, in Figure 14, we compared Quad Core Intel Xeon (2x6MB L2) running at 2.0GHz and 3.0GHz respectively. Table 4 shows that for 2.0GHz/3.0GHz Quad Core Intel Xeon / 2x6MB L2, ssj_ops@100% improves by ~24% while power consumption@100% increases by ~10%. Overall ssj_ops/Watt improves by ~76%.

Table 4. Frequency Scaling

Frequency Scaling Intel Xeon QuadCore processors	%increase
2.0 GHz to 3.0 GHz	50%
ssj_ops@100%	24%
Power@100%	10%

6.13   Platform Generation Scaling

Often a new generation of platforms delivers more performance, consumes less power and exhibits overall better energy efficiency. We measured three distinct generations of Intel platforms starting from the year 2005. Figure 15 compares the results from three publications [15]: Single Core Intel Xeon 3.6GHz/1M L2 with HT, Dual Core Intel Xeon 3.0GHz/4M L2 and Quad Core Intel Xeon 2.0GHz/2x4M L2. Data in Table 5 clearly shows that latest generation has improved ssj_ops@100% by >4x while reducing power@100% by ~10% resulting in overall ssj_ops/watt improvement of >4x.

Table 5. Platform Generation Scaling

Processor	Performance ssj_ops@100%	Power(watts) @100%	Overall ssj_ops/watt
Single Core Intel Xeon 3.6GHz	40,852	336	87
Dual Core Intel Xeon 3.0GHz	163,768	291	338
Qual Core Intel Xeon 2.0GHz	220,306	276	468

7   Benchmark as Load Generating Tool

This benchmark has many built-in capabilities which can be used to create various system utilization characteristics. A note of caution is that such changes make the run non-compliant but nonetheless they are very useful in creating different use scenarios. In this section we have listed many such characteristics which can be set just by modifying the file "SPECpower_ssj_EXPERT.props" as well as shared some results and conclusion from some experiments following this methodology.

7.1   Impact of Different Batch Sizes

A batch is "fine grained transactions contained in each batch of high-level transactions" where both default and compliant size is 1000. This property can be set by changing "input.scheduler.batch_size=1000". For a given throughput, a smaller batch size will result in smaller size of batches arriving more frequently and vice versa for large batch size. This feature is very interesting for understanding the impact of complex power saving algorithms. Figure 16 shows the impact on ssj_ops/watt for different batch sizes of 1, 10, 100, 1000 and 10,000 and 100,000.

Above data indicates that a batch size from 10 to 10,000 is well within narrow range while either small batch size of 1 or a very large size >10,000 are showing expected behavior of being out of range. A very small batch size results in very frequent arrival of transactions denying power saving opportunities while a very large batch size results in arrival of large batches at very infrequent interval leaving lots of opportunity to transition into sleep states. Also the large batch size makes it hard to hit the load level target because of granularity.

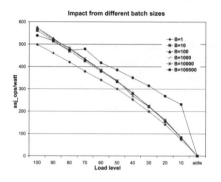

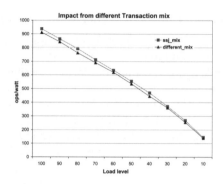

Fig. 16. Impact from Different Batch Sizes

Fig. 17. Impact from Different Transaction Mix

7.2 Impact of Different Transaction Mix

There are six different type of Java transactions which have a fixed probability distribution. For compliant runs, the transaction mix is following:

$$input.transaction\_mix.new\_order \quad = 10$$
$$input.transaction\_mix.payment \quad = 10$$
$$input.transaction\_mix.order\_status = 1$$
$$input.transaction\_mix.delivery \quad = 1$$
$$input.transaction\_mix.stock\_level \quad = 1$$
$$input.transaction\_mix.cust\_report \quad = 10$$

Each transaction have different characteristic and as a result changing this mix stresses a system differently. In our experiment we have compared the compliant settings with the alternate mix as below while all others are same as above:

$$input.transaction\_mix.new\_order \quad = 15$$
$$input.transaction\_mix.cust\_report = 5$$

Since we changed the transaction mix and hence the average instruction executed per ops are also changed resulting in a change in ops/watt. For more detailed study, this transaction mix could be changed more significantly to understand the impact on total average power at different load levels and also to replicate if some application are closer to different transaction mix in characteristic.

7.3 Impact of More Threads

This benchmark tests the system where number of threads (each warehouse is one thread) equals number of logical cores on that system. Property *input.load_level.number_warehouses* was set to test two configurations of 1 thread/ logical core vs. 2 threads/logical core to understand the impact on performance and power consumption. When running 2 threads/logical core, ssj_ops@100% dropped by ∼2%. Figure 18 shows that ssj_ops/watt is similar at lower load

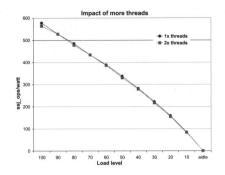

Fig. 18. Impact of More Threads

levels while a bit lower at higher load levels when comparing 1 thread/logical core vs. 2 threads/logical core.

A further study of increasing the number of threads/logical core beyond 2 will be very interesting to understand the impact of more context switching on power and performance.

7.4 Single Queue vs. Dedicated Queue

The processing queue of applications for handling incoming requests could be categories in two broad categories: single queue vs. multiple queues. For compliant runs, this benchmark deploys multiple queues (one queue for each warehouse called dedicated scheduler queue) as that type of approach is more scalable to large systems, but, using the property "input.scheduler.single_queue" to "=true" a characteristic of application using a single queue for that JVM instance can be tested. We have compared the power and performance for single queue vs. dedicated scheduler queues. Figures 19 and 20 have power and performance data for

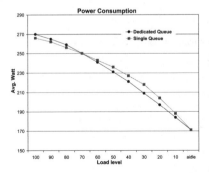

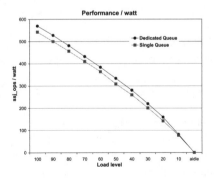

Fig. 19. Power Consumption for Dedicated Queue vs. Single Queue

Fig. 20. Performance/Watt for Dedicated Queue vs. Single Queue

these two configurations. Since single scheduler queue implementation has more lock contention, it produces ~6% less ssj_ops@100% compared.

Figure 19 shows very interesting data that single queue implementation consumes more power at lower load levels while dedicated queue consumes more power at higher load levels. A note of caution here as this unique phenomena could be h/w and s/w stack configuration specific and not generic in nature. Figure 20 shows that overall performance/watt at all load levels is better for dedicated scheduler queue as it has less lock contention and producing more ssj_ops.

7.5   Numerous Other Experiments

There are many other settings which we described in brief below which can be set to simulate characteristics of various applications. There are:

$input.load\_level.target\_max\_throughput = \#$

A target throughput can be given by setting this property. This is very useful when a user want to evaluate various h/w and s/w settings while executing same amount of transactions at load level for different settings.

$input.load\_level.throughput\_sequence = \#\#\#\#$

Rather than executing fixed load levels, a user can set specific throughput at each load level. Alternately a user can set $input.load\_level.percentage\_sequence$ to set target in terms of % load level rather than throughput. Both settings are excellent tool to let a user test impact of h/w and s/w settings while executing same amount of transactions.

$input.override\_itemtable\_size = 20000$

This setting decides the itemtable_size which impacts the data footprint of each warehouse which is at default value around 25MB/warehouse. A larger data footprint will put more pressure on memory sub-system of a platform.

$input.warehouse\_population = 60$

This setting decides the active population inside a warehouse and increasing this results in lot more contention on objects.

$input.scheduler.log\_arrival\_rates = false$

When set to true, it enables logging of various time points of a batch. It logs arrival time, wait time by a batch in the queue, total response time for batch (defined as wait time in queue + execution time of a batch). This also slightly increases the I/O activity. More important is that at various load levels throughput just indicates the given throughput while response time measure the real response time of a batch and could help in testing and tuning of various architecture features which will show variation in response time at a load level even when throughput remains similar. More understanding of variation in response time will make this logging data extremely useful.

In our evaluation, this benchmark provides unprecedented amount of flexibility to simulate various characteristics for research purposes. All these built-in capabilities provides excellent mechanism to evaluate and test future power saving algorithms and settings at OS and driver level as well as at hardware components level including processors and chipsets.

8   System Configuration Considerations

The SPECpower_ssj2008 benchmark metrics have two primary components: performance (ssj_ops) and power consumption (average Watts). In this section, software and hardware choices are listed that may impact performance, power or both.

8.1   Performance Factors

The following factors can have a significant impact on performance with unknown impact to power consumption.

Java Virtual Machine (JVM). Different JVMs will deliver different performance.

JVM Parameters. A JVM can run by default (no options) but very likely will not deliver optimal performance. To find parameters for optimal performance, one can search published results at SPEC website or otherwise will need to find their own best tuning parameters for a JVM.

Multiple SSJ Instances. If a system has large number of logical cores, often increasing the number of SSJ instances with each JVM instance at no more than ~8 warehouse threads results in better performance.

Affinity of SSJ Instances. When running multiple SSJ instances, affinitizing them to shared caches or each socket or each NUMA node results in better performance.

HW and OS Settings. Some HW settings like enabling or disabling features in BIOS or OS settings and use of large pages can result in better performance.

8.2   Power Factors

The following factors can impact power consumption significantly while minimally impacting performance. They are provided here for awareness purposes. Systems vary widely with options; consult the manufacturer's documentation.

BIOS Power Management Options. Many systems provide BIOS options for power management. The best choice of options depends on your priorities. It is wise to check the BIOS options since the best setting may or many not be enabled by default.

One such power management option on Intel processor based systems is called "Intel EIST". Another is "C states" or C1. Both should be enabled if your objective is to reduce power consumption.

Fan Speed Control in BIOS. Fans consume significant amount of power. Selecting optimal settings for fan speed control, when available, can reduce power consumption without performance impact. In some cases if fan speed is drastically reduced, it could lead to lower performance due to system level thermal throttling.

OS Power Management. Most operating systems have some power management settings. With Microsoft Windows Server 2003 for example, choosing "power options" from the control panel and then the option "balanced power and server performance" will conserver power without severe impact on performance.

Power Supplies (PSUs). Many systems are ordered with optional redundant power supplies. Reducing the number of power supplies (without going below the minimum needed) will result in lower power consumption.

Memory Size and Performance. The most important factor in this category is total system RAM size and configuration. The platform configuration is the primary determinant of power consumption. Memory configuration can have following impact:

As RAM size is increased, both performance and power consumption will increase. Performance will increase (with associated heap size adjustments) to some limit up to the optimal amount of RAM. If RAM size is beyond the optimal size, there may be no measurable increase in performance but power consumption will increase with the number (and type of) DIMMs. RAM configuration or slot placement can have an impact on performance if the platform supports more than one memory channel and memory interleaving which can improve performance. Consult system documentation.

9 Conclusions

The SPECpower_ssj2008 benchmark and the associated Full Disclosure Reports present an unprecedented amount of data on the power consumption and performance of server systems across the graduated load levels. The benchmark framework, with the power data capture from the Power and Temperature Daemon combined with the OS counters collection daemon, with information captured by the logging capability in CCS and SSJ makes this benchmark a powerful and capable toolset for new areas of behavioral data collection exposing new fields of systems analysis.

Based on the information presented in this paper, we observe that most system resource utilizations are following the expected patterns. Processor Utilization follows the load line for Intel Core 2 based platforms (note that this is architecture dependent and CPU utilization is no part of the benchmark). Power consumption tracks the transaction load. % time in C1 state is inversely proportional to processor utilization at each load level. When the min and max heap sizes are the same, memory committed is constant across load line. Disk I/O has regular bursts of ~140K byte writes with overall average of ~3.3K bytes/sec for all load levels while disk reads are none. Network I/O is ~1.5K bytes/sec and is almost constant across load line. The basic OS events interrupts and context switches/sec have some unique behavior which requires further investigation. .

Experiments using different JVM options, processor scaling, frequency scaling and platform generation scaling show that primary metric and associated data for SPECpower_ssj2008 fairly reflect configurations and OS settings for performance, power and overall ssj_ops/Watt. All these results are specific to the platform and OS measured. We expect similar data from different architectures and OS(s) will be very valuable. This initial characterization is just a first look and more measurements are required to continue in-depth characterization.

In summary, we are just getting started!

Acknowledgment

Special thanks to Christopher B. Jorgensen, a graduate student intern from Portland State University, for multiple series of measurements collecting the bulk of the data shown in this paper. Many thanks to Kai Sach from TU Darmstadt for typesetting this paper in LaTeX2e format and other suggestions to improve the format and appearance.

Intel and Xeon is a trademark or registered trademark of Intel Corporation or its subsidiaries in the United States and other countries. SPEC and the benchmark names are trademarks of the Standard Performance Evaluation Corporation. Other names and brands may be claimed as the property of others.

References

1. Gray, L., Kumar, A., Li, H.: Characterization of SPECpower_ssj2008 Benchmark. In: SPEC Benchmark Workshop 2008 (2008)
2. SPEC, http://www.spec.org
3. SPECpower_ssj2008, http://www.spec.org/power_ssj2008
4. SPECpower_ssj2008 User Guide, http://www.spec.org/power_ssj2008/docs/SPECpower_ssj2008-User_Guide.pdf
5. SPECpower_ssj2008 Hardware Setup Guide, http://www.spec.org/power_ssj2008/docs/SPECpower_ssj2008-Hardware_Setup_Guide.pdf
6. SPECpower_ssj2008 FAQ, http://www.spec.org/power_ssj2008/docs/SPECpower_ssj2008-FAQ.html

7. SPECpower_ssj2008 Run and Reporting rules,
   http://www.spec.org/power_ssj2008/docs/SPECpower_ssj2008-Run_Reporting_Rules.pdf
8. SPECpower_ssj2008 Result File Fields,
   http://www.spec.org/power_ssj2008/docs/SPECpower_ssj2008-Result_File_Fields.html
9. SPECpower_ssj2008 Design Overview, http://www.spec.org/power_ssj2008/docs/SPECpower_ssj2008-Design_overview.pdf
10. SPECpower_ssj2008 CCS Design, http://www.spec.org/power_ssj2008/docs/SPECpower_ssj2008-Design_ccs.pdf
11. SPECpower_ssj2008 PTD Design, http://www.spec.org/power_ssj2008/docs/SPECpower_ssj2008-Design_ptd.pdf
12. SPECpower_ssj2008 SSJ Design, http://www.spec.org/power_ssj2008/docs/SPECpower_ssj2008-Design_ssj.pdf
13. SPEC Power and Performance Methodology,
    http://www.spec.org/power_ssj2008/docs/SPECpower-Methodology.pdf
14. SPECpower_ssj2008 Release, http://www.spec.org/power_ssj2008/press/SPECpower_ssj2008-Press%20Release.html
15. SPECpower_ssj2008 Intel publication, www.spec.org/power_ssj2008/results/res2007q4/power_ssj2008-20071129-00015.html
    www.spec.org/power_ssj2008/results/res2007q4/power_ssj2008-20071129-00016.html
    www.spec.org/power_ssj2008/results/res2007q4/power_ssj2008-20071129-00017.html
16. Morin, R., Kumar, A., Ilyina, E.: A multi-level comparative performance characterization of SPECjbb 2005 versus SPECjbb 2000. In: Proceedings of the IEEE International Workload Characterization Symposium, 2005, pp. 67–75 (2005)
17. BEA JRockit 6 P27.4.0 JDK,
    http://dev2dev.bea.com/jrockit/releaseupdate.html
18. BEA JRockit Command Line Reference,
    http://edocs.bea.com/jrockit/jrdocs/refman/index.html

Trace-Context Sensitive Performance Profiling for Enterprise Software Applications[*]

Matthias Rohr[1], André van Hoorn[1], Simon Giesecke[2], Jasminka Matevska[1], Wilhelm Hasselbring[1], and Sergej Alekseev[3]

[1] Software Engineering Group, University of Oldenburg, Germany
[2] OFFIS Institute for Information Technology, Oldenburg, Germany
[3] Nokia Siemens Networks GmbH & Co KG, Berlin, Germany

Abstract. Software response time distributions can be of high variance and multi-modal. Such characteristics reduce confidence or applicability in various statistical evaluations.

We contribute an approach to correlating response times to their corresponding operation execution sequence. This provides calling-context sensitive timing behavior models. The approach is based on three equivalence relations: caller-context, stack-context, and trace-context equivalence. To prevent model size explosion, a tree-based hierarchy provides timing behavior models that provide a trade-off between timing behavior model size and the amount of calling-context information considered.

In the case study, our approach provides response time distributions with significantly lower standard deviation, compared to using less or no calling-context information. An example from a performance analysis of an industry system demonstrates that multi-modal distributions can be replaced by multiple unimodal distributions using trace-context analysis.

1 Introduction

Response time monitoring data is a valuable artifact for software performance analysis of software systems, such as enterprise information systems based on Java EE. For instance, response time data from such systems is used for online performance evaluation, such as performance optimization and failure diagnosis, and for offline performance evaluation, such as performance tuning, benchmarking, profiling, and performance prediction. Typically, not only end-to-end response times are considered, but also response times of operations (alternatively called methods, routines, procedures, or sometimes services), i.e., software architecture entities that group statements to larger blocks of software.

Enterprise software applications are usually deployed in middleware environments that do not provide real-time properties and show non-trivial scheduling and queueing behavior. These systems typically have to serve large numbers of concurrent and heterogeneous user requests competing for computational resources. Therefore, the timing behavior of such systems tends to be of high

---

[*] This work is supported by the German Research Foundation (DFG), grant GRK 1076/1.

S. Kounev, I. Gorton, and K. Sachs (Eds.): SIPEW 2008, LNCS 5119, pp. 283–302, 2008.

variance and follows complex distributions. Unfortunately, many analytical and statistical performance evaluation approaches may produce low quality results for such timing behavior or cannot handle complex distribution families.

Operation executions show specific timing behavior for the calling-context of an operation execution, which is given by the call trace that corresponds to the execution of an operation. We discovered that a significant part of undesired distribution characteristics result from calling-context specific timing behavior of software operations. Our approach is to derive calling-context specific response time distributions by correlating response times to sequences of operation executions (see also Rohr et al. [1]). The resulting timing behavior model consists of multiple, calling-context specific response time distributions for each operation.

For large and dynamic systems, the number and size of traces might be very large. To prevent model size explosion [2], a hierarchy of abstraction levels for calling-context information is provided. Three abstraction levels are given by three equivalence relations: caller-context, stack-context, and trace-context equivalence. A tree-based hierarchy provides timing behavior models that provide a trade-off between timing behavior model size and the amount of calling-context information considered.

We contribute new empirical data on trace-context specific timing behavior distributions from a commercial telecommunication software system and a detailed analysis for a non-trivial Java online store demo application. Trace-context analysis is also compared to two other types of calling-context types (stack-context, caller-context). Furthermore, it is analyzed how the number of instrumented software operations relates to the calling-context analysis. Finally, the case study provides quantitative data showing that trace-context information is a major source of dispersion in response time distributions. In contrast to our former results [1], the reduction of standard deviation is studied for a large number of random instrumentations, to provide results that are independent from the selection of monitoring points.

The document is structured as follows. Section 2 discusses calling-context dependence in software timing behavior. Our approach to modeling timing behavior in dependence to calling-contexts is presented in Section 3 in combination with an example based on monitoring data from an industry system. Section 4 presents a step to optimize the timing behavior model. The case study is presented in Section 5. A discussion of our approach is in Section 6 before the related work and the conclusions follow in Section 7 and 8.

2   Calling-Context Dependence of Software Response Time Distributions

2.1   Software Response Time Distribution Characteristics

In this paper, the duration between the start and the end of an operation execution is denoted its response time [3]. This response time metric does not distinguish CPU time for the operation execution from other times, such as I/O processing time, resource waiting time, and response times of invoked operations (sub-calls). Hence, this metric less accurately describes the resource demands (e.g., CPU and I/O) than other timing metrics that do that distinction. The advantage of this simple response time metric is that it can be efficiently monitored and it does not require platform-specific monitoring functionality such as hardware performance counters.

Response time distributions of operations in software systems, such as in Java EE applications, often show high variance and do not follow simple distribution families, such as exponential or normal distributions. For instance, we measured the software operation response times displayed in Figure 1(a) during a performance evaluation of a large industry software system of Nokia Siemens Networks. The system evaluated is one of the leading commercial software platforms for implementing signaling services in telecommunication networks. The shape of the response time distribution (Figure 1(b)) of this operation cannot be accurately described by a single exponential or normal distribution.

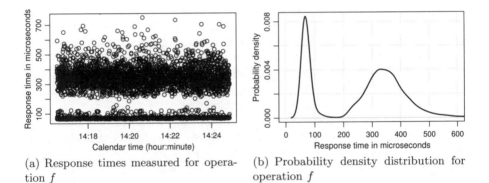

(a) Response times measured for operation f

(b) Probability density distribution for operation f

Fig. 1. "Clusters" and multi-modality in the software operation response times monitored in an industry telecommunication signaling system

Another example of multi-modal timing behavior distributions is provided by Bulej et al. [4]. These authors reported multi-modal response time distributions in different versions of CORBA middleware and use the term "cluster" for each group of similar response times. Bulej et al. [4] illustrate that clusters in timing behavior measurements reduce the potential to detect changes in the timing behavior of software. The authors experienced this problem in the context of performance regression benchmarking, which aims at detecting regressions in software performance between different versions of a software product.

High variance in response time distribution reduces the confidence in various statistical evaluations. An example for such an evaluation is the statistical hypothesis test that two response time observation sets belong to the same distribution. The confidence of this test usually decreases by increasing standard deviation, or more samples are required to reach the same confidence. Complex distributions, e.g., showing multi-modality, are not usable in many performance evaluation approaches because of mathematical tractability. Approximating complex distributions of response time measurements using simple distribution families is an option to satisfy requirements of performance evaluation approaches, but may lead to low quality results.

2.2   Calling-Context Specific Timing Behavior

Different timing behavior can correspond to multiple calling-contexts for the same software operation. Possible reasons are that the contexts correspond to particular software system states or operations show different timing behavior when they are used in different types of service requests. An example for the first is that a system provides different levels of personalization depending on the current workload intensity [5]; an example for the latter is that the response time of a service might heavily depend on the type of the request e.g., a watermarking service in an online media store might show different response time distributions for different media types that use individual watermarking techniques.

Calling-context is the set of circumstances or facts that surround an operation call. Software operation executions are embedded in sequences of interacting operation executions that participate in answering external service requests (from users or other systems). We consider three simplified models of the general calling-context that take into account different parts of the execution sequence of an execution: caller-context, stack-context, and trace-context. These models will be described in more detail in the next section.

Many aspects of the context of an operation execution are relevant to performance behavior. A key activity of performance modeling is the selection of the relevant aspects to consider. Obviously, the more such aspects are included, the higher precision can be expected from performance analysis. Modeling all relevant aspects to timing behavior is usually not an option, since the overall modeling and analysis effort grows by increasing modeling detail. Additionally, in some cases such as performance modeling during the early design of a software system, relevant context information may be unknown and it has to be decided, whether unknown relevant context information is estimated and included, or if it is excluded from the performance model.

The response time distribution of an operation is composed of response times made in different calling-contexts. It is our hypothesis that this causes a significant part of the distribution variance or multi-modality. If this hypothesis is true, it follows that including relevant calling-context information into timing behavior modeling can improve timing behavior evaluation approaches that are sensible to high variance or multi-modality in response time distributions, such as many anomaly detection approaches.

3   Approach to Calling-Context Sensitive Timing Behavior Modeling

In this section, we describe how calling-context information can be used in timing behavior modeling. We compare three different types of calling-context information: caller-context, stack-context, and trace-context. Caller-context and stack-context information have been used in performance evaluation before by Ammons et al. [6] and Graham et al. [7].

3.1   Software Behavior and Its Monitoring

We assume that software systems are composed of components. The components provide *operations* that might be requested by other components, external users, or systems.

Primary artifacts of runtime behavior are *executions* of the operations. We define a monitored execution as a tuple (o, i, r, st) of an operation o, its response time r, a start time st, and an identifier i, which is a number to distinguish executions of the same operation. As described in Section 2.1, we define the *response time* of an execution to be the number of time units (e.g., milliseconds) between the start and the end of an execution.

A *trace* is a finite sequence of operation executions that results from a user request or a request of an external system. We limit the scope to synchronous communication between executions as defined in the UML [8]: the caller of an operation is blocked and has to wait until the callee returns a result before it continues its own execution. Figure 2 provides the UML Sequence Diagrams for the running example.

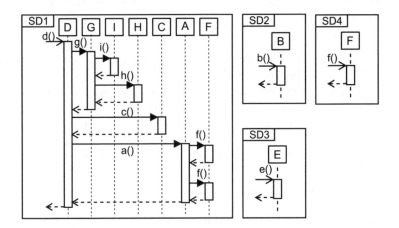

Fig. 2. UML Sequence Diagrams from a module of a partially instrumented telecommunication signaling system of Nokia Siemens Networks derived from monitoring data. (Operation names changed, operations omitted).

A trace can be represented by a dynamic call tree [6]. Each node of such an *ordered* tree represents an operation execution by its operation name. An edge from one node to another, i.e. their parent-child relation, corresponds to the caller/callee relation within the trace. Figure 3 shows the four trees (three consisting of one node only) that represent the traces shown in Figure 2.

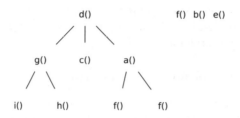

Fig. 3. Tree representation of each of the traces illustrated in Figure 2

3.2 Types of Calling-Context Equivalence

It is our goal to partition operation response times that are within equivalent calling-contexts. In the following we specify three equivalence relations:

- *Caller-context equivalence:* Two executions of the same operation are caller-context equivalent if they are called from operations with the same name.
- *Stack-context equivalence:* Two executions of the same operation are stack-context equivalent if the paths from the corresponding nodes to their roots are equal.
- *Trace-context equivalence:* Two executions of the same operation are trace-context equivalent if the corresponding trees are equal and both executions correspond to dynamic call tree nodes with the same position within the tree.

Trace-context equivalence implies stack-context equivalence and stack-context equivalence implies caller-context equivalence.

Each of the three equivalence relations specifies a partitioning of the monitored executions and its response times into equivalence classes. In the following, we use the terms *caller-, stack-,* and *trace-context* to refer to an equivalence class of executions that are caller-, stack-, and trace-context equivalent respectively. The term calling-context refers to any of those three equivalence classes.

3.3 Example: Trace-Context Analysis

As presented in Section 2.1, operation f has a multi-modal response time distribution (Figure 1(b), page 285). Applying calling-context analysis to the monitoring data and corresponding traces, shown as trees in Figure 3, identifies sets of calling-contexts. This set is consists of three trace-contexts, two stack-contexts $(d(), a(), f()$ and $f())$, and two caller-contexts ($\$()$, denoting the external caller, and $a()$). The stack-contexts and caller-contexts are identical for this operation. Therefore, stack-context information does not allow one to distinguish more calling-context than using caller-context information in this case.

Stack-Context Analysis and Caller-Context Analysis. Figure 4 shows the corresponding probability density distributions that would result from stack-context analysis and caller-context analysis for this operation. The first stack-context still shows a multi-modal distribution (Figure 4(a)).

The standard deviation of all response times for that operation is 136.47, the standard deviation corresponding to stack-context 1 is 155.54 and for stack-context 2 it is 49.74. The average standard deviation for the stack-context sensitive model, weighted by the observed calling frequency, is 120.13. This means that 11.97% of the standard deviation for the monitoring data of this operation can be removed using stack-context information.

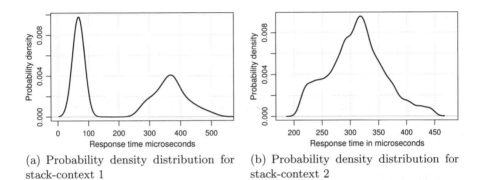

(a) Probability density distribution for stack-context 1

(b) Probability density distribution for stack-context 2

Fig. 4. Stack-context analysis identifies two stack-contexts for operation f

Trace-Context Analysis. Trace-context analysis allows one to distinguish three response time distributions as illustrated in Figure 5. These trace-contexts correspond to different calls of operation f shown in the UML Sequence Diagrams in Figure 2 on page 287: Trace-context 1 (solid line in Figure 5(a)) corresponds to the first call of $f()$ in SD1, trace-context 2 (Figure 5(b)) to the second call of $f()$ in SD1, and trace-context 3 (dashed line in Figure 5(a)) to the call of $f()$ in SD4.

The three probability distributions for these trace-context are not multimodal. This demonstrates that a multi-modal response time distribution can be replaced by multiple unimodal distributions using trace-context analysis, in an industrial software system. Caller-context analysis or stack-context analysis is not able to resolve multi-modality in this case.

The standard deviation corresponding to trace-context 1 is 53.83, for trace-context 2 it is 2.20, and for stack-context 2 it is 49.74. Weighted by the calling frequency of the monitoring data, the average standard deviation for a trace-context sensitive model is 35.94. This means that 73.66% of the standard deviation for the monitoring data of this operation can be removed using stack-context information. Hence, most of the dispersion in the response time distribution of this particular operation can be removed by making trace-context dependence explicit.

In this case, the benefit in terms of removing standard deviation, is much higher for trace-context analysis than for stack- or caller-context analysis. To

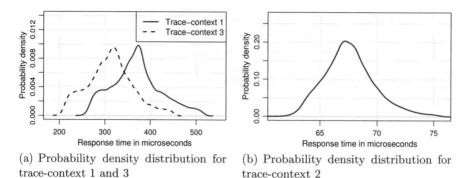

(a) Probability density distribution for trace-context 1 and 3

(b) Probability density distribution for trace-context 2

Fig. 5. Trace-context analysis identified three trace-contexts for operation f

study this for all operations of a software system, Section 5 presents a quantitative analysis on how much standard deviation of operation response time distributions depends on which type of calling-context information for random partial instrumentations.

4   The Calling-Context Tree

Using the same calling-context analysis detail for all operations of a system may uncover some undesired model properties (see Section 4.1). To overcome this, we present an additional step to find a more adequate context-sensitive timing behavior model than trace-context analysis alone would provide. This step consists of the representation of the results from caller-, stack-, and trace-context analysis in a tree (Section 4.2) and the application of tree modification operators (see Section 4.3). The application of these operators reduces the resulting number of calling-contexts and amount of calling-context information used to model the timing behavior of a system.

4.1   Undesired Calling-Context Analysis Results

The analysis presented in Section 3 may produce results with undesired properties:

- Too many calling-contexts: The efficiency and feasibility of performance analysis methods may depend on the size of the timing behavior model.
- Calling-contexts with an insufficient number of measurements: Many basic statistical methods require a minimum number of observations in order to provide robust results.
- Calling-contexts may be distinguished that do not differ in their timing behavior distributions.
- Trace-context analysis may be used in cases for that the computationally cheaper stack- or caller-contexts would produce an equal result.

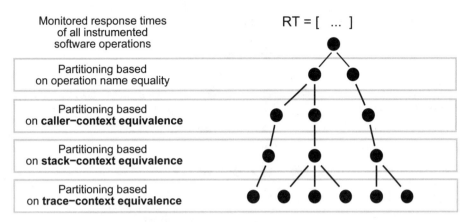

Fig. 6. The monitored operation response times of a system are partitioned according to their calling-contexts. The calling-context equivalence relations organize the monitored observations into a tree.

4.2   Construction of the Calling-Context Tree

To form a timing behavior model free of the undesired properties presented above, the results of all three calling-context analyses are connected within a tree, denoted *calling-context tree* (CCT). Moreover, the implication relationship between the three equivalence relations allows to organize the calling-contexts into a tree, denoted . An example of an CCT is illustrated in Figure 6. A calling-context tree is constructed as follows:

- The root of the calling-context tree is given by all observations monitored.
- The nodes of the first level of the CCT represent calling-contexts for the observations corresponding to the software operation with the same name.
- The nodes of the second level of the CCT represent the caller-contexts. Based on the callee's operation name, each second level node is connected to its corresponding first level node.
- The third CCT level is defined by stack-context equivalence. Each third level node is connected to its corresponding second level node.
- The fourth level of the CCT is the partitioning defined by trace-context equivalence. Each trace-context node has an edge to its corresponding stack-context node.

A complete *timing behavior model* consists of any node subset of the CCT that is a complete partitioning of all monitored observations. For instance, each subset of all tree nodes that resulted from the same type of calling-context analysis is a complete partitioning, and hence, is a complete timing behavior model. A set of tree operators, described next, is applied to the tree to identify the node subset that both considers as much calling-context information as possible and is free of the undesired properties.

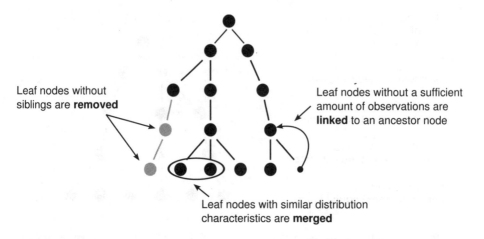

Leaf nodes without siblings are **removed**

Leaf nodes without a sufficient amount of observations are **linked** to an ancestor node

Leaf nodes with similar distribution characteristics are **merged**

Fig. 7. Node merging, removing, and linking to reduce the number of calling-contexts, avoid unrequired trace evaluations, and to have leaf nodes corresponding to a sufficient number of observations

4.3   Modification of the Calling-Context Tree

The maximum level of calling-context information would be included in the timing behavior model given by the nodes of the fourth layer of the CCT, i.e., the trace-contexts. However, this timing behavior model may have the undesired properties described in Section 4.1. We define three operators to the CCT tree leafs to remove the undesired properties:

1. Leaf nodes that have no siblings are **removed** from the tree. The removal of leaf nodes reduces the size and computational costs for applying the calling-context tree as performance model in some evaluations, e.g., when it is used as a reference model in anomaly detection or regression benchmarking. For instance, a trace-context node that has no siblings is removed, since it makes no sense to compute and evaluate the complete trace for trace-context analysis, while stack-context analysis already provide the same response time distributions for the corresponding operation calls.

2. Leaf nodes having similar response time distribution characteristics and that are siblings may be **merged**. Merging is performed until some stop criterion, such as that the number of leafs in the tree is equal or below a user-specified maximum number of timing behavior model entities. An alternative stop criterion is the absence of additional sufficiently similar merging candidates. Similarity is defined based on a user-defined similarity metric for probability distributions. Only nodes are merged that have enough observations to robustly determine the distribution similarity.

3. Nodes in the CCT without a sufficient number of observations are **linked to** an ancestor node that has a sufficient number of observations. The linking semantics is that all corresponding executions and response times of the linked node are used for the node that links to it. How many observations

are sufficient depends on two aspects: the underlying probability distribution for the sample observations [9], and the statistical analysis that is to be performed in the subsequent performance evaluation.

These three operators are repeatedly applied in random order to the CCT until no further applications of operator 1 and 3 are possible and a user-defined stop criterion for operator 2 is satisfied. An example for the application of the three operators is illustrated in Figure 7. The final context sensitive timing behavior model is given by the leaf nodes of the CCT.

A detailed discussion of similarity metrics between response timing distributions is out of the scope of this paper. We used a distance metric based on inter-quartile-range and distribution median. These two metrics are considered more robust to characterize a distribution than the more common sample mean and standard variation, which are sensitive to extreme outliers. We experienced that few extremely large response times are not uncommon, especially for small software operations. This confirms to models that use log-normal distributions for response time data, which is for instance suggested by the research of Mielke [10] for end-to-end response times in Enterprise Resource Planning (ERP) systems.

5   Case Study

This case study explores the relation between the number of monitoring points and the number of resulting calling-contexts, and compares the calling-context specific response time distributions to the response time distributions without calling-context analysis. The most important empirical result of this analysis is that trace-context information is responsible for a significant part (20% to 40%) of the average standard deviation for the large majority of random partial instrumentations. Trace-context analysis outperforms stack-context and caller-context analysis that show relatively similar results.

5.1   Setting

The software system analyzed in the case study is the iBATIS JPetStore[1], which is a demo Java Web application implementing an online store scenario. The instrumentation to monitor response times of the internal operations of the JPetStore is given by the software instrumentation package Kieker [11].

The evaluation abstracts from the problem selecting monitoring points by evaluating more than 95,000 random partial instrumentations of the 2^{199} possible partial instrumentations. The traces and response times are taken from several fully instrumented experiment runs of 20 minutes. The first 3 minutes are considered the warm-up period and are ignored in the evaluation.

The JPetStore is deployed in the Apache Tomcat Servlet container (version 5.5.23) running on a desktop computer equipped with an Intel Pentium 4 3.00 GHz hyper-threaded CPU and 1 GB physical memory and Linux 2.6.17.13.

---

[1] http://ibatis.apache.org/

The application server software employs Sun Java SE 1.6.0_03. JPetStore uses a database management system (MySQL 5.0.18) for storing business data running on a GNU/Linux 2.6.15 system with two Intel Xeon 3.00 GHz CPUs and 2 GB of physical memory. The application server and the database back-end are connected via 100 Mbit Ethernet. A workload generator runs on a separate desktop computer being identically equipped and configured as the application server node above.

The workload for the JPetStore is generated by the workload driver Apache JMeter 2.2 extended by our probabilistic workload driver Markov4JMeter [12]. This tool allows to emulate users based on an application model and a mix of corresponding probabilistic user behavior models. The think time between user requests is configured to be normally distributed. The number of concurrent users is set to 10, which can be handled without any problems by the system under monitoring. A detailed description of the workload can be found in van Hoorn et al. [12].

5.2   Results

Table 1 outlines characteristics of the monitoring data collected during the experiment runs and the range of the number of caller-, stack-, and trace-contexts resulting from calling-context analysis.

Table 1. Summary of case study characteristics

Instrumentation	Full (199 mon.pts.)	Random
# Instrumented Operations	199	1–198
# Monitored Executions	2,032,573	1–2,032,572
# Traces	36,036	1–36,036
# Caller-contexts	290	1–312
# Stack-contexts	368	1–368
# Trace-contexts	7021	1–7021

The number of resulting calling-contexts is illustrated in Figure 8 (1,500 samples of 95,000 plotted) in dependence to the number of monitoring points. The number of stack-contexts and caller-contexts both grow linearly with similar rates by the number of monitoring points, as shown in Figure 8(a). In most of the instrumentation scenarios (80%), the number of stack-contexts was larger than the number of caller-contexts for the same instrumentation. In contrast to the number of distinct stack- and trace-contexts, the number of caller-contexts is not at its maximum for full instrumentation. This demonstrates that adding monitoring points can reduce the number of caller-contexts. Figure 8(b) visualizes the numbers of trace-contexts resulting from the random instrumentation scenarios. The number of trace-contexts increases much faster than the number of stack-contexts and caller-contexts does.

In general, the number of distinct calling-contexts tends to grow with the number of monitoring points. Adding a new monitoring point to an existing

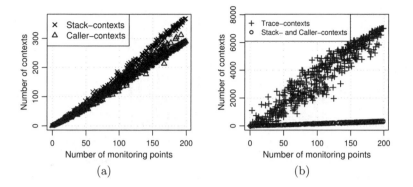

Fig. 8. The number of monitoring points in relation to the number of contexts

instrumentation also increases the number of trace-contexts and stack-contexts, while adding a monitoring point may reduce the number of caller-contexts. However, the fact that an instrumentation with n monitoring points has m calling-contexts does not imply that a second instrumentation with $n' > n$ monitoring points has more than m calling-contexts (in the same software system and for the same workload), since different monitoring points can increase the same numbers of calling-contexts differently.

Response Time Distribution Variance Related to Calling-Context Information. Figures 9(a) – 9(c) show the average standard deviation reduction in the timing behavior model resulting from caller-, stack-, and trace-context analysis. These diagrams show the distribution of this metric as boxplotted for bins of numbers of monitoring points.

Figure 9(a) reveals that caller-context information corresponds to about 6.8% of average standard deviation of all response times in a fully instrumented experiment run. For less monitoring points, there is a larger uncertainty on how much average standard deviation could be removed by caller-context analysis. If half of the operations are instrumented, 75% of the instrumentations result in an average standard deviation isolation of more than 6.2%. For smaller numbers of monitoring points, a majority of instrumentations results in below 2% but the boxplot also shows a large number of outliers (observations above an upper whisker in a boxplot [13]) representing cases in which up to 45% percent of standard deviation can be removed. In summary, cases exist where caller-context analysis is very effective. The benefit of caller-context analysis to average standard deviation reduction is in most cases below 7%.

Stack-context analysis (see Figure 9(b)) shows slightly more benefits than using caller-context analysis. For instance, for higher numbers of instrumented operations approx. 11% of the average standard deviation can be removed.

Figure 9(c) shows that much more average standard deviation is connected to trace-context information than to the other calling-context types. For full instrumentation, trace-context analysis leads results in about 42% less average

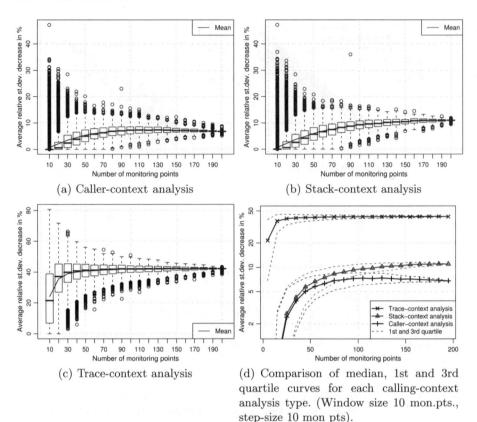

(a) Caller-context analysis   (b) Stack-context analysis

(c) Trace-context analysis   (d) Comparison of median, 1st and 3rd
                               quartile curves for each calling-context
                               analysis type. (Window size 10 mon.pts.,
                               step-size 10 mon pts).

Fig. 9. Average decrease in standard deviation for different numbers of monitoring points using calling-context information compared to standard deviation using no calling-context information

standard deviation in the trace-context sensitive response time distributions than using no calling-context information. For more than the half of the evaluated instrumentations with around 40 monitoring points, 40% of average standard deviation could be removed and only few instrumentations of that size were in the results that had less than 10% of average standard deviation reduction.

This shows that a large part of the standard deviation of the monitored and evaluated scenarios is related to trace-context information.

Figure 9(d) compares the amount of average standard deviation that can be removed by each of the calling-context types. It underlines that stack-context analysis performs slightly better than caller-context analysis, and that trace-context analysis outperforms stack-context analysis and caller-context analysis. Trace-context analysis removes for most instrumentation scenarios, in particular for those with more than 25 monitoring points, more than 10% of the standard deviation. For most instrumentation scenarios with more than 50 monitoring points, more than 40% standard deviation decrease was observed.

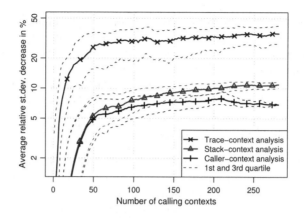

Fig. 10. Average decrease in standard deviation for different numbers of calling-contexts using calling-context information compared to standard deviation using no calling-context information. Comparison of Median, 1st and 3rd quartile curves for caller-, stack-, trace-context analysis. (Window size 10 contexts, step size 2 contexts).

Figure 10 presents how much standard deviation is connected to the calling-contexts in dependence of the number of calling-contexts. Figure 10 reveals that trace-context information is connected to more calling-context information than the other two calling-context types. This means that it does not "just" provide more different equivalence classes for each monitoring point, but also defines calling-contexts that are connected to more average standard deviation than using caller-, or stack-context analysis.

6 Discussion and Limitations

In the following, application issues and limitations related to continuous runtime behavior monitoring during regular operation in distributed software applications are discussed.

6.1 Monitoring Overhead

As discussed in the introduction, typical application scenarios are runtime QoS management and failure diagnosis based on anomaly detection, such as [14,15,16]. This requires continuous monitoring during regular operation of the software system. Therefore, the monitoring overhead should be reasonably low. It is our experience that imposing less than 20% overhead on response times and throughput is accepted by the industry in exchange for monitoring and supervision.

A detailed discussion on monitoring overhead is not part of this paper. In the case studies using our instrumentation prototype Kieker, we observed an overhead on response times of below 15% for systems that consist of one execution environment. For distributed software systems, an additional overhead exists for remote communication. This results from the absence of a distributed clock that could be used to order executions within a sequence, and from the requirement to pass unique trace identifiers together with remote methods calls in order to distinguish multiple concurrent executions within the system.

Kieker uses aspect-oriented programming (AOP), similar to the monitoring framework InfraRED, for which an overhead of about 10% was reported [17].

6.2 Distributed Software Systems

Our monitoring infrastructure allows to trace execution paths through multiple execution environments for certain types of remote communication such as the Hessian Web Service protocol[2], which is for instance supported by the Spring Java EE application framework. Support for other remote communication methods, such as Remote Method Invocation, may be future work. The context-dependent profiling technique presented in this paper is limited to synchronous communication, i.e. a caller is blocked and waits until the callee returns a result. Traces with parallel asynchronous communication, are automatically split into multiple execution traces that only contain synchronous communication. Therefore, the calling-context analysis cannot benefit from correlations between timing behavior and the execution traces characteristics that are not within the sequence of synchronous communication. This limitation could be resolved by using an alternative monitoring approach, such as Briand et al. [18].

6.3 Representativeness and Completeness of Monitoring Data

In our approach, timing behavior distributions and calling-contexts result from monitoring data. This results in the two major risks that the monitoring data is not representative for normal behavior and that not all calling-contexts are detected. For instance, calling-contexts are missing if possible execution sequences were not activated during the monitoring period, which depends on the system workload. These risks can be minimized by using a sufficient amount of monitoring data from real system usage. For instance, for a typical online store, we consider few weeks of monitoring data to be sufficient for timing behavior anomaly detection. For the identification of calling-contexts, static (source code) analysis provides an alternative to monitoring data analysis, since it does not depend on system workload. Since the performance behavior of a software system changes over time (e.g., improving of algorithms, changes in user behavior, changes in hardware), it is required to update software performance models regularly.

6.4 Considering Other Types of Calling-Context Information

This paper explored the correlation between operation response time distributions and operation execution sequences, represented as dynamic call trees. The results showed that especially trace-context information can be strongly connected to response time distribution characteristics.

---

[2] http://hessian.caucho.com/

As mentioned before, trace-, stack- and caller-context analysis only consider a part of the calling-context, i.e. the set of circumstances or facts that surround an operation call. It has been suggested to also consider parameter values [19] or workload intensity [20] in timing behavior modeling. Additionally, the information provided on lower system layers, such as performance counter metrics on cache hits and on the number of context switches, are also often correlate to timing behavior. In this paper, these other types of calling-context information were not studied. It is not known, to what extend these are beneficial for considering in the analysis of response times in enterprise software systems. Furthermore, we did not address whether multiple object instances of the same class show different timing behavior.

Considering these other types of calling-context information may be beneficial as well, and should be subject to future research.

7   Related Work

Related work comes from the domains of profiling and trace analysis, performance evaluation, online failure diagnosis, and performance prediction.

There is much literature in the domain of software profiling that addresses to connect response time behavior to method calls and context information. Graham et al. [7] introduced the profiler *gprof*. Gprof provides caller-context information (i.e., makes caller-callee relations explicit). The trace-context analysis studied in this paper is an extension of the concept of caller-contexts. Most modern profiling tools, such as Intel's VTune Performance Analyzer follow gprof by providing caller-context information (see Xie and Notkin [21]). Ammons et al. [6] go beyond the caller-callee relationship and introduces what we call stack-context equivalence. We extend the concept of stack-context equivalence by using the complete sequence of operations for the definition of equivalence. These authors do not discuss the timing behavior distributions resulting from calling-context analysis, which is a major focus of our paper. A more recent approach to evaluating runtime behavior in the context of execution traces is given by the work on monitoring trace representation of Hamou-Lhadj [22]. This approach and other trace analysis approaches, such as those surveyed by Hamou-Lhadj and Lethbridge [2], apply high levels of abstraction in order to achieve compact models for very large traces. The amount of preserved calling-context information of such trace models are at stack-context level or below (e.g., caller-context). Those techniques do not focus on combining trace-context analysis with timing behavior evaluation.

Bulej et al. [4], report and analyze timing behavior clusters for two CORBA implementations in the context of regression benchmarking of different software versions. The k-means clustering approach is used to identify clusters in timing behavior measurements. In contrast to our approach, this does not require to connect single execution observations to traces, therefore the requirements on the monitoring infrastructure are lower than in our approach. Our approach uses the trace information as additional information, which allows the precise distinction of timing behavior classes (if there are correlations to the trace-contexts). The k-means clustering approach is a heuristic that performs well, if the correct number of clusters is known in advance and the values of the clusters are well separated.

Various approaches have been presented to use timing behavior monitoring data of software systems in order to implement preemptive quality of service management. For instance, in the Magpie project by Barham et al. [23] it has been motivated to correlate monitored events for specific requests to timing behavior measurements to identify anomalies and perform failure diagnosis. The Magpie approach shares the general idea of correlating monitored events within a request to timing behavior with our approach, but details on the correlation or empirical data have not been presented, so far.

The performance modeling approach of Koziolek et al. [19] considers parameter values as part of usage profiles in order to increase performance prediction precision. Parameter values can also be considered calling-context information. The three calling-context types described in this paper are not part of Koziolek et al. [19]'s software performance model.

8   Conclusions

Summary. This paper presents empirical data from a lab case study and from monitoring data of an industry system that both show that a large part of the standard deviation in software response time distributions can be related to calling-context information. This allows to conclude that using calling-context information can significantly improve timing behavior evaluations, such as those that depend on the variance of response time distributions.

In this paper, we presented our approach to evaluating operation response time measurements in dependence to their calling-contexts. Our approach creates a trace-context sensitive timing behavior model from monitoring data. We introduced trace-context equivalence, which extends the concepts of caller-context equivalence and stack-context equivalence. In a second step, our approach organizes equivalence classes of monitored observations in a tree-structure to reduce the number of resulting calling-contexts and to remove unrequired distinctions of calling-contexts.

Additionally, we demonstrated for monitoring data of a commercial telecommunication signaling system that multi-modal distributions can be removed from timing behavior models by trace-context analysis.

Future Work. Currently, the approach requires the complete trace to be recorded before an estimation of a response time for an execution within the trace is possible. This is not necessarily a problem in failure diagnosis approaches such as anomaly detection, but in some cases it can be desirable to estimate the expected response times of a method before its execution. In that case, only a part of the full trace for that request is recorded. In contrast to using the full trace, a prefix could be used to estimate the future response time of the method currently executed. This information could be useful to organize scheduling in multi-user systems.

Acknowledgement

We would like to acknowledge Nokia Siemens Networks Berlin, Business Service Solution for supporting this project.

References

1. Rohr, M., van Hoorn, A., Giesecke, S., Matevska, J., Hasselbring, W.: Trace-context sensitive performance models from monitoring data of software-intensive systems. In: Workshop on Tools Infrastructures and Methodologies for the Evaluation of Research Systems (TIMERS 2008) at IEEE International Symposium on Performance Analysis of Systems and Software (April 2008)
2. Hamou-Lhadj, A., Lethbridge, T.C.: A survey of trace exploration tools and techniques. In: Conference of the Centre for Advanced Studies on Collaborative research CASCON 2004, pp. 42–55. IBM Press (2004)
3. Jain, R.: The Art of Computer Systems Performance Analysis: Techniques for Experimental Design, Measurement, Simulation, and Modeling, 1st edn. John Wiley & Sons, Chichester (1991)
4. Bulej, L., Kalibera, T., Tůma, P.: Repeated results analysis for middleware regression benchmarking. Performance Evaluation 60(1-4), 345–358 (2005)
5. Arlitt, M.F., Krishnamurthy, D., Rolia, J.: Characterizing the scalability of a large web-based shopping system. ACM Transactions on Internet Technology 1(1), 44–69 (2001)
6. Ammons, G., Ball, T., Larus, J.R.: Exploiting hardware performance counters with flow and context sensitive profiling. In: Conference on Programming Language Design and Implementation (PLDI 1997), pp. 85–96. ACM, New York (1997)
7. Graham, S.L., Kessler, P.B., McKusick, M.K.: gprof: a call graph execution profiler. SIGPLAN Notes 17(6), 120–126 (1982)
8. Object Management Group (OMG): Unified Modeling Language: Superstructure Version 2.1.1 (February 2007)
9. Barrett, J.P., Goldsmith, L.: When is n sufficiently large? The American Statistician 30(2), 67–70 (1976)
10. Mielke, A.: Elements for response-time statistics in ERP transaction systems. Performance Evaluation 63(7), 635–653 (2006)
11. Rohr, M., van Hoorn, A., Matevska, J., Sommer, N., Stoever, L., Giesecke, S., Hasselbring, W.: Kieker: Continuous monitoring and on demand visualization of Java software behavior. In: IASTED International Conference on Software Engineering 2008, pp. 80–85. ACTA Press (February 2008)
12. van Hoorn, A., Rohr, M., Hasselbring, W.: Generating probabilistic and intensity-varying workload for web-based software systems. In: SPEC International Performance Evaluation Workshop (SIPEW 2008). LNCS, vol. 5119. Springer, Heidelberg (2008)
13. Montgomery, D.C., Runger, G.C.: Applied Statistics and Probability for Engineers, 3rd edn. John Wiley & Sons, Inc., Chichester (2003)
14. Duzbayev, N., Poernomo, I.: Runtime prediction of queued behaviour. In: Hofmeister, C., Crnković, I., Reussner, R. (eds.) QoSA 2006. LNCS, vol. 4214, pp. 78–94. Springer, Heidelberg (2006)
15. Diaconescu, A., Mos, A., Murphy, J.: Automatic performance management in component based software systems. In: First International Conference on Autonomic Computing (ICAC 2004), pp. 214–221. IEEE, Los Alamitos (2004)

16. Agarwal, M.K., Appleby, K., Gupta, M., Kar, G., Neogi, A., Sailer, A.: Problem determination using dependency graphs and run-time behavior models. In: Sahai, A., Wu, F. (eds.) DSOM 2004. LNCS, vol. 3278, pp. 171–182. Springer, Heidelberg (2004)
17. Govindraj, K., Narayanan, S., Thomas, B., Nair, P., P, S.: On using AOP for Application Performance Management. In: AOSD 2006 - Industry Track Proceedings (Technical Report IAI-TR-2006-3, University of Bonn), pp. 18–30 (March 2006)
18. Briand, L.C., Labiche, Y., Leduc, J.: Toward the reverse engineering of UML sequence diagrams for distributed Java software. IEEE Transactions on Software Engineering 32(9), 642–663 (2006)
19. Koziolek, H., Becker, S., Happe, J.: Predicting the Performance of Component-based Software Architectures with different Usage Profiles. In: 3rd International Conference on the Quality of Software Architectures (QoSA 2007). LNCS, vol. 4880, pp. 145–163. Springer, Heidelberg (2008)
20. Rohr, M., Giesecke, S., Hasselbring, W.: Timing Behavior Anomaly Detection in Enterprise Information Systems. In: 9th International Conference on Enterprise Information Systems (ICEIS 2007), June 2007, pp. 494–497. INSTICC Press (2007)
21. Xie, T., Notkin, D.: An empirical study of Java dynamic call graph extractors. Technical Report UW-CSE-02-12-03, University of Washington Department of Computer Science and Engineering, Seattle, WA, USA (December 2002)
22. Hamou-Lhadj, A.: Techniques to Simplify the Analysis of Execution Traces for Program Comprehension. PhD thesis, Ottawa-Carleton Institute for Computer Science, School of Information Technology and Engineering (SITE), University of Ottawa (2005)
23. Barham, P., Isaacs, R., Mortier, R., Narayanan, D.: Magpie: online modelling and performance-aware systems. In: 9th Conference on Hot Topics in Operating Systems (HOTOS 2003), USENIX Association, p. 15 (2003)

Performance Monitoring and Analysis of a Large Online Transaction Processing System

Manoj Nambiar and Hemanta Kumar Kalita

Performance Engineering Research Center
TATA Consultancy Services, Gateway Park (Akruti Business Port)
Road No. 13, Andheri (E), Mumbai–400093, India
{m.nambiar, hemanta.kalita}@tcs.com

Abstract. A large Employee Appraisal System is accessed by clients from different international locations using the Internet. Being a distributed system, it is not easy to monitor and assess performance of such a large online transaction processing (OLTP) system. Performance Monitoring and Analysis of such a system requires pinpointing to the box or link in the system that is responsible for the overall slow performance. In this paper, we elaborate on our approach of performance monitoring and analysis of a large OLTP system using an employee appraisal system as an example.

1 Introduction

A large IT company, which has offices in different countries and employees at different locations, hosts a large employee appraisal system . The employees use this system to initiate their appraisals, select appraisers, and enter their self ratings. The supervisors use the system to rate the employees. Within the application, there is a workflow system which notifies the status of an employee's appraisal to whomever (supervisor or employee) against whom action is pending.

Fig. 1 shows the architecture of the appraisal system. The system has a separate Workflow Server and Workflow Database Server only to manage workflow processing. The Application Server and Database Server of the system process the remaining transactions. There are multiple instances of the Application Server and Workflow Server connected through the SSL[1] Accelerator. The Application Server acts as the front ending server for the appraisal application, and it makes calls to the Workflow Server for workflow related transactions. The Database Server is also partitioned according to the functionality as Database Server and Workflow Database Server .

All employees are required to enter appraisal details on a half-yearly basis. The appraisal system for a half year period is kept open for two months. A large number of employees, however, access the system in the last week of the appraisal cycle. As a result, the system response becomes very slow; thereby, impacting productivity considerably. For the system managers, it is essential that they identify all the bottlenecks in the system, so that they can provide a solution to improve the system performance.

---

[1] Secure Sockets Layer.

S. Kounev, I. Gorton, and K. Sachs (Eds.): SIPEW 2008, LNCS 5119, pp. 303–313, 2008.

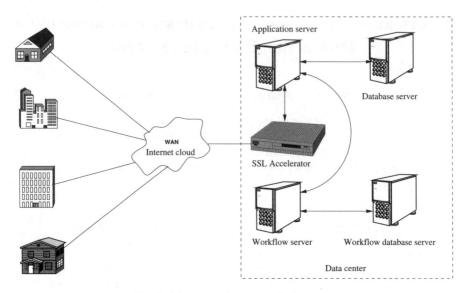

Fig. 1. A large employee appraisal system

This paper highlights how the performance of a large employee appraisal system was analyzed using data provided by ScrutiNet[1]. Also shown in the specific measurements is how simple context specific data can be used to aid analysis.

The remainder of this paper is divided into five sections. Section 2 discusses related work and existing performance monitoring and analysis tools. Section 3 explains our approach to performance monitoring and analysis using ScrutiNet. Section 4 discusses deployment of ScrutiNet in the large employee appraisal system . A detailed result analysis is done in Section 5, and Section 6 concludes the paper.

2   Related Work

There are many approaches to performance monitoring and analysis of OLTP system. For the purpose of discussion, we categorize them into active monitoring, application logging, and passive monitoring.

Active Monitoring. In this method, application specific scripts are developed and scheduled to be run at specific intervals. Instances of these scripts are deployed across strategic locations on the Internet. These scripts monitor transaction response times and upload the measurement details to a centralized database so that all data can be seen from a single console. HP/Mercury Business Availability center [7] is a good example of an active monitoring tool. Apart from script development, there is a lot of dependency on the availability of measurement agents to gather data. These agents themselves can add to the load on the server. Moreover, not all transactions can be run by agents especially those that change the state of the application. For example, a bank withdrawal transaction cannot be run by an agent.

Application Logging. Embedding application code with time stamps can provide enough detail about the location of the bottlenecks. Often, these logs are not easy to read because they require the development of application log readers for the purpose of reading. Also, increasing the amount of logging itself can cause serious drops in performance levels. Application Response Measurements (ARM)[8] is one specification that attempts to standardize code level performance logging.

Passive Monitoring. Analyzing the network packets coming in and out of a transaction server can help gain valuable insight into application performance. And this can be done with the aid of network switches in such a way that the application being measured is not impacted at all. This is the basis of passive monitoring, and it is a desirable way to monitor application performance. Passive monitoring, therefore, is the focus of this document. There are many passive transaction performance monitoring tools commercially available. Iwatch[2] is one such software based tool, which provides good graphical reporting capabilities. Network General[3] provides a hardware based solution, which stores network packets. The reporting tools of Network General work on the packet store and compute transaction response time and correlation across tiers. Software based tools include Crannog software Response Watch[5], which can monitor web applications, and Compuware Vantage[4] that has most of the features for aiding bottleneck analysis. In open source, the authors found one passive monitoring tool called PastMon[6] that reports detailed transaction specific metrics at the Transmission Control Protocol (TCP) level. However, string matching rules need to be built into PastMon to help classify specific transactions.

Apart from this, [9] discusses on designing tools that would enable isolating performance bottlenecks in distributed systems composed of black-box nodes. [10] highlights steps in performance analysis as instrumentation/measurement and analysis (online, automatic and postmortem).

3   Performance Monitoring and Analysis Using ScrutiNet

ScrutiNet is a passive performance monitoring and analysis tool designed at the Performance Engineering Research Center, TATA Consultancy Services (TCS), Mumbai. ScrutiNet can be used to monitor online applications non-intrusively. For any OLTP server, ScrutiNet monitors its network packets to identify transactions and measure performance. For every transaction, ScrutiNet can provide details like response time and its breakup between processing time and network delay. For multitier transactions, it also aids in isolating the delays for a transaction across tiers.

What sets ScrutiNet apart from other passive monitoring tools is that it is application agnostic and can be used to detect the bottleneck in any request–response based OLTP transaction. It does not attempt to decode the application level protocol in the network packets. For ScrutiNet, a transaction is simply a request message sent by the client to the response message sent from the server on the same TCP connection. The request and response messages are split into packets when transmitted over the network. So, pipelined transactions in which two requests appear back to back in the same TCP connection can't be analyzed completely using ScrutiNet. However, it does not diminish the value of ScrutiNet as a performance bottleneck detection tool.

3.1 ScrutiNet Report Format

Some relevant transaction performance data reported by ScrutiNet are listed below.

Transaction Start time. The time when the first request packet from the client was seen on the network.

Client IP Address and Port. This information identifies the TCP connection on which the transaction is being executed.

Request Send Time. Time taken by the client to send the request message to the server.

Response. Time Taken for the server to push the last packet of the response message back to the client since the arrival of the last request packet of the transaction.

Network Overhead. Network overhead is the sum of times elapsed during data transfer phases when the server is responding. A data transfer phase is identified as time during which there is at least one response packet unacknowledged by the client. A data transfer phase is complete when the client acknowledges all outstanding response packets.

Client Window Zero Delay. Client window zero is the sum of times elapsed during all client delay phases of the transaction when the server is in the responding state. A client delay phase is identified as the time starting from when a client sends a TCP window update packet with a window size of zero to when the client sends a TCP window update packet with a non zero receive window size.

Average Round Trip Time. Average of all the TCP round trip time samples taken in the course of the transaction.

Total Bytes In. The sum of sizes of all network packets sent from the client to the server during the transaction.

Total Bytes Out. The sum of sizes of all network packets sent from the server to the client during the transaction.

Request Contents. The contents of the first packet of the request message in ASCII.

3.2 Correlation Functionality in ScrutiNet

A correlate functionality is available in ScrutiNet, which helps a user to find transactions in the next tier related to any selected transaction in the current tier. For example, ScrutiNet can be used to identify the database transactions when the selected HTTP transaction is in progress. The following data appears in the correlation report.

- Transaction performance details regarding the selected transaction ($seltxn$). We will call this set of selected transactions the candidate next tier transactions.
- All the transaction performance details of transactions in the next tier (txn) that match the following criteria:

$$startTime_{txn} \geq startTime_{seltxn} \tag{1}$$

$$startTime_{txn} + respTime_{txn} \leq startTime_{seltxn} + respTime_{seltxn} \tag{2}$$

$startTime$ and $respTime$ are transaction start time and transaction response time.

– Each transaction of this kind belongs to a specific TCP connection. For each connection, all the transaction response times are added and reported as connection response times. This method of analysis relates response time of one tier to that of its neighboring tier. As such it does not depend on the total number of tiers in the system architecture.

It should be noted that all connections to the next tier will not contribute to the selected transaction. To know the number of connections that are opened to the next tier can be taken as input from the application support team. Otherwise, this information can be obtained by analyzing ScrutiNet output at a time when there is only one user in the system.

3.3 Performance Monitoring and Analysis – ScrutiNet Based Approach

A general heuristic analysis algorithm to identify bottlenecks in a multi-tier application when using measurement data from ScrutiNet is as follows:

1. Sort all transactions in the front tier server based on response time functionality available in ScrutiNet.
2. Identify the transactions of interest. For each transaction, follow the subsequent steps.
   (a) Is *Client Window Zero Delay* greater than zero? If so, review the TCP socket buffer settings in the client host. These problems are typically seen when the response message size is large, so reducing/compressing the response message can also help.
   (b) Is the *Network Overhead* a significant part of the response time? If so, check the *Total Bytes Out* measure. This is generally very large in case of high network overheads. Compressing the response message sizes can help. Also, check if the average round trip time is large. In such a case, the routing from the client to server and back should be verified.
   (c) Is the *Request Send Time* non negligible? If so, check the *Total Bytes In* measure for the transaction. Again if this measure is very large, then it points to the request message size. The application should be tuned to reduce this size.
3. If none of the preceding three measures are significant, then it points to processing overhead within the server. This overhead includes processing time in the server being monitored or processing time in the next tier server.
4. To determine contribution of next tier to the response time, obtain a correlation report for the selected transaction. This functionality is available in ScrutiNet.
5. Obtain the number of connections n made to the next tier as input.
6. Sort the connections in the correlation report for connection response time. Select the top n connections and sum up their response times. In many cases just based on top active n connections, it can be deduced whether the current tier or the next tier is the bottleneck. Otherwise, application specific data needs to be taken into account to identify the relevant n connections. One method of getting application specific data is to collect a ScrutiNet trace of a single user transaction in a test setup of the same system.

If the above steps are repeated recursively from first tier to last tier, then we get a breakup of transaction across tiers.

4   Deployment of ScrutiNet in a Large Employee Appraisal System

ScrutiNet as shown in Fig. 2 is deployed to the data center for collection of data. The network switch connecting all the servers and SSL Accelerator in the data center is port mirrored[2] to collect data at ScrutiNet workstation.

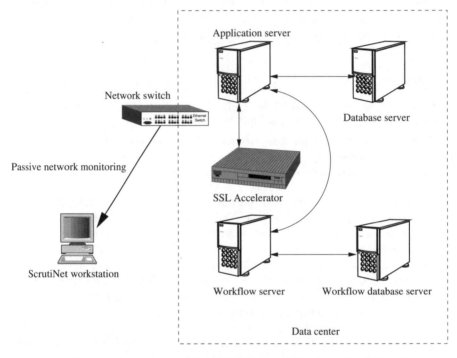

Fig. 2. Large employee appraisal system monitoring using ScrutiNet

The following four servers were monitored using ScrutiNet for a period of 45 minutes.

Application Server   APS
Database Server   DBS
Workflow Server   WFS
Workflow Database Server   WFDBS

The four servers are logically connected to each other as shown in Fig. 3. Note that in tier 1, the client is *SSL Accelerator* , and the servers are *Application Server* and *Workflow Server*. In tier 2, the clients are *Application Server* and *Workflow Server* whereas servers are *Database Server* and *Workflow Database Server* .

---

[2] For passive network monitoring.

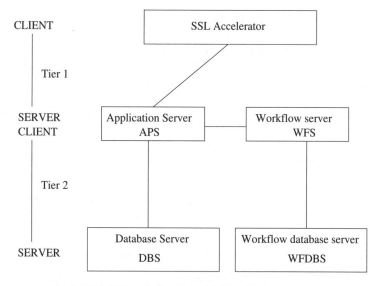

Fig. 3. Two–tier connection in the employee appraisal system

5   Result Analysis

ScrutiNet collects and analyzes data to produce a report as shown in Fig. 4. From this report, we can identify the top n number of slow transactions.

Request No	Client	Client Port	Percentage client network request delay	Server Reaction Time (seconds)	Server Response Time (seconds)	Average Network time (seconds)	Network Overhead in the Server Response Time	Percentage Network Overhead in the Server Response Time	Client Window zero Interval	Total Bytes In	Total Bytes Out	Request contents
6785		3673	0	0.229001	56.12432	0.065364	2.734473	4.872171	49.52164	7864	163373	POST./pages/goalSettingHome.jsf.HTTP/1.1
2817		3596	95.94055	0.318773	33.51618	0.06017	3.521455	10.506731	26.05994	24049	161844	POST./pages/individualGoalSheetHome.jsf.H
10492		3701	95.94367	0.271653	29.01595	0.036071	1.179319	4.064381	58.68056	23002	139704	POST./pages/individualGoalSheetHome.jsf.H
13170		3736	93.31853	0.56624	27.05198	0.029673	0.900574	3.32905	22.44872	23849	174452	POST./pages/individualGoalSheetHome.jsf.H
9907		3688	98.29304	0.55814	20.58293	0.053934	2.169634	10.540938	14.01995	22547	159694	POST./pages/individualGoalSheetHome.jsf.H
1760		3810	1.453199	20.27197	20.27475	0.001029	0.002783	0.013726	0	2517	24502	POST./pages/changeAllocationHome.jsf.HT

Fig. 4. ScrutiNet report shows the top two slow transactions in the Application Server

5.1   Application Server Transaction Analysis

Fig. 4 (rows 2 and 3, columns 1 and 6) shows that transactions having request numbers 6785 and 2817 have server response time of 56.12 seconds and 33.51 seconds, respectively. Note that the meaning of all these columns are given in the Section 3.1. As the server response time for these transactions is higher than the remaining ones, these two transactions are considered as the top two slow transactions. Hence, the top two slow HTTP transactions in the Application Server are:

1. POST./pages/goalSettingHome.jsf.HTTP/1.1
2. POST./pages/individualGoalSheetHome.jsf.HTTP/1.1

The detailed ScrutiNet output for the two slow transactions are shown in Fig. 5 and Fig. 6.

From Fig. 5, we can infer that request no 6785 passes from the SSL Accelerator (port 3673) to the Application Server (APS) and the Application Server takes 56.12 seconds to respond.

Request No	Transaction start time	Client	Client Port	Request Send Time (seconds)	Server Reaction Time (seconds)	Server Response Time (seconds)	Average Network Round trip time (seconds)	Network Overhead in the Server Response Time	Client Window zero Interval	Total Bytes In	Total Bytes Out
6785	12/07/2007	████████	3673	0	0.229001	56.12432	0.065364	2.734473	49.52164	7864	163373
2817	12/07/2007	████████	3596	1.767359	0.318773	33.51618	0.06017	3.521455	26.05994	24049	161844

Fig. 5. ScrutiNet report (Column 1 – 26) shows the top two slow transactions in the Application Server (some columns are hidden)

Request No	Request contents
6785	POST./pages/goalSettingHome.jsf.HTTP/1.1..Accept:.image/gifcomma.image/x-xbitmapcomma.image/jpegcomma.image/pjpegcomma.application/vnd.ms-excelcomma.application/vnd.ms-powerpointcomma.application/mswordcomma.application/xaml+xmlcomma.application/vnd.ms-xpsdocumentcomma.application/x-ms-xbapcomma.application/x-ms-applicationcomma.application/x-shockwave-flashcomma.*/*..Referer:.https://gspeed.ultimatix.net/pages/goalSettingHome.jsf..Accept-Language:.en-us..Content-Type:.application/x-www-form-urlencoded..Accept-Encoding:.gzipcomma.deflate..User-Agent:.Mozilla/4.0.(compatible;.MSIE.6.0;.Windows.NT.5.1;.SV1;.InfoPath.1;..NET.CLR.1.1.4322;..NET.CLR.1.0.3705;..NET.CLR.2.0.50727;..NET.C LR.3.0.04506.30)..Host:.gspeed.ultimatix.net..Content-Length:.78..Cache-Control:.no-cache..Cookie:.JSESSIONID=yZ6HYhbQQTYQLJhGJ3vSMt985HR6SkLX9N3BrvJ1nf7H3NpHnbw/729940139..X-Forwarded-For:.68.82.100.84.... idJsp29 SUBMIT=1&jsf sequence=4& idJsp29%3A link hidden = idJsp29%3AhyperLink
2817	POST./pages/individualGoalSheetHome.jsf.HTTP/1.1..Accept:.image/gifcomma.image/x-xbitmapcomma.image/jpegcomma.image/pjpegcomma.application/vnd.ms-excelcomma.application/vnd.ms-powerpointcomma.application/mswordcomma.application/xaml+xmlcomma.application/vnd.ms-xpsdocumentcomma.application/x-ms-xbapcomma.application/x-ms-applicationcomma.application/x-shockwave-flashcomma.*/*..Referer:.https://gspeed.ultimatix.net/pages/individualGoalSheetHome.jsf..Accept-Language:.en-us..Content-Type:.application/x-www-form-urlencoded..Accept-Encoding:.gzipcomma.deflate..User-Agent:.Mozilla/4.0.(compatible;.MSIE.6.0;.Windows.NT.5.1;.SV1;.InfoPath.1;..NET.CLR.1.1.4322;..NET.CLR.1.0.3705;..NET.CLR.2.0.50727;..NET.C LR.3.0.04506.30)..Host:.gspeed.ultimatix.net..Content-Length:.15692..Cache-Control:.no-cache..Cookie:.JSESSIONID=yvPbHYJc2ybN4RvKhxJ3CWDWi5jwh93kBNGHJndQ1NC5vYhWfn16l729940139..X-Forwarded-For:.68.82.100.84....

Fig. 6. ScrutiNet report (Column 27) shows the top two slow transactions in the Application Server

In Fig. 7, the response time breaks up for both the POST request transactions. It shows percentage of delay of client, network, and other factors (for example, server reaction time) contributed to the total response time. In both the transactions, client delay is the major contributor.

When we follow the analysis algorithm presented in Section 3, we conclude that the client delay is a major component of the response time for the POST request. This means that the SSL Accelerator has been the major source of delay for this transaction.

As the client delay component has been identified as the major source of delay, we will skip the step of correlation analysis for the next tier (database tier) for this transaction.

Thus, the main findings for HTTP transactions on the Application Server are:

– Both the transactions have about 75% of client delay. As the SSL Accelerator is the client to the Application Server, this delay can be attributed to the SSL Accelerator. In general, this problem occurs when the response message is more than 150 KB as can be seen in Fig. 5 in the column *Total Bytes Out*.

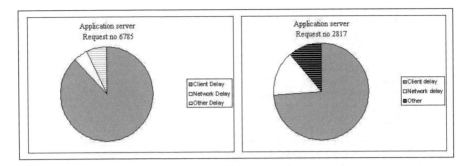

Fig. 7. Response time breakups of the top two slow transactions in the Application Server

5.2 Workflow Server Transaction Analysis

Similarly, as per the ScrutiNet report, the slowest transaction in the Workflow Server is an XML based query called QUERY PROPERTY (see Fig. 8 and Fig. 9), which is sent by the Application Server. For this transaction, when we follow the analysis algorithm, we see that the client window zero delay, request send time, or network overhead hardly contribute to the response time. The delay, therefore, is either in the Workflow Server or in the Workflow Database Server.

Request No.	Transaction start time	Client	Client Port	Request Send Time (seconds)	Server Reaction Time (seconds)	Server Response Time (seconds)	Round Trip Time (seconds)	Average Network Round trip time (seconds)	Network Overhead in the Server Response Time	Client Window zero Interval	Total Bytes In	Total Bytes Out
582	12/07/2007		53307	0	19.37399	19.37402	0.062015	0.03107	0.000034	0	1300	3765

Fig. 8. ScrutiNet report (Column 1–26) shows the top slow transaction in the Workflow Server (some columns are hidden)

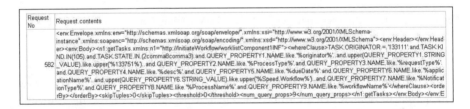

Fig. 9. ScrutiNet report (Column 27) shows the top slow transactions in the Workflow Server

From the development team, it is understood that only one connection to the Workflow Database Server is made for each workflow transaction. As per the correlation report in Fig. 10, we can see that the connection on port 62277 contributes significantly to the response time of the workflow transaction QUERY PROPERTY. Fig. 11 shows the requests made to the Workflow Database Server on connection 62277. The sum of response times of all these transactions is 19.356 seconds as seen in the correlation report in Fig. 10 (row 16).

Response Time of selected txn = 19.374 seconds			
Final txn resp time = 19.374			
Network overhead = 3.4e-005 (0.000175493 %)			
Client Delay = 0.000000 (0%)			
Next Tier overheads per connection			
Response Time in next tier for connection on port 55695 = 0.178429 (0.92097%)			
Response Time in next tier for connection on port 55697 = 0.206702 (1.0669%)			
Response Time in next tier for connection on port 49427 = 0.00307 (0.015846%)			
Response Time in next tier for connection on port 61982 = 1.31589 (6.79203%)			
Response Time in next tier for connection on port 62232 = 0.895182 (4.62053%)			
Response Time in next tier for connection on port 65439 = 0.000432 (0.00222979%)			
Response Time in next tier for connection on port 55685 = 0.132921 (0.686079%)			
Response Time in next tier for connection on port 65440 = 0.00067 (0.00345824%)			
Response Time in next tier for connection on port 65441 = 0.000555 (0.00286466%)			
Response Time in next tier for connection on port 62276 = 0.363481 (1.87613%)			
Response Time in next tier for connection on port 62277 = 19.3564 (99.9089%)			
Response Time in next tier for connection on port 62278 = 1.53336 (7.91451%)			
Response Time in next tier for connection on port 55694 = 0.02255 (0.116393%)			
Response Time in next tier for connection on port 58042 = 0.004071 (0.0210127%)			
Total overhead in next tier = 24.0137 (123.948%)			

Fig. 10. ScrutiNet generated correlation report for the next tier of the top slow transaction in the Workflow Server

Request No	Request contents
73592	.........g.....WASD.$.6.....<.........O.......".3.jv..l......a.:..M.......O......".3.jv..l......a.:..M..
73593	...........^...).....W.........................SELECT.DISTINCT.TA.TKIID.comma.TA.ACTIVATED.comma.TA.APPLIC_NAME.comma.TA.COMPLETED.comma.TA .LAST_MODIFIED.comma.TA.NAME.comma.TA.ORIGINATOR.comma.TA.OWNER.comma.TA.TKTID.comma.TA.STATE.commaQP1.NAME..QP1NA ME.comma.QP1.STRING_VALUE..QP1SVALUEcomma.QP2.NAME..QP2NAME.comma.QP2.STRING_VALUE..QP2SVALUEcomma.QP3.NAME..Q P3NAME.comma.QP3.STRING_VALUE..QP3SVALUEcomma.QP4.NAME..QP4NAME..comma.QP4.STRING_VALUE..QP4SVALUEcomma.QP5.NA ME..QP5NAME.comma.QP5.STRING_VALUE..QP5SVALUEcomma.QP6.NAME..QP6NAME..comma.QP6.STRING_VALUE..QP6SVALUEcomma.Q P7.NAME..QP7NAME.comma.QP7.STRING_VALUE..QP7SVALUEcomma.QP8.NAME..QP8NAME.comma.QP8.STRING_VALUE..QP8SVALUEcom ma.QP9.NAME..QP9NAMEcomma.QP9.STRING_VALUE..QP9SVALUE.FROM.QUERY_PROPERTY.QP3comma.QUERY_PROPERTY.QP8comma. QUERY_PROPERTY.QP5comma.QUERY_PROPERTY.QP7comma.QUERY_PROPERTY.QP1comma.QUERY_PROPERTY.QP2comma.QUERY_P ROPERTY.QP6comma.QUERY_PROPERTY.QP4comma.WORK_ITEM.WIcomma.TASK.TAcomma.QUERY_PROPERTY.QP9.WHERE.(WI.OBJEC T_ID.=.TA.TKIID.AND.TA.CONTAINMENT_CTX_ID.=.QP5.PIID.AND.TA.CONTAINMENT_CTX_ID.=.QP7.PIID.AND.TA.CONTAINMENT_CTX_ID.=.QP1. PIID.AND.TA.CONTAINMENT_CTX_ID.=.QP2.PIID.AND.TA.CONTAINMENT_CTX_ID.=.QP6.PIID.AND.TA.CONTAINMENT_CTX_ID.=.QP4.PIID.AND.TA
73594	...............m..
76104	.M.......g.....WASD.$.6.....<..............WASD......$......6.....O.......".3.jv..l......a.:..M.......O......".3.jv..l......a.:..M...............................
76105	.....w..........O.......".3.jv..l......a.:..M.......O......".3.jv..l......a.:..M..

Fig. 11. Transactions on connection port 62277 on the Workflow Database Server for the execution of QUERY PROPERTY transaction on the Workflow Server

The Workflow Database Server query in the connection was verified with the development team to validate that the Workflow Database Server, indeed, was the bottleneck for the workflow transaction.

6   Conclusion

In this paper, we have discussed our approach to the performance monitoring and analysis of a large OLTP system, with an example of employee appraisal system. From the observations made in this paper, it is clear that performance monitoring and analysis of a large OLTP system requires analytical ability to determine the bottlenecks, but tools can aid in this regard. ScrutiNet, a tool designed by TCS's Performance Engineering

Research Center was used to monitor and analyze the performance of OLTP transactions regardless of the application type. Currently, the patent application for ScrutiNet is pending. The tool, however, can be used by obtaining a user license from TCS. For more information please contact the authors of this paper.

References

1. Nambiar, M., Parab, O.: ScrutiNet (2006),
   `http://tatainfotech.com/Solutions/TechProd_TPS.html`
2. Iwatch – A non-intrusive performance monitoring solution for client/server application environments, `http://www.exact-solutions.com/`
3. Network General, `http://www.netscout.com/products/`
4. Compuware Vantage, `http://www.compuware.com/`
5. Crannog Software Response Watch, `http://www.2crannog-software.com/`
6. PasTmon – The Passive Application Response Time Monitor, `http://pastmon.sourceforge.net`
7. HP Business Availability Center software,
   `http://www2.hp.com/solutions/bac/ds/4aa0-9272enw_bac_ds.pdf`
8. Application Response Measurement, `http://www.opengroup.org/management/arm/`
9. Aguilera, M.K., Mogul, J.C., Wiener, J.L., Reynolds, P., Muthitacharoen, A.: Performance Debugging for Distributed Systems of Black Boxes. In: SOSP 2003, Bolton Landing, New York, USA, October 19–22 (2003)
10. Roy, R.: Performance analysis for parallel applications. In: Monitoring Distributed Systems for Diagnostic Purposes Workshop at Ericsson, Montral, January 29-30 (2008)

Speeding up STL Set/Map Usage in C++ Applications

Dibyendu Das, Madhavi Valluri, Michael Wong, and Chris Cambly

IBM
{dibyendu.das@in.ibm.com, mvalluri@us.ibm.com,
michaelw@ca.ibm.com, ccambly@ca.ibm.com}

Abstract. In this work we augment the red-black tree implementation of STL set<...>/map<...> with a doubly linked list that is in sorted order. This is done for the purpose of speeding up C++ applications that use set<>/map<>::iterator considerably. In such cases, the doubly linked list helps in iterating over the set<>/map<> quickly. Usually the ++/-- operations have an amortized cost of $O(1)$ for a red-black tree implementation. The linked list augmentation helps in improving the ++/-- operations to $\Theta(1)$. In addition, our experiments for IBM's P5+ and P6 processors show that this mechanism improves performance for two SPEC CPU2006 benchmarks and there is no adverse cache effect when we support two additional pointers per node of a red-black tree.

1 Introduction

As modern-day programming becomes more involved and complex, programmers are increasingly using tailor-made data structures that provide the correct functionality as well as good performance. Standard Template Libraries (STL) are a part of C++ standard [7] that are provided by all C++ vendors and compilers. STL eases the burden of the programmers by providing a number of ready-made data structures like vector<...>, dequeue<...>, list<...>, set<...>, map<...> etc that allow programmers a faster turnaround time. These data structures and their supporting methods are also sufficiently generic so that they can be easily tailored to a wide range of situations. In addition, these are written with performance and memory usage in mind. Such STL implementations are hard to surpass both in terms of usability and performance by code implemented from scratch.

In this work, we focus on two specific STL structures called the set<...> and the map<...> (and its variants the multiset<...> and the multimap<...>). A set<...>/map<...> is an associative container which is a collection of elements which are unique (unless one uses the multiset<...>/multimap<...>). A map<...> differs from a set<...> in storing additional satellite information with each key. Most STL vendors like SGI, HP, STL Port and Dinkumware implement a set<...>/map<...> in the form of a red-black tree [7]. The set/map is thus kept both unique and sorted as a virtue of its implementation. Also, since set/map uses a tree as its underlying data structure in this work we will use set<...> to represent either a set<...> or a map<...> and its variants.

The implementation of a set<...> as a tree places some restriction as far as iterators of a set<...> are concerned. Iterators are data structures that move to the next/previous element (by using ++ or --) of a STL data structure – the concept of next and previous

S. Kounev, I. Gorton, and K. Sachs (Eds.): SIPEW 2008, LNCS 5119, pp. 314–321, 2008.
© Springer-Verlag Berlin Heidelberg 2008

elements being defined by the data structure. For example for a vector<...> the statement

```
(vector<...>::iterator itr=vec.begin();itr!=vec.end(); ++itr)
```

will traverse the entire vector from vec[0] to vec[vec.size()-1]. Since, by definition, the elements of a vector are not sorted, the ++ itr operation just moves over the vector elements in no particular order other than the order in which these elements have been stored in the vector. On the other hand, if an iterator is defined over a set<...>, then its corresponding ++/-- operations move to the next sorted element in the set<...>. Thus

```
(set<...>::iterator sitr=xSet.begin(); sitr!=xSet.end(); ++sitr )
```

results in the `sitr` traversing the `xSet` in such a way that the iterator points to the next sorted element in non-decreasing order in the set with every ++ operation. For a tree, such a traversal is not O(1) for every ++/-- operation, but has an amortized O(1) complexity for a group of ++/-- operations. However, due to each ++/-- not working in $\Theta(1)$ time, applications which use set<...> iterators heavily, may perform poorly as we have observed in some SPEC CPU2006 applications [6].

We have found that by supporting an additional sorted linked list on top of the red-black tree implementation while implementing the set<...> STL, we perform much better when applications use set<...> iterators. Our experiments show that we gain substantially for two SPEC CPU2006 benchmarks – dealII and xalancbmk when compiled and run on the IBM Power5+ and Power6 processors.

2   Traditional Implementation of Set<...>

The traditional set<...> implementation in the C++ STL (originally published by HP [7]) can be found in set* and xtree* files in the header include paths. Most of the other vendors follow a very similar implementation. As mentioned earlier, a set<...> is usually implemented as a balanced binary tree – specifically as red-black trees[5]. Red-black(RB) trees allow insertion and deletion in O(logn) and help maintain the other complexity bounds prescribed in the C++ Standards. IBM's xlC compiler [10] uses STL provided by Dinkumware. Its set<...> implementation is also based on red-black trees. In the following example in Fig 1, we show a set of integers defined as set<int> being represented as a RB tree.

Consider the set iSet defined as set<int> iSet, which has 9 nodes represented as a red-black balanced binary tree. The red nodes are shaded lightly while the darker ones are the black nodes. Now, consider an iterator for this set defined as

```
set<int>::iterator sitr = iSet.begin();
```

This positions `sitr` on the node marked 1.Applying the ++ operator on `sitr` moves the iterator to the next sorted element in the set. This implies that if we invoke ++sitr 4 times, `sitr` will be positioned on the node marked 8 as shown in the Fig 1. If we invoke ++sitr once more, the iterator needs to climb up the nodes 7 and 2 before it reaches 11 which is the next sorted element in the list. This requires 3 link traversals. The subsequent ++sitr invocation results in 2 link traversals downwards,

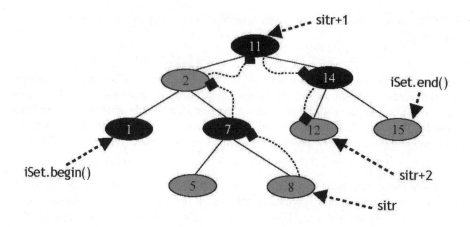

Fig. 1. A set<int> iSet as a red-black tree

to 12. Thus it is fairly clear that we may need to traverse more than one link every time we apply the ++ operator on sitr. If we do the arithmetic we will find that sitr needs to traverse 12 links if we have sitr move from the begin() to the end() of the set using a statement like the one shown below:

```
for (sitr = iSet.begin() ; sitr != iSet.end(); ++ sitr)
```

This averages to 12/9 = 1.3 links for the ++ operator when amortized. Though such an amortized cost is well within the O(1) bound prescribed by the C++ STL standards, it can have quite a negative impact on performance – especially for applications which indulge in set iteration to a large extent.

3   Our Implementation of Set<...>

Our implementation of set<...> maintains a doubly linked list on top of the red-black tree as shown in Fig 2. Each tree node maintains two additional _Next and _Prev pointers pointing to the next sorted tree node in the non-decreasing order and non

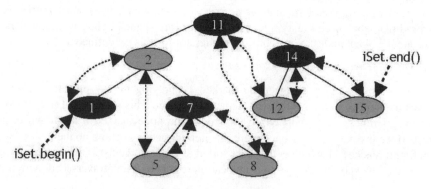

Fig. 2. Our implementation

increasing order respectively. These pointers are shown as double edged dotted pointers in the Fig 2. The list is sorted with respect to the elements of the set<...> so that the ++ and -- operation on a set iterator can be supported in $\Theta(1)$ time complexity instead of O(1). If sitr now points to 8 its _Next pointer points to 11 while its _Prev pointer points to 7. 8 is also pointed at by 11's _Prev pointer. This implies exactly 1 link traversal for supporting every ++/-- operation.

The additional time required for insert() or delete() operations in set<...> to support the doubly linked list is of complexity O(1). This implies very little overhead for these operations while honouring the O(logn) time complexities prescribed in the standards.

4 Implementation Overview

This section outlines the main code changes carried out to implement our set<...> as outlined above. We have modified the Dinkumware provided STL for that purpose. At the current stage, the changes to the Dinkumware set<...> STL comes into effect only under the special compiler #define ___IBM_FAST_SET_MAP_ITERATOR.

We add two _Prev and _Next pointers to the basic red-black tree node class so that we can support the sorted doubly linked list using these pointers. In this class we support two new methods RB_next() and RB_prev() to navigate the doubly linked list in both directions. The insert() method is invoked during set<...> insertion which eventually inserts a node in a red-black tree. During insertion, depending on whether the node is inserted as a left child or a right child, the _Next and _Prev pointers are updated accordingly to reflect the position of the inserted node in the sorted list. Fig 3 illustrates a general case when a new node _Z is inserted to the left of a node _Y. The dotted edges represent the doubly linked list. In order to insert _Z at the proper position in the sorted list, the relevant fields of RB_Prev(_Y), _Y and _Z should be modified. The resultant tree with the new sorted list is shown on the right of Fig 3.

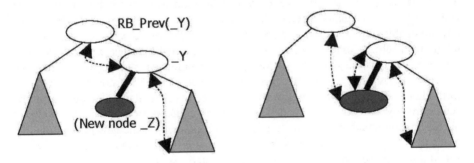

Fig. 3. Insertion of a node in set<...> and its list update

In case of erase() the _Next/_Prev pointers are updated at the start of the method body. This ensures that the node to be deleted is removed from the sorted linked list even before the child and parent pointers are changed for actual deletion

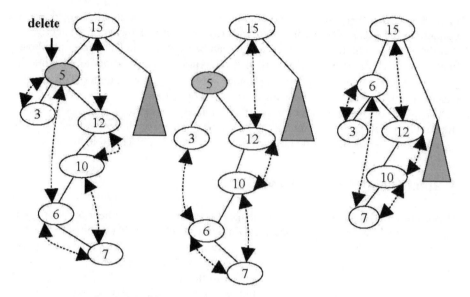

Fig. 4. Deletion of a node and its list update

and subsequent rotation. Some implementations (ex the HP STL set<...>) may call
::swap(a,b) to swap the contents of two nodes before deleting one of them (say
b). In such implementations, the code needs to be modified accordingly, so that we
can back up the _Next/_Prev pointers of a and restore it after the ::swap has
been called. Our implementation does not require this change as the erase()
implementation does not invoke swap for copying contents of a node but manipulates
the parent pointers to carry out the actual deletion.

The following example in Fig 4 illustrates how the sorted list is maintained in case
of a generic deletion of a node via the erase() method. If the node marked 5 is to
be deleted, then, the sorted list is updated to reflect this as shown in Fig 4b. When the
node marked 5 is actually deleted, the _Left/_Right/_Parent pointers of the
tree are modified to create the tree shown in Fig 4c. The operator++ and operator-- in
the original set<...> implementation need to traverse multiple links to reach the next
sorted element in the tree. But, in our implementation we just need to follow the
_Next/_Prev links to correctly increment or decrement an iterator. The _Copy()
method of a set<...> is invoked from the operator=. This creates a new tree out of the
source tree by allocating new nodes and copying contents from the source nodes to
the destination nodes. Since the _Next/_Prev pointers of the new destination tree
needs to be created, we need to scan from the first to the last node in the new tree in
sorted order and set up the _Next/_Prev pointers accordingly. To do this we need
to traverse multiple links and traverse up/down the tree using the original ++/--
algorithms. The original ++ method does not use the _Next/_Prev pointers but
only the _Left/_Right/_Parent pointers. Setting up the _Next/_Prev
pointers of a copied tree takes an additional O(1) amortized time for every copied
node.

5   Performance

Our implementation of set<...> supported by a sorted doubly linked list has been found to benefit a couple of SPEC CPU2006 benchmarks – dealII and xalancbmk. Among the SPEC CPU2006 benchmarks omnetpp, dealII and xalancbmk use set/map. dealII uses set<...>::iterator heavily while xalancbmk uses map<...>::iterator. The effect of our implementation is more pronounced on dealII than on xalancbmk as the iterators are hotter in the former. Also the map usages in omnetpp are cold. The performance numbers are summarized in the tables below for P6 and P5+. We have done peak runs using the highest optimization flag -O5 of the xlC compiler and with profiling (pdf) enabled. Both the benchmarks pass the specdiff validation test.

Table 1. P6 Performance

Benchmark	Original Time	Modified Time	% Improvement
dealII	502	398	20.7

Table 2. P5+ Performance

Benchmark	Original Time	Modified Time	% Improvement
dealII	918	776	15.5
xalancbmk	754	732	2.9

6   Correctness

The correctness of our mechanism – that of supporting a sorted doubly linked list over a tree, is based on several key observations. Firstly, when a node N is inserted into or deleted from the tree, we update the _Next/_Prev links of the doubly linked list of N even before rotation happens for rebalancing. This ensures that the list remains correctly sorted before rotation starts. Secondly, rotation for balance does not disturb the sorted linked list. Rotation changes the heights of nodes to maintain the red-black properties. Also, rotation re-positions the _Left/_Right/_Parent pointers of various nodes to achieve the balance, without actually creating new nodes or copying from one node to another. Since changing only the _Left/_Right/_Parent pointers have no bearing on the already constructed sorted list, the list remains correctly sorted after rotation that may follow an insert or delete operation. Neither during insertion nor during deletion, nodes are copied to or from other nodes at any stage of the algorithms, ensuring correctness. For STL implementations that may use node copying for deletion some extra code will be required to ensure correctness.

7   STL and Other Performance Implications

As stated earlier, our set<...> implementation honors all the performance complexities prescribed by the C++ standards. Insertion and deletion are still O(logn) as we just add constant time to an insertion/deletion in order to fix the sorted doubly linked list.

Iteration time improves to $\Theta(1)$ for every operation instead of the amortized $O(1)$ time complexity prescribed by the standards. Since we add two pointers to every node of the tree, the size of the node increases. This raises the usual concern of whether this may have cache performance implications [2, 3]. However, we noted that for P5 and P6 processors, increasing the size of the node has almost no bearing on the cache performance. This has been verified through the use of the performance monitoring tool for P5 and P6 called pmcount[9].

8 Related Work

None of the existing implementations of the set<...>/map<...> STL that are used by the commercial compilers, deviate too much from the red-black tree of the original HP implementation [7]. The research work in [3] on the other hand uses a B-tree to improve upon the set/map implementation. But their experimental results show that while they are faster for scans and searches and comparable on insertions, they are more than twice as costly for deletions when compared to a RB tree. AVL trees have also been used instead of RB trees to implement sets and maps in [4]. The authors saw small degradation for all operations when using the AVL tree implementation as opposed to the RB tree implementation. The work in [2] evaluates various techniques to speed up RB tree implementation for sets and maps. The techniques evaluated range from removal of parent pointers, threading, compacting colour bits to providing rank searches. Their experiments on basic insertion/deletions and search show that their implementation is more space-efficient than the RB tree implementation used in [7] and is usually as fast as the RB tree implementation. On some occasions their implementation is faster. Their work on using threaded RB trees comes closest to our work on supporting a doubly linked list on a RB tree. However, threading has several disadvantages in having a high deletion time and the inability to work with multisets and multimaps.

9 Conclusions

In this work we have shown that supporting a doubly linked list in the sorted order on the tree that implements the STL set<...>/map<...>, enables performance gain for some SPEC CPU2006 benchmarks that use set<...>/map<...>. It especially affects the dealII and xalancbmk benchmarks in a positive way. Our implementation also honors the C++ complexity bounds and does not have any detrimental effect on cache performance due to the increased size of the nodes used to store the additional fields that support the doubly linked list.

References

1. Meyers, S.: Effective STL. Addison Wesley Professional Computing Series (2001)
2. Bronimann, H., Katajainen, J.: Efficiency of Various Forms of Red-Black Trees. CPH STL Report 2006-2, University of Copenhagen (2006)

3. Hansen, J.G., Henriksen, A.K.: The Multi map/set of the Copenhagen STL. CPH STL Report 2001-6, University of Copenhagen (2001)
4. Lynge, S.: Implementing the AVL Trees for the CPH STL. CPH STL Report 2004-1, University of Copenhagen (2004)
5. Cormen, H., Leiserson, C.E., Rivest, R.L., Stein, C.: Introduction to Algorithms. Prentice-Hall, India (2006)
6. SPEC CPU 2006 benchmarks, `http://www.spec.org`
7. Stepanov, A., Lee, M.: The Standard Template Library, Technical Report HPL-95-11, Hewlett Packard (1995)
8. ISO/IEC 14882:1998 and ISO/IEC 14882:2003(E) Standard for the C++ Programming Language
9. pmcount, http://www-128.ibm.com/developerworks/power/library/pa-cpipower2/
10. IBM XL Compilers and White Papers,
    `http://www.ibm.com/software/awdtools/ccompilers`
    `http://www1.ibm.com/support/docview.wss?rs=32&context=SSEP5D`
    `&uid=swg27007322`
    `http://www-1.ibm.com/support/docview.wss?rs=43&context=`
    `SSEP9Q&uid=swg27005175`

Author Index

Printing: Mercedes-Druck, Berlin
Binding: Stein+Lehmann, Berlin

Lecture Notes in Computer Science

Sublibrary 2: Programming and Software Engineering

For information about Vols. 1– 4468
please contact your bookseller or Springer

Vol. 4807: Z. Shao (Ed.), Programming Languages and Systems. XI, 431 pages. 2007.

Vol. 4799: A. Holzinger (Ed.), HCI and Usability for Medicine and Health Care. XVI, 458 pages. 2007.

Vol. 4789: M. Butler, M.G. Hinchey, M.M. Larrondo-Petrie (Eds.), Formal Methods and Software Engineering. VIII, 387 pages. 2007.

Vol. 4767: F. Arbab, M. Sirjani (Eds.), International Symposium on Fundamentals of Software Engineering. XIII, 450 pages. 2007.

Vol. 4765: A. Moreira, J. Grundy (Eds.), Early Aspects: Current Challenges and Future Directions. X, 199 pages. 2007.

Vol. 4764: P. Abrahamsson, N. Baddoo, T. Margaria, R. Messnarz (Eds.), Software Process Improvement. XI, 225 pages. 2007.

Vol. 4762: K.S. Namjoshi, T. Yoneda, T. Higashino, Y. Okamura (Eds.), Automated Technology for Verification and Analysis. XIV, 566 pages. 2007.

Vol. 4758: F. Oquendo (Ed.), Software Architecture. XVI, 340 pages. 2007.

Vol. 4757: F. Cappello, T. Herault, J. Dongarra (Eds.), Recent Advances in Parallel Virtual Machine and Message Passing Interface. XVI, 396 pages. 2007.

Vol. 4753: E. Duval, R. Klamma, M. Wolpers (Eds.), Creating New Learning Experiences on a Global Scale. XII, 518 pages. 2007.

Vol. 4749: B.J. Krämer, K.-J. Lin, P. Narasimhan (Eds.), Service-Oriented Computing – ICSOC 2007. XIX, 629 pages. 2007.

Vol. 4748: K. Wolter (Ed.), Formal Methods and Stochastic Models for Performance Evaluation. X, 301 pages. 2007.

Vol. 4741: C. Bessière (Ed.), Principles and Practice of Constraint Programming – CP 2007. XV, 890 pages. 2007.

Vol. 4735: G. Engels, B. Opdyke, D.C. Schmidt, F. Weil (Eds.), Model Driven Engineering Languages and Systems. XV, 698 pages. 2007.

Vol. 4716: B. Meyer, M. Joseph (Eds.), Software Engineering Approaches for Offshore and Outsourced Development. X, 201 pages. 2007.

Vol. 4709: F.S. de Boer, M.M. Bonsangue, S. Graf, W.-P. de Roever (Eds.), Formal Methods for Components and Objects. VIII, 297 pages. 2007.

Vol. 4680: F. Saglietti, N. Oster (Eds.), Computer Safety, Reliability, and Security. XV, 548 pages. 2007.

Vol. 4670: V. Dahl, I. Niemelä (Eds.), Logic Programming. XII, 470 pages. 2007.

Vol. 4652: D. Georgakopoulos, N. Ritter, B. Benatallah, C. Zirpins, G. Feuerlicht, M. Schoenherr, H.R. Motahari-Nezhad (Eds.), Service-Oriented Computing ICSOC 2006. XVI, 201 pages. 2007.

Vol. 4640: A. Rashid, M. Aksit (Eds.), Transactions on Aspect-Oriented Software Development IV. IX, 191 pages. 2007.

Vol. 4634: H. Riis Nielson, G. Filé (Eds.), Static Analysis. XI, 469 pages. 2007.

Vol. 4620: A. Rashid, M. Aksit (Eds.), Transactions on Aspect-Oriented Software Development III. IX, 201 pages. 2007.

Vol. 4615: R. de Lemos, C. Gacek, A. Romanovsky (Eds.), Architecting Dependable Systems IV. XIV, 435 pages. 2007.

Vol. 4610: B. Xiao, L.T. Yang, J. Ma, C. Muller-Schloer, Y. Hua (Eds.), Autonomic and Trusted Computing. XVIII, 571 pages. 2007.

Vol. 4609: E. Ernst (Ed.), ECOOP 2007 – Object-Oriented Programming. XIII, 625 pages. 2007.

Vol. 4608: H.W. Schmidt, I. Crnković, G.T. Heineman, J.A. Stafford (Eds.), Component-Based Software Engineering. XII, 283 pages. 2007.

Vol. 4591: J. Davies, J. Gibbons (Eds.), Integrated Formal Methods. IX, 660 pages. 2007.

Vol. 4589: J. Münch, P. Abrahamsson (Eds.), Product-Focused Software Process Improvement. XII, 414 pages. 2007.

Vol. 4574: J. Derrick, J. Vain (Eds.), Formal Techniques for Networked and Distributed Systems – FORTE 2007. XI, 375 pages. 2007.

Vol. 4556: C. Stephanidis (Ed.), Universal Access in Human-Computer Interaction, Part III. XXII, 1020 pages. 2007.

Vol. 4555: C. Stephanidis (Ed.), Universal Access in Human-Computer Interaction, Part II. XXII, 1066 pages. 2007.

Vol. 4554: C. Stephanidis (Ed.), Universal Acess in Human Computer Interaction, Part I. XXII, 1054 pages. 2007.

Vol. 4553: J.A. Jacko (Ed.), Human-Computer Interaction, Part IV. XXIV, 1225 pages. 2007.

Vol. 4552: J.A. Jacko (Ed.), Human-Computer Interaction, Part III. XXI, 1038 pages. 2007.

Vol. 4551: J.A. Jacko (Ed.), Human-Computer Interaction, Part II. XXIII, 1253 pages. 2007.

Vol. 4550: J.A. Jacko (Ed.), Human-Computer Interaction, Part I. XXIII, 1240 pages. 2007.

Vol. 4542: P. Sawyer, B. Paech, P. Heymans (Eds.), Requirements Engineering: Foundation for Software Quality. IX, 384 pages. 2007.

Vol. 4536: G. Concas, E. Damiani, M. Scotto, G. Succi (Eds.), Agile Processes in Software Engineering and Extreme Programming. XV, 276 pages. 2007.

Vol. 4530: D.H. Akehurst, R. Vogel, R.F. Paige (Eds.), Model Driven Architecture - Foundations and Applications. X, 219 pages. 2007.

Vol. 4523: Y.-H. Lee, H.-N. Kim, J. Kim, Y.W. Park, L.T. Yang, S.W. Kim (Eds.), Embedded Software and Systems. XIX, 829 pages. 2007.

Vol. 4498: N. Abdennahder, F. Kordon (Eds.), Reliable Software Technologies - Ada-Europe 2007. XII, 247 pages. 2007.

Vol. 4486: M. Bernardo, J. Hillston (Eds.), Formal Methods for Performance Evaluation. VII, 469 pages. 2007.

Vol. 4470: Q. Wang, D. Pfahl, D.M. Raffo (Eds.), Software Process Dynamics and Agility. XI, 346 pages. 2007.